KT-378-896

The **European Science Foundation** (ESF) is an association of its fifty-five member research councils, academies and institutions devoted to basic scientific research in twenty countries. The ESF assists its Member Organisations in two main ways: by bringing scientists together in its Scientific Programmes, Networks and European Research Conferences, to work on topics of common concern; and through the joint study of issues of strategic importance in European science policy.

The scientific work sponsored by ESF includes basic research in the natural and technical sciences, the medical and biosciences, the humanities and social sciences.

The ESF maintains close relations with other scientific institutions within and outside Europe. By its activities, ESF adds value by cooperation and coordination across national frontiers and endeavours, offers expert scientific advice on strategic issues, and provides the European forum for fundamental science.

One speaker, two languages

Cross-disciplinary perspectives on code-switching

Edited by

LESLEY MILROY and PIETER MUYSKEN

CAMBRIDGE
UNIVERSITY PRESS

BLACKBURN COLLEGE
LIBRARY

Acc No. _B819630_____

Class No. HSC 404.2 MIL

Date 19.2.09_____

Published by the Press Syndicate of the University of Cambridge
The Pitt Building, Trumpington Street, Cambridge CB2 1RP
40 West 20th Street, New York, NY 10011-4211, USA
10 Stamford Road, Oakleigh, Melbourne 3166, Australia

© Cambridge University Press 1995

First published in 1995

A catalogue record for this book is available from the British Library

Library of Congress cataloging in publication data

One speaker, two languages: cross-disciplinary perspectives on code-
    switching / edited by Lesley Milroy and Pieter Muysken.
        p.   cm.
    Includes index.
    ISBN 0 521 47350 0 (hardback) ISBN 0 521 47912 6 (paperback)
    1. Code-switching (Linguistics) I. Milroy, Lesley. II. Muysken,
    Pieter.
P115.3.054 1995   94-23047 CIP
306.4'4–dc20

ISBN 0 521 47350 0 hardback
ISBN 0 521 47912 6 paperback

Transferred to digital printing 1999

TS

Code-switching – the alternating use of several languages by bilingual speakers – does not usually indicate lack of competence on the part of the speaker in any of the languages concerned, but results from complex bilingual skills. The reasons why people switch their codes are as varied as the directions from which linguists approach this issue, and raise many sociological, psychological and grammatical questions. This volume of essays by leading scholars brings together the main strands of current research in four major areas: the policy implications of code-switching in specific institutional and community settings; the perspective of social theory on code-switching as a form of speech behaviour in particular social contexts; the grammatical analysis of code-switching, including the factors that constrain switching even within a sentence and the implications of code-switching in bilingual processing and development.

CONTENTS

NOTES ON CONTRIBUTORS

Louise Dabène (University of Grenoble) and Danièle Moore (CREDIF, Saint Cloud) have been engaged in research on the bilingual behaviour of migrants in Europe for many years. Louise Dabène has published on Maghrebin migrants in France, showing how the actual language behaviour of migrants must be seen in the context of their often complex biographies and circumstances. Danièle Moore has carried out research amongst Panjabi/English bilingual speakers in Bradford, in the North of England, focussing particularly on communication patterns within the family.

Anna Giacalone Ramat (Facolta di Lettere, University of Pavia) was trained in general and historical linguistics and has carried out research in various areas, including the acquisition of Italian by migrant workers, with particular reference to temporality and modality, and Italian socio-dialectology. A focus in her work has been grammaticalisation phenomena in second language learning.

Penelope Gardner-Chloros (Birkbeck College, University of London) has carried out extensive research on French–Alsatian bilingualism in Strasbourg, developing an integrated perspective in which macro-social, psychological and pragmatic factors interact. More recently, she has carried out research in the Cypriot community in metropolitan London, developing a cross-generational perspective on the language use patterns of this bilingual group.

Marilyn Martin-Jones (University of Lancaster) worked for several years as a researcher on the Linguistic Minorities Project at the University of London. Those working on the project were the first to describe systematically the nature and extent of the linguistic diversity in England resulting from the labour migrations of the decades after the Second World War. In 1985, she co-authored with her colleagues a book entitled *The other languages of England*. Since then she has published extensively on community-based research on bilingualism and on educational issues related to bilingualism. She is also overall co-ordinator of two recent research projects on multilingualism, funded by the Economic and Social Research Council: the first one was based in primary schools in the north-west of England, and the second is an ethnographic project (1993–5) which is based in the Gujerati-speaking community in Lancaster.

Peter Auer (University of Hamburg) has published widely in the fields of dialectology, sociolinguistics and bilingualism, and phonology. He has published a number of volumes dealing with issues in these fields, and has also carried out an extensive study of the bilingual conversational behaviour of Italian/German speaking children of migrant origin in Konstanz, South Germany. More recently he has carried out research on bilingualism in Canada.

Lesley Milroy and Li Wei (University of Michigan and University of Newcastle upon Tyne) are engaged in a large project studying code choice and code-switching in the Tyneside Chinese community, across several generations.

Monica Heller (Ontario Institute for Studies in Education (OISE), Toronto) was trained as a sociolinguist at Berkeley and has studied the relation between the political dimensions of bilingualism and code-switching in specific settings, in both the public and private sectors. She has carried out fieldwork in the French/English bilingual setting of a large brewery in Montreal, and more recently in bilingual classrooms in the Toronto metropolitan area. She has edited a well-known volume on code-switching (Mouton de Gruyter, 1988).

Pieter Muysken (University of Amsterdam) has worked in the Andes on Quechua and on Quechua–Spanish language contact, and with different creole languages of the Caribbean, including Papiamentu and Negerhollands.

Shana Poplack (University of Ottawa) has carried out extensive research on diverse bilingual communities, including the Puerto Rican community in New York, the French-speaking community in the Ottawa-Hull region and Finnish, Tamil and West African immigrants in Canada, as well as on Early African American English as reflected in the English Samanà, Nova Scotia and the Ex-Slave Recordings.

Majory Meechan is in the doctoral programme in Linguistics at the University of Ottawa. Her dissertation focusses on phonological and syntactic variability in Canadian English. She has been working in the Ottawa project on Wolof and Fongbe.

Carol Myers-Scotton (University of South Carolina) is best known for her work on Swahili/English bilingualism in eastern Africa, which she has approached from a number of perspectives. A (socio-)linguist by training, Myers-Scotton has written on strategies of neutrality, and on code-switching as a marked/unmarked choice. She has recently completed two books: *Social motivations for codeswitching* (Oxford: Clarendon Press, 1993) and *Duelling languages: grammatical structure in codeswitching* (Oxford: Clarendon Press, 1993).

François Grosjean (University of Neuchâtel) was trained as a psychologist and has been working on the psycholinguistics of bilingual processing for a number of years. While much of his research has been done with French/English bilinguals, the wide scope of his knowledge is revealed in his *Life with two languages* (Cambridge, Mass.: Harvard University Press, 1982).

Regina Köppe and Jürgen Meisel (University of Hamburg) have been engaged in a large project on the simultaneous acquisition of French and German as first languages by bilingual children. Meisel has also collaborated in a study on the acquisition of German as a second language by Spanish and Italian migrant workers and a study of the bilingual acquisition of Basque and Spanish.

Kenneth Hyltenstam (University of Stockholm) has worked on several aspects of the psycholinguistics of bilingualism, on which he has edited a book conjointly with Loraine Obler, *Bilingualism across the lifespan: aspects of acquisition, maturity, and loss* (Cambridge University Press, 1989). In earlier work he focussed on the adult second language acquisition of Swedish, and at present he is engaged in studying the effects of Alzheimer's dementia on the bilingual competence and on the code-switching behaviour of elderly Finnish/Swedish bilinguals.

Andrée Tabouret-Keller heads the LADISIS Laboratory, dedicated to the psychological study of language, at the Université Louis Pasteur in Strasbourg. She has first-hand experience with bilingual communities in a large number of countries, including Belize, and has acted as a consultant in a number of educational planning projects. She has published on a wide range of subjects in bilingualism, including language shift and code shifting in the Alsace, and is well known for the work carried out conjointly with R. B. Le Page, which culminated in *Acts of Identity* (Cambridge University Press, 1985).

ACKNOWLEDGMENTS

This volume grew out of a network activity, the Network on Code-switching and Language Contact, funded by the European Science Foundation (ESF). We are grateful to the ESF, and particularly to Wouter Hugenholtz and Pat Cosgrove for helping to set up the Network and to keep it on course. Pat Cosgrove was also subsequently instrumental in co-ordinating the preparation of this book, and in assisting us as editors.

We also would like to acknowledge the crucial role of Georges Lüdi in chairing the Co-ordinating Committee of the Network. His part in piloting the original Network proposal through the European Science Foundation's decision-making bodies, his major contribution in helping to organise the Network meetings and in providing an overall balance to the perspectives adopted should not be underestimated.

Other members of the Co-ordinating Committee were Hugo Baetens Beadsmore, Norbert Dittmar, François Grosjean, Shana Poplack, Anna Giacalone Ramat, Andrée Tabouret-Keller and Miquel Strubell i Trueta, as well as the editors. This book owes a great deal, both in the way it is structured and in its contents, to the input by the members of the Co-ordinating Committee and the other researchers participating in the Network.

Finally we acknowledge the assistance of Lisa McEntee and Jette Bolle in helping to prepare the manuscript for publication and for assistance with the index.

1 INTRODUCTION: CODE-SWITCHING AND BILINGUALISM RESEARCH

Lesley Milroy and Pieter Muysken

1 The contemporary setting of bilingualism studies

In the last forty years or so, developments such as the expansion of educational provision to many more levels of society, massive population shifts through migration, and technological advances in mass communication have served to accentuate our sense of a visibly and audibly multilingual modern world. Other large-scale social changes have combined to lead to a considerable increase in bilingualism, not only as a European but as a world-wide phenomenon.

First, modernisation and globalisation have stimulated the expansion in numbers of people speaking national languages located within relatively limited boundaries alongside international languages such as English, French and Spanish. As a consequence of centuries of colonisation, these have spread far beyond their original territories, and there is every sign that their spread as second or auxiliary languages for large numbers of speakers is continuing. Indeed, they are being joined by other languages of economically powerful nations, such as Japanese and Arabic. Furthermore, new multilingual nations have emerged in the years since the Second World War, where linguistic minorities are increasingly becoming bilingual, not only in the language of their own social group and the national language, but often additionally in one of these international languages.

A second development leading to increasing bilingualism is the relatively recent phenomenon of large-scale language revival. There are many nation states in Europe – Switzerland and Belgium are well-known examples – where bilingualism is institutionalised and historically deep-rooted. In addition to this stable type of bilingualism, there has been a resurgence throughout this century, accelerated in recent years, of regional and ethnic movements. This has often led to the preservation, resuscitation and expansion in the use of minority languages which policy makers had already declared moribund and relegated to the scrapheap of history. This language revival phenomenon, in conjunction with the considerable expansion in use of ethnic, national and international languages already noted, leads to many more instances of bilingualism at the level both of the community and the individual. While regional languages and languages of small nations often survive, they are spoken side by side with politically legitimised national languages.

The migration of people from poor countries to the rich industrial West leads to yet further multiplication of bilingual communities; in Auckland, Toronto, Los Angeles and Melbourne any number of languages may be heard. In Europe also we find many bilingual communities of migrant origin; Arabic is spoken alongside Dutch in Holland and alongside French in France; Panjabi and Cantonese are spoken alongside English in England, and Turkish and Italian are spoken alongside German in Germany. The kind of bilingualism which emerges from economically motivated migration is often socially submerged and difficult to study. Frequently there is pressure on immigrants, both direct and indirect, to assimilate culturally and linguistically as rapidly as possible, and countries vary in the quality and kind of provision offered to migrant workers and their families. Migrant communities themselves vary in their attitude to their two languages. Nearly all make some attempt to maintain their original language and culture and their contact with relatives left behind in the homeland. Their dilemma is to balance this human need against a conflicting desire to assimilate to the host language and culture. Bilingualism in migrant communities differs from the more stable and (to some extent) institutionally legitimised types of bilingualism already outlined above. Characteristically, it spans three generations, the oldest speakers sometimes being monolingual in the community language, the economically active generation being to varying degrees bilingual but with greatly differing levels of competence in the host language, while children born in the host community may sometimes be virtually monolingual in the host language.

2 Linguistics and bilingualism

Taken together, the developments set out above lead to a widespread bilingualism as a pervasive phenomenon in the modern world, which seems set to increase in the future. European linguistics (and indeed Western linguistics generally) has been slow to catch up with this contemporary situation. The historical roots of European linguistics can be located in the Romanticism of von Humboldt and Grimm, and the discipline flourished with particular vigour in officially monolingual nation states with powerful standard languages (such as Britain, France and Germany, and later the United States). The assumption dominating linguistics continues to be one which views as the normal or unmarked case the monolingual speaker in a homogeneous speech community. Academic linguists trained in this tradition have sometimes assumed that speakers who mix languages know neither language adequately. Particularly well-known is Bloomfield's (1927) account of the inadequacy in both languages of English/Menomini bilinguals, some of whom he describes individually. A distinction between such speakers and supposedly 'ideal' bilinguals who are fully competent in both languages has been drawn quite frequently in academic linguistic discourse in the years since Bloomfield, and has sometimes been developed into fully fledged and often quite influential theories with profound consequences for educational policy and practice. The theory of semilingualism developed by educational psychologists in Canada and Sweden is a case in point. Semilingualism is a term used to describe a condition where bilingual children are said to know neither of their two languages well enough to sustain the advanced cognitive processes which enable them to benefit from mainstream education. As Martin-Jones and Romaine point out (1986), and as is evident from the material in several of the chapters of this book, such a deficit-based type of analysis cannot easily be sustained in the face of sociolinguistic evidence. This becomes clear if we examine Cummins's (1979) definition of bilingual competence in terms of some ideal bilingual speaker with perfect knowledge of both languages; in fact bilingual speakers characteristically use each of their languages in different social contexts and would not be expected to use either of them in all contexts.

Noam Chomsky's meta-theoretical focus on the ideal native speaker in the ideal speech community is perhaps the most famous modern embodiment of this monolingual and non-variationist focus. While generative grammar has flourished by focussing on simple cases and ignoring more complex situations such as bilingualism, generativists are not alone amongst modern linguists in reflecting such a traditional orientation. William Labov is renowned for his achievements in facing up to the challenges posed by variable and non-ideal everyday spoken language data. Yet even he excluded non-native speakers from consideration in his study of New York City, that city of non-English speaking immigrants *par excellence*. More recently, Horvath's (1985) comparable study of the social varieties of English spoken in Sydney, another great immigrant city, has included ethnic minority speakers within the sample, with interesting results.

Work such as Horvath's suggests some move to redress the balance in modern linguistics, and the chapters of this book, along with their references to a copious research literature, show that many other linguists are also beginning to do so. It is important that they should; for not only is it difficult for linguistics as a discipline to turn its back on the complex issues facing the world community, with their sociolinguistic, psycholinguistic and educational implications, but it is also arguable that mainstream monolingually oriented linguistics has a good deal to learn from research into bilingualism. For example, by observing how people from the same community selectively use several languages in their everyday lives we can learn a lot about language use and language variation in general; the act of switching between languages is much more visible than the style-shifting characteristic of the monolingual speaker. The complex interactions resulting from the storage and simultaneous processing of several languages in one human brain are revealing of general features of neurolinguistic and psycholinguistic processing. The mixing of sounds and of grammatical patterns of different languages in bilingual speech informs us about general features of language structure.

Let us now turn from these essential background issues to focus more specifically on the topic of bilingualism itself. Before turning to comment on the range of orientations to code-switching presented in the following chapters, and the linkages between them, we summarise briefly, with particular (but not exclusive) reference to the European context, a range of issues which have persisted historically as major concerns in bilingualism research. Such a summary can help us understand how the field came to be constituted in the way it is, and can tell us something of the concepts and models employed within it.

3 A selective history of bilingualism research

We cannot hope to do full justice to this topic in a short introduction such as this. We approach it here by mentioning briefly in very rough historical order a small number of individual scholars who have been particularly influential in defining many of the issues that are discussed further in this book. We are aware that not everyone will agree with our selection, and conscious that it is too early to evaluate this work fully and to expound the strands of research of the last fifty years and the interconnections between them. Many of the references provided in the following chapters will flesh out the outline presented here.

Apart from early studies such as that of Ronjat (1913), who described the early balanced French/German bilingual development of his son Louis in great detail, the classic study of child bilingualism remains Leopold (1939–49). In this diary study Leopold records how his daughter Hildegard grew up bilingually with both her father's language, German, and with English, the language of her mother and the wider environment. Many of the central themes of child bilingualism research are highlighted: the separation of the two languages; the influential role of the interlocutor; the asymmetrical character of bilingual competence; the influence of the dominant language on the weaker one.

Without doubt Uriel Weinreich's *Languages in contact* (1953) is the single most influential earlier study. Drawing on a wide range of sources, but with particular attention to the bilingual situation in Switzerland, Weinreich has managed to introduce from several perspectives – psycholinguistic, grammatical and sociolinguistic – every issue that is being researched today. Well known is his typology of bilinguals as co-ordinate (systems kept apart), compound (systems drawing on common mental representations), and subordinate (one system is represented in terms of the other). Though psycholinguistic research has not confirmed empirically anything like these distinctions, the notions inherent in them continue to play an important role. Weinreich was interested in the psycholinguistic basis for, and sociolinguistic conditions underlying, what he terms interference, i.e. interlingual influence. This notion also is now rejected by many researchers as being too broad (covering (nonce) borrowing, switching, mixing, and so on), but it is only fair to mention that Weinreich was keenly aware of many of the conceptual refinements required.

In the period between Ronjat and Weinreich we may briefly refer to a number of studies on the European continent, carried out from various viewpoints and ideological perspectives and linked with issues of nationalism, statehood, language minorities, language change, purism etc. A useful summary of this literature is given in Vildomec (1963).

Einar Haugen's *The Norwegian language in America*, which appeared in two volumes in 1953, but was based on research and fieldwork carried out during the late thirties and the forties, is still one of the most detailed studies of language contact and bilingualism in print. It is innovative in its focus on an immigrant community, and combines historical, dialectological and sociolinguistic perspectives and techniques. As stated in the title, Haugen particularly deals with the original native language of the immigrants, and takes as his point of departure phonological, grammatical and psycholinguistic dimensions of the process of borrowing. Haugen developed a particularly complex and subtle set of categories with respect to which borrowing phenomena can be classified and studied, and it is here that his most influential contribution is to be found.

Joshua Fishman studied the phenomenon of language loyalty among various immigrant groups in the United States and Spanish–English bilingualism among Puerto Ricans in New York, before turning to issues involving language policy in later work. In his well-known article from 1965 he presents his key concept, domain, defined as a 'cluster of social situations typically constrained by a common set of behavioral rules', to account for patterns of language choice in bilingual communities. Fundamentally, domain analysis is a macro-level approach informed by a sociological analysis, which views the language behaviour of individuals as derived from, and constrained by, higher-order societal structures.

Much influential work focussing on a range of issues, from political to social–psychological and even neurolinguistic, has been carried out in French-speaking Canada. Mackey (1972, 1980) has systematically placed the issue of bilingualism in the political sphere and documented the diversity of bilingual situations around the world. In this volume, Heller explores new perspectives on language politics. Lambert (e.g. 1972) has introduced research techniques from social psychology to the study of bilingualism and explored the complex attitudes towards the different languages and their speakers in a bilingual community. Finally, Paradis (e.g. 1978), has linked the issue of bilingualism to the neurolinguistic study of language disorders. This perspective is further taken up in this book in the chapter by Hyltenstam.

A pioneer in Australia in the field of bilingualism and code-switching is Michael Clyne. In early studies on German and Dutch immigrants in Australia (1967, 1972) Clyne has explored key notions such as lexical triggering and language convergence in relation to bilingual usage, linking psycholinguistic and sociolinguistic aspects.

A very different perspective on the bilingualism of migrant communities is offered by the innovatory work of Klein and Dittmar (1979) who make reference to contemporary research on second language learning. They make use of relatively sophisticated grammatical frameworks to characterise the structural properties of the 'developing grammars' of migrant workers as their bilingualism develops from a very limited base to a much more advanced ability in German. As well as being linguistically sophisticated, their work is characterised by a sensitivity to the effects of social factors on language. For example, they note that duration of residence in Germany is a much poorer predictor of competence in German than is the proportion of social ties contracted by migrants with monolingual German speakers.

We can conclude this short historical survey with a comment on the work of Le Page in multilingual situations in the Creole-speaking Caribbean and amongst West Indian communities in London. Following extensive fieldwork and analysis over many years, Le Page has adopted a fundamentally social–psychological perspective. To a considerable extent this aligns with the accommodation theories which Giles and his colleagues have developed to account for variation at the level of face-to-face interaction, in stylistic or dialect choice by monolinguals, or language choice by bilinguals (Giles and Coupland 1992). Le Page also sees particular choices as responses to other participants in the interaction, and as symbolising the kind of identity which a speaker at any given time wishes to communicate. He has referred to each utterance a speaker makes and the language choice which it embodies as an 'act of identity' associated with the different sources of influence (Spanish, English, Creole, for example) in his or her multilingual and multicultural community. Speakers use one or other of the choices available to them to express aspects of a fluid social identity as they move through a multidimensional sociolinguistic space, and the metalinguistic concept of a single language or a multilingual repertoire as consisting of a number of languages is seen as problematic and liable to obscure the nature of these communicative processes. A clear account of Le Page's orientation may be found in Le Page and Tabouret-Keller (1985).

One striking feature of much of the central and influential bilingualism research described here is how closely it is linked to important historical developments in this century. For example, Leopold and Haugen come to grips with the linguistic consequences of North European migration to North America; Vildomec deals with some linguistic consequences of the aftermath of the Second World War; the Canadian research can be situated in the complex and dynamic set of relations there, particularly in Quebec between French and English; Clyne's research emerged in response to the complex bilingual situation in post-war Australia, and Fishman analyses the influence of migration from the Third World on language practices in the industrial West; Le Page's work bears on rapid changes in the Caribbean in the sixties and seventies; Klein and Dittmar deal with the bilingualism of guest workers in the Germany of the seventies. All of this work reflects contemporary preoccupations (see also Bratt Paulston 1988; Mackey 1972).

4 Code-switching research

Perhaps the central issue in bilingualism research is code-switching, the alternative use by bilinguals of two or more languages in the same conversation. Under this general term, different forms of bilingual behaviour are subsumed. Sometimes switching occurs between the turns of different speakers in the conversation, sometimes between utterances within a single turn, and sometimes even within a single utterance. Readers will discover that the reasons proposed for, and the accounts given of, these switching behaviours are as various as the directions from which linguists approach code-switching.

At this point some terminology is useful; often the term 'intra-sentential' is used for switches within the sentence, in contrast with 'inter-sentential' used for switches between sentences. Sometimes the terms 'tag-switching', 'emblematic switching', or 'extra-sentential switching' are used to refer to a switching between an utterance and the tag or interjection attached to it.

In contrast with the research on bilingualism in general, and on borrowing and interference, the study of code-switching was slow in starting. Weinreich (1953) focusses mostly on lexical issues. Even cases from American Yiddish like:

er hot *gečéjndt* zajn *majnd*
he changed his mind

are treated as 'transfer of analyzed compounds' (1953: 50). A little later, listing reasons for borrowing, Weinreich writes:

> Finally, a bilingual's speech may suffer from the interference of another vocabulary through mere OVERSIGHT; that is, the limitations on the distribution of certain words to utterances belonging to one language are violated. In affective speech, when the speaker's attention is almost completely diverted from the form of the message to its topic, the transfer of words is particularly common. (p. 60)

About the same time, Haugen writes:

> Except in abnormal cases speakers have not been observed to draw freely from two languages at once. They may switch rapidly from one to the other, but at any given moment they are speaking only one, even when they resort to the other for assistance. The introduction of elements from one language into the other means merely an alteration of the second language, not a mixture of the two. (1950: 211)

It is not easy to understand the reasons for the relative invisibility of code-switching and particularly code-mixing to researchers such as Weinreich and Haugen. Four possible factors come to mind:

(a) a focus ultimately on 'langue', the bilingual language system, rather than on 'parole', bilingual language use, in spite of paying considerable attention to language use;

(b) a structuralist bent towards integrity of the grammatical system, for which code-switching and code-mixing were seen as a potential disturbance;

(c) lack of sophisticated recording equipment, which makes it possible for contemporary researchers to unobtrusively gather high-quality recordings of naturalistic bilingual conversations. This may have had two effects: first, more obtrusive recording techniques will yield bilingual language data that contain much less code-switching and code-mixing; second, when no recordings are made and the researcher has to rely afterwards on his or her recall of what was said, the principle of categorial perception will tend to filter out at least part of the language mixes;

(d) finally, the study of immigrant communities undergoing rapid language shift towards the dominant language may initially have been less propitious for discovering and analysing the phenomenon of switching than the much more stable bilingual communities that became the focus of research in the seventies. When Spanish–English and Hindi–English bilingualism were studied, code-switching soon came to the fore.

We have already mentioned above the research of Joshua Fishman in the Puerto Rican community in New York. While Fishman's work continues to be influential, many researchers have sought a supplementary framework which addresses in detail at a 'micro' level of analysis the interactional dynamics underlying code-switching and language choice.

Such an approach is provided by Gumperz's pioneering work on bilingual interactive strategies. Furthermore, his analyses directly contradict the view of code-switching as representing a deficient knowledge of language, a grammarless mixture of two codes. Language alternation is conceptualised not as a deficit to be stigmatised, but as an additional resource through which a range of social and rhetorical meanings are expressed (Gumperz 1982a, 1982b). Typically, he focusses not on details of constituent structure but on the discourse and interactional functions which code-switching performs for speakers. Gumperz examines this in terms of the influence of situational factors such as topic, participants and setting, and to this extent he is indebted to Fishman.

The oft-cited distinction between 'situational switching' (switching triggered by a change in the situation) and 'metaphorical switching' (switching that itself expresses a 'comment' on the situation) was made in a work by Blom and Gumperz (1972). This paper focusses on Norway, and introduces switching between related varieties. In this volume the chapter by Giacalone Ramat also focusses on switching involving dialects of the same language.

Since much switching occurs within a single conversation or utterance (conversational code-switching), Gumperz has also emphasised the strategic activities of speakers in varying their language choice within an agreed framework of social values and symbols. From this perspective, code-switching is an element in a socially agreed matrix of contextualisation cues and conventions used by speakers to alert addressees, in the course of ongoing interaction, to the social and situational context of the conversation (Gumperz, 1982: 132–52; 1984: 112). In recent years, Gumperz's approach has been developed by a number of scholars (particularly Peter Auer, whose work is represented in this volume).

A rather different perspective is taken in work by Georges Lüdi and colleagues (e.g. Lüdi 1987). In this work two intersecting but separate distinctions are drawn: (a) between 'exolingual interaction' ['interaction exolingue'], where speakers of different languages interact, and 'endolingual interaction' ['interaction endolingue'], involving speakers with the same language-background; (b) between 'unilingual' and 'bilingual' interaction. The combination of the two distinctions allows us to define four types of interaction:

exolingual	exolingual
bilingual	unilingual
(interactants with	(native and non-native speak-
different languages)	ers in one language)
endolingual	endolingual
bilingual	unilingual
(among bilinguals)	(among monolinguals)

A cover term 'marque transcodique' is used to refer to any phenomena indicative of the influence of one language upon the other, such as code-switches, borrowings and loan translations.

It is impossible to write about code-switching research entirely from a historical perspective. The authors of the pioneering studies in this field are often still actively contributing. While the earliest studies were often focussed on Spanish–English code-switching in the US or on the bilingual situation in the Indian subcontinent, now a wide variety of bilingual communities and language pairs is at present under study, using a variety of approaches and analytical techniques. Some of that variety is shown in the chapters of this book.

5 This volume: some comments on orientation and structure

There is a general lesson about co-operation to be learnt from this book as a whole and the chapters which comprise it, for these spring from a major research initiative supported by the European Science Foundation. The authors were all involved, to varying extents, in the activities of a European Science Foundation Research Network, which held a number of meetings between 1990 and 1993. At these meetings participants attempted to identify and focus on the principal issues which researchers into bilingualism needed to address, and to co-ordinate and make available information on a wealth of existing but largely uncoordinated research, particularly in Europe. Participants came from very different subdisciplines of linguistics; some had a social orientation, some a psychological or developmental one, some specialised in educational issues, some focussed on theoretical issues in linguistics, some had a particular interest in migrant communities, while yet others saw themselves as specialists working with particular language situations in their native countries. Gradually, all came to realise the benefits of an interdisciplinary perspective; bilingualism particularly is a topic which needs such a perspective. Following intensive interactions at a series of workshops and symposia, network members became able to contemplate the orderly treatment of a dauntingly heterogeneous field which is embodied in these specially commissioned chapters. This book is intended to provide, for the first time, an orderly, comprehensive and integrative treatment of the field as a whole.

Surprising as this may seem to non-linguists, a linguistics text which systematically deals with a single issue from as wide a range of subdisciplinary perspectives as the ones represented here is as rare as a pink rhinoceros. In addition to offering a comprehensive account of contemporary issues in bilingualism research, we hope to set here an example of integrative research and writing, to counter the trend of hyperspecialism which increasingly isolates linguists from other practitioners of the *sciences humaines* as well as from each other. This is a further and equally compelling reason for the multiple authorship of this volume. Each chapter is written by an acknowledged specialist in his or her subdiscipline, and no-one, even if s/he had unlimited time at his or her disposal (which we all lack, alas) could have written all these chapters with the authority and confidence of the specialists whose work is assembled here. While attempting to provide a much needed integrated and comprehensive coverage of a complex field with a flourishing research tradition, the book is structured with attention to the needs of researchers who are attempting to come to grips with the heterogeneous research literature. It is also intended to be of value to the lay reader who wants to find out about the state of the art in bilingualism research.

We commented above on the heterogeneous nature of bilingualism research. The intensive discussions at the meetings of the European Science Foundation Network on Code-Switching and Language Contact were the scene of (often strenuous) attempts to identify the principal issues in the field. The organisation of this book embodies our conviction that these issues can best be presented as clustering around four major topics, each of which has been addressed in some form by one or more of the influential scholars whose work we summarised above; recall particularly Weinreich's presentation of research perspectives as sociolinguistic, psycholinguistic and grammatical. These perspectives correspond to the four parts of this book, the first two parts embodying broadly (but not exclusively) a sociolinguistic perspective. The four parts deal in turn with code-switching in institutional and community settings, code-switching and social life, grammatical constraints on code-switching and code-switching in bilingual development and processing.

We conclude this introduction with some brief comments on two particular aspects of our editorial practice.

Firstly, the field of code-switching research is replete with a confusing range of terms descriptive of various aspects of the phenomenon. Sometimes the referential scope of a set of these terms overlaps and sometimes particular terms are used in different ways by different writers. When we started working together in the Research Network, one of our first endeavours was to standardise this terminology, with a view to imposing some order on a heterogeneous field of enquiry and ultimately producing rather more reader-friendly publications. This soon turned out to be an impossible task, and as a consequence no clear set of defined terms uniformly used by all authors can be found in this book. However, each author has attempted to locate his or her position within the overall field, and to clarify the particular terms used so as to minimise potential confusion.

Secondly, given the multidisciplinary nature of this book and the fact that the authors approach their topic from the perspective of a range of different disciplines and frameworks, it has proven neither sensible nor possible to achieve a uniform standard of complexity across all chapters. Some writers have concentrated on introducing new models (for example Myers-Scotton) while others (such as Martin-Jones) have found it more appropriate to locate their own work within quite extensive summaries of a developing research tradition. Furthermore, readers differ in their perceptions of complexity; one will perhaps find a chapter on grammatical constraints rather technical, another will not be familiar with the psycholinguistic background literature to some of the chapters on bilingual processing, and yet a third will need to concentrate on the sociological theories described in some of the chapters which deal with code-switching from a social perspective. Despite these problems however, the authors have tried to presuppose as little technical knowledge as possible, and in our role as editors we have attempted to ensure that every unfamiliar concept is briefly explained. We hope we have succeeded in producing, in close collaboration with the authors, an integrated and comprehensive volume which is a valuable tool to researchers in this dynamic and exciting multidisciplinary field.

Bibliography

Blom, J.-P. and Gumperz, J. J. (1972) Social meaning in linguistic structures: code-switching in Norway. In J. J. Gumperz, D. Hymes eds., *Directions in sociolinguistics. The ethnography of communication.* New York: Holt, Rinehart & Winston, 407–34.

Bloomfield, L. (1927) Literate and illiterate speech. *American Speech*, 2: 432–9. Reprinted in D. Hymes ed. (1964), *Language in culture and society.* New York: Harper and Row, 391–6.

Bratt Paulston, C. (1988) (ed.) *International handbook of bilingualism and bilingual education.* Westport, Conn.: Greenwood Press.

Clyne, M. (1967) *Transference and triggering.* The Hague: Nijhoff.

(1972) *Perspectives on language contact.* Melbourne: Hawthorne.

Cummins, J. (1979) Linguistic interdependence and the educational development of bilingual children. *Review of Educational Research*, 49: 222–51.

Fishman, J. A. (1965) Who speaks what language to whom and when? *La linguistique*, 2: 67–88.

Giles, H. and Coupland, N. (1992) *Language: contexts and consequences.* Milton Keynes: Open University Press.

Gumperz, J. J. (1982a) *Discourse strategies.* Cambridge University Press.

(1982b) *Language and social identity.* Cambridge University Press.

Haugen, E. (1950) The analysis of linguistic borrowing. *Language*, 26: 210–31.

(1953) *The Norwegian language in America.* 2 vols. Philadelphia: The University of Pennsylvania Press.

Horvath, V. (1985) *Variation in Australian English.* Cambridge University Press.

Klein, W. and Dittmar, N. (1979) *Developing grammars.* Berlin: Springer.

Labov, W. (1966) *The social stratification of English in New York City.* Washington: Center for Applied Linguistics.

Lambert, W. (1972) *Language, psychology, and culture.* Stanford University Press.

Le Page, R. B. and Tabouret-Keller, A. (1985) *Acts of Identity, creole-based approaches to language and ethnicity.* Cambridge University Press.

Leopold, F. (1939–49) *Speech development of a bilingual child; a linguist's record.* 4 vols. Evanston, Ill.: Northwestern University Press.

Lüdi, G. (1987) Les marques transcodiques: regards nouveaux sur le bilinguisme. In G. Lüdi ed., *Devenir bilingue–parler bilingue. Actes du 2e colloque sur le bilinguisme, Université de Neuchâtel, 20–22 Septembre, 1984.* Tübingen: Max Niemeyer Verlag, 1–21.

Mackey, W. F. (1972) *Bibliographie internationale sur le bilinguisme.* Quebec: Université Laval.

(1980) *Le bilinguisme et contact des langues.* Paris: Klinksieck.

Martin-Jones, M. and Romaine, S. (1986) Semi-lingualism: a half-baked theory of communicative competence. *Applied Linguistics*, 7: 26–38.

Paradis, M. (1978) *Aspects of bilingualism.* Columbia, S.C.: Hornbeam Press.

Ronjat, J. (1913) *Le développement du langage observé chez un enfant bilingue.* Paris: Champion.

Vildomec, V. (1963) *Multilingualism.* Leyden: A. W. Sythoff.

Weinreich, U. (1953) *Languages in contact.* The Hague: Mouton.

1

CODE-SWITCHING IN INSTITUTIONAL AND COMMUNITY SETTINGS

Louise Dabène and Danièle Moore

Bilingualism and language contact phenomena have attracted a lot of attention over the past decades and research on bilingualism is now well documented. Language contact research centres on different types of language contact situations and different forms of bilingualism. Nonetheless, most contributions appear to concentrate on a number of particular instances of language contact, and two main sociolinguistic fields of investigation seem to have attracted unequal academic attention. On the one hand, numerous studies have been devoted to observing the language behaviour of bilingual communities in long-established contact situations. Examples of such settings include indigenous linguistic minorities, whose languages survive within a higher-prestige language dominance (as Welsh and Gaelic speakers in Great Britain, or Alsatians in France; see for example chapter 4), or former immigrant populations (as Puerto Ricans in New York, or French-speaking Canadians in Ottawa; see for example Poplack 1980). A second research tradition focusses on the language behaviour of newly established populations, who settled in industrial urban areas largely as a result of labour migration during the years following the Second World War. In spite of some impressive research, there is still little known about the development of bilingualism and specific speech patterns in the latter context. Our emphasis here is on the complex issue of bilingualism in the specific contexts of labour migrations in Europe, and more specifically on aspects of the bilingual speech of two distinct Mediterranean groups of immigrants: the Iberian and Algerian communities living in France.

1 Migrant groups in Europe

1.1 Diversity in migration patterns

The incentives for migration are usually explained in terms of both push and pull factors united to encourage people to leave their homelands for a better future: the political and/or economic situation in the home country on the one hand, and the perceived work opportunities and social mobility in the receiving country on the other. Migratory situations in Europe give rise to diversified contact configurations, including movements of populations between European countries (for example, from Portugal to France) and the arrival of new extra-European groups (in particular from Asia or Africa). Immigration in Europe therefore reveals high degrees of heterogeneity.

1.1.1 The migratory process

Despite the above differences, it remains possible to classify migrant groups along a time axis and two intersecting dimensions: the place of origin, and the motivation underlying the original migration. It is then possible to establish a broad distinction between two main populations: (i) those originating from former European colonies whose distribution is dependent on the historical and political links prevailing between the host and home countries. Such populations include Indians, Pakistanis, Hong Kong Chinese and West Indians in England, or Algerians, Tunisians and Moroccans in France; (ii) those originating from poor European countries, such as Italians, Greeks, Spaniards and Portuguese, or from Eastern Europe (mainly as a result of refugee immigration between 1945 and 1950).

Interesting parallels mark the settlement patterns of migrant groups in Europe. Four clear phases can be identified, although time scales vary according to different situations.

(i) Early migration usually started with the arrival of single males who spontaneously left their homelands either for economic gain or for sheer adventure. As the first 'pioneers', they opened the path to many future followers. Agnihotri (1979) and Robinson (1986) note the example of temporary settlements of Sikh seamen in England. After only a few years, the majority of them returned to India. Nevertheless, they were immediately replaced in their occupations in England by close relatives or friends in a system of rotating transience. The very short periods of establishment inhibited the development of residential clusterings in the early stages of migration. Rather than geographical origins or a common language, a shared poverty was the foundation for groupings in the poor neighbourhoods of industrial cities:

> The small numbers involved in the pioneer phase and the imperma-
> nence of settlement prevented the development of uniquely ethnic
> areas in British cities. Even in 1949, for example, there were still
> fewer than 100 Indians in Birmingham. As a result, the pioneers
> occupied scattered accommodation in the twilight zone of Britain's
> cities where they followed the Poles and other East Europeans in a
> loose ecological succession. (Robinson 1986: 27)

(ii) The years after the Second World War marked a radical change in population movements in Europe. Because of the high demand for cheap labour to deal with war losses and reconstruction, migration swelled, peaking in the 1960s, but was still considered temporary. The migratory phenomenon evolved and shifted, as older intra-European migrations steadily declined while the number and variety of both sending and receiving countries increased: 'in addition to such traditional immigrant nations as Canada, the United States, Australia, New Zealand and Argentina, countries throughout Western Europe, notably Germany, France, Switzerland, Sweden and the Netherlands, now attract immigrants; and for the first time Europe has become an area of immigration rather than emigration' (Massey 1990: 62).

(iii) The implementation of new entry regulations in most European countries in the 1970s transformed immigration patterns once again. Whereas migration entered a consolidation phase spurred by the reunification of families, restrictive policies suddenly speeded new arrivals. The fear of not being allowed to gain access to major industrial European countries stimulated a new wave of migration, regardless of new economic circumstances and labour demand. Restrictive policies largely contributed to the selection of migrants, in terms of places of origin and membership in migratory networks already well-established in the receiving countries.

(iv) Migration enters its fourth phase with the emergence of a new population: the new generations, born or settled at an early age in the host country, and educated in a language and a culture different from those reinforced in school and the society at large.

1.1.2 Receiving contexts and linguistic configurations

Fundamental differences in the legal treatment granted to various categories of migrants in various receiving contexts in Europe can be attributed to many factors: whether the migrants belong to former colonies or not, originate from Europe or not, are considered as refugees, etc. The legal status granted to migrants is linked closely to the image attached to migration in the eyes of the receiving community. In addition, people from particular groups continue to be considered as foreigners, whereas their legal status gives them citizenship in the host country. This is the case, for example, of the Harki children and numerous young Algerians in France, and the members of many ex-Commonwealth countries in England.

The status attributed to minority languages in education is another critical issue. Whether or not the country of origin is European is a key factor shaping the migrants' status, and subsequently the status attributed to their home language within the dominant school system. Learning high-prestige European languages (such as Italian, Portuguese or Spanish) still plays a key role in gaining upward social mobility. Other languages such as Turkish, Arabic and Urdu traditionally hold marginal positions in the education system, although efforts have been made to counteract their devaluation in recent years.

The lack of prestige of minority languages, closely bound to the socio-economic and legal position of the speakers, is worsened when the parents' language variety is different from the standard taught in school. Such is the case with Panjabi children in England who learn Urdu (see Moore 1992) or Algerian children in France exposed to classical Arabic in the school system (see Falip and Deslandes 1989). Lüdi (1990: 122) highlights even more complex polyglossic situations with the example of Sicilian children in Zurich, a German-speaking part of Switzerland. These children may use their parents' Sicilian dialect at home, learn standard Italian as their home language at school and German (hochdeutsch) as the official school language. To complicate matters, they must also develop sufficient knowledge of Schwyzertütsch to communicate in ordinary conversations in the host area. Such multiple-level discrepancies often contribute to further marginalisation:

> It is only natural that, to validate languages and cultures (both in the eyes of the children and families of the guest and host communities), they are presented in their most legitimate and normative forms. It is no less surprising that some children feel a double minorization in

their own language practices when compared to the linguistic models offered through school, and the image given of their home language and culture. (Coste 1989: 176; see also Dabène 1989)

1.2 Common features in migration patterns

1.2.1 The importance of chain migration and social networks

Despite a large variety of situations, common patterns characterise migratory biographies, specifically in relation to the access modes to the new country and the restructuring of social networks in the new environment. For most groups, recurrent patterns of settlement seem to obey common mechanisms. First, the early settlers incite family and village members to travel to the host country and join the work force. Specific migratory chains rapidly emerge, and directly foster a selection amongst would-be candidates for migration. At the same time, chain migration funnels new arrivals into specific reception areas in the host country, and therefore accentuates voluntary clustering and social encapsulation.

One can thus observe a number of recurring traits which characterise labour migration. First, the separation of nuclear families dislodges an otherwise coherent grouping. Single men, fathers and husbands immigrate in search of economic opportunities that will better the lives of the families they left behind, while women and children typically come and join them only years later. This two-step immigration process further distances the immigrants from the host society, labelling them as an unstable fringe group.

Such migration mechanisms are not new. In the 1930s, Algerian pioneers in Paris set up comprehensive networks of lodgings to accommodate their newly arrived fellow-workers (Dubet 1989). Up to 80 per cent of the present-day workers at Renault's automobile factories immigrated from northern Africa, and are distributed in four different provincial groups (MIGRINTER 1986). Similarly, Boubakri (1984) notes that the high concentration of Tunisian restaurants and shops in specific Parisian streets corresponds to a high homogeneity in the owners' places of origin: most of them come from Ghoumrassen and the Tunis area. Salem (1984) shows that the circulatory movements of various groups from Africa follow highly organised networks, functioning both as reception and credit centres. An example of such a phenomenon is the Senegalese pedlars' commercial network in France. The strong internal cohesion and the success of the migratory chain are reinforced by the fact that pedlars belong to the same ethnic groups, mostly the Laobe Mbouky (from Thies), but also the Laobe Diula and Yett. Patterns of settlement in various French cities confirm the constitution of highly organised networks for each particular group, supported by common housing and food shelters as the foundations for their different commercial systems.

Similar phenomena can be observed in other parts of Europe. For example, Saifullah-Khan (1987) shows that the Indo-Pakistanis in the English industrial city of Bradford (Yorkshire) originate principally from the Punjab, and more specifically from the Mirpur region. Nortier (1989) explains the over-representation of Moroccans in Utrecht in the Netherlands by labour-recruiting practices that led to massive arrivals in the country, frequently in a second phase of migration that first led them to France or Belgium. The mechanism of migratory chains also explains the highly concentrated geographical origins. Moroccans in the Netherlands belong to three main groups, originating respectively from the Rif mountains in northern Morocco, the Casablanca region in the west, and the Anti-Atlas in the south: 'Moroccans who have only recently arrived in the Netherlands often have friends and acquaintances in the closed group of people they already knew, directly or via other people, in their place of region or origin' (Nortier 1989: 18).

A mainly urban settlement, whereas most migrants are themselves from rural areas, and the discrepancies linked to the migration situation itself, lead to the quick reconstitution of relation networks based on the village models. These different factors explain spatial distributions and the emergence of ethnic enclaves in cities with large migrant populations: Chinatowns in London or Paris, Pakistani clusterings in the industrial cities and towns of northern England, Arabic concentrations in Marseille, and Turkish groupings in Berlin. Clustering, reinforced by the arrival of women and children, allows groups to function as a micro-society – or an extended family – and to reactivate social duties between community members. Embracing these social obligations allows the community to protect itself from out-group values, as well as to validate in-group linguistic and behavioural models.

The mechanisms of chain migrations highlighted in these various examples have important repercussions on the restructuring of the different groups' social networks, and subsequently on linguistic behaviours, as we will discuss later. In particular, autonomisation of migrant communities, and their recourse to a social structure based on the models offered by the home culture, allows members who do not have to maintain close links with the host society (for example, housewives) to develop minimal skills in the majority language. Women usually seem to be the most affected by such phenomena. Their central position in families imposes the extensive usage of the original language as the privileged code for daily conversation. It is then essentially through the mediation of school-age children that the majority language penetrates the home context.

1.2.2 The evolution of the migrant group concept

Group membership *a priori* is first determined by birth, and is strengthened through family and kinship relations. *A posteriori*, it is determined by the individual's decisions (Dittmar 1989). The group, by establishing the boundaries between members and non-members, organises social functioning based on intimacy and strong moral obligations.

Group membership is a central notion. Conformity to the demands and obligations attached to group adherence allows assessment of members' loyalty: 'the patrimony dimension is suffused with moral implications, with judgements of good or bad, with specifications (stereotyped "markedness") in terms of which one is evaluated and in terms of which one evaluates others vis-à-vis the fulfilment of own-group membership requirements' (Fishman 1989: 28). Language therefore plays the part of an 'emotional cement' in own-group recognition and the determination of in- and out-group boundaries.

Group membership is not a static phenomenon: it can develop and change over time and according to situations. As stated earlier, first migrants tend to muster because of their difference from the host community. With the increase of newcomers and the consequential reinforcement of groups, the bases for aggregations progressively modify. A higher selectivity in terms of place of origin, common language and often religion, determines group formation.

Identification with a community language is probably the key factor in group strengthening and stabilisation. Language can be invested and recognised as the guide to kinship-interpreted group membership, and as the open demonstration of it. Language then undertakes once again its role as 'the supreme symbol system [that] quintessentially symbolizes its users and distinguishes between them and others' (Fishman 1989: 217). In other words, the need to display identity increases with the need to assert differentiation. Language acts as a strong federative medium, and entails emblemacy of group membership claims: 'three fundamental factors – race, religion, language – partake of a power no other possible factors of ethnic identities have: language, because, while being one element of culture among others, it transcends all other elements in so far as it has the power to name, express and convey them' (Abou 1981: 33).

As a result, the groups' autonomy increases, while they tend to develop their own social and cultural resources, in particular through the establishment of community shops, associations, schools and churches. At the same time, an elite emerges which serves as an intermediary between the two communities and ensures the necessary intergroup communication.

As such, language is much more than a simple means of communication; it is clearly invested with symbolic boundary functions. Language represents a reliable guide for the interpretation of eligibility for group membership. Because of its strong emblematic power, language choice defines adherence to group values and sets the limits between those who can speak the language and those who cannot. Loyalty to the endo-group is thus measured on a language choice based on conflict, rather than agreement, with other groups in contact (Martin-Jones 1987).

Sometimes two languages, rather than one, can act as group-membership symbols and demonstrate ethnic identity. Such is the case with Urdu and Panjabi for Muslim Punjabis in the north of England. Panjabi is the oral language used for everyday interactions, whereas Urdu marks membership and faithfulness to the Pakistani Muslim community, as opposed to Sikh Punjabis, who assert their difference by adhesion to a written form of spoken Panjabi: the gurmukhi script.

Individuals in contact situations may wish to assert various degrees of loyalty towards different groups, and adapt their language choices accordingly. The phenomenon is therefore a dynamic one; it can vary in time and is dependent on situation. Young adolescents in post-migratory situations, who have been socialised in rival cultural and linguistic systems, often feel part of both home and host cultures, and demonstrate convergence through language choice to one or the other according to the situation. They can also develop attachment to a completely new group, generally constituted of their peers, with a new system of values and norms, and adopt a vernacular language not accessible to non-members.

1.2.3 The evolution of the notion of return

While all migrations are assumed to be temporary, numerous indications attest that migration in Europe has clearly entered a permanent phase (see Lüdi 1990: 119). The schooling of young generations in the host state's education system probably acts as one of the major factors hindering return to the home country. Added to this is the difficulty of going back after a lengthy period of time, and the anxieties linked to labour shortage and housing scarcity in the home country. The fact that an increasing number of women from migrant backgrounds have taken up employment is a further reason inhibiting leaving, although their percentage varies greatly according to group of origin. The example of migrant women workers in France provides a clear indication of the heterogeneity of situations since no less than 62% of Portuguese women were employed in 1982 compared to 22% amongst Tunisian women (Dubet 1989: 15). Lastly, the migrants' fear of unfulfilled aims and hopes is a further hindrance to returning to the homeland. For example, surveys carried out in France and Germany with Portuguese and Turkish populations showed that their returns to the homeland were linked to severe failure in the migratory enterprise, and only rarely motivated by financial success (Dubet 1989: 17).

The aspiration to return to the homeland, however unlikely such a return may be, remains a powerful motivation for first-generation immigrants. Most of them keep close ties with their relatives and home country, through letters, audio and video tapes, and holiday trips. These long-lasting and multiplex relationships play a crucial part in the reactivation of home-language use within the families, and more especially when interacting with the youngest children. The focus on an eventual return highlights the wide discrepancy observable between the migrants and their home country, described by Oesch-Serra as 'the cultural loyalty to the original matrix, often stretching to the limits of hyperconservation' (1990: 214).

2 The development of bilingual linguistic behaviour in migratory situations

2.1 Current research on bilingual speech and migrants

2.1.1 Perspectives and field investigation

We follow here Gumperz's definition of code-switching as 'the juxtaposition within the same speech exchange of passages of speech belonging to different grammatical systems or subsystems' (1982: 59).

Code-switching mechanisms in bilingual speech constitute an important aspect of bilingualism, and a dynamic and promising research field, although the awareness that code-switching is linguistically constrained, and not haphazard or the result of lack of competence in one, or both, of the languages, is a rather recent development in research.

Although different orientations underlie studies of bilingual speech, much research has been devoted to long-standing language contact settings. These specific situations usually entail a relative stabilisation between two linguistic groups and generally involve typologically close language pairs. Noteworthy examples include Poplack's work on bilingual speech patterns of Francophones in Canada, and the numerous studies on the speech behaviour of Chicanos in the

United States. Groups under observation generally share common features, notably rather symmetrical competence in both of the languages in contact, with each of them being assigned to fairly well-defined domains of use. Bilingual verbal repertoires appear therefore fairly stable, and unlikely to undergo dramatic stages of development and change.

The observation of bilingual speech specifically in work situations is better developed in research which focusses on newly established migrant populations, rather than on long-term, stable contact situations. From a linguistic perspective, these contact situations involve either typologically close languages (see research on Spanish and Portuguese immigration, Araujo Carreira 1991, and the work reported in this chapter) or typologically distant languages such as Turkish and Dutch (Boeschoten and Verhoeven 1987), Moroccan Arabic and Dutch (Nortier 1989), or Algerian Arabic and French (see present work). Recently established groups share distinct traits, including unstabilised repertoires at an initial stage of contact, asymmetrical competence in the different languages, and differences in repertoire structure according to age and birth order. Moreover, particularly complex linguistic behaviours can be at work when code-switching does not arise from the migration situation: in Algeria, code-switching between French and Algerian Arabic is part of ordinary everyday conversation. Therefore, immigration does not initiate bilingual speech, but because of immigration bilingual speech undergoes drastic structural alterations. In such contexts, the symbolic value attached to the languages in contact is an active component of identity reconstruction processes for the newly settled. Evaluative reactions to code-switching amongst community members and non-members, and social categorisation of speakers on the basis of their switching behaviour therefore deserves full attention on the part of researchers.

2.1.2 Methodological options and data collection

It is quite clear that linguists do not adhere to a common standard of research design and their options in data collection can vary extensively in relation to research fields and objectives. Broadly speaking, three main perspectives underlie research orientations and contribute to providing valuable and complementary insights into bilingual speech and code-switching phenomena.

(i) A traditional approach consists of using standardised experimental procedures to elicit speech samples. Informants are generally recruited according to strict selection criteria.

(ii) A second approach favours informal recorded interviews with bilingual interviewers. Here again, informants are chosen according to various defined criteria whilst test situations are most often socially marked (interviews are for instance recorded at school).

(iii) A third orientation aims at collecting natural language in interaction situations which are as authentic as possible. A high value is placed upon participant observations carried out by investigators from the same groups. Other procedures require self-recordings in situations within self-constituted groups and without the intervention of outsiders (even when they are bilingual and members of the same communities).

2.1.3 An example: the Iberian and Algerian communities in Grenoble, France

Our research in the Grenoble area in France has been designed with similar perspectives in mind and centres on the observation of natural speech in authentic interaction situations within self-constituted groups. Data should then be collected in situations where the alternate use of two languages is ensured by the dual competence of the interlocutors and a shared feeling of in-group membership. Although close attention is given to adult speech patterns, our main interest lies principally in the attitudes and linguistic behaviour of young adolescents, often inappropriately labelled as 'second-generation immigrants'.

We sought to develop research procedures capable of integrating various dimensions for the empirical study of bilingualism phenomena in migratory settings, especially through the study of the different *strategies* which these groups have been developing to deal with two languages in contact. By strategies, we mean (i) the attitudes (high or low regard for the languages involved), (ii) the degrees of linguistic awareness (metalinguistic, sociolinguistic), and (iii) the different types of language practices (differentiated use of their bilingual competence according to situations, speakers, settings, topics, relationships between the participants in the interchange etc.).

Although the first two aspects were analysed by means of surveys based on data from interviews and individual conversations, it was necessary to collect actual language samples produced in the most authentic contexts possible in order to analyse the subjects' verbal behaviour. This step was greatly facilitated by the fact that the field-workers belonged to the same ethnic community as the subjects and consequently faced less difficulty than outsiders would have faced in collecting data.

Our original hypothesis can be summarised as follows: it seemed that the children of immigrant parents were developing a particular form of bilingualism based on a more or less functional distribution of their available codes, as pointed out by Mackey (1982). Born and educated in France, the majority of these adolescents can be considered native French speakers. Nevertheless, this does not mean that their parents' original language has disappeared from their linguistic repertoire. Even though we cannot speak of a traditional diglossic situation here, it is necessary to emphasise that the original language assumes specific functions even if the number of occurrences varies according to the individual level of bilingualism (generally higher among the Iberian population than among the Algerian one) and the context.

According to our initial assumption, two constraints were imposed. Firstly, we had to observe language behaviour in situations which allowed the subjects to use their entire linguistic repertoire. These situations were essentially found in two different social networks: family and peer group. Secondly, we had to pay particular attention to the way in which the two codes were articulated, code-switching being considered a strong indication of the type of bilingualism the subjects resorted to.

Given that our study emphasised verbal exchanges in a family context, we felt it was also necessary to analyse the parents' speech in order to take into consideration its specific characteristics. As a result, we had to deal with a double corpus: two populations, one Spanish or Portuguese and the other Algerian, further divided into two age groups corresponding to the respective generations under study. The analysis should help answer the following questions: (i) what contextual contraints condition the use of code-switching (CS) as identified by the principal types of code-switches found in our corpus? (ii) what conditions regarding the situation and the type of bilingualism noted seem to encourage the use of code-switching?

2.2 Social networks and in-group communication

Despite the evidence of numerous common points between the different groups of migrants settled in Europe (as discussed earlier), research on language contact and bilingualism insists on the variety that marks their language behaviour. Heterogeneity is observable in three particularly salient contexts: (i) the way languages are transmitted (and the inter-generational evolution of that transmission); (ii) language usage within the family and for outside interactions (in particular at school and in the neighbourhood); (iii) identity allegiances attached to language choice or to code-switching (de Heredia-Deprez 1991).

Linguistic repertoires of the various groups settled in Europe include a wide range of oral and written skills. Nonetheless, individual members in each group can show various degrees of competence within the potential linguistic repertoire accessible to their community. Competence is partly dependent on the degree of schooling in the country of origin, and the subsequent access to information and literature available in that language in the host country. Some individuals have little opportunity to use their home language outside the nuclear family, and therefore need to develop a certain degree of proficiency in the host language in order to communicate. Others need not do so since use of the home language allows them to participate in a wide range of daily situations. All different factors involve differential access to the languages in contact, and a subsequent unequal distribution of language skills. We shall not comment further on the influence of social network structure on language maintenance and language use (see Milroy and Li, this volume). Various groups manage to retain extensive in-group relations. Language choices depend to a considerable extent on the type of social networks favoured within the communities, and on linguistic norms and value systems that community networks protect and impose on members.

Special attention should thus be given to the study of speech patterns and language behaviour in two key social networks: the family, because families function as micro-societies largely reflecting language choice rules in the community at large; and adolescent peer groups, as adolescents are the most important link between home and host communities. While considered to be of extreme interest, communication patterns within migrant families and adolescent peer groups still remain an open field for investigation, mainly because they are so difficult to observe.

In the following sections we shall first provide a general overview of language behaviour prevalent in the two communities under study, depending on situations and interlocutors, and later discuss in greater detail why, when and how people switch from one language to the other.

2.2.1 Intra-family communication

Iberian populations from Spain and Portugal and Algerian communities constitute two large groups heavily represented in Grenoble and its surroundings. The history and motives for migration, and the structure of the groups once settled differ considerably. They nevertheless reveal strong similarities with respect to family relations, and to the role of women in preserving original values.

Because of their social position within the migrant group, women often need not maintain extensive relations with the host society. They consequently tend to develop more limited skills in the host language than do men and children. Women therefore generally assign themselves the role of guardians of home language retention and use within nuclear and extended families. Observation shows that they more systematically resort to the home language in family interaction, while other members of the community appear to comply with the same language choice when conversing with them. Nevertheless, adolescents' language behaviour and linguistic preferences can vary to a large degree across the two communities, as will be emphasised in the next section.

Non-reciprocal language use seems to be a very frequent pattern within the migrant families under observation. Most often, parents use the home language to address their children whereas the young generations prefer to answer back in the host language. This pattern, commonly observed by researchers in France (see Dabène and Billiez 1986; de Heredia-Deprez 1991; Merabti 1992; Merabti and Moore 1993), is not a general phenomenon among migrant communities (see, for a counter-example, Moore 1992). Beyond possible variation in the adoption of specific conversation rules, migrant families seem to evolve into unique settings of linguistic mediation between parents and children, older and younger children, home and host languages. The mutual teaching of languages developed within families is conducive to linguistic creativity; as a result, each family cell becomes a privileged setting for specific linguistic behaviour and interactional patterns (Dabène 1991).

2.2.2 Adolescent peer groups and peer vernacular

The language young adolescents from Iberian and Algerian backgrounds identify with, and consider themselves to be fluent in, is seldom the language they have learned in early childhood and continue to use in daily interaction in the family. Although the preferred language in peer groups is most often the host one, home languages still play an important role as symbolic markers of group membership. The values attached to their use are nonetheless clearly different from those linked to home-language retention for the older generations. In particular, new linguistic phenomena appear with the emergence of plurilingual vernacular languages. The use of new interethnic vernaculars, based on the host language and enriched with linguistic contributions from various other languages, has been under observation in contexts where high concentrations of multilingual children are in close contact (Dabène and Biliez 1986). Youngsters are confronted with the peer vernacular early on, when playing in the streets or going to school.

The learning and use of minority languages by adolescents from different linguistic backgrounds allow multilingual adolescent peer groups to define in-group identity through a refocussing of norms and exclusion of non-speakers. The emergence of a new multilingual youth code marks a remarkable expansion in both the numbers of speakers and the domains of minority language use. Hewitt (1982) mentions similar phenomena in England with Afro-Caribbean adolescent peer groups in London, and Edwards (1986) cites the example of British-born West Indians in the West Midlands. Rampton (1991) reports that the learning and use of the various languages used in multilingual peer groups (Panjabi, Creole and English) imply see-saw motions in prestige hierarchy, since each speaker in turn is considered a linguistic expert or novice, and so on.

The multilingual repertoire draws in-group boundaries and signals group solidarity. The resort to the vernacular for interaction marks its users' youth and membership of pluriethnic backgrounds. It also consolidates their opposition to out-group values and, more especially, adult norms. In other words, bilingual speech patterns in peer groups can present drastic differences from adult bilingualism and speech patterns favoured within families, in terms of the number of languages involved, the structure of language change, and the symbolic value attached to language choice.

2.3 Types of code-switching and their constraints

In the previous section, we discussed language use in migrant communities, focussing our attention on the general conversational rules governing language choices in two key networks: family and peer group. This section will provide an overview of bilingual language usage, and classify types of code-switching and their constraints. All following examples are excerpts from recordings of family and peer group conversations.

2.3.1 Inter-utterance code-switching

One type of code-switching can occur between two utterances spoken by the same speaker. Since the two utterances can be fairly far apart from each other in the course of a dialogue, we tend to consider this type of linguistic behaviour as an instance of change of code rather than an example of code-switching. Researchers have frequently observed that this phenomenon is often conditioned by the utterance that immediately precedes it. It also allows the interlocutors to switch from one type of interaction to another.

Children of immigrant parents in our study in Grenoble tend to switch codes in this manner when they are in a family context, according to whether they are addressing their brothers and sisters (more often French-speaking) or their parents – and especially their mothers (see above). In previous studies, we called this phenomenon of convergence in language choice between two speakers *homodialectal adhesion*. Homodialectal adhesion can be said to be discourse-related, if the choice is determined by the immediately preceding utterance

(1)   (during an exchange in Spanish)
        A– Ben moi, je suis pour la télé
           [If you want my opinion, I am for television]
        B– Ben moi, je vais te dire
           [If you want my opinion, I will tell you]

Homodialectal adhesion can be said to be participant-related if the choice is dependent on the interlocutor, even in the event that the interlocutor chose the other language. The following example illustrates this phenomenon:

(2)   (discussion between parents and children concerning potential guests at Christmas)

A (son)	– Luis, il vient?
	[Is Luis coming?]
B (Luis's friend)	– J'sais pas
	[I don't know]
C (mother)	– No t'a pe dit?
	[He didn't tell you?]
B	– *No porque hay sus primos*
	[*No, because his cousins are there*]

Despite the fact that B's mother momentarily abandons her native language to ask B a question in a rather approximate version of French, B responds in Spanish.

2.3.2 Inter-sentential or intra-sentential code-switching?

Inter-sentential vs intra-sentential CS is a difficult notion to maintain with respect to an oral corpus in which incomplete sentences are predominant. It seems more appropriate to base our analysis on the notion of *act* (Sinclair and Coulthard 1975; Roulet 1981) as a functional unit. Certain instances of code-switching separate different acts and indicate changes in discourse orientation, as in the following example, in which CS marks the passage from a statement to a request for information:

(3)   (mother–son dialogue)

    Son   – *¿Qué hiciste de comida?*
            [*What did you make to eat?*]

    Mother – *Carne de cocido*
            [*stew . . .*]

    Son   – *Pero está rojo el caldo* – comment ça se fait?
            [*But the broth is red* – how come?]

2.3.3 Segmental or unitary code-switching

Within this definition of an act, it is possible to distinguish between two types of switching, involving either CS modifying a segment of an utterance or a single item. In the first case, we propose the term segmental code-switching. This can involve either an entire clause, which can be juxtaposed as follows:

(4)   – *La semana próxima tengo cada vez de las doce a las dos y luego tengo que venir otra vez*, pendant au moins trois jours je fais ça
       [*Next week, I'm working from noon to two and afterwards I have to come back,* I have to do that for three days]

or it can involve a phrase which can take on different functions in the utterance. In the following example, the phrase functions as a circumstantial:

(5)   (within an exchange almost entirely in Spanish)
    Avant, ben c'est vrai, avant non, *no existía eso en España*
    [Before, that's true, before, *that didn't exist in Spain*]

In the second case, which we call unitary code-switching or insert, only one element is affected. We can find two possible configurations. In the first configuration (insert 1), the L2 element is treated syntactically as an L1 element:

(6)   (L1 French–L2 Arabic   – Quelle *hEts*
                [What *a shame*]

(7)   (L1 Spanish–L2 French) – *Era bueno aquel* gâteau
                                    [*That cake was* good]

The above examples illustrate mainly lexical items. However, CS can also affect discourse connectors:

(8)   (L1 Spanish–L2 French) – Mais, *es por eso que nunca las he probado*
                                    [But, *that's why I never tasted them*]

modifiers:

(9)   (L1 French–L2 Arabic)   – *Belek* ils sont déjà partis
                                    [*Maybe* they are already gone]

or an adverb:

(10)   (L1 French–L2 Arabic)   – Platini *walla* Platino maintenant
                                    [Platini *has become* Platino now]

In the second configuration (insert 2), the L2 element is simply inserted in the L1 utterance without taking on a predetermined syntactic function. These terms generally fulfil an exclamatory function.

(11)   (L1 French–L2 Arabic)   – Les soeurs musulmanes se balladent avec
                                    une chemise, *wallah*, c'est vrai!
                                    [Muslim sisters go around in shirts, *I swear*,
                                    it's true!]

The sociolinguistic function of this type of code-switching, frequently used in the speech of the young Algerian subjects, but practically nonexistent in the speech of the Spanish- and Portuguese-speaking subjects, will be commented on later in the text. Figure 1.1 illustrates the different types of CS.

One can obviously ask to what extent the instances of code-switching we have labelled 'unitary' could also be considered as 'loan-words'. In our opinion, considering the specific linguistic characteristics of the communities under study, the notion of loan-words is rather awkward and we prefer not to use it. The reasons for our position are as follows.

Firstly, one of the deciding factors in identifying a loan-word is its recurrent use in a community (Poplack 1989). However, the immigrant populations living in France are not confined to a specific geographic area; even though they tend to maintain certain associative relationships, there has been no sign of the emergence of a systematically organised intermediary dialect (or interlect) of any type which

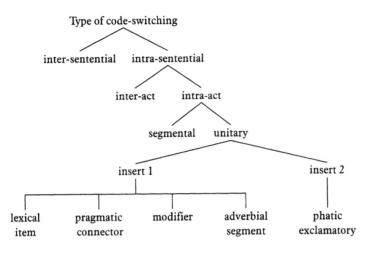

Figure 1.1

could be easily described. Rather, what has been observed is a series of highly variable contact phenomena, dependent on both the interlocutors and the situation and affecting different levels of language.

In the case of the Spanish-speaking subjects, such variability is further accentuated by the linguistic diversity of their native country (the interlect of a Galician is very different from that of an Andalusian). As for the Algerian immigrants, the problem is no less complex, but for a different reason. As was emphasised before, the practice of using French and Arabic dates back to a period long before the beginning of the migratory movement to France with the result that it can be considered a constitutive aspect of the dialectal form of Arabic spoken in Algeria. Consequently, it is difficult to situate with any precision the moment of entry of an L2 term into the L1 repertoire and thus classify it as a loan-word rather than an instance of code-switching.

Secondly, at a theoretical level, it seems more profitable to consider the subjects as possessors of a 'linguistic repertoire' that could be described as 'linguistically heterogeneous', but functionally homogeneous; each individual assigns a distributional function to each code. Contrary to a typical diglossic situation in which the functions are determined more or less permanently by the social constraints that govern the bilingual context, our subjects must resort to a continual renegotiation of the conditions that allow CS, based on a large number of different parameters. Some parameters depend on the setting (global environment, types of interaction, relationships between the interlocutors, topic of the interaction); others depend on discursive factors (pragmatic or stylistic intent, change of register, metalinguistic intent, etc.; Gumperz 1982; Dabène and Billiez 1986). Furthermore, these parameters are dependent upon the linguistic repertoire of the speaker, that is, his specific type of bilingual behaviour.

This complex alchemy varies greatly from one individual to another, but as far as our subjects are concerned, we noticed the recurrence of certain types of behaviour which allowed us to determine several major categories.

2.4 Types of bilingual behaviour and their conditions of emergence

The following two examples clearly emphasise the diversity of linguistic behaviour observed in our study.

2.4.1 Family C (of Spanish origin)

The participants in this interaction are J, J's parents and two friends, a boy, L, and a girl, C (our field-worker).

If we compare the number of CS tokens produced by the participants, we note a clear difference: despite a similar number of tokens, inter-act CS represents 63% of J's code-switching patterns, as illustrated by the following example in which the change of code allows the speaker to comment on what she has just said.

(12)   *Yo mañana empiezo, me levanto a las siete de la mañana,* je suis malade rien que de le savoir
[*Tomorrow, I start working, I've got to get up at 7 o'clock,* I feel sick only to think about it]

The only instances of intra-act code-switching used by J are lexical items which constitute the main point of a metalinguistic discussion:

(13)   J   – C'était 'sans blagues', pour dire 'sans blagues' il disait '*sin bragas*'
[It was 'no kidding', to say 'no kidding' he said '*without pants*']
Father – *No, no tu lo has comprendido mal. Yo he dicho 'sans blaga'*
[*No, no you didn't get it right. I said 'sans blaga'*]

On the other hand, the father's use of intra-act code-switching, accompanied by syntactic transfers, rises to 84.4%:

(14)   – C'est les mieux conserves *que hay, es de Galicia*
          [They are the best, *from Galicia*]

There are also many examples of the influence of one language on the other in the parents' speech: lexical transfers from French to Spanish ('hemos ida en "vila"') or from Spanish to French ('conte-nous ton histoire') as well as grammatical transfers (confusion between 'mieux' and 'meilleur' due to the existence of only one corresponding term in Spanish, 'mejor' for 'better': see ex. 14).

Two major types of speech patterns thus emerge: (i) CS is frequent, syntactically integrated, and it accompanies other indications of the language contact (such as transfers: 'mieux' instead of 'meilleur'); (ii) CS is juxtaposed and stylistically integrated (a commentary). There is no evidence of restructuring one language under the influence of the other.

We can then say that for this family there are two fundamentally different types of bilingual behaviour:

(i) the younger generation tends to use elements from both languages as a discourse strategy that allows stylistic or pragmatic differences. We will speak in this case of a *functional bilingualism*;

(ii) the older generation (the parents) tends to use elements from the two languages in contact in order to compensate for the insufficient mastery of either code. We will refer to such a phenomenon as *complementary bilingualism*.

2.5 A group of young Algerians in the Grenoble area

This group, which has been the focus of our research for several years, is made up of young Algerians living in the same residential complex. Their speech samples were taped in settings where they were among members of their respective families. They consisted of conversations among themselves or with native French-speakers from the same age group, usually classmates. Within this group, let us examine in some detail the linguistic behaviour of one of the girls, S.

We obtain Table 1.1 by classifying the types of CS produced by S and by distributing the types according to different communicative settings:

A look at this table as well as a detailed analysis of the corpus leads us to the following observations: in the family setting, change of language choice appears to be the dominant type of code-switching. This is largely due to a discourse-related homodialectal adhesion phenomenon, as previously defined: S is talking primarily with her mother who speaks almost exclusively Arabic. When the girls are talking together, the dominant type of CS is once again a change of language choice, but

Table 1.1

Types of CS	Setting family	peer group girls only	(mixed)
Change in choice	11	9	4
Inter-act	2	7	0
Incidental CS	3	3	4
Insert 1	0	5	5
Insert 2 (phatic)	1	4	2

more diversified forms also appear. When the boys enter into the conversation, the dominant type of CS is of the insert type. An analysis of the speech patterns of the boys amongst themselves reveals that the dominant type is also the insert, more notably the phatic insert (see above). However, the boys tend to use much more French in the family setting than the girls.

The communicative setting seems, therefore, to determine certain types of code-switching.

(i) The family context and the exclusively female interactions, which can be considered an extension of mother–daughter dialogue, constitute settings which condition a certain type of CS;

(ii) Peer group interactions encourage the emergence of a particular type of CS, labelled insert 2, which predominantly makes use of phatic and exclamatory terms. This type of behaviour does not require a high degree of competence in the language from which the element is borrowed; in fact, this same practice is noted in the speech of native French-speakers who have Algerian friends. Moreover, this speech pattern does not seem to correspond to a specific linguistic function. It plays an essentially symbolic role and provides a procedure for the group to affirm its identity. This explains why it is paradoxically absent in family interactions where the subjects feel less of a need to display signs of their identity.

For many young men of Algerian descent, this type of linguistic behaviour seems to be the only sign of what we will call a residual bilingualism from a linguistic point of view, and a symbolic bilingualism from a sociolinguistic one.

2.6 Conclusion: from complementary to functional bilingualism

Through the two examples presented and our earlier comments, we hope to have underlined the distinctive modes of bilingual behaviour of speakers in migrant or post-migrant situations, and to add to the understanding of current research issues. From our observations, two major points clearly stand out.

On the one hand, the first-generation speakers under observation use a type of code-switches that tend to be of an essentially remedial nature: a combination of the two languages is often necessary to express communicative intent. We can assume – and this assumption has been partially verified – that their speech behaviour would be essentially the same in settings other than the family. Earlier, we referred to this pattern as complementary bilingualism. This type of bilingualism seems to be specific to a certain category of the population as well as to a particular geographical area. First-generation immigrants, with little formal schooling, have a lower degree of normative consciousness which may account for the permeability of the linguistic system in which they are less linguistically competent. This type of behaviour, however, remains within the limits of individual or, possibly, familial variation since there has been no sign of the emergence of a contact dialect, probably due to the fact that the migrant population is too widely spread over the French territory.

On the other hand, second-generation speakers tend towards types of code-switches that varied according to the degree of command of the two languages: relative mastery of the parents' language correlated with greater ability to use both languages metalinguistically and stylistically, enabling the subjects to produce balanced bilingual speech, whereas a weaker grasp of the original language, especially orally, reduced the possibility of code-switching to a single type which fulfilled more of a symbolic function than a linguistic one. We use the term *functional bilingualism* to describe this type of speech behaviour.

An analysis of code-switching has proved extremely useful for highlighting and characterising the different kinds of linguistic behaviour as presented above. It would now be of the greatest interest to compare our observations with those found in other contexts in order to shed more light on the relationship between language and social identity, which seem to play a major part in determining the type of code-switching used.

Bibliography

Abou, S. (1981) *L'identité culturelle, relations interethniques et problèmes d'acculturation*. Paris: Editions Anthropos.

Agnihotri, R. K. (1979) Processes of assimilation: a sociolinguistic study of Sikh children in Leeds. Unpublished Ph.D. dissertation, University of York.

Alber, J. L. and Oesch-Serra, C. (1987) Aspects fonctionnels des marques trans-codiques et dynamiques d'interaction en situation d'enquête. In Lüdi (1984), 23–54.

Ammon, U. (1989) ed. *Status and function of languages and language varieties*. Berlin: Mouton de Gruyter.

Ammon, U., Dittmar, N. and Mattheier, K. (1987) eds. *Sociolinguistics, an international handbook of the science of language and society*. Berlin: Mouton de Gruyter.

Ammon, U., Mattheier, K. and Nelde, P. (1990) eds. Minorities and language contact, International Yearbook of European Sociolinguistics, *Sociolinguistica* IV. Tübingen: Max Niemeyer Verlag.

Appel, R. and Muysken, P. (1987) *Language contact and bilingualism*. London: Edward Arnold.

Araujo Carreira, M.-H. (1991) La nature et les mécanismes du contact des langues. Une étude de l'expression écrite d'adolescents portugais en France. In *Papers for the symposium on code-switching in bilingual studies: theory, significance and perspectives*. (Held in Barcelona, 21–23 March 1991.) Strasbourg: European Science Foundation, 157–80.

Baetens Beardsmore, H. (1986) *Bilingualism: basic principles*. Clevedon, Avon: Multilingual Matters.

Benattig, R. (1987) *Les migrants en Europe. Quel avenir éducatif et culturel?* Paris: L'Harmattan.

Billiez, J. (1985) Les jeunes issus de l'immigration algérienne et espagnole à Grenoble: quelques aspects sociolinguistiques. *International Journal of Sociology of Language*, 54: 41–56.

Billiez, J. and Merabti, N. (1991) Communication familiale et entre pairs: variations du comportement langagier d'adolescents bilingues. *Plurilinguismes*, 1: 34–52.

Boeschoten, R. and Verhoeven, L. (1987) Language mixing in children's speech: Dutch language use in Turkish discourse. *Language Learning*, 37 (2): 191–215.

Boubakri, H. (1984) La restauration tunisienne à Paris. *Etudes Méditerranéennes*, 7: 51–114.

(1985) Modes de gestion et réinvestissements chez les commerçants tunisiens de Paris. *Revue Européenne des Migrations Internationales*, 1 (1), 49–65.

Cadiot, P. (1987) Les mélanges de langues. In Vermes and Boutet (1987), 50–61.

(1989) On language mixtures. In Ammon (1989), 570–80.

Cadiot, P. and Dittmar, N. (1989) eds. *La sociolinguistique en pays de langue allemande*. Presses Universitaires de Lille.

Camilleri, C. (1985) *Anthropologie culturelle et éducation*. Neuchâtel: Bureau international de l'education, UNESCO, Delachaux et Niestlé.

Castles, S. (1984) *Here for good, Western Europe's new ethnic minorities*. London: Pluto Press.

Chana, U. and Romaine, S. (1984) Evaluative reactions to Panjabi/English code-switching. *Journal of Multilingual and Multicultural Development*, 6 (5): 447–71.

Coste, D. (1989) Minorisation et majorisation en situation d'apprentissage institutionnel. In Py and Jeanneret (1989), 169–77.

Dabène, L. (1981) ed. *Langues et migrations*. ELLUG, Université de Grenoble III.

(1987) Caractères spécifiques du bilinguisme et représentations des pratiques langagières des jeunes issus de l'immigration en France. In Lüdi (1987a), 77–95.

(1989) Problèmes posés par l'enseignement des langues minorées. In Py and Jeanneret (1989), 179–84.

(1990) Le parler bilingue issu de l'immigration en France. In R. Jacobson (ed.), *Code-switching as a worldwide phenomenon*. New York: Peter Lang.

(1991) Quelques aspects du rôle de l'environnement familial dans un contexte multilingue. *Revue Enfances*, 4: 159–69.

Dabène, L. and Billiez, J. (1986) Code-switching in the speech of adolescents born of immigrant parents. *Studies on Second Language Acquisition*, 8: 309–25.

Dabène, L., Flasaquier, M. and Lyons, J. (1983) eds. *Status of migrants' mother-tongues*. Strasbourg: European Science Foundation.

De Heredia, C. (1983) Les parlers français des migrants. In F. Francois, *J'cause français, non?* Paris: Ed. Maspero.

(1987) Du bilinguisme au parler bilingue. In Vermes and Boutet (1987), 91–127.

De Heredia-Deprez, C. (1991) Des langues en famille. *Plurilinguismes*, 1: 1–4.

Del Coso-Calame, F., Oesch-Serra, C. and De Pietro, F. (1985) La compétence de communication bilingue. Etude fonctionnelle des code-switchings dans le discours de migrants espagnols et italiens à Neuchâtel (Suisse). In Gülich and Kotschi (1985), 377–98.

Dittmar, N. (1989) De la théorie en sociolinguistique, éléments pour une perspective globale en sociolinguistique. In Cadiot and Dittmar (1989), 23–64.

Dubet, F. (1989) Immigrations; qu'en savons-nous? Un bilan des connaissances. La Documentation Française, 4887, Paris.

Eastman, C. (1992) ed. Codeswitching, special issue, *Journal of Multilingual and Multicultural Development*, 13 (1 & 2).

Edwards, V. (1986) *Language in a black community*. Clevedon, Avon: Multilingual Matters.

Etudes Méditerranéennes (1984) *Marchands ambulants et commerçants étrangers en France et en Allemagne fédérale*. Fascicule 7, Réseau MIGRINTER, Centre Interuniversitaire d'Etudes Méditerranéennes, Université de Poitiers.

Falip, M. and Deslandes, B. (1989) Une langue un peu plus étrangère que les autres: l'enseignement de l'arabe en France, continuités et ruptures. *LIDIL*, 2: 51–89.

Fishman, J. (1989) *Language and ethnicity in minority sociolinguistic perspective*. Clevedon, Avon: Multilingual Matters.

Gardner-Chloros, P. (1987) Code switching in relation to language contact and convergence. In Lüdi (1987a), 99–111.

Gendron, J. D. and Nelde, P. H. (1986) eds. *Plurilinguisme en Europe et au Canada, perspectives de recherche*. Bonn: Dümmler.

Gretler, A., Gurny, R., Perret-Clermont, A. N. and Poglia, E. (1989) eds. *Etre migrant. Approches des problèmes socio-culturels et linguistique des enfants migrants en Suisse*. Berne: Peter Lang.

Grosjean, F. (1982) *Life with two languages. An introduction to bilingualism*. Cambridge, Mass.: Harvard University Press.

Grosjean, F. and Py, B. (1991) La restructuration d'une première langue, l'intégration de variantes de contact dans la compétence de migrants bilingues. *La
Linguistique*, 27: 35–60.

Gülich, E. and Kotschi, T. (1985) eds. *Grammatik, Konverssation, Interaktion*.
Tübingen: Max Niemeyer Verlag.

Gumperz, J. J. (1982) *Discourse strategies*. Cambridge University Press.

(1989) *Sociolinguistique interactionnelle, une approche interprétative*. Paris:
L'Harmattan.

Heath, J. (1989) *From code-switching to borrowing: foreign and diglossic mixing in
Moroccan Arabic*. London: Kegan Paul International.

Heller, M. (1987) Language and identity. In Ammon, Dittmar and Mattheier
(1987), 781–4.

Hewitt, R. (1982) White adolescent creole users and the politics of friendship.
Journal of Multilingual and Multicultural Development, 3. (3).

Labov, W. (1977) *Language in the inner city: studies in the Black English Vernacular*.
Oxford: Basil Blackwell.

Le Page, R. B. and Tabouret-Keller, A. (1985) *Acts of identity, creole-based
approaches to language and ethnicity*. Cambridge University Press.

LIDIL (1989) 2: Les langues et cultures des populations migrantes: un défi à
l'école française. (Presses Universitaires de Grenoble (PUG).)

(1992) 6: Autour du multilinguisme. PUG.

Lüdi, G. (1987a) ed. *Devenir bilingue – parler bilingue. Actes du 2e colloque sur le
bilinguisme. Université de Neuchâtel, 20–22 Septembre 1984*. Tübingen: Max
Niemeyer Verlag.

(1987b) Les marques transcodiques: regards nouveaux sur le bilinguisme. In
Lüdi (1987a), 1–19.

(1990) Les migrants comme minorité linguistique en Europe. In Ammon *et al.*
(1987), 113–35.

Lüdi, G., De Pietro, J. F. and Papaloizos, L. (1990) Etranger dans son propre pays:
dimensions linguistiques de la migration interne en Suisse. *Ethnologica
Helvetica* (Berne), Images de la Suisse, 13 & 14: 269–97.

Lüdi, G. and Py, B. (1990) La Suisse: un laboratoire pour l'étude de la dynamique
des langues en contact. *Langage et Société*, 50 & 51: 87–92.

Mackey, W. F. (1982) Interaction, interférence et interlangue. Rapport entre
bilinguisme et didactique des langues. *Actes due 3ème colloque sur la didactique
des langues*. Quebec: Centre International de Recherche sur le Bilinguisme
(CIRB), Université Laval.

Martin-Jones, M. (1987) Les modèles sociolinguistiques dans l'étude du bilinguisme: le cas des minorités linguistiques. Paper presented at colloquium
on *Contacts de langues: quels modèles*, 28–30 Sept. 1987, IDERIC, Nice.

Massey, D. (1990) The social and economic origins of immigration. *Annals*,
AAPSS, 510 (July 1990): 60–72.

Merabti, N. (1992) Variations des pratiques bilingues d'un groupe d'adolescents
issus de l'immigration algérienne. *LIDIL*, 6: 93–114.

Merabti, N. and Moore, D. (1993) Pratiques bilingues d'adolescents issus de
l'immigration en France et en Angleterre. *TRANEL* (Institut de linguistique
de l'Université de Neuchâtel), 19 (March 1993): 95–110.

MIGRINTER (1986) Les Maghrébins de la régie Renault: solidarités commu-
nautaires et implications au Maghreb. *Revue Européenne des Migrations
Internationales*, 2 (1): 137–60.

Moore, D. (1992) Perte, maintien ou extension des langues d'origine? Réflexions à
partir de la situation indo-pakistanaise en Angleterre. *LIDIL*, 6 (June 1992):
53–68.

Naït M'Barek, M. and Sankoff, D. (1988) Le discours mixte arabe/français:
emprunts ou alternances de langue? *Canadian Journal of Linguistics/Revue
Canadienne de Linguistique*, 33(2): 143–54.

Nortier, J. M. (1989) *Dutch and Moroccan Arabic in contact: code-switching among
Moroccans in the Netherlands*. Academic Proefschrift, Universiteit van
Amsterdam.

Oesch-Serra, C. (1990) Italiens vendus et Suisses à quat'sous. In P. Centlivres, G.
Kreis, P. Bois *et al.* eds., *Devenir Suisse: adhésion et diversité culturelle des
étrangers en Suisse*. Geneva: Georg Editeur SA, 211–28.

Poplack, S. (1980) Sometimes I'll start a sentence in Spanish Y TERMINO EN
ESPAÑOL: toward a typology of code-switching. *Linguistics*, 18: 581–618.
Also in J. Amaslae, L. Elias-Olivares (1982) eds. *Spanish in the United
States. Sociolinguistic aspects*. Cambridge University Press, 230–63.

—— (1989) Statut des langues et accommodation langagière de long d'une frontière
linguistique. *TRANEL*, 14: 59–91.

Porquier, R. (1988) Processus d'acquisition et interactions sociales chez des
adultes migrants en milieu naturel et chez des adolescents migrants en
milieu scolaire. *Bulletin CILA*, 47: 43–51.

Py, B. (1981) Quelques aspects du bilinguisme des enfants de travailleurs
migrants. In Gretler *et al.* (1989), 105–24.

—— (1986) Un exemple de diglossie instable: la famille migrante. *LENGAS*, 20: 17–
20.

Py, B. and Jeanneret, R. (1989) eds. *Minorisation linguistique et interaction. Actes du
symposium de Neuchâtel, Septembre 1987*. Geneva: Droz.

Rampton, M. B. H. (1991) Second language learners in a stratified multilingual
setting. *Applied Linguistics*, 12 (3): 229–48.

REMISIS – Réseau d'information sur les migrations internationales. (Centre National
de la Recherche Scientifique (CNRS)).

Robinson V. (1986) *Transients, settlers and refugees, Asians in Britain*. Oxford:
Clarendon Press.

Romaine, S. (1981) Problems in the socio-linguistic description of communicative
repertoires among linguistic minorities. In Dabène *et al.* (1983), 119–30.

—— (1989) *Bilingualism*, Language in Society 13. Oxford: Basil Blackwell.

Roulet, E. (1981) L'analyse des conversations authentiques. *Etudes de Linguistique
Appliquée*, 44: 7–40.

Saifullah-Khan, V. (1974) Pakistani villagers in a British city. Unpublished Ph.D.
dissertation, University of Bradford.

—— (1987) The role of the culture of dominance in structuring the experience of
ethnic minorities. In C. Husband ed., *Race in Britain, continuity and change*.
London: Hutchinson University Library.

Salem, G. (1984) Les marchands ambulants et le système commercial sénégalais en France. *Etudes Méditerranéennes*, 7: 7–50.

Schatz, H. (1989) Code-switching or borrowing? English elements in the Dutch of Dutch-American immigrants. *ITL*, 83–4: 125–62.

Sinclair, J. M. and Coulthard, R. M. (1975) *Towards an analysis of discourse: the English used by teachers and pupils*. Oxford University Press.

Vermes, G. and Boutet, J. (1987) eds. *France, pays multilingue. Pratiques de langues en France* I & II. Paris: L'Harmattan.

3 CODE-SWITCHING IN THE CONTEXT OF DIALECT/STANDARD LANGUAGE RELATIONS

Anna Giacalone Ramat

1 On principles and conditions underlying code-switching

In the current state of language-contact research, code-switching (CS) studies have been mainly concerned with clearly separated, often typologically distant, pairs of languages.[1] One question that has been insufficiently explored is whether both syntactic models and pragmatic functional models which are intended to account for code-switching patterns can straightforwardly be applied to situations where the languages in contact are the standard language and a genetically related dialect.[2] It is reasonable to assume that conditions and constraints may be shaped differently depending on different contact situations. This could lead us to claim that different models of CS can be selected heuristically on the basis of types of contact situations to be accounted for.

As a case in point, I shall focus on the Italian situation because I assume that investigating this specific situation might provide us with broader insights into a range of comparable cases. So far, contact phenomena in Italy have attracted the attention of traditional dialectologists interested in the process of italianisation of dialects or, conversely, in the influence of dialects on Regional Italian. Indeed, switching behaviour between Italian and dialects has scarcely been investigated, either empirically or theoretically.

The structure of this chapter is as follows: I will first discuss some general issues by relating them to the Italian situation (section 1), and will later describe at some length the presence and uses of varieties in the Italian repertoire (section 2). I will then attempt some generalisations on social factors constraining CS and on discourse functions CS serves (sections 3 and 4). I will subsequently turn to a mainly linguistic perspective discussing linguistic constraints and models (section 5). This will finally allow for some consideration of the role of CS in language shift (section 6).

In the search for general principles underlying CS, one should keep in mind that the sociolinguistic approach has a kind of priority over the grammatical or structural approach in CS studies, since the choice and the alternation between different languages or varieties is triggered by social or psychological factors rather than by internal linguistic factors of the languages involved. Social conditions may, and in fact do, change bilingual behaviour and CS patterns, in the sense that they may determine which permissible patterns are preferred (Myers-Scotton 1990). Examples can be found in Gal's (1979) account of changing bilingualism in a village on the Austrian–Hungarian border, or in Giacalone Ramat's (1979) report on the German-speaking community of Gressoney, Aosta Valley.

Obviously, this is not to say that grammatical models are not relevant to CS or are bound to fail as explanatory tools. It is widely agreed that CS processes are systematic and structured in some way, that switches do not occur at just any point. This means that a structural analysis of CS patterns is needed for an adequate understanding of this form of bilingual interaction (Muysken, this volume).

Many terms have been used to describe switching between standard variety and dialects: code-switching, code shifting, code fluctuation, style shifting (Auer 1976, 1990). Abundance of terms does not by itself increase conceptual clarity, and conditions on the application of such terms should be explicitly stated.

When speaking of dialects and standard variety, the debate as to whether we are dealing with separate systems or a single system with internal variation is crucial. A closer analysis of real speech reveals that within sets of varieties many gradients can be found that tend to constitute a continuum with fuzzy boundaries. For purposes of analysis the linear continuum in discourse will be broken up into a number of points, of discrete structures and categories. In the Italian situation, the two extremes of the continuum are very clearly identifiable as separate systems, both morphosyntactically, and phonologically and lexically (Mioni 1976; Mioni and Trumper 1977; Trumper 1989).

For this reason I decided to use the term 'code-switching' to refer to the alternation of Italian and Italian dialect in discourse. Contrary to Hymes (1974) and Auer (1976), I take CS as being different in nature from monolingual 'style shifting', the change of formality levels within the same language. The latter is a quite common phenomenon in spoken Italian, but is found also in dialects: dialect speakers may shift between a restricted local dialect and a more extended *koiné*-like dialect. Although monolingual style shifting and code-switching may be seen as equivalent with respect to the social meanings they can convey (Romaine 1989: 155), from a linguistic point of view speaking of switching makes sense only if the two systems are independent.[3] The fact that conversations among bilingual speakers reveal some problematic cases for the linguist, where it is difficult to decide whether an utterance or a piece of utterance belongs or not to the 'same system' as the contiguous elements, does not invalidate the claim. Despite such borderline cases, the notion of separate systems should prove to be conceptually relevant and fundamental for descriptive purposes.

In trying to contribute to the development of a structural model that adequately accounts for switching patterns in dialect–standard situations, I will focus on some linguistic generalisations holding for the type of situations under scrutiny. In particular, it will be shown that the notion of a continuum can apply also to grammatical constraints on CS and that the morphological typology of the languages involved plays a role in allowing for patterns of switching.

2 The Italian situation in the European context

By way of introduction, I shall briefly discuss the use of varieties in the Italian repertoire. As I said, Italian dialects show sufficient structural and typological differences from Italian to form separate languages (Mioni and Arnuzzo Lansweert 1979; Trumper 1989; Berruto 1993; etc.). Speakers of Standard Regional Italian who also speak one (or more) dialects can be appropriately viewed as bilingual speakers and the observation of their behaviour belongs to the issues of bilingualism and language choice.[4] There is on the whole a diglossic distribution, and the two languages are used in complementary domains. As noted by Sobrero (1992: 17), however, the structural distance between the variety of dialect and the variety of language which come into contact can vary. On the one hand, it can be very small as in the cases of Tuscan, which genetically coincides with Standard Italian, and of the urban speech of big cities such as Milan and Rome; on the other hand, it is considerable in the cases of Piedmontese, which is typologically closer to French than to Tuscan, and Friulan.

So far two parameters have been proposed along which variation in the use of dialect and in the practice of CS may be located: the rural/urban opposition and the regional distribution. Differences between urban and rural situations in the use of CS have been described by Sobrero (1988a) drawing on data from Salento in southern Italy. Generally speaking, such notions as linguistic loyalty, social network and prestige differentiate the patterns of choice in urban and rural bilingual communities. In urban communities a tendency has been found to limit CS to tag switching, whereby dialectal microstructures such as deictics, or pragmatic locutions or interjections penetrate into Italian. In villages in Salento, on the other hand, the choice of dialect is dominant, with some CS in the direction of Italian. However, a dynamic process can be observed in Sobrero's data between a younger 'vanguard' oriented towards a monolingual speech mode and an older rearguard oriented towards a bilingual speech mode.

A model of the relations between dialects and Italian based on regional distribution as determined by historical and economic factors has been proposed by Trumper (1977, see also 1984 and 1989). He draws a distinction within the diglossia category between 'macro-diglossia' and 'micro-diglossia'. The first case can be exemplified by Veneto, a region in north-eastern Italy characterised by a strong dialectal *koiné*. Both codes – Italian and dialect – are distributed over a large number of domains with a great deal of overlapping between codes in functionally ambiguous contexts (1984: 36). The second case, micro-diglossia, is characterised by the absence of a dialect *koiné* and by a more clear-cut functional separation between codes. The dialect is used when talking to people who are known as dialect speakers and members of the community, and mostly for interactions falling inside the expected domains. Trumper (1977) suggests a correlation with CS patterns: in macro-diglossic situations CS should be very frequent and accompanied by a fairly high amount of fusion between the codes. In microdiglossic situations on the other hand CS would be limited.

The Italian situation is a particularly clear instance of dialect–standard switching phenomena which occur elsewhere in Europe as well, even if few studies are available on the topic apart from the classical study of Blom and Gumperz (1972) in Norway.[5] More recently, Giesbers's (1989) investigation deserves particular attention. He has studied the relations between dialect and standard Dutch in Ottersum, a bilingual community in Limburg, where a local dialect considerably distant from the national standard is spoken. The overall picture seems to be similar to the Italian one,[6] although the linguistic distance between the dialect and the standard is smaller in the Dutch case.

As to the Swiss situation, Swiss German dialects are clearly different language forms from High German and regionally and locally distinct. Swiss German has, however, political and social characteristics that are peculiar to Switzerland: as a widely spoken language it has the function of an 'Umgangssprache' more than that of a dialect, as noted by Sieber and Sitta (1984). CS from a dialect towards (Swiss) High German has been described on the functional and linguistic levels and a large range of variation has been shown (Werlen 1988). In southern Germany, on the other hand, the dialect–standard language differences are not treated as belonging to separate linguistic systems, but rather as a continuum of speech forms. Auer (1976) calls 'code shifting' the conversational variation from more dialect-like to more standard-like forms and vice versa. While a coherent account of these and other comparable situations need not be further pursued here, we suggest that the analysis presented in this chapter is appropriate for our understanding of language choice and code-switching behaviour in Italy and in similar dialect–standard situations as well. What is needed, however, is a principled definition of linguistic distance, a thorny issue that cannot be tackled here.

3 The sociolinguistic significance of patterns of choice in dialectal communities

Drawing on data gathered from different sources (Giacalone Ramat 1990; Sobrero 1988a; Berruto 1990; Alfonzetti 1992) I will attempt some generalisations on the functions which CS most frequently fulfils in bilingual dialectal communities in Italy.[7] It is important to specify that in this section I will use only data gathered from adults who can be considered stable bilinguals; children or others acquiring the language are not considered here. Insufficient knowledge of the language or dialect as a possible motivation for CS can thus be ruled out. Such cases will be discussed in the last section.

The approach proposed here tends to highlight the functions of CS both as an individual ability to re-interpret conventional patterns of language use and as a social activity involving multiple intergroup relations. On the whole, the data gathered confirm that CS is a quite widespread form of bilingual interaction. In particular, rural community members switch codes as part of their normal behaviour and for some speakers the dialect represents the usual unmarked choice for most situations, except formal ones. The amount of CS towards Italian may, however, vary considerably according to the interlocutor and tends to increase where the latter prefers to speak Italian. For other speakers the pattern may be reversed and in this case the shift proceeds from an Italian base towards dialect with in-network interlocutors.

A bilingual behaviour of this type can be explained in the light of the speech accommodation theory formulated by Giles and his associates, based on the notion of convergence and divergence between speakers (Giles and St. Clair 1979; Thakerar, Giles and Cheshire 1982). In general, when speakers desire each other's approval they tend to adapt to each other's speech in order to narrow the social distance between them. The adaptation is achieved by modifying a wide range of linguistic features, and CS may be considered an aspect of this modification. The fact that the theory can also be applied to monolingual interactions is an argument in favour of its validity, even if it is not possible to explain all choices in terms of accommodation or non-accommodation to the addressee.

To illustrate the adaptation to the interlocutor I will below report an extract from a conversation in a food store in Nibbiano, a village in the province of Piacenza. The owners – a middle-aged couple – speak both Italian and dialect and alternate both according to fairly clear and routinised patterns. Dialect is mostly used with people from the village, but Italian is chosen in the following cases: (i) with unknown customers, (ii) with children and young people from the village, whose preferred code is Italian.

In what follows the owner's wife (M), who acts as a cashier, addresses a child in Italian, and talks to the accompanying person (D) in dialect:[8]

(1)   M   Oh+ che bel bimbo
            [Oh, what a nice little baby]
       D   *L-è 'l bagaj dla Lice*
            [*It's Lice's child*]
       M   Ah sì *ma l-è zamò gnit grand*+ *l-è tyt la facia d'so maar*++ prendi pure
            le patatine caro+ te le regalo io quelle
            [Oh, really? *but he has grown up so much* + *he looks like his mother*++
            take the crisps, dear: I'm giving them to you]
       D   Sù+ ringrazia la signora
            [Come on, say thank you to the lady]

Since dialect is best viewed as the unmarked code in such service encounters in a rural situation, switches to Italian are somehow marked. Their general motivation seems to be – as I said – a convergence towards the interlocutor with the effect of establishing a closer relationship with him or her, and of facilitating communication at the interpersonal level. On the generalisability of this bilingual behaviour in rural communities in the negotiations between seller and customers, see also Sobrero (1992).

Divergent speech behaviour where each participant uses a different code is much less frequent in our data: if it occurs, it may be taken as a signal of less conversational co-operation. Generally speaking, bilingual dialectal speakers tend to accommodate rather than to build barriers (as has been reported in other situations across the world: see Heller 1988a; Dittmar and Schlobinski 1988). However, in asymmetric communications, it is the dialect speaker who is submitted to a stronger pressure to adapt to the interlocutor's code. This condition could be formulated as a principle of dialect–standard interactional behaviour where there are divergent linguistic preferences.

A second main class of functions for CS can be subsumed under the label of conversational functions, or 'discourse related' CS (Auer 1983; Gumperz 1982; Giacalone Ramat 1990; Alfonzetti 1992). Some switches occur at points of conversational relevance and mark the organisation of conversations in sequences, the change of topic, the beginning of, or the exit from, a topic, the introduction of a side sequence, of a facetious comment, etc.

As an illustration I will cite the following extract from the Sicilian corpus. The passage is taken from a conversation between university researchers who are doing some editorial work for a journal. At a certain moment one of them interrupts the ongoing topic with a comment on the pouring rain. To mark this side comment, he shifts to the dialect.

(2)   M   Sì sì+ tu quando ci vai? se passi da me+ andando da A + che ti
              viene di passaggio+ ti lascio ti dò una cosa da dargli? (pausa)
              Va bene+ magari ci sentiamo+ d'accordo? come vuoi tu . . . io . . .
              comunque lo chiamo+ magari+ lo chia/è (. . .) *ma comu ni nni*
              iemu ccu st'acqua?

              [Okay, okay. When are you going there? if you drop in at my place
              on your way to A, which *is* on your way, I'll leave . . . I'll give you
              something for him?
              (pause)
              Okay, maybe we'll talk about it again, okay? as you like . . . at any
              rate I'll call him, maybe, I'll call/it's just that (. . .) *but how can we*
              get out of here with this rain?]

4 Some conclusions on functions

Generally, the dynamics of alternating Italian and dialect follows both sociolinguistic strategies of convergence between participants, and discourse-oriented strategies aimed at organising bilingual discourse. In addition to what has been said, the following points should be taken into consideration:

4.1 The preferred code

The preference for dialect or for Italian (other factors being equal, such as competence, absence of conflicts or social barriers) seems to be an overall condition motivating a number of choices and switches in bilingual interactions. Bilingual speakers appear to have a preference for one of the two codes, and when they do not follow rules of appropriateness of language selection connected to domains or topics, or do not accommodate to the interlocutor, they tend to insist on the preferred code or to switch back to it (Auer 1983; Alfonzetti 1992).

This preference depends largely on individual life histories, which in turn may be the result of a set of social and educational factors, and particularly of age. Thus, the notion of preferred code partially overlaps with the marked/unmarked distinction which depends on the community norms holding for any specific communicative situation, but is based on a different dimension of individual characteristics. For instance, somebody addressing in dialect the staff of a post office may be using his or her preferred code, but makes a marked choice with respect to the social norms.

4.2 The direction of switching

As a methodological remark it should be stressed that to obtain valid information on this point we should rely on entire corpora rather than on occasional observations; this allows for some kind of quantitative statement. In Alfonzetti's data switching from Italian towards dialect is more frequent (59%); in Giesbers's data, on the other hand, 60% of the total of switches is from dialect to Standard Dutch. Both studies however agree on an important point: that the direction from Standard Dutch to dialect and from Italian to the Sicilian dialect occurs chiefly in the category of switches labelled as 'pragmatic' and reflects the function of CS as an 'emotional device'. This observation also fits a number of cases discussed in Berruto 1990.

While we accept CS to be an interactional resource (Auer 1983; Lüdi and Py 1986, among others), we claim that the direction of switching is not relevant in terms of social meaning or function in our data, because it depends on the pre-ferred code: we expect that speakers using the dialect more frequently will switch to Italian for contrasting effects, and vice versa. This point is of some theoretical relevance. The main function of switching seems to be that of achieving a contrast: both directions are viable and also predictable, provided that the change gives rise to a contrast with the language used before the switching point. In example (2) above, the situation is the same as far as participants, topic and setting are con-cerned. The switch is stimulated by no external feature, rather by an emotional attitude of the speaker.

This conclusion holds for the situations I have examined (see also Sobrero 1992 for similar data), but caution would be needed before generalising it to other settings where the access to important social and economic resources is controlled by language choice (Heller 1988a). However, the Italian case is theoretically interesting precisely because it shows how CS functions in situations where there are no ethnic conflicts and cultural identity problems.

4.3 A typology of functions

I will not attempt here to elaborate a typology of CS functions to fit all exchanges. Quite apart from constraints on space, it seems difficult in principle to draw up an exhaustive list beyond the six functions distinguished by Gumperz (1982) or the classification adopted by Auer (1983). As stated by Poplack (1980), it is the overall pattern of switching that is significant in the communities observed, but it is not necessary to view each switch as fulfilling a specific function. In slightly different terms, Trumper (1984) also remarks that his corpus does not support the idea that each switching is socially meaningful on its own. The social norms and conditions holding in Italian bilingual communities clearly point to a smooth switching as the strategy normally used for mixing languages. However, in communities abroad, where an Italian immigrant group is in contact with speakers of other languages, strategies of flagging have been reported. Commenting on Italian–English contact in Australia, Kinder (1987) discusses a number of 'transference markers' which can consist of so-called 'hedges' ('words or phrases which attenuate or accentuate the force with which a statement is made' – in uppercase in example (3)):

(3)   c'era:/c'era uno/dello STAFF qua INSOMMA, uno dell'UFFICIO INSOMMA

        [there was/there was/someone from the STAFF here LIKE, someone from the OFFICE LIKE) (Kinder 1987: 42)

Kinder suggests that these different ways of marking a transfer may originate in the potential risks of non-comprehension associated with language mixing, or in negative attitudes towards the switching practice. As we might expect, in the dialect-speaking communities in Italy much of this flagging is neutralised. Speakers who live in contact with each other in a bilingual community do not need to reassess the linguistic norms of their behaviour.

5 The constraints issue

This section will focus on the issue of constraints which govern the behaviour of CS in the individual and on linguistic models proposed to account for them.

5.1 Types of switching

In our data from the provinces of Pavia and Piacenza a great deal of CS occurs at sentence boundaries, i.e. it is of the inter-sentential type (Poplack 1980). This may be due to the fact that in those villages bilingualism follows what has been described as a micro-diglossic pattern, where varieties are not mixed within the sentence boundaries (see section 2). In the Sicilian corpus the following distribution was found: 49.95% of a total of 999 code switches was intra-sentential, 43.14% inter-sentential and 6.91% tag switches (Alfonzetti 1992: 180).

When we are faced with intra-sentential CS, constituent insertion at syntactic boundaries which are congruent in the two languages turns out as the most frequent type. Here are two examples: in the first VP is switched, in the second the subject NP.

(4)   Devi stare attento, Mario, perché il Maci *l-è teribil*

      [You have to pay attention, Mario, because Maci *is terrible*]

      (from a conversation between two young people in Pavia)

      non pàvunu tutti sti tassi i dottori . . . *chiddi ca pàvunu semu nuàtri pureddi*

      [the doctors *do not pay all these taxes* . . . *those who pay are we poor people*]

      (Alfonzetti 1992: 194)

As to a frequency hierarchy of switched constituents, insertion of a noun phrase is most frequent in the Sicilian corpus (97 cases), followed by that of a subordinate clause (78 cases) and of bare determiners. In particular, 43 cases of switched object NPs have been counted. It is noteworthy that 57 cases were found where the switched element is the dialectal determiner (definite or indefinite article) or the demonstrative, contrary to a formerly suggested constraint that closed class items are not switched or at least show low frequency (Pfaff 1979):

(5)   prima di tutto *u* portiere non c'è, sarà minimo cinque sei anni

      [first of all there has been no porter for at least five or six years]

      (Alfonzetti 1992: 203)

(6)   *u* nucleare! minchia! erano loro a favore del nucleare, che c'erano bat-
       taglie epiche

       [*the* nuclear power! fuck it! they were in favour of nuclear power, and
       there were epic fights] (Alfonzetti 1992: 204).

Other phenomena involving language mixing appear with notable frequency in
our dialect–standard data. As is to be expected, a considerable number of lexical
borrowings, both established borrowings and nonce borrowings (Poplack and
Sankoff 1988; Poplack 1990) have been observed.

Word-internal CS between a base and a bound morpheme is also found.
Whatever criteria we use, this type of language contact phenomena is not easy
to distinguish in a principled way from nonce borrowing. In Myers-Scotton's
(1988, 1990) 'frame process model' a 'system morpheme principle' is proposed
which requires that inflections come from the matrix language for those forms
made up of elements from both the matrix language and the embedded language.
Myers-Scotton's principles crucially depend on determining the matrix language,
but precisely this requirement is difficult to meet in language contact situations
where convergence and interchangeability of codes are very high. According to
another line of research, cases of phonologically and morphologically integrated
lexical items transferred from a dialect into the standard variety and vice versa are
considered 'hybrid forms' (Berruto 1989, 1990).[9]

In our corpora word-internal CS, however, occurs with relatively low frequency,
probably because of the greater cohesion of morphemes within the word boundaries as a general constraint holding for fusional languages. A further reason for
its marginality may reside in the overt stigmatisation that bilingual speakers often
exert against such types of switching. In spite of this, however, switching inflections such as plural endings or infinitive endings, an operation which would make
an Italian word look like a dialectal word or vice versa, is relatively easy for the
bilingual speakers and can readily be used as a routinised morphological integration (see Treffers-Daller 1991 for French–Dutch contact data). Through this
route, as a matter of fact, borrowings have traditionally been integrated into the
Italian language: e.g. *stoppare*, from English *stop* + infinitive inflection *-are*, or,
recently, *computerizz-are*. Indeed such morphological adaptation significantly
includes more verbs than nouns because of the central role played by the verb
in structuring the clause.

Analysis of the Italian materials suggests some typological considerations. Both
Italian and dialects are fusional as far as their morphological typology is concerned. In fusional languages the morphological integration of a lexical element

into a host language may easily take the form of a switch between a lexical morpheme and an inflectional morpheme derived from the host language. This is what we get in cases like *papariavano* [they were splashing about] – a form produced with a playful intention – or *pavare* [to pay], both formed with a dialectal lexeme and Italian verbal morphology (Alfonzetti 1992: 237). Morphological integration can be expected especially for language pairs where categories such as tense/aspect marking or case marking are equivalent (for example Spanish/Italian; see also Giesbers (1989: 161–2) for cases of word-internal CS involving derivations and compounds).

5.1.1

Let us turn to the models issue. What was observed on word-internal CS is obviously relevant to the 'Free Morpheme Constraint', proposed by Poplack (1980) as one potentially universal restriction on CS. Poplack (1988: 219) describes the constraint as follows: 'the free morpheme constraint . . . prohibits mixing morphologies within the confine of the word'. In such a form the principle has been disconfirmed by several empirical investigations (Myers-Scotton 1988, 1990; Eliasson 1990; Romaine 1989; etc.). The typological distance between the pair of languages involved in a contact situation deserves to be further investigated as a potential motivation of divergent behaviour. One might assume that in genetically related languages the possibility of morpheme switching is favoured by the structural similarity of the languages in contact.

A reasonable conclusion could be that the constraint as formulated above is too powerful. Poplack herself has more recently tried to relativise the claim of universality by introducing a distinction between code-switching and nonce borrowing, and between 'smooth' versus 'flagged' switching. In the latter case, exemplified – for instance – by the Canadian French–English situation, syntactic constraints would not be operative.

5.1.2

As for the perhaps most widely discussed constraint, the 'Equivalence Constraint' (Poplack 1980), it should not have much relevance for our corpus of data, since the syntactic linear order for Italian and dialects is very similar.

Interestingly enough, however, one is not entitled to conclude that the surface structures of Italian and dialects map strictly onto each other in all cases. Recent investigations in the field of syntax have pointed out significant differences between dialects and Italian with respect to subject clitics, position of negation and interrogative sentences, and suggested that dialects are at a closer examination even more distant from Standard Italian than it was earlier assumed (Benincà and Vanelli 1984; Brandi and Cordin 1989). Here I will briefly discuss a crucial case, namely, the position of negation, which is postponed to the inflected verb in a number of Northern Italian dialects, like Piedmontese and Lombard, while it is preposed in Standard Italian (Molinelli 1988). Compare Milanese dialect:

(7)   *El mé fradèl l-*   *è no rivà*
        [My brother he-SUBJECT CLITIC is not arrived]

with Italian:

(8)   Mio fratello non è arrivato
        [My brother not is arrived]

or Bergmasque:

(9)   *L- piöf mia*[10]
        [It-SUBJECT CLITIC rains not]

with Italian:

(10)   non piove
        [not rains]

The equivalence constraint would prohibit the switch: *Mio fratello non *l-è rivà*, since the two elements Neg and V are ordered differently in the two languages. Since I did not find any instance of such switching, as far as I know the equivalence constraint is not violated in our data.

An interesting point is made by Alfonzetti: some Southern Italian dialects essentially differ from Standard Italian in the verb position which easily takes final place, while Standard Italian is SVO. Cases such as

(11)   venticinque anni *avi*
        [twenty five years *has* = he is twenty-five years old]
                                                    (Alfonzetti 1992: 221)

could in principle represent a crucial test for the equivalence constraint because word order patterns are divergent in this case for Italian and Sicilian dialect. Yet in fact they do not tell us much because final position of the verb is a feature that is rather common in Regional Standard Italian spoken in Sicily. Compare, again from the Sicilian corpus:

(12)   Arrivato a un certo momento l'ultima lettera

     [at a certain moment   the last letter

     gli mandai, cci rissi . . .

     I sent him, I told him . . .]

Therefore, what we actually find in example (11) is most probably a case of switching at congruent syntactic boundaries.

Anyway, structural equivalence has proved to be an adequate tool to describe CS patterns between Italian and dialects. Although the equivalence constraint is often neutralised by the structural convergence between Italian and dialect in discourse, as far as we know CS is avoided whenever dialectal syntax diverges in word order patterns from Italian syntax.

5.1.3

The 'government constraint' (DiSciullo, Muysken and Singh 1986) based on the government and binding theory would forbid CS between a preposition and the governed NP, between a verb and the governed object (unless a 'neutralising element' in the same language as the governing element facilitates the switching). In fact, violations of this constraint have been frequently reported. I will quote some cases where the governed object is not in the same language as the governing verb:

(13)   No, *ca iu vùogliu vide* mio figlio, *ca iu cce l'aju lu jatu*

     [No, I want to see my son, I've got enough breath]

     (Trumper 1984: 43, from Rende, Calabria)

(14)   *picchì ccà, cchiossài di vinti miliuni cci vòlunu pp'abbissari* il locale

     [*because here much more than twenty million are necessary to fix* the place]

     (Alfonzetti 1992: 228)

More recently, a probabilistic perspective on constraints has been taken, in an attempt to find out which types of switching are most frequent (Treffers Daller 1991; Muysken, this volume). In this perspective, the data collected from dialect–standard interactions provide us with evidence showing that switches may occur at any juncture in the sentence, although with different frequencies, and confirm that absolute restrictions do not appear to be operative.

5.1.4

The role of *neutral sites* deserves particular attention: they are frequent in closely related languages and may have the effect of favouring CS and, in the long run, convergence of systems. Clyne (1969, 1987) has developed the notion of 'triggering' whereby an element that can belong to both systems and is alike in form and meaning in both languages triggers off a switch from one language to another. The importance of such 'homophonous diamorphs' in creating neutral sites where CS is likely to appear has also been stressed by Muysken (1990). An interesting list of neutral sites from the Sicilian corpus can be found in Alfonzetti (1992: 240ff.) and indeed this seems to be a common feature in all our dialect–standard data:

(15)   *ma picchì non m'a potti n* **campagna** *quest'estate c'a m'ai a spiccicari u cori*
       [*but why don't you bring her to me* to the country this summer *for I am really fond of her*]

5.1.5

To sum up, CS between Italian and dialects has proved to have a number of specific features both on the structural and on the social level:
   (i) owing to the structural affinity of the languages and the long and stable nature of their contact, there are many points of equivalence and hence many potential switch sites;
   (ii) moreover, a fairly high amount of neutral sites where elements occur which are the same in both languages can be found;
   (iii) there is absence of separateness (in the sense of the 'we code' and 'they code' of Gumperz) between a dialect-speaking and a standard-speaking community, since bilingual speakers belong to a monocultural community. This holds true especially in rural areas and in small towns;
   (iv) as a consequence of (iii), there is a large reversibility in the switch direction since the main function of switches is to create contrast. This allows the conclusion that the marking achieved through switching is mostly stylistic and only secondarily functional and social.
   These results seem to support the suggestion I put forward at the outset of this chapter: morphosyntactic constraints regulating intra-sentential CS should be seen as building a continuum with respect to their applicability. This continuum should be based on a typological consideration of the languages involved, ranging

from typologically distant languages such as English and Maori, through genetically related, but still distant, languages such as English and Spanish, to more closely related and similar ones, such as Italian and its dialects. As one moves along this cline, the number of permissible junctures for CS is enlarged because equivalence conditions based on linear order increase, although a total equivalence may prove difficult to find (as shown above, closely related languages may still maintain differently structured areas). The possibility of finding at one extreme of the cline a pair of languages that do not allow for any strategy of switching should also be ruled out. Languages, inasmuch as they allow for interference from other languages, will also allow for some kind of juxtaposition in discourse. CS is potentially a universal phenomenon.

I might add that the relaxation of linguistic constraints that is found along such a continuum is not intended to support the notion of uncontrolled variation, nor to undermine the ultimate goal of building a CS theory.

6 Effects of CS on language shift

In this section I shall sketch the problem of the effects of code-switching in bilingual communities with regard to such issues as language shift and/or language maintenance. There is a wealth of evidence that is suggestive of a close relation between the social and political meaning of a language and its fate in a bilingual community (Dressler 1988; Gal 1979; Dorian 1981; Giacalone Ramat 1979, 1989, among others). It has been observed that in such situations monolinguals in the dominant language do not usually learn the minority language. From a social point of view the result will be the minority adaptation to the majority norm. The issue is particularly relevant for the fairly large number of linguistic minorities which live within the borders of the Italian Republic (Giacalone Ramat 1982; MPI 1985) and which are all undergoing a more or less rapid process of language shift. However, it seems important to me to use the same interpretative framework also in analyses of data sets from dialectal communities.

I suggest indeed that the dialectal communities in Italy can be equated, at least to some extent, with linguistic minorities since in both cases situations of language contact are observed where two languages are in an asymmetric relationship to each other. It seems difficult to draw a sharp and principled distinction. Social are present in both, although they may carry different implications with institutions, school life or interpersonal interactions. On the whole, we a larger use of conflict-overcoming rather than conflict-raising stratal communities.

As is well known, a shift towards Italian is taking place in dialectal communities in Italy (see Coveri 1978 and 1986 discussing nationwide statistical data). While a number of other variables may interact with language choice behaviour in different communities, we wish to focus here on the relation between language convergence and shift. A long-term contact generally induces processes of change, interference or convergence even among quite distant languages, as contact situations such as the Balkan Sprachbund or the Kupwar languages in India teach us (Thomason and Kaufman 1988). In the contact between Standard Italian and the dialects, convergence has been reported by various studies, both at the structural and at the conversational level (see Grassi 1993 for a survey on Italian and dialects in contact). The mechanisms of convergence are those proposed by Pfaff (1979) for code-switching: the role of bilingual speakers in favouring structures shared by both languages is crucial.

The question can be raised whether, and to what extent, the adoption by individuals of CS practices may contribute to convergence (Woolard 1989). We suggest the following hypothesis:

CS is a factor promoting convergence and at the same time a consequence of convergence, with a bidirectional relationship between the two phenomena which is particularly favoured in those bilingual communities where linguistic choice is not effected as a result of social sanctions.

The role of code-switching represents an intriguing question with respect to different diglossic types found in the Italian situation (see section 2). Mioni and Arnuzzo Lansweert (1979: 94) suggest that the 'purity' of the dialect in micro-diglossic situations is the hallmark of a dying language rather than of a living one. On the other hand, Berruto (1985: 75) claims that CS, insofar as it promotes the interpenetration of Italian and dialects, is a possible forerunner of the dissolution of dialects into the corresponding regional variety of Italian. However, adaptation and convergence may in fact enable a language to survive, as found elsewhere (Woolard 1989). Also Trumper and Maddalon (1988: 240) find that in Veneto the structural convergence between a largely used dialectal *koiné* and regional varieties of Italian has led to a situation where Italian is *less used* and the *koiné* offers evidence of greater resistance to language shift. These different patterns of regional bilingual behaviour may suggest caution when making diachronic predictions about effects of CS in language shift. It is however important to emphasise that in bilingual situations, where dialects are still currently used, CS is evidence of widespread bilingual behaviour, rather than an indicator of language shift. It presupposes fluency on both sides and the ability of alternating codes in the easiest way. Yet, obviously, the very notion of a 'stable' bilingual community is questionable. Members of the same bilingual community and even members of the same family may show very different patterns of use and proficiency levels in the two languages.

Decline of bilingualism may indeed determine a change in CS strategies. Poplack (1980) has observed that lesser fluency in one language correlates with inter-sentential rather than intra-sentential CS. The results of several investigations in the Italian area fully support this claim. Younger generations may dispose of a reduced competence of dialect which is reflected in the preference for inter-sentential CS or even for limiting CS to tag switches and stereotypes (all expressions which can be produced with minimal knowledge of the dialect grammar) inserted in what is basically Italian speech (Sobrero 1988a; Giacalone Ramat in press). In such cases CS may be related to the poor competence of the speakers, in much the same way as in imperfect language learning.

At this point it is not easy to make predictions about the fate of Italian dialects. Their extinction has been expected for a long time, but is still far from occurring. Anyway, in the light of the stand on CS as a mode of bilingual interaction which I have taken here, it is clear that no generalisation about its role as a causal factor of language shift can be drawn.

Further research should include the analysis of the development of CS patterns over time. This issue is important to determine the impact of non-linguistic social factors underlying language loss. It has been suggested (McClure and McClure 1988: 44ff.) that the process of language shift runs from context-free, interlocutor-bound language choice to conversational CS. Indeed, there is some evidence in the case of the Walser (German) minority in Aosta Valley (Zürrer 1986; Giacalone Ramat 1989) that the use of Italian in conversations within the family domain has progressed from a marked choice, often restricted to interactions with younger generations, to a more frequent and neutral choice as a symptom of progressive language shift. For many families the process has come to an end (Giacalone Ramat 1979). One might assume that code-switching is concurrent and co-occurring with this evolution. At present, however, the evidence available does not allow any firm conclusions or diachronic predictions.

Notes

[1] Examples are Poplack (1980) and Pfaff (1979) on Spanish–English contact, Romaine (1989) on Panjabi–English, Poplack et al. (1987) on Finnish–English, Bentahila and Davies (1983) on Arabic–French, Myers-Scotton (1988, 1990) on Swahili–English and many others.

2   The term 'bidialectalism' has been deliberately avoided in this paper. I follow the Continental European usage of the term 'dialect' rather than the Anglo-Saxon usage (according to which 'dialect' is the generic term for standard and non-standard varieties (Ammon 1987)).

3   In addition to the real differences in linguistic structure, we may also note that members of dialect communities view their dialects as quite separate from Italian. Admittedly, the speakers' awareness of the language separateness is an important cue, but one that must be validated by linguistic investigation, as noted by Blom and Gumperz (1972: 411).

4   For simplicity's sake I shall speak in this paper of 'Standard Italian' as an entity opposed to dialects. Of course, the reality is far more complicated and the composition of the linguistic repertoire has been debated at length by scholars (among others, Trumper 1989; Berruto 1993). Without going into detail, we can say that the term 'standard' is best seen as applying to the written variety, while spoken varieties of Italian are regionally differentiated, especially on the phonological level. For them the label Standard Regional Italian is more appropriate.

5   Nevertheless, Blom and Gumperz's description of a bilingual situation in Norway is different from the Italian case. After having defined the two systems as separate, the authors conclude that 'the narrow range of variation we find lends support to our view of dialect features as variables within a single grammatical system' (p. 416). I would not take this as an adequate description of the Italian situation, where the dialects and the standard vary strongly at all linguistic levels (see section 5.2 for some discussion on syntax).

6   Indeed the sociolinguistic characterisation of Ottersum recalls a development pattern common in Italy: Ottersum is a community where, over a relatively short period, the dialect has lost ground, particularly in children's education, and the Standard has developed into a variety that also plays a role in family interactions, even in informal situations between adults.

7   Some of the data discussed here have been collected under my supervision in little towns or villages located in the provinces of Pavia or Piacenza. Recordings were made by students, mostly with a hidden tape recorder. Notes were also taken for each informant concerning traditional sociological variables: social class, education, occupation.

    G. Alfonzetti (1992) has carried out a major research on CS in a Sicilian urban community, Catania. The investigation is based on spontaneous inter-actions recorded in communicative situations of a moderate to low degree of formality.

8   In all the examples throughout this paper the italicised sequences are in dialect. As to the transcription conventions note that:
    +, ++, +++ = pause from 1 to 3 seconds
    (. . . .) = unintelligible segment
    A transcription system has been used for dialects which adopts conventions current for Standard Italian. Note that: *é, ó* are close-mid vowels, *è, ò* are open-mid vowels and that *c, g* + front vowels are palatal affricates.

9   Focussing on morphological criteria in order to decide on hybrid forms is not new: Mioni had already suggested in 1976 that the decision whether a mixed

lexical item should be assigned to Italian or to a dialect could be taken on the basis of its morphology. The suggestion is taken up by Berruto (1989): a word with a lexical morpheme in Italian and a dialectal grammatical morpheme should be assigned to dialect and vice versa.

[10] Compare the interrogative form *piö-el mia?* with obligatory clitic subject postposed. The two forms imply a phonological underlying form /piöv/ which is never realised as such, but only through the word-final unvoiced allophone /f/ and zero between vowels. Such rules are unknown to Italian (I thank G. Bernini for this suggestion).

Bibliography

Alfonzetti, G. (1992) Il discorso bilingue. Italiano e dialetto a Catania. *Materiali Linguistici*, 8. Milan: F. Angeli.

Ammon, U. (1987) Language-variety/standard variety/dialect. In U. Ammon, N. Dittmar, K. J. Mattheier eds., *Sociolinguistics I*. Berlin: Mouton de Gruyter, 316–35.

Auer, P. (1976) Konversationelle Standard/Dialekt-Kontinua (code shifting). *Deutsche Sprache*, 2: 97–124.

(1983) Zweisprachige Konversationen. Code-switching und Transfer bei italienischen Migrantenkindern in Konstanz. *Papiere des Sonderforschungsbereichs 99* (Universität Konstanz, Fachgruppe Sprachwissenschaft), 79.

(1990) *Phonologie der Alltagssprache*. Berlin: Mouton de Gruyter.

Auer, P. and di Luzio, A. (1988) eds. *Variation and convergence*. Berlin: Mouton de Gruyter, 94–124.

Benincà, P. and Vanelli, L. (1984) Italiano, veneto, friulano: fenomeni sintattici a confronto. *Rivista Italiana di Dialettologia*, 8: 165–94.

Bentahila. A. and Davies, E. E. (1983) The syntax of Arabic–French code-switching. *Lingua*, 59: 301–30.

Berruto, G. (1985) "'l pulman l-è nen ch-a *cammina tanto forte*". Su commutazione di codice e mescolanza dialetto-italiano. *Vox Romanica*, 44: 59–76.

(1989) Tra italiano e dialetto. In G. Holtus, M. Metzeltin, M. Pfister eds., *La dialettologia italiana oggi. Studi offerti a Manlio Cortelazzo*. Tübingen: G. Narr, 107–22.

(1990) Italiano regionale, commutazione di codice e enunciati mistilingui. Paper presented at the 18th Congress of the Società di Linguistica Italiana, Padova 1984. In A. Mioni and M. Cortelazzo eds., *L'italiano regionale*. Rome: Bulzoni, 105–30.

(1993) Le varietà del repertorio. In A. Sobrero ed., *Introduzione all'italiano contemporaneo. La variazione e gli usi*. Bari: Laterza, 3–36.

Bettoni, C. and Gibbons, J. (1987) Italian speakers in Australia: creative in practice, but traditional in attitudes. *Australian Review of Applied Linguistics*, Series S.4, 66–80.

Blom, J.-P. and Gumperz, J. J. (1972) Social meaning in linguistic structures: code-switching in Norway. In J. J. Gumperz and D. Hymes eds., *Directions in sociolinguistics. The ethnography of communication.* New York: Holt, Rinehart & Winston, 407–34.

Brandi, L. and Cordin, P. (1989) Two Italian dialects and the Null Subject Parameter. In O. Jaeggli and K. J. Safir eds., *The Null Subject Parameter.* Dordrecht: Kluwer, 111–42.

Clyne, M. G. (1969) Switching between language systems. In *Actes du Xème Congrès internationale des linguistes* I. Bucharest: Editions de l'Académie, 343–9.

——— (1987) Constraints on code-switching: how universal are they? *Linguistics*, 25: 739–64.

Coveri, L. (1978) Chi parla dialetto, a chi e quando, in Italia? Un'inchiesta Doxa. *La ricerca dialettale*, 2: 341–2.

——— (1986) Chi parla dialetto in Italia? *Italiano e oltre*, 1: 198–202.

DiSciullo, A.-M., Muysken, P. and Singh, R. (1986) Government and code mixing. *Journal of Linguistics*, 22: 1–24.

Dittmar, N. and Schlobinski, P. (1988) Convergence, discourse and variation. In P. Auer and A. Di Luzio, *Variation and convergence.* Berlin: Mouton de Gruyter, 157–75.

Dorian, N. C. (1981) *Language death: the life cycle of a Scottish Gaelic dialect.* Philadelphia: University of Pennsylvania Press.

Dressler, W. (1988) Language death. In F. Newmeyer ed., *Linguistics. The Cambridge Survey* IV. Cambridge University Press, 184–91.

Eliasson, S. (1990) Models and constraints in code-switching theory. In *Papers for the workshop on constraints, conditions and models.* (Held in London.) Strasbourg: European Science Foundation, 17–50.

Gal. S. (1979) *Language shift: social determinants of linguistic change in bilingual Austria.* New York: Academic Press.

Giacalone Ramat, A. (1979) *Lingua, dialetto e comportamento linguistico. La situazione di Gressoney.* Aosta: Musumeci.

——— (1982) Le minoranze tedescofone al di fuori dell'Alto Adige. *Sociologia della Communicazione*, 1: 47–55.

——— (1989) Per una caratterizzazione linguistica e sociolinguistica dell'area walser. In E. Rizzi ed., *Lingua e communicazione simbolica nella cultura walser. Atti del VI Convegno internazionale di Studi Walser.* Anzola d'Ossola: Fondazione Monti, 37–66.

——— (1990) Code switching in dialectal communities: effects on language shift. In *Papers for the workshop on impact and consequences: broader considerations.* (Held in Brussels, 22–24 November 1990.) Strasbourg: European Science Foundation, 189–223.

——— (In press) Language choice, code-switching and language shift in bilingual communities. *Journal of Pragmatics.*

Giesbers, H. (1989) *Code-switching tussen dialect en standaard taal.* Amsterdam: P. J. Meertens Instituut.

Giles, H. and St. Clair, R. (1979) *Language and social psychology.* Oxford: Blackwell.

Grassi, C. (1993) Italiano e dialetti. In A. Sobrero ed., *Introduzione all'italiano contemporaneo. La variazione e gli usi.* Bari: Laterza, 279–310.

Gumperz, J. J. (1982) *Discourse strategies.* Cambridge University Press.

Heller, M. (1988a) Strategic ambiguity: code-switching in the management of conflict. In Heller (1988b), 77–98.

(1988b) ed. *Code-switching: anthropological and sociolinguistic perspectives*. Berlin: Mouton de Gruyter.

Hymes, D. (1974) *Foundations in sociolinguistics: An ethnographic approach*. London: Tavistock.

Kinder, J. J. (1987) Code switching and social integration in bilingual conversation. *Australian Review of Applied Linguistics*, Series S.4: 37–51.

Lüdi, G. and Py, B. (1986) *Etre bilingue*. Berne: P. Lang.

McClure, E. and McClure, M. (1988) Macro- and micro-sociolinguistic dimensions of code-switching in Vingard (Romania). In M. Heller (1988b), 25–51.

Mioni, A. (1976) Per una sociolinguistica del Veneto Centrale. In *Atti del XIV Congresso internaz. di linguistica e filologia romanza* II. Naples: G. Macchiaroli. Amsterdam: G. Maccharoli J. Benjamins, 327–33.

Mioni, A. and Arnuzzo Lansweert, A. M. (1979) Sociolinguistics in Italy. *International Journal of the Sociology of Language*, 21: 81–107.

Mioni, A. and Trumper, J. (1977) Per un'analisi del 'continuum' linguistico veneto. In R. Simone and G. Ruggiero eds., *Aspetti sociolinguistici dell'Italia contemporanea*. Rome: Bulzoni, 329–72.

Molinelli, P. (1988) *Fenomeni della negazione dal latino all'italiano*. Firenze: La Nuova Italia.

MPI Ministero della Pubblica Istruzione (1985) Rapporto sulle minoranze linguistiche in Italia. *Scambi Culturali* (Direzione Generale per gli scambi culturali del Ministero della Pubblica Istruzione), 7 (1–3).

Muysken, P. (1990) Concepts methodology and data in language contact research: ten remarks from the perspective of grammatical theory. In *Papers for the workshop on concepts, methodology and data*. (Held in Basel, 12–13 January 1990). Strasbourg: European Science Foundation, 15–30.

Myers-Scotton, C. (1988) Codeswitching as indexical of social negotiations. In M. Heller (1988b), 151–86.

(1990) Intersections between social motivations and structural processing in code-switching. In *Papers for the workshop on constraints, conditions and models*. (Held in London, 27–29 September 1990). Strasbourg: European Science Foundation, 57–82.

Pfaff, C. W. (1979) Constraints on language mixing: intrasentential code-switching and borrowing in Spanish/English. *Language*, 55: 291–318.

Poplack, S. (1980) Sometimes I'll start a sentence in Spanish Y TERMINO EN ESPAÑOL: toward a typology of code-switching. *Linguistics*, 18: 581–618. Also in J. Amastae, L. Elías-Olivares (1982) eds. *Spanish in the United States. Sociolinguistic aspects*. Cambridge University Press, 230–63.

(1988) Contrasting patterns of code-switching in two communities. In Heller (1988b), 215–44.

(1990) Variation theory and language contact: concepts, methods and data. In *Papers for the workshop on concepts, methodology and data*. (Held in Basel, 12–13 January 1990.) Strasbourg: European Science Foundation, 33–66. Also in D. Preston (1993) ed., *American dialect research: an anthology celebrating the 100th anniversary of the American Dialect Society*. Amsterdam: Benjamins, 251–86.

Poplack, S. and Sankoff, D. (1988) Code-switching. In U. Ammon, N. Dittmar, K. J. Mattheier eds., *Sociolinguistics*. Berlin: Mouton de Gruyter, 1174–80.

Poplack, S., Wheeler, S. and Westwood, A. (1987) Distinguishing language contact phenomena: evidence from Finnish–English bilingualism. In P. Lilius, M. Saari eds., *The Nordic Languages and Modern Linguistics*, 6. (Proceedings of the Sixth International Conference of Nordic and General Linguistics in Helsinki, 18–22 August 1986.) 33–56. Also in K. Hyltenstam, L. K. Obler (1989) eds., *Bilingualism across the lifespan. Aspects of acquisition, maturity and loss*. Cambridge University Press, 132–54.

Romaine, S. (1989) *Bilingualism*, Language in Society 13. Oxford: Basil Blackwell.

Sieber, P. and Sitta, H. (1984) Schweizerdeutsch zwischen Dialekt und Sprache. *Kwartalnik Neofilologiczny*, 31: 1, 3–40.

Sobrero, A. (1988a) Villages and towns in Salento: the way code-switching switches. In N. Dittmar and P. Schlobinski eds., *The sociolinguistics of urban vernaculars*. Berlin: Mouton de Gruyter, 207–16.

   (1988b) Conversational microconvergences between dialect and language. In Auer and di Luzio (1988), 195–216.

   (1992) Sociolinguistic variables of code switching in dialectal communities. In *Code-switching Summer School* (Held in Pavia, 9–12 September 1992). Strasbourg: European Science Foundation, 17–33.

Thakerar, J., Giles, H. and Cheshire, J. (1982) Psychological and linguistic parameters of speech accommodation theory. In C. Fraser and K. R. Scherer eds., *Advances in the social psychology of language*. Cambridge University Press, 205–55.

Thomason, S. G. and Kaufman, T. (1988) *Language contact, creolization, and genetic linguistics*. Berkeley: University of California Press.

Treffers-Daller, J. (1991) Towards a uniform approach to code-switching and borrowing. In *Papers for the workshop on constraints, conditions and models*. (Held in London, 27–29 September 1990.) Strasbourg: European Science Foundation, 259–77.

Trumper, J. (1977) Ricostruzione nell'Italia settentrionale: sistemi consonantici. Considerazioni sociolinguistiche nella diacronia. In R. Simone and U. Vignuzzi eds., *Problemi della ricostruzione linguistica*. Rome: Bulzoni, 259–310.

   (1984) Language variation, code switching and the migrant question. In P. Auer and A. Di Luzio eds., *Interpretive sociolinguistics*. Tübingen: Narr, 29–52.

   (1989) Observations on sociolinguistic behaviour in two Italian regions. *International Journal of the Sociology of Language*, 76: 31–62.

Trumper, J. and Maddalon, M. (1988) Converging divergence and divergent convergence: the dialect–language conflict and contrasting evolutionary trends in modern Italy. In Auer and di Luzio (1988), 217–59.

Werlen, I. (1988) Swiss German dialects and Swiss Standard High German. In Auer and di Luzio (1988), 94–124.

Woolard, K. A. (1989) Language convergence and language death as social processes. In N. C. Dorian ed., *Investigating obsolescence. Studies in language contraction and death*. Cambridge University Press, 355–67.

Zürrer, P. (1986) *Deutscher Dialekt in mehrsprachiger Gemeinschaft*. (*Zeitschrift für Dialektologie und Linguistik*, Beiheft 53). Wiesbaden: F. Steiner.

4 CODE-SWITCHING IN COMMUNITY, REGIONAL AND NATIONAL REPERTOIRES: THE MYTH OF THE DISCRETENESS OF LINGUISTIC SYSTEMS

Penelope Gardner-Chloros

Dedicated to Norman Denison

In this paper I shall draw attention to a paradox. On the one hand, the study of code-switching coincided with, and was partly the product of, a realisation within linguistics that bilingualism was not an abnormal situation and that the linguistic behaviour which results from bilingualism could not be dismissed as arbitrary or aberrant. On the other hand, a lot of effort has been expended within the field of code-switching on setting up a new orthodoxy to replace the old orthodoxy of monolingual norms. This consists in defining code-switching as a special form of skilled bilingual behaviour, *to be distinguished* from the aberrant manifestations of bilingualism which involve one language influencing another. I will try to show that this new type of ideal speaker–listener, whose existence depends on such discrete alternation, is as much of a rare bird as Chomsky's monolingual original, and that code-switching should instead be considered as a much broader, blanket term for a range of interlingual phenomena within which strict alternation between two discrete systems is the exception rather than the rule.

Code-switching is found in a variety of linguistic contexts, ranging from that where highly educated bilinguals are talking among themselves, alternating between two codes which closely reflect the relevant monolingual norms, to situations where societal multilingualism is the general norm. These in turn can include, at one extreme, wholly bilingual communities where everyone uses the same language to their peers and another to say, the servant class, as in nineteenth-century Russia, and at the opposite extreme, cases where groups which have no common language are thrown together and have to find a means to communicate. Le Page (1992) gives as an example of a situation where some form of code-switching is a matter of desperate survival, that which obtained in slave-depots on the west coast of Africa in the eighteenth and nineteenth centuries. There speakers of various tribal languages *had* to acquire a few words of Portuguese or French or English, filtered through their native West African phonology and syntax, in order to communicate with their captors, who in return probably used a similar way of speaking to the slaves if they came to think this was the best way to communicate with them. Each side would be forced to switch back into their native language when the *ad hoc* pidgin failed.

In Western societies today, where education, government and the media all exert linguistic levelling pressures and encourage us to think of 'a language' as a clearly defined entity which we must strive to acquire, many people's lives, be they immigrants or dialect speakers who came into contact with the standard or with other dialects, are still conducted between two (or more) cultures and languages. Whether we view such groups of people and their modes of speaking as being a composite of two or more monolingual/monodialectal entities, or as new entities in their own right, is not the most interesting issue. Any mixture sooner or later is associated with a new identity. The emergence of new linguistic forms, as of new cultural practices, is usually a matter of time. There may appear to be no 'third grammar' to be observed, no new paradigms of syntax or word-formation or phonology which cannot be traced back to one of the monolingual reference points. That is either because we need to dig deeper in order to find them in their emerging form or because they have not yet had time to develop. In ten, twenty or thirty years' time, when the community's identity has crystallised, they will, from the point of view of the analyst, be codifiable. From the point of view of any individual born into that community, what others call a mixture is the given, the starting-point; we should not lose sight of the fact that our so-called standard languages are all mixtures in origin. A linguistically appropriate analysis of code-switching depends on our keeping sight of the psychological realities of how individuals create their own first language from the options around them, be it a pidgin, a code-switched variety, a regional dialect or a standard language.

In this paper I shall make use of the notion of focussed and diffuse varieties developed by Le Page (1989) and Le Page and Tabouret-Keller (1985):

> By verbalizing as he does, [the individual] is seeking to reinforce his models of the world, and hopes for acts of solidarity from those with whom he wishes to identify. The feedback he receives from those with whom he talks may reinforce him, or may cause him to modify his projections, both in their form and in their content. To the extent that he is reinforced, his behaviour in that particular context may become more regular, more focussed; to the extent that he modifies his behaviour to accommodate others it may for a time become more variable, more diffuse, but in time the behaviour of the group – that is, he and those with whom he is trying to identify – will become

more focussed. Thus we may speak of focussed and of diffuse, or non-focussed, linguistic systems, both in individuals and in groups, with each individual's knowledge of the systems of his groups the lynch-pin upon which the shared concept of communal languages or vari-eties turns. (Le Page and Tabouret-Keller 1985: 181–2)

There is a marked contrast between the fluidity of language choices implied by this formulation and the 'hard edges' implicit in the notion of code-switching. There are two reasons why this term has become a victim of its own success. The first has to do with the relationship between code-switching and other interlingual phenomena. Its use encourages us to believe that we are studying a unitary phe-nomenon with objective reality rather than a fuzzy-edged construct. Soon, like Monsieur Jourdain in Molière's *Le bourgeois gentilhomme*, who was so delighted to discover that he was speaking prose, bilinguals the world over will doubtless humiliate the linguistic purists who disapprove of their 'mixing' languages with the revelation that what they are in fact doing is 'code-switching'. Like Frankenstein's monster, once invented, code-switching has taken on an existence of its own which is blurring our recognition of its conceptual origins.

The second reason has to do with the nature of the phenomena subsumed under the heading of code-switching. The use of the term code-switching implies a binary choice – that at any given moment speakers are either operating in one mode or in another, which is clearly distinguishable from the first. This is an oversimplification. The type of language mixing which occurs in a given setting depends on a number of factors including the relative prestige of the varieties in question and the extent to which they are considered separate, identifiable lan-guages. Moreover, it is very unlikely that in any language contact situation only one kind of interlingual phenomenon is to be found, and that this kind can be neatly parcelled off from the rest

I shall therefore show firstly that what has been called code-switching in fact merges into various other interlingual phenomena, and that drawing clear lines between these phenomena is an ideological, rather than an objective linguistic, activity. Secondly, I will provide arguments as to why I do not believe that the two languages, varieties or codes which make up code-switching can be discretely categorised in all but the most exceptional cases. Although this is easiest to prove in relation to communities where a range of unfocussed varieties co-exist – and I shall of course be referring to such cases – I shall draw most of my evidence from the community whose code-switching I am most familiar with, the French-Alsatian bilingual community in Alsace. The examination of this data from a qualitative angle shows that, even within what are generally accepted as code-switches, we are dealing with a number of overlapping phenomena whose individuality cannot be captured within traditional grammatical categories.

Two further theoretical issues are relevant to the argument that the varieties which interact within code-switching are non-discrete. These can be termed the *base-language issue* and the *rules-and-exceptions issue*.

The *base-language issue* concerns the question of whether it is right to postulate that in language-mixing of any kind, there is always a base-language which is opposed to a 'donor' language. Myers-Scotton (1993a) makes use of this concept to propose a new framework to describe the regularities of code-switching, which goes beyond traditional grammar. Although Myers-Scotton is prepared to concede that shifts in base-language can occur within a single sentence, one can argue that an even more flexible framework is required for describing the shifting grammatical parameters which we find in mixed codes. The solution advocated by Myers-Scotton is that we should have greater resort to lexically based grammars such as that described in Levelt (1989). Yet whether or not such a grammar constitutes a useful framework for describing code-switching does not necessarily depend on our always being able to identify a base-language. We should consider the possibility that speakers can simply let down the mental barriers between the two languages at various different levels – for example, switching can take place at the phonological level only – rather than assuming that they constantly shift from one pre-set frame to another.

The *rules-and-exceptions issue* concerns the question of whether it is right to view the linguistic *regularities* within a given community's code-switching – whose existence, at a variety of levels, is uncontroversial – in terms of observed patterns with predictive power ('the rules') and to contrast these with the cases which they do not explain, and for which no pattern has yet been found ('the exceptions'). A number of largely unquestioned assumptions lie behind this procedure, in particular regarding the *locus* of code-switching – individual or community – for the rules used by any individual do not coincide with those which are abstracted from the behaviour of the group (Le Page and Tabouret-Keller 1985: Ch. 5). So what are exceptions from the point of view of the analyst who is working (for example) with a construct such as 'group average' may be guiding principles within the speech of a given individual. Above all, this paradigm, like the base-language paradigm, implies that one is either operating within one set of linguistic norms or another; in the next section I will argue that this is too rigid a view of bilingual behaviour.

1. Code-switching as a fuzzy-edged construct

Within any bi- or plurilingual society the varieties at issue may be more or less functionally separate, depending partly on what proportion of the population is plurilingual and partly on the degree of separateness of the domains where they are used. Scotton (1986) has shown, for example, how under strict traditional diglossia, which is now increasingly seen as a theoretical ideal rather than a reality, no intra-sentential code-switching could occur. On the other hand communities are now being described where *only* code-switched varieties are ever used in everyday life (Agnihotri and McCormick, forthcoming).

On the whole, linguists are finding that situations described as involving the discrete use of separate codes involve more contact between the varieties than was originally thought. A recent example of this is Maehlum (1990), in which Blom and Gumperz's influential (1972) study of code-switching in Hemnesberget, Norway, is re-examined. The two codes, Dialect and Standard, which were described by Blom and Gumperz as being in complementary distribution, are seen by Maehlum as 'idealized entities' which are in fact the subject of 'interference at different linguistic levels'. Maehlum asserts that:

> It would surely be very difficult to use these data to argue that any distinct, systematic switching between the two varieties occurs. Most probably, the switching strategies which Blom and Gumperz recorded in Hemnes actually represent some form of *variant switching* whereby, in certain contexts, single words, (idiomatic) expressions and grammatical forms from the standard are introduced into otherwise dialectal utterances. That does not mean, however, that there is any *systematic and distinct* alternation here between two structurally defined varities. (1990: 351)

Fasold (1984: 57) views this breaking down of the distinctions between High and Low partly as a historical trend, parelleling the breakdown of hierarchical social organisation. He describes the four linguistic case-studies which Ferguson (1959) gave as his original exemplars of diglossia as evolving gradually towards a position where 'Diglossia will begin to be expressed through a more unified set of linguistic options, that is, more what we have called style-shifting and less what we call superposed bilingualism or classic diglossia'. Modern Greek provides a good example of this process. The *de facto* existence of a continuum between High and Low has now been compounded by the official abandoning of the High (*katharevousa*) for education and government affairs.

In showing that code-switching cannot be kept separate from whatever manifestations of language contact are prevalent within the society at issue, I shall consider three stages or types of interlingual phenomena: borrowing, language mixing/interference and pidginisation. The first two have often been deliberately distinguished from code-switching in existing studies (e.g. Poplack *et al.* 1987) for reasons which will be discussed below. As to pidginisation, oddly enough it has so far, to my knowledge, never been systematically compared with code-switching. Although both are language contact phenomena, they seem to be treated as occurring under quite different social circumstances. Yet although code-switching in focussed linguistic communities is not necessarily accompanied by pidginisation, the reverse does not hold, and there is evidence from a variety of sources that code-switching occurs in pidgin/creole-speaking areas (Mühlhäusler 1982; Le Page and Tabouret-Keller 1985; Crowley 1990; Romaine 1992). Moreover, there are linguistic phenomena which might be conceptualised both as code-switching and pidginisation, as we can see through the example of new compound verb-formations discussed below. The similarities and differences between the two processes therefore merit some discussion.

1.1 Code-switching and borrowing

The distinctions and similarities between code-switching and borrowing have been amply discussed (for reviews of these discussions see Romaine 1989; Myers-Scotton 1992) and will only be touched on briefly here. The reason why this question has so often been raised is partly that in many communities, single-word switching is the commonest kind, and partly that any bilingual data-set contains examples of loans alongside instances of code-switching. The researcher transcribing and analysing code-switched data therefore inevitably has to face the problem of drawing the line between the two categories. This turns out to be less straightforward than one might imagine. For example the following are three criteria which, contrary to expectation, do *not* distinguish reliably between code-switches and loans:

(i) *morphophonemic integration with the surrounding language*: both loans and code-switches can be morphologically and phonologically integrated or un-integrated with the surrounding language, depending on a wide variety of personal and linguistic factors;

(ii) *native synonym displacement*: there are examples of both loans and code-switches filling 'lexical gaps' in the surrounding language *and* of them adding themselves as a further option to the 'native' equivalent.

(iii) *grammatical category*: although loans are often nouns, all grammatical categories are potentially borrowable; conversely, in many, though not in all, contexts, noun code-switching is statistically the most common kind to occur in the data.

Although everyone would probably agree that loans used by completely monolingual speakers in highly focussed communities should be regarded as being psychologically separate from code-switching, this provides little help when what you are dealing with is bilingual or plurilingual speakers in bilingual or plurilingual contexts. One problem is that many of the words which occur in the data and which are candidates for loan/code-switch status in fact 'belong' equally to both codes (Clyne 1987). In Alsace for example phatic greeting formulas of French origin ('Bonjour Madame', 'Merci', 'Au revoir' etc.) are used invariably, whether the speakers are using French, Alsatian or code-switching. Diachronically speaking, they have been borrowed from French by the dialect; but in a synchronic context, such a remark is of little relevance. When a team of three native judges were presented with a list of French words used in Alsatian conversations (and vice versa) and asked to classify them as loans, code-switches or to place them in an in-between category, they only agreed among themselves in approximately one third of cases (Gardner-Chloros 1991: 162). In the case of a word like 'piscine' ['swimming pool'] they all agreed that the word was neither a full loan-word nor simply an *ad-hoc* code-switch. Their general lack of agreement can be explained if one takes the view that every loan starts off life as a code-switch, and that some of these code-switches gradually become generalised and spread through the community. Like other linguistic changes, they spread irregularly, and in some sub-sections of the community they acquire currency sooner than in others. In spite of being born-and-bred bilinguals from the same town, the three Alsatian judges' experience of different linguistic groups around them was, understandably, non-identical.

1.2 Code-switching and mixing/interference

Like the distinction between borrowing and code-switching, the distinction between mixing/interference and code-switching has been much discussed, and so will only be treated briefly here (for a review of these concepts and how they have been used see Hamers and Blanc 1989: 143–54). Haugen (1956) distinguished between code-switching on the one hand, in which the distinct character of the codes is said to be preserved, and interference/integration on the other, which are instances of the levelling down of differences between them. This distinction was very influential, and is basically the same one that was used by Sankoff and Poplack in devising the rules of their 'code-switching grammar'

(1981). Such a grammar depends on a distinction being drawn between language alternation, in which the two languages are said, thanks to the application of additional code-switching rules, to preserve their monolingual characteristics even though they may be closely interwoven within the fabric of the sentence, and cases where one language influences the form of another owing to contact between them.

> What is important is that this phenomenon [*i.e. code-switching*] be clearly distinguished, first conceptually, and then operationally as much as possible, from all other consequences of bilingualism which involve not alternate use, but the truly simultaneous use of elements from both codes . . . Not least important, all of these phenomena should be distinguished from speech errors which involve elements of both languages, and which may be properly considered 'interference'. (Poplack 1987: 72)

Linguistic quick-change acts such as those Poplack refers to, in which the monolingual stretches in each language are indistinguishable from those which would be uttered by the speakers' (hypothetical) monolingual peers, are indeed sometimes performed. However these constitute a small minority of bilingual code-switched utterances. For one thing they arise only in communities where linguistic focussing and adherence to standards are the norm. They are outnumbered by those where the code-switched passages *do* show departures from the two monolingual norms. Myers-Scotton (1993a) reviews studies carried out over the last twenty years to test the applicability of the grammatical constraints on the occurrence of code-switching, which alone can guarantee this degree of separateness of the two systems. She concludes that the implied universality of such constraints is heavily qualified by the number and the variety of counter-examples of which we now have evidence: 'First, the counter-examples are not so few that they can be attributed to part of the natural variation inherent in any speech community. Second, because they come from such typologically diverse languages, the counter-examples cannot be ascribed to typological differences among languages.' (1993a: 34).

Mougeon and Beniak (1991: 9) suggest that Poplack over-emphasised internal explanations of minority-language change, at the expense of explanations based on language contact, as a reaction to exaggerated claims that such languages are hybrid and that their speakers are inferior. They themselves set out to rehabilitate the role of *interference* in language change, as they consider that its role has been minimised in recent studies of language contact; code-switching is mentioned mainly as the likely source of specific borrowings.

In the Panjabi–English data collected by Agnihotri in Leeds (1987, 1992), 'interference' and code-switching go hand in hand. He gives numerous examples of lexemes which are used apparently indifferently with the morphological markings of either language:

aːntiːz/aːntiyā	('aunties')
wiːks/wiːkā:	('weeks')
aːr̤iːz/aːr̤iyā:	(Panjabi, 'prayer') (1992)

He gives other examples of the closely parallel use of lexical items (found in the same output, indeed in some cases in the same sentence) with modifiers in either language:

tu: sistəːz	(two sisters)
ikk brʌdər	(one brother)
yelo pagz	(yellow turbans)
fə biːd	(the holy book) (1992)

Such arbitrariness in the switching patterns – and the attendant lack of any plausible motivation – is characteristic of code-switching as an unmarked choice (Myers-Scotton 1993b). It is in such contexts that a blurring of the distinction between code-switching and interference occurs.

Various general attempts have been made to specify the conditions under which code-switching is likely to occur. Gumperz and Hernandez (1969: 2) said that it could be found 'each time minority language groups come into contact with majority language groups under conditions of rapid social change'. Others (see Giacalone Ramat, this volume) have on the contrary described it as a feature of stable bilingualism in a community where most speakers possess both of the codes in question. Heller (1988) identified this problem and suggested that, among the issues which code-switching research still has to address, we look at: 'the extent to which different types of code-switching are related to different types of boundary maintenance/change processes' and 'the generalizability of findings concerning the social conditions under which code-switching is or is not found' (1988: 268–9).

What is now certain is that code-switching *can* arise in linguistic situations of widely varying stability. It can be a feature of stable bilingualism for an extended period, and then, if circumstances alter and language shift sets in, it may persist as a *vehicle* of that shift. Only careful analysis of the community patterns may allow the differences in the two types of code-switching to appear.

This is the case of Sauris in the Carnian Alps, described by Denison (1971, 1984, 1986). This small community had preserved a local variety of German for some 600 years, Friulian being the regional norm and Italian the national norm, with which speakers, until this century, had relatively little contact. Now the local dialect is giving way, above all to Italian, but is as yet still evident in the – frequently code-switched – speech of the community.

1.3 Code-switching and pidginisation/creolisation

In many part of the world, code-switching is found alongside creolisation and decreolisation, and contributes, like the latter, to the processes of language convergence or divergence. For example Crowley (1990), in rejecting the idea that the history of Melanesian Pidgin can be divided into chronologically distinct developmental phases, argues that access to the substratum persists at all levels; stabilisation, destabilisation and creolisation should all be regarded as contributing simultaneously to the gradual evolution of the language (1990: 384–6). As to code-switching, its presence or absence seems to be largely a function of the prestige attached to the pidgin. Comparing usage on the radio in Vanuatu and the Solomon Islands, Crowley finds much more code-switching in the Solomon Islands, where the pidgin's prestige is low, than in Vanuatu – to the extent that in the case of Solomon Islands announcers, 'It is sometimes difficult to know which language they would claim to be speaking.'

In Papua New Guinea, Romaine (1992) shows how code-switching occurs within the context of a post-creole continuum which has emerged in the last twenty years: 'In town, Standard English, English spoken as a second language with varying degrees of fluency, highly anglicized Tok Pisin, more rural Tok Pisin of migrants, and the creolized Tok Pisin of the urban-born coexist and loosely reflect the emerging social stratification' (1992: 323).

Le Page and Tabouret-Keller (1985) give examples of creole speech from various different sources in the Caribbean, Belize and from London Jamaican. At its most fluid level, code-switching involves shifting at particular linguistic levels rather than a wholesale transition from one discrete code to another – indeed discrete codes are difficult to come by in linguistic contexts as unfocussed as those they describe. Sometimes, as in the case of London Jamaican, the switching between codes is more symbolic than real:

> 'London Jamaican' is more a set of norms to be aimed at than an internally coherent and consistent system. Speakers behave as if there

were a language called 'Jamaican', but often all they do (perhaps all they *know how* to do) is to make gestures in the direction of certain tokens associated with Jamaican Creole which have a stereotypical value. (1985: 180)

There are practical consequences, also, which arise from the fluidity characterising the transitions between creoles and their attendant substrata and superstrata. For example in Papua New Guinea, but also in Haiti (Valdman 1975, discussed in Romaine 1992) and in the Central African Republic (Gerbault 1990), there are difficulties in selecting a variety sufficiently distinguishable from the others to be the subject of standardisation.

As in pidginisation, so within code-switching, linguistic convergence phenomena can arise which follow recognisable patterns across typologically diverse combinations, as in the case of the compound verb formation described in Romaine (1986). In English–Panjabi code-switched speech of bilinguals living in Birmingham, Panjabi verbal operators meaning 'do, make' etc. are commonly combined with a major category (noun, verb, adjective) taken from English to make new verbal compounds which function as a single syntactic/semantic unit, e.g. '*ple* kerna', where *ple* comes from English 'play' and 'kerna' means 'do, make' in Panjabi. The new formation means 'to play' and can be replaced by a single, synonymous verb in Panjabi.

Romaine shows how this formation violates all the major grammatical constraints proposed for code-switching, such as for example those based on the government and binding theory. It cannot be satisfactorily analysed in terms of English or Panjabi grammar. Parallel creations have been attested in other, typologically diverse studies of language contact, *whether or not* any native model exists in one of the two languages. For example in a study of the Greek Cypriot community in London, I found examples of English major categories being combined with the Greek verb 'kano', meaning 'do/make', here in its Cypriot form 'kamno'. In Standard Modern Greek, as in the Greek Cypriot dialect, 'kano' is only used to create new verbal compounds when the second element of the compound is the direct object of 'kano', and therefore a noun (e.g. 'kano γimnastiki' ['I do gymnastics']). Neither English nor Greek provides a model for the double verbal formation attested in code-switching.

Mixed compound verb formations in Cypriot/English

kamno *use*	to use
kamno *respect*	to respect
kamno *developed*	to develop

kamno *spelling*   to spell
(Gardner-Chloros 1992: 127)

The use of the same structure in Greek–English switching in Montreal is reported in Maniakas (1991). A parallel formation found with 'εχο' ('have') in the London community further demonstrates that we are dealing with a new verbal formation rather than simple switching between the two languages. In example (1):

(1)   ksero oti εχis *very busy*
             [I know that you have (i.e. you are) very busy]

we are clearly dealing with a new verbal formation as there is no reason why the speaker should not use the Greek verb to be and say 'I know you *are* very busy', exactly as in the English and in the Greek monolingual models.

The most linguistically intense and constraint-defying forms of code-switching do not arise only in unfocussed situations. Educated bilinguals whose two languages have been presented to them in quite separate contexts, are also capable of such switching. Its presence is a function of the lack of inhibition and intimacy of the situation in which they find themselves. For example Maters (1979) was surprised to find numerous examples of bound morpheme switching, such as the past participle 'ge*coverd*' ['covered'] and, in the other direction, the present participle 'beschouw*ing*' ['considering'] even in modest data samples taken from her Dutch relatives speaking English to each other. She found that the code-switchers themselves found sentences where such integration *had* taken place more acceptable than those where it had not, her explanation for this being that the violation of the free morpheme constraint *helped repair the ungrammaticality* caused by violations of the equivalence constraint. The antagonistic functioning of these two constraints has not, to my knowledge, yet been investigated, though it makes perfect sense of much 'educated bilingual' data. Maters also reports the use of code-switched sentences which do not conform to either the grammar of Dutch or that of English, commenting that 'Ungrammaticality can and does occur in the code-switches of very balanced bilinguals (such as my informants)' (1979: 15).

Others, from different theoretical backgrounds (Giles *et al.* 1978; Bourhis *et al.* 1979; Coupland 1985; Sachdev and Bourhis 1990), have drawn attention to the uses of code-switching for purposes of *accommodation*. The difference between these approaches and that of Le Page and Tabouret-Keller lies principally in the latters' emphasis on individuals in their relations to the group as opposed to intergroup relations. Thus we see that code-switching takes its place within a range of occurrences which characterise bilingual/plurilingual situations in varying configurations. It can be the vehicle of quite opposite tendencies, from accommodation to divergence and from language maintenance to language shift. Chameleon-like, it reflects social tendencies, and differences within the same society and language combination (Bentahila and Davies 1991) just as it reflects those between different societies and different language combinations (Poplack 1987).

In the next section we will have a closer look at the chameleon, particularly in the context of Strasbourg, with a view to observing its internal anatomy, as opposed to its relationship with other species.

2 The internal description of code-switching: the case of Strasbourg

The case of Strasbourg will be used here as an example to show how even within a relatively constrained macrolinguistic situation, code-switching can cover a complex range of overlapping linguistic phenomena.

2.1 The macrolinguistic context

The border area of Alsace is part of the Germanic dialect continuum, but has been part of France since the end of the Second World War. Before that, it belonged alternately to Germany and to France between 1648 and 1945, changing hands five times in 300 years. Since 1945, in spite of the strong pressures towards centralisation and uniformity which characterise the influence of the French state, Alsace has preserved a strong cultural identity of its own, which is clearly distinct from that of neighbouring Germany as well as that of the rest of France. It is only relatively recently that socio-economic pressures have led, there as elsewhere, to an erosion of that identity and to a falling off in the use of the traditional Alemannic dialect (Tabouret-Keller and Luckel 1981a,b; Ladin 1982; Gardner-Chloros 1991). This trend is most marked in the capital, Strasbourg, owing to its cosmopolitan nature and to the presence of large numbers of 'Français de l'Intérieur' – French from other parts of France. It is also the place where code-switching is most prevalent. There it is not only a 'strategy of neutrality', to use Scotton's term (1986), i.e. the most universally acceptable means of communication with people of differing linguistic competence. It is also the only 'we code' now available to a large number of younger Alsatian speakers, who are no longer able to speak the dialect in an unmixed form.

The type of code-switching which occurs is partly determined by the overt status enjoyed by the two varieties, and a comparison carried out by Treffers-Daller (1991) between code-switching patterns in Brussels and Strasbourg clearly illustrates this point. The comparison was possible owing to similarities between the two cities, which are both situated in the border zone of a Germanic and a Romance language. Both the Germanic languages in question are in contact with French, from which they have borrowed extensively, borrowing in the opposite direction being much less frequent. Differences between the code-switching patterns are therefore very likely to be attributable to sociolinguistic factors, and Treffers-Daller's results confirm their significance in determining the prevailing linguistic patterns. In Brussels, where both the languages enjoy the status of standard languages, intra-phrase switching is shown by Treffers-Daller's data to be much less common than in Strasbourg, where the Alemannic dialect enjoys less overt prestige than French. At a qualitative level, there is evidence in Brussels that French words borrowed into Brussels Dutch are morphophonologically integrated. In Strasbourg the French words can preserve their French morphology; again, this is consistent with the fact that Alsatian enjoys a lower status in Strasbourg than Dutch does in Brussels.

The overt status-balance of the varieties is also reflected in the lack of symmetry in patterns of code-switching and borrowing. These partly reflect speaker-related factors such as individual language dominance, but are also attributable to the cultural influence of one variety on another. The easiest type of code-switching to quantify for this purpose is single-word switching. In order to draw up a linguistic profile of the type of code-switching which occurs, six conversations, recorded in natural circumstances, three in work settings and three in homes, were transcribed (Gardner-Chloros 1991). After having eliminated loan-words, there were between four and five times as many French words embedded in Alsatian as there were Alsatian words embedded in French (1991: 163–4). The commonest category among the French words was nouns, and the commonest by far among the Alsatian words was interjections/tags and other phatic markers, indicating that the switching was not only quantitatively different but was also fulfilling a different function depending on the direction of the switch.

This lack of symmetry in bilingual usage is identifiable at all levels, for example in the prevailing rules of linguistic etiquette. There are still widely accepted norms as to when the different varieties can/should be used, and there are settings from which Alsatian is still almost completely excluded, such as the school setting. It is much harder to find any from which French is totally excluded: outside the towns, the unmixed use of the dialect is still associated with the older, male, farmworkers, though these represent under 5 per cent of the population (Tabouret-Keller and Luckel 1981a,b). Yet in Strasbourg it is difficult to find any setting from which younger and non-Alsatian speakers are totally excluded, and I was unable to locate dialect-speaking bastions in Strasbourg in spite of a deliberate attempt to do so (Gardner-Chloros 1991: 101–2).

One of the most widely mentioned rules is that one should not use the dialect in the presence of non-dialect speakers. The reverse, i.e. speaking French in front of non-French-speakers is (i) much less likely to occur (almost everyone understands French even when they do not speak it), and (ii) more acceptable on the basis that 'Alsace is part of France' and that the older generation, for whom that has not always been true, have to accept this as a modern fact of life.

2.2 The microlinguistic continuum

We have seen that the situations where French and Alsatian can be used in their unmixed form are relatively clearly mapped out in Strasbourg, with French being used in particular whenever a non-dialect speaker is present. We have also seen that code-switching fulfils two principal functions, one as a compromise code between speakers with differing degrees of competence in French and Alsatian, and another as a 'we code' opposed to the 'they code' of French. Diachronically, in this second function it has taken over the role assigned to Alsatian a generation earlier.

Let us now look at what happens at a linguistic level when speakers make use of this second function, that is when they use switching as an unmarked choice. This occurs in situations where they are sure to be understood whichever language, or whichever elements from each language, they use. The only 'rule' which need prevail *within* this type of unmarked code-switching is that speakers should exploit the maximum number of communicative conventions which are shared; as a result, code-switching among peer groups is likely to be more linguistically intense than that which is found, say, between different generations, even within the same family, and more intense than that which characterises out-group inter-action, even between bilinguals. There is evidence for this from various sources in the Strasbourg data, as there is from other settings.

(i) Firstly, the amount of code-switching found in family conversations, where different generations were present, was more limited than that found in work-place conversations where bilinguals of a similar background were interacting with their work-mates (Gardner-Chloros 1991: 164).

(ii) Secondly, in a survey carried out in an insurance office, where the conversations taking place over a whole day between co-workers and between employees and clients were recorded, and then analysed and compared, switching among employees talking to each other took place in over 40% of cases, whereas switching when an employee was talking to a client only took place in 14% of the exchanges observed (Gardner-Chloros 1991: 88–9).

(iii) Thirdly, in a survey of language use in three department stores, modelled on Labov's 1966 New York study (described in Labov 1978), overall the same pattern prevailed, with switching between salespeople being more common than switching in conversations between salespeople and customers (Gardner-Chloros 1991: 79). The main finding of the survey was, however, that the different motivations which could lead to code-switching did not lead to a clearly predictable or linear pattern of switching at a quantitative level (Gardner-Chloros 1991: 86).

The ability of individual speakers to adjust the rate and type of switching which they use in different circumstances is a function of their bilingual skills. To take an extreme example, one employee in the insurance office, Mrs F, in the course of a day's work, produced instances of Standard French with no trace of regional characteristics; strongly accented regional French; interlocutor-related switching; fluent Alsatian (she lived in a village outside Strasbourg and so was in touch with monolingual dialect-speakers); and intensive unmarked switching which I have been able to use as a classic example of that mode (Gardner-Chloros 1991: 92–9). The analogy with monolingual style-shifting is clear, and the range available to play on is probably broader.

The puzzle which still remains to be elucidated, in the face of the flexibility of individual behaviour, is this: what is the real effect of the macrolinguistic or societal 'rules', such as the linguistic etiquette rules outlined above, on individual behaviour? Since individuals clearly *are* affected by these social norms, how is it that on certain occasions they can apparently shake them off, and behave like Maters's educated Dutch–English bilinguals, who indulge in inter-morpheme switching between what are *to them* two highly focussed 'languages'? What are the mechanisms by which diffuseness is instituted within a basically non-diffuse situation? In Strasbourg for example we are not dealing with a dialect continuum between two related varieties. The lack of standardisation of Alsatian is a factor which increases its permeability, as compared, for example, with the situation in Brussels. Yet we are still dealing with the mixing of this dialect with an *unrelated and highly focussed standard language*, French.

The answer to the question as to how this is achieved is to be found at several different levels.

First of all, there are *linguistic techniques* for achieving the degree of mixing which is necessary in order to place oneself within a distinct code, without having to resort to dense grammatical mixing which could cause raised eyebrows when a focussed, standard language is involved.

One of these techniques, found repeatedly in the data, involved exploiting the characteristics of the spoken language, such as its frequently occurring paratactic and appositional constructions. Like the inter-morpheme switching described by Maters (1979), the use of such structures, which would be unthinkable in writing, legitimises the language changes which would otherwise require taxing inter-grammatical gear changes – for example:

(2)   *D'meischte wie drinne spiele*, ils sont costauds
       [*Most of those who play there*, they're tough]

       La cassette, *wie lang ass se geht?*
       [The cassette, *how long does it run for?*]

       Ah ja,'s geht als an, la lumière
       [*Oh yes, it always goes on*, the light]

More generally, the characteristics of natural conversational speech, now seen as significant for monolingual conversational coherence (Milroy and Milroy 1985: 141–2), are also exploited in bilingual code-switching. They frequently serve to let the speaker get around the grammatical puzzle of conjoining two languages, especially where these, like French and Alsatian, show typological differences, such as in the placement of the main verb in the sentence. Other examples of this are given in Gardner-Chloros 1991 (pp. 175–7). One would therefore expect to find that (i) switches coinciding with conversational breaks, self-interruptions etc., correspond with the use of structures where there is a lack of parallelism between the two monolingual grammars, and that (ii) other factors being equal, the amount of such switching is correlated with the extent of typological mismatch between the two languages. Both these questions remain to be investigated.

The other technique for circumventing the pressure of external norms is more psychological or structural. It consists in allowing speakers to do quite a range of things with their two languages while ostensibly all operating within the same speech mode. Thus 'unmarked code-switching' in fact includes a range of variation in actual linguistic behaviour, both as regards quantity and quality. Code-switching is a highly individualistic phenomenon, and some speakers' particular 'brand' of it is characterised by grammatically dense switches, while others' is not.

Some speakers come up with intra-sentential switching which violates every conceivable grammatical constraint:

(3)   *Il* koch guet
         [*He* cooks well]

or:

(4)   *Tee het er immer zamme*mélangé
         *Tea has he always together*mixed
         [He has always mixed tea together]

Others provide not a single example of this grammatically intense mixing, but
switch more often. In one conversation within which a lot of unconstrained code-
switching takes place, for instance, one speaker is in fact switching in 30% of his
utterances, another in 20%, and the other two participants in under 10% of cases
(Gardner-Chloros 1991: 118). These are considerable differences. Yet the overall
picture is an integrated one, there is no interlocutor-related switching within this
group (though there is earlier when members of the younger generation are present), and there is certainly no evidence that anyone regards the most intense
switcher as odd.

    Within what one can call the 'unconstrained switching mode', a range of beha-
viour profiles are therefore acceptable. Because of this, speakers of widely varying
linguistic competence in the two varieties can be accepted within conversations
which are taking place in the unmarked, code-switching mode – they need only
make the most symbolic 'gestures' to indicate their allegiance to this speech-mode.
Tag switching is the clearest example of this. There are speakers in Strasbourg
whose only form of switching consists in adding the Alsatian tag 'gel?' [= 'isn't
that so, eh?'] to the end of each French sentence. The extent to which this is a
symbolic process is illustrated by a conversation in which a monolingual French-
speaker is being persuaded to become a 'proper Alsatian' by his heavily code-
switching colleagues; the linguistic issue becomes blurred with a culinary one as
they discuss where to go for lunch, finally insisting that if he eats a particular dish
with them two or three times like a good Alsatian, he too will be able to speak the
dialect (Gardner-Chloros 1991: 144).

    It is very likely, of course, that at other levels, especially prosodic and para-
linguistic, such speakers display features which place them squarely within this
discourse-type more conclusively than it appears from their code-switching patterns as such. Prosodic and paralinguistic aspects of code-switching therefore
deserve more attention than they have so far received.

3 Conclusion

Code-switching should be viewed as an analyst construct rather than as an observable fact. It is a product of our conceptualisations about language contact and language mixing, and it is not separable, either ideologically or in practice, from borrowing, interference or pidginisation.

In an attempt to set up a theoretically satisfying taxonomy, the term has often been applied to a particularly focussed type of language-mixing, defined by the grammatical independence and discreteness of the contributing varieties. This is held to be a feature of stable bilingual communities, and to contrast with the interpenetration of varieties which characterises situations involving language shift.

However, there are a number of problems with this definition. First of all, it is an illusion to consider the stability of bilingual situations as an absolute. The one universal which is uncontentious to linguists of all schools is that languages change over time, and contact between varieties is now accepted as a major mechanism of change. Code-switching may be only the first step in the process, but it is nonetheless part of it.

Secondly, that very grammatical independence on which the definition rests appears to be, at best, one extreme of a continuum. The number of examples of intermediate codes and intermediate phenomena is ever-growing and as this process continues, the cases where monolingual standards apply unequivocally to the monolingual segments within code-switched speech will be recognised for the exceptions that they are. Certainly the idea that there is a one-to-one correspondence between the type of switching which is used, and the degree of bilingual ability of the speaker, must be seen as an oversimplification. Sociolinguistic and individual factors should be seen as equally important; typological and paralinguistic aspects require further investigation; and the description of both inter- and intra-individual variation in the same communities has hardly even begun.

What we are left having to explain, in order to understand the overall phenomenon of code-switching is therefore not how speakers keep their languages separate, but how they manipulate the overall sociolinguistic situation to create their own linguistic sub-groups and sub-codes. In this connection we have seen that *what speakers do* is much more subtle than what the external rules would lead us to expect. This is because the linguistic behaviour of individuals is not only a barometer of social forces but also of micro-level identifications which sociological description as such cannot capture. A whole range of linguistically diverse features can be present in, or absent from, a 'we code'. It is the symbolic intentions which underlie such a code, along with the way in which they are understood, that give it its significance. These structural processes are the same whatever the status and relationship of the contributing varieties, be they dialects or standards.

It is time to concentrate on the distinctions in language behaviour which are organising principles for speakers, leaving to last any positive linguistic categorisation of the units or varieties involved. We should observe the behaviour of the molecules, and the waves which they generate, without worrying about what either waves or molecules should be called. Nevertheless, those who do consider names important would do well to reflect that code-switching deserves a name less misleading as to its nature.

Bibliography

Agnihotri, R. K. (1987) *Crisis of identity: the Sikhs in England*. New Delhi: Bahri.
(1992) Code-mixing among Sikh children in Leeds, U.K. Paper presented at Sociolinguistics Symposium IX, University of Reading, April 1992.

Agnihotri, R. K. and McCormick, K. (forthcoming) *Just a normal way of talking: language mixing*. Real Language Series. Longman.

Bentahila, A. and Davies, E. E. (1991) Constraints on code-switching: a look beyond grammar. In *Papers for the symposium on code-switching in bilingual studies: theory, significance and perspectives*. (Held in Barcelona, 21–23 March 1991.) Strasbourg: European Science Foundation, 369–403.

Blom, J.-P. and Gumperz, J. J. (1972) Social meaning in linguistic structures: code-switching in Norway. In J. J. Gumperz and D. Hymes eds., *Directions in Sociolinguistics. The ethnography of communication*. New York: Holt, Rinehart and Winston, 407–34.

Bourhis, R. G., Giles, H., Leyens, J. P. and Tajfel, H. (1979) Psycholinguistic distinctiveness: language divergence in Belgium. In H. Giles and R. St. Clair eds., *Language and social psychology*. Oxford: Basil Blackwell, 158–85.

Clyne, M. G. (1987) Constraints on code-switching: how universal are they? *Linguistics*, 25: 739–64.

Coupland, N. (1985) Hark, hark the lark: social motivations for phonological style-shifting. *Language and Communication*, 5 (3): 153–71.

Crowley, T. (1990) *Beach-la-Mar to Bislama: the emergence of a national language in Vanuatu*. Oxford: Clarendon Press.

Denison, N. (1971) Some observations on language variety and plurilingualism. In J. B. Pride and J. Holmes, *Sociolinguistics: selected readings*. Harmondsworth, Middx.: Penguin Books, 65–78.
(1984) Language acquisition in a plurilingual environment. *Grazer Linguistische Studien*, 21 (Spring 1984): 35–64.
(1986) Sociolinguistics, linguistic description, language change and language acquisition. In Fishman *et al.* (1986), I: 83–98.

Fasold, R. (1984) *The sociolinguistics of society*. Oxford: Basil Blackwell.

Ferguson, C. A. (1959) Diglossia. *Word*, 15: 325–40. Reprinted in Giglioli, P. (1972) ed. *Language and social context*. Harmondsworth: Penguin Books, 232–52.

Fishman, J. A., Tabouret-Keller, A., Clyne, M., Krishnamurti, B. and Abdulaziz, M. (1986) eds. *The Fergusonian impact*. 2 vols. Berlin: Mouton de Gruyter.

Gardner-Chloros, P. (1991) *Language selection and switching in Strasbourg*. Oxford: Clarendon Press.

(1992) The sociolinguistics of the Greek-Cypriot community of London. In M. Karyolemou ed., *Sociolinguistique du grec et de la Grèce*, 4 (June 1992). Plurilinguismes. CERPL Paris: Université René Descartes, 112–36.

Gerbault, J. (1990) Conflicting forces in the standardization of Sango and the development of vernacular literacy in the Central African Republic. In *Abstracts and transcriptions of the discussion, York workshop 1990*. International Group for the Study of Language Standardization and the vernacularization of Literacy. Department of Language and Linguistic Science, University of York, 8–12.

Giles, H., Mulac, A., Bradac, J. J. and Johnson, P. (1987) Speech accommodation theory: the first decade and beyond. In M. L. McLaughlin ed., *Communication yearbook*, 10. Beverley Hills, Calif.: Sage, 13–48.

Gumperz, J. and Hernandez, E. (1969) *Cognitive aspects of bilingual communication, Working Paper No. 28, Language Behavior Research Laboratory*. Berkeley: University of California Press.

Hamers, J. and Blanc, M. (1989) *Bilinguality and bilingualism*. Cambridge University Press.

Haugen, E. (1956) *Bilingualism in the Americas: a bibliography and a research guide*. Publications of the American Dialect Society, 26, University of Alabama Press.

Heller, M. (1988) *Code-switching: anthropological and sociolinguistic perspectives*. Berlin: Mouton de Gruyter.

Labov, W. (1978) *Sociolinguistic patterns*. Oxford: Basil Blackwell, 43–69.

Ladin, W. (1982) *Der elsässische Dialekt – museumsreif? Analyse einer Umfrage*. Strasbourg: Salde.

Le Page, R. B. (1989) What is a language? *York Papers in Linguistics*, 13: 9–24.

(1992) Personal communication.

Le Page, R. B. and Tabouret-Keller, A. (1985) *Acts of identity, creole-based approaches to language and ethnicity*. Cambridge University Press.

Levelt, W. J. M. (1989) *Speaking: from intention to articulation*. Cambridge, Mass.: MIT Press.

Maehlum, B. (1990) Codeswitching in Hemnesberget – myth or reality? In E. Hakon Jahr and O. Lorentz, *Tromso linguistics in the eighties*. Oslo: Novus Press. Forthcoming, *International Journal of the Sociology of Language*.

Maniakas, T. M. (1991) KANO+INF: the case of a Greek auxiliary verb in a language contact situation. *Journal of Applied Linguistics*, 7: 114–31.

Maters, K. (1979) An evaluation of syntactic constraints on code-switching and their potential application to Dutch/English. Unpublished M. Phil. thesis, University of Cambridge.

Milroy, J. and Milroy, L. (1985) *Authority in language: investigating language prescription and standardization*. London: Routledge & Kegan Paul.

Mougeon, R. and Beniak, E. (1991) *Linguistic consequences of language contact and restriction: the case of French in Ontario, Canada*. Oxford: Clarendon Press.

Mühlhäusler, P. (1982) Code-switching in Papua New Guinea: local languages versus New Guinea Pidgin, Hiri Motu and English. In S. A. Wurm ed., *New Guinea and neighbouring areas: a sociolinguistic laboratory*. The Hague: Mouton.

Myers-Scotton, C. (1992) Comparing codeswitching and borrowing. *Journal of Multilingual and Multicultural Development*, 13 (1–2): 19–39.

   (1993a) *Duelling languages: grammatical structure in code-switching*. Oxford: Clarendon Press.

   (1993b) *Social motivations for code-switching: evidence from Africa*. Oxford: Clarendon Press.

Poplack, S. (1987) Contrasting patterns of code-switching in two communities. In E. Wande, J. Anward, B. Nordberg, L. Steensland and M. Thelander eds., *Aspects of multilingualism: proceedings from the fourth Nordic symposium on bilingualism, 1984*. Sweden: University of Uppsala, 51–77.

Poplack, S., Wheeler, S. and Westwood, A. (1987) Distinguishing language contact phenomena: evidence from Finnish–English bilingualism. In P. Lilius, M. Saari eds., *The Nordic Languages and Modern Linguistics*, 6. (Proceedings of the Sixth International Conference of Nordic and General Linguistics in Helsinki, 18–22 August 1986.) 33–56. Also in K. Hyltenstam, L. K. Obler (1989) eds., *Bilingualism across the lifespan. Aspects of acquisition, maturity and loss*. Cambridge University Press, 132–54.

Romaine, S. (1986) The syntax and semantics of the code-mixed compound verb in Panjabi-English bilingual discourse. In D. Tannen and J. Alatis eds., *Language and linguistics: the interdependence of theory, data and application*. Washington, D.C.: Georgetown University Press, 35–49.

   (1989) *Bilingualism*, Language in Society 13. Oxford: Basil Blackwell.

   (1992) *Language education and development: urban and rural Tok Pisin in Papua New Guinea*. Oxford: Clarendon Press.

Sachdev, I. and Bourhis, R. (1990) Bilinguality and multilinguality. In H. Giles and W. P. Robinson eds., *Handbook of language and social psychology*. Chichester: J. Wiley, 293–308.

Sankoff, D. and Poplack, S. (1981) A formal grammar for code-switching. *Papers in Linguistics: International Journal of Human Communication*, 14 (1): 3–45.

Scotton, C. M. (1986) Diglossia and codeswitching. In Fishman *et al.* (1986), II: 403–15.

Tabouret-Keller, A. and Luckel, F. (1981a) La dynamique sociale du changement linguistique: quelques aspects de la situation rurale en Alsace. *International Journal of the Sociology of Language*, 29: 51–66.

   (1981b) Maintien de l'alsacien et adoption du français: éléments de la situation linguistique en milieu rural en Alsace. *Languages*, 61: 39–62.

Treffers-Daller, J. (1991) French–Dutch language mixture in Brussels. Unpublished Ph.D. thesis, University of Amsterdam.

5 CODE-SWITCHING IN THE CLASSROOM: TWO DECADES OF RESEARCH

Marilyn Martin-Jones

Research on code-switching in bilingual classrooms now spans almost two decades. It has been cross-disciplinary in nature and has thus reflected different currents of influence: from educational research on classroom interaction and teacher talk styles and, more recently, from conversational analysis, pragmatics and the ethnography of communication. It has also been international in nature: the early studies were carried out in the United States in bilingual education programmes for linguistic minority children. The 1970s and early 1980s saw the development of a substantial body of classroom-based research in this particular context. However, since the early 1980s, research on bilingual classroom processes has also been undertaken in other bilingual and multilingual settings such as Canada, South America, Europe, Africa and South East Asia.

Most research has been undertaken in settings where there is an ongoing debate about language education policy: in situations where a new form of language education programme has been implemented or where there has been a change in the medium of instruction or, in contrast, in situations where a change in medium needs to be considered because current policies are inappropriate. The principal motivation in undertaking most classroom-based research seems to have been to establish how language education policies are being translated into communicative practice in the day-to-day cycles of classroom life. As Merritt *et al.* have pointed out: 'Determinants of language choice and code-switching in the classroom are necessarily more complex than can be "legislated" by language policy on medium of instruction' (1992: 105).

My aim, in this chapter, is to provide a critical review of the developments that have taken place in research conducted in bilingual and multilingual classrooms over the two decades since the mid 1970s. I will examine two broad strands of research:

(i) early studies where the first attempts were made to conduct classroom discourse analysis in bilingual contexts. This research focussed primarily on the

90

communicative functions of code-switching in teacher-led talk and on the frequency with which particular languages were employed to perform different functions.

(ii) more recent studies which have taken more account of the sequential flow of classroom discourse and of the way in which code-switching contributes to the interactional work that teachers and learners do in bilingual classrooms. This research has incorporated elements of a conversational analytic approach to code-switching and has generally been grounded in ethnographic observation.

My focus will be on the cross-disciplinary currents of influence and the different research approaches reflected in these two strands of work. I will refer to a small selection of studies to illustrate the points I want to highlight in each section. In my discussion of the first strand of research, I will refer to two studies carried out in bilingual education programmes in the United States. In my account of the second strand of research, I will refer to two studies carried out in different learning environments and policy contexts.

In the next two sections of the chapter, I will then go on to describe two other significant developments in research in bilingual classrooms: first, changes in the approach to the analysis of code-switching in bilingual classroom discourse; and, second, the development of micro-ethnographic work in bilingual education settings. In this part of my chapter, I will refer to a study of bilingual classroom interaction that I have recently been conducting with colleagues here in the north west of England.[1]

In the final section, I will indicate how I feel research in bilingual classrooms still needs to be developed. I will first show how recent ethnographic research has helped us to grasp the importance of the cultural dimension of bilingual classroom communication. However, I will then go on to argue that the social component of research on code-switching in bilingual classrooms still needs to be more fully explored.

1 The development of research on bilingual classroom interaction

During the latter half of the 1970s, classroom-based research in American bilingual education programmes focussed almost exclusively on documenting the amount of time devoted to the use of the learners' L1 (usually Spanish) and to the use of English. (For detailed reviews of this research, see Ovando and Collier 1985; Ramirez 1980; Wong Fillmore and Valadez 1986.) During this period, there was considerable controversy in educational circles in the United States about the impact of bilingual classroom communication on children's language development. It was argued that the use of English predominated in this type of classroom communication, even where teachers aimed for equal use of both languages and that this was likely to have a negative effect on the development of the children's L1.

The policy debate determined the nature of the questions that were posed in research conducted at that time and the way in which studies were actually designed. Sometimes, classroom observations were combined with quantitative analyses of test scores (Legaretta 1979; Wong Fillmore 1980). Comparisons were made between different types of bilingual education programmes: those organised on a 'language separation' basis, where different languages were used on different days or for different subjects in the curriculum; and those where two languages were used 'concurrently'.

The quantitative evidence generated by some of these early studies of bilingual classrooms fuelled the educational debate taking place in the United States about the pros and cons of different forms of bilingual education provision. However, it soon became apparent that this evidence was of a very limited nature. Some researchers began to investigate the communicative dimensions of classroom talk in addition to gathering evidence of a quantitative nature. This was generally done by adopting coding schemes that had already been devised for studies of classroom behaviour. A number of researchers (Townsend 1974, 1976; Townsend and Zamora 1975; Legaretta 1977) employed an adapted version of the Flanders (1970) system for on-the-spot coding of teacher/learner interactions being observed in bilingual classrooms.

1.1   Code-switching and the functions of classroom discourse

The first significant breakthroughs were made when researchers began to work with audio-recordings of classroom interactions and when analyses took a more linguistic turn. Researchers such as Milk (1981, 1982) and Guthrie (1984) were among the first to adopt a more linguistic approach in their work. They gave particular prominence to the analysis of classroom discourse functions. Milk (1981) argued that a more accurate account of the status accorded to each language in a bilingual programme would be obtained by focussing on classroom discourse functions. He said 'It is quite conceivable . . . that even in a classroom where Spanish and English are being used for an equal amount of time, Spanish might be unconsciously relegated to a lower status in the eyes of students because of the different functions to which it is allocated in the classroom as compared to English.' (1981: 12).

This shift of focus to the accomplishment of communicative acts in bilingual classroom discourse represented an important step forward. More attention was now given to the ways in which teachers and learners get things done with two languages in bilingual classrooms and to the way in which language values are transmitted through communicative choices.

These researchers worked with audio-recorded data. They also drew on descriptive frameworks developed by those who were working on monolingual classroom discourse. For instance, Milk (1981) used an adapted version of the model proposed by Sinclair and Coulthard (1975) in his study of a twelfth-grade civics class in San Jose, California. The class was taught bilingually by a young Mexican-American teacher. The original inventory of twenty-two classroom discourse acts devised by Sinclair and Coulthard was adapted so as to focus on the patterns of code-switching in the data.

Another quite different analytic framework was used by Guthrie (1984) in a comparative study of two teachers (one bilingual and one monolingual) working with Chinese learners in a Californian elementary school. Guthrie adapted the system of conversational acts developed by Dore (1977) for the study of child language. He then used this adapted system to code all the teacher utterances in his audio-recorded corpus.

The analysis of code-switching in data gathered in classrooms such as these was guided by such questions as: what types of communicative acts can be identified? In what language are acts of different types performed? How often and how consistently? What values are conveyed to learners by the teachers' patterns of bilingual communication?

Milk (1981) found that the only act that was realised equally often in Spanish and in English was elicitation. English predominated in all other acts. It was used most frequently in directives and metastatements. Milk inferred from these findings that a hidden agenda was operating in this classroom. He argued that the predominance of English in directives signalled to learners that it was the language of power and authority. He also commented on the predominance of English in metastatements – this is the category of act where the main function is to 'help the students to see the structure of the lesson . . . to help them to understand the purpose of the subsequent exchange and see where they are going' (Sinclair and Coulthard 1975). Milk suggested that the predominance of English in metastatements, an act crucial to grasping the significance of a particular stretch of classroom discourse, put Spanish-dominant students at a disadvantage.

Guthrie (1984) found that the bilingual teacher in his study was very consistent in her use of language with groups of both higher and lower proficiency in English. However, the range of communicative acts in the discourse of the mono- lingual teacher varied according to the group he was working with. Guthrie reports that: 'Interactions with the lower group . . . were characterized by a higher proportion of attention getters, requests for action, and protests' (1984: 44). The inference he drew from this quantitative finding is that the monolingual teacher was less able to manage teaching/learning interactions with the group of Chinese children who were still at an earlier developmental stage in their English. Guthrie argued that this placed him at a disadvantage as compared with the bilingual teacher.

The quantitative evidence gathered in this study was then complemented with a qualitative analysis of the audio-recorded interaction between the teachers and the two groups of learners. Focussing in on the bilingual teacher's switches into Chinese, Guthrie identified five communicative functions. Chinese was appar- ently used: (i) for translation, (ii) as a 'we code', (iii) for procedures and directions, (iv) for clarification, (v) to check for understanding (1984: 45). Guthrie also noted that the monolingual teacher did not tolerate code-switching into Chinese. He reprimanded the learners when they spoke Chinese assuming that they were not paying attention to the lesson. This happened even when the children's Chinese utterances had a direct bearing on the lesson content.

Studies such as these gave fairly detailed insights into teachers' attitudes and into the functions of teacher-talk in the bilingual classes observed. This was achieved primarily because the researchers carried out extensive observations of classroom interactions and then complemented these with close analyses of class- room language. They also began to address the difficult task of demonstrating how values and attitudes were conveyed to learners through the teachers' code-switch- ing practices.

Yet, with hindsight, we can see that this work was constrained by the approach adopted to discourse analysis. As in early studies that had relied on Flanders-type coding schemes, the analytic approach was still a relatively static, taxonomic and quantitative one. The focus is still on individual acts rather than on the sequential flow of classroom discourse.

In classroom contexts, teachers and learners exchange meanings with each other in intricate and highly routinised sequences of interaction. They attend to each others' contributions to the interaction and, in a bilingual setting, they also attend to each others' proficiency in the languages involved in the interaction. What was still lacking in the early studies of bilingual classroom talk was an account of what Mehan has called: 'the mutual synchronization of behaviour' (1981: 40).

1.2 Code-switching in the sequential flow of classroom discourse

In a more recent strand of work in bilingual classrooms, the central focus has been on the ways in which teachers and learners achieve this mutual synchronisation of behaviour in different types of bilingual teaching/learning events. In this section, I will first give a brief account of two studies which illustrate the kind of descriptive work that has been done. The first study by Zentella (1981) was conducted in a bilingual education programme in the United States. The second study was carried out in Anglo-Chinese secondary schools in Hong Kong (Lin 1988, 1990).

1.2.1 The first illustrative study

Zentella's (1981) study was carried out in two bilingual classes in New York: one third-grade and one sixth-grade class. The learners and teachers were all of Puerto Rican origin. Zentella conducted ethnographic observations in these two classes over a four-month period. She audio-recorded the bilingual interactions that took place in different kinds of teaching/learning events. She then transcribed and analysed this corpus of bilingual classroom discourse. In her analysis of teacher–learner interactions, Zentella focussed initially on Initiation–Response–Evaluation (IRE) sequences. She identified three recurring patterns of language switching from one IRE exchange to another. Table 5.1 summarises the interactional rules governing these patterns.

Zentella also provided an account of the pragmatic functions of local switches between languages which represented departures from these recurring patterns. The two teachers in her study alternated between Spanish and English to mitigate the effect of admonitions, to make asides, and to make metalinguistic commentaries.

Zentella's analysis of the code-switching practices in her audio-recorded corpus was grounded in the ethnographic work she had carried out in the two classrooms. She found that the two teachers in her study had clearly contrasting patterns of code-switching. In approximately 8 hours of recorded classroom interaction, one teacher code-switched 127 times and the other only 26 times. Zentella was able to explain these differences in the bilingual discourse of the two teachers because she had built up a profile of their language histories, their educational backgrounds,

Table 5.1

Rules governing language choices	Teacher initiation language*	Student reply language	Teacher evaluation language
1 Teacher and student: 'Speak what you are spoken to' or 'follow the leader'	English Spanish	English Spanish	English Spanish
2 Teacher: 'Follow the child'	English Spanish	Spanish English	Spanish English
3 Teacher: 'Include the child's choice and yours'	English Spanish	Spanish English	Code-switching Code-switching

*The teachers also code-switched for translation during initiations
Source: (adapted from Zentella (1981: 119))

their values and their attitudes to bilingual communication in the classroom. She also described in detail the circumstances in the classes they were teaching.

1.2.2 The second illustrative study

The second study was carried out in a very different setting. Lin (1988, 1990) investigated patterns of code-switching in English language lessons in Anglo-Chinese secondary schools in Hong Kong. Four different classes were audio-recorded. They were all large classes and the interactions between teachers and learners were predominantly teacher-led. There was frequent code-switching between English and Cantonese because the learners had considerable difficulty understanding and using English.

The strength of this study lies in the way in which conversational analysis was employed. Lin made audio-recordings of selected teaching/learning events and looked closely at the interactional work that the teachers and learners were doing in different events. She observed that the teachers made ample use of Cantonese in teaching English vocabulary and grammar and noted that they did so 'in highly ordered patterns of alternation between English and Cantonese' (Lin 1990: 115). The following sequential pattern recurred in the discourse of one of the teachers:

the teacher first introduced a grammar point in English, then repeated the point and/or elaborated on it in Cantonese. Then, key elements were reiterated in English. Lin comments as follows on the consistency of this routine in the teacher's discourse:

> It is unlikely that these patterns have evolved only by accident. Rather they seem to reflect the teacher's response to some conflicting demands on her. On the one hand, they reflect her attempt to fulfill the requirement of teaching L2 grammar in L2; that explains why she always presents the examples and teaching points in L2 first and last. On the other hand, they reflect her attempt to ensure thorough understanding of the teaching points by reiterating and elaborating them in L1 between the L2 initial and final presentations (the L2–L1–L2 sequence). (Lin 1990: 116)

Another salient feature of the bilingual discourse recorded in these Hong Kong classrooms was the use of code-switching to negotiate and renegotiate the tenor of teaching/learning events. Lin (1988) notes that, through their persistent use of Cantonese, 'most of the time, the students were trying to redefine the English language lesson as a less formal, less serious and more play-like situation' (1988: 79). A detailed example is given of how a teacher tries to get the learners to work through a sentence pattern drill in pairs. The proposed activity is explained in English and then in Cantonese. She uses the term 'partner' to describe the pair work she has in mind. The students respond by teasing the teacher about her use of the Cantonese word for 'partner'. The teacher briefly goes along with this bantering in Cantonese. Her switch to Cantonese is realised at a lower pitch and volume. She then switches back to English to reassert her authority as teacher and to redefine the situation as 'a formal, serious lesson' (1988: 81).

I have described the two studies above in some detail because they provide good examples of how descriptions of bilingual classroom interaction have moved away from the taxonomic and quantitative approaches adopted in earlier studies. The principal contribution made by Zentella (1981) and Lin (1988, 1990) to research in bilingual classrooms has been that they have insisted on taking account of learners' contributions to classroom interactions and they have focussed our attention on the sequential structuring of bilingual classroom discourse as well as on the negotiation of meanings moment by moment. In the two sections below, I will now go on to examine two other significant ways in which research in bilingual classrooms has been developed.

1.3 Classroom code-switching: a conversational analytic approach

In the early studies of classroom code-switching, there was a tendency to characterise the social meaning of code-switching in terms of a two-way choice between an in-group code (a 'we code') and an out-group code (a 'they code') (e.g. Guthrie 1984). Whilst the languages used in a bilingual classroom are bound to be associated with different cultural values, it is too simplistic to claim that whenever a bilingual teacher who has the same language background as the learners switches into a shared code, s/he is invariably expressing solidarity with the learners. Code-switching is employed in more subtle and diverse ways in bilingual classroom communication. Teachers and learners exploit code contrasts to demarcate different types of discourse, to negotiate and renegotiate joint frames of reference and to exchange meanings on the spur of the moment.

As Gumperz (1982) has pointed out, code-switching is one of a number of possible contextualisation cues or communicative resources available for constructing and interpreting meanings in context. Other cues operate at the gestural, kinesic and prosodic level. Contextualisation cues do not carry meaning in and of themselves. They convey meaning only when they co-occur with verbal cues in particular moments of interaction. Code-switching can therefore be seen as a resource similar to some punctuation features in written discourse: a means of conveying pragmatic information to interlocutors as to how a particular utterance is to be 'read' in context.

The exploitation of code-switching as a contextualisation cue in bilingual classrooms is comparable to the use of contrasting modalities by monolingual teachers in the management of classroom interactions. Merritt (1982) provided examples of this kind of monolingual modality switching in a study carried out in primary classrooms in the United States. She noted that teachers made strategic use of contrasts between verbal and non-verbal communication to distinguish between a teaching frame and a classroom management frame. She also observed that differences in pitch and volume were exploited to distinguish between talk addressed to the class as a whole and talk addressed to one student. The patterns of switching between modalities in these classes were highly consistent.

Researchers investigating code-switching in bilingual community contexts have become increasingly aware of the need to take account of code-switching related to the language proficiencies and preferences of the hearer(s) as well as code-switching which signals the communicative intentions of the speaker. Drawing on his research on bilingual discourse in peer-group interactions, Auer (1984, 1990, chapter 6 of this volume) has identified two main ways in which code contrast is employed as a contextualisation cue. He refers to these as discourse-related and participant-related code alternation. This distinction is particularly relevant to the study of bilingual classroom interaction.

1.3.1 Discourse-related switching

According to Auer (1990), discourse-related switching is speaker-oriented: it serves as a resource for accomplishing different communicative acts at specific points within interactional sequences, e.g. changing footing, moving in and out of different discourse frames, doing a side sequence, representing the voices of different characters in a narrative, marking topic changes.

Remarkably similar discourse-related functions of code-switching were documented in the studies conducted by Zentella (1981) and by Lin (1988, 1990). These were communicative functions such as making an aside, quoting, specifying a particular addressee, moving in and out of the teaching/learning frame. Certain uses of code-switching as a contextualisation cue may well recur across different types of bilingual learning environments. However, as Auer (1990) points out, it is impossible to compile a comprehensive inventory of the functions of code-switching. The number of possible functions is infinite. A more productive task is to attempt to gain more insights into how code contrasts are strategically exploited in specific types of communicative encounters. We therefore need more detailed analyses of the different kinds of teaching/learning events which occur in bilingual classrooms and, as I will argue in the next section, these analyses need to be grounded in ethnographic observation and they need to take account of interactants' own understandings of each communicative event.

One striking feature of the use of code-switching as a discourse-related cue in the studies by Zentella (1981) and by Lin (1988, 1990) is the way it co-occurs with other cues, prosodic and non-verbal. For example, Lin (1990) notes that one teacher in her study changed pitch and volume on switches into Cantonese which changed the tenor of exchanges with her pupils. This aspect of classroom code-switching clearly merits closer inspection. Contextualisation cues may co-occur with particularly high frequency in bilingual *classroom* discourse, particularly in situations where teacher-talk predominates.

1.3.2 Participant-related switching

Participant-related switching is hearer-oriented: it takes account of the hearer's linguistic preferences or competences. This notion is an especially useful one for the study of classroom discourse because classrooms are settings where conversational participants typically have differing language abilities and communicative repertoires.

Participant-related switching is likely to be particularly salient in some contexts. Take, for example, the classrooms described by Lin (1988, 1990) in Hong Kong. There, the communicative problems facing teachers and learners are primarily due to the fact that a foreign language is still retained as a medium of instruction in Anglo-Chinese schools. This presents an enormous challenge to learners who have very little exposure to English in their lives outside the school context. It also presents a major communicative challenge to their bilingual teachers in their day-to-day classroom practice.

In bilingual education programmes for linguistic minority children, such as the one in New York described by Zentella (1981), participant-related switching is also likely to predominate, particularly in the early years. In situations such as these, code-switching appears to be a crucial communicative resource for managing teaching/learning interactions. As one of the teachers in Zentella's study put it: 'Sometimes I have to be bouncing from one language to the other . . . but that's the only way sometimes they'll understand' (1981: 119).

During children's first year at school, especially in bilingual programmes which have primarily transitional goals, there may well be considerable changes that take place in patterns of participant-related switching, as children develop greater proficiency in the dominant language. We know from the early studies of bilingual classroom interaction that the dominant language eventually takes over, but we do not yet know *how* patterns of participant-related code-switching change over time. This points to the need to develop longitudinal studies designed specifically to capture changes over time.

1.4 An ethnographic approach to bilingual classroom interaction

In the early 1980s, specific proposals were made as to how ethnographic research should be developed in bilingual classrooms (Mehan 1981; Moll 1981; Moll *et al.* 1985; Trueba and Wright 1981). Over the last decade, research on bilingual classroom interaction has begun to incorporate some of these proposals, but it has been a very gradual development. I will not recycle the proposals here but I will illustrate some of the ways in which ethnographic work has been developed. I will do this by examining one aspect of this work: namely, the move towards micro-ethnographic observation and analysis of different teaching/learning events in the communicative cycles of daily life in bilingual classrooms. I will highlight the advantages that accrue from adopting a micro-ethnographic focus.

The examples in this section will be drawn from the ethnographic research on bilingual classroom interaction that I have been conducting with colleagues in schools in the north west of England. The study was based in inner-city primary schools. Our focus was on a policy initiative implemented by the local education authority. Bilingual classroom assistants who were speakers of South Asian languages such as Panjabi or Gujarati were appointed by the authority in September 1989 to work in the nursery and reception classes of local schools alongside monolingual class teachers.[2]

Our aim, as researchers, was to provide an account of how this new form of educational provision was being translated into communicative practice in the classroom. Over a two-year period, we carried out classroom observations in local reception classes where bilingual assistants were working. Our principal research activity was carrying out focussed observations in two classes over a full school year. In these two classes, we audio- and video-recorded different types of teaching/learning events that were conducted bilingually.

1.4.1 Micro-ethnographic accounts of classroom events

From our initial observational work in our two main classrooms, it became clear that teaching/learning events would need to be our principal unit of observation and analysis. Day-to-day life in these reception classes revolved around small-group activities such as the following: art work; baking activities; computer-assisted learning activities; story-telling; guided play at the water-tray; carrying out a small experiment or going on a small expedition (e.g. around the local neighbourhood); story-telling; other small-group activities related to a cross-curricular theme during which the children might be reading, writing, drawing, colouring or cutting and pasting. There were also news-sharing events at the start of the school day and story-telling sessions towards the end of the school day which involved the class as a whole.

Focussing in on events as a unit of observation and analysis enabled us to capture a crucial dimension of the pedagogy in the classrooms we were observing. As Enright (1984) points out: 'Classroom events are *emic* units of interaction in that they represent the teacher's own conceptualisation of how the flow of interaction in his or her classroom is divided up and conducted' (1984: 31). Our participant observation work also involved informal conversations with the teacher and the bilingual assistant in each class, during breaktimes and during lunch hours. This enabled us to check our own understanding of the purpose and organisation of classroom events against theirs.

The focus on different types of classroom event also helped us to get a sense of how monolingual teachers perceived the value and purpose of bilingual support work in their classes. The monolingual teachers made the main decisions day by day as to which events should be conducted bilingually and as to what role the bilingual assistants should play as participants in those events. There was considerable variation from one classroom to another in the way in which bilingual support work was organised. The details of this variation are described at some length in Martin-Jones (1994) and Martin-Jones and Saxena (in press).

I will focus briefly here on two clearly contrasting participant roles that were defined for the bilingual assistants by class teachers in different types of teaching/ learning event. These were: (i) leading a teaching/learning event alone with a small group of children in one corner of the classroom and thereby retaining control over the allocation of turns at talk; (ii) doing small-group work 'alongside' a monolingual teacher and translating or reformulating the contributions of the monolingual adult into the children's home or community language. In teaching/learning events of the latter type, the monolingual adult kept control over the distribution of turns.

Sometimes, overt turn-giving signals were given. These included utterances addressed to the bilingual assistant by the class teacher, such as 'Carry on, Miss Khan'[3] or utterances addressed to the children which made explicit reference to the discourse role of the bilingual assistant. For example, in one primary science activity on electricity, the class teacher introduced a point in English then turned to the children and said 'Mrs Anwar will explain . . . '.[4] This served as a cue for the bilingual assistant to take a turn in Panjabi. Thus, the organisation of the bilingual support work in each event shaped the patterns of bilingual talk. When bilingual assistants were positioned as interpreters, they had much less scope for using the child's home or community language and for responding to contributions made by the children.

Finally, there was one other significant dimension of variation in the bilingual discourse we observed and recorded: the patterns of code-switching in the discourse of the bilingual assistant varied according to the language backgrounds of the learners. Sometimes, all the bilingual children taking part in a particular event would have the same language background and the same language as the bilingual assistant. An example of this would be an event where a Panjabi-speaking bilingual assistant was working with a group of bilingual children who all spoke Panjabi at home. However, sometimes, the constellation of participants in an event was quite different. The groups sometimes included children whose home language was Gujarati or Urdu. When faced with the communicative challenge of working with groups of mixed language backgrounds like this, the Panjabi-speaking bilingual assistants usually continued to use Panjabi and English with the group as a whole but code-switched into Urdu and/or Gujarati when addressing individual children.[5]

2 Developing the social component of research on code-switching in the classroom

Thus far, I have argued that a conversational analytic approach to code-switching in classroom discourse, grounded in ethnographic observation, can give us fine-grained descriptions of the ways in which teachers and learners get things done bilingually in the classroom. I have also shown how ethnographic observation can give us insights into the ways in which views about bilingual education provision get translated into classroom practice in different contexts.

We clearly need more studies in different bilingual learning environments, which combine conversational analysis with ethnographic observation. In this way, we can build up a comparative picture. Schools and classes vary enormously in their ethos, in their social organisation and in their 'language climate' (Masemann 1978 cited in Ytsma 1988) even within the same policy context. Teachers' styles and beliefs about pedagogy also vary in significant ways. However, studies that are confined to the micro-level of classroom routines and discourse strategies fail to take account of social factors that have a crucial influence on bilingual classroom communication.

In an early review of research conducted in bilingual classrooms in the North American context, Fishman (1977) noted the need to take account of the social dimensions of teaching/learning processes. He argued that 'Social dimensionality must be recognised *within* the bilingual education classroom, rather than merely *outside* of it in "the community" and "in society". Societal factors dictate much of *what* is taught and *to whom*; as well as *how* it is taught and by whom; and finally how all of those involved in the teaching–learning process interact with each other.' (1977: 32).

Fishman posed this challenge well over a decade ago and offered clear pointers as to how we could develop the social component of studies of bilingual classroom discourse. He argued that there were three dimensions of teaching/learning in bilingual classrooms which need to be taken into account: curriculum organisation, pedagogy and social relations. In this final section of my chapter, I will focus on one of these dimensions of teaching/learning: the social relations between the participants in classroom interactions. Though, as Fishman himself implied, all three dimensions of the social life of classrooms are closely imbricated.

2.1 Cultural congruence between bilingual teachers and learners

A paper written over a decade ago by Cazden *et al.* (1980) was the first to consider whether there had been any research in a bilingual education context which had taken up Fishman's challenge. The authors noted that ethnographic work in bilingual classrooms had been slow to develop, despite evidence from early anthropological research on cross-cultural communication in the classroom (Philips 1972) which pointed clearly to the need to take account of the cultural background and cultural values of participants in classroom conversations.

Cazden *et al.* (1980) put forward a convincing case for focussing ethnographic descriptions on bilingual teaching/learning situations where there is cultural congruence between teacher and learners. They cited as examples several ethnographic studies which were in progress at the time, including one of their own (Au and Jordan 1981; Erikson and Mohatt 1982; Erikson *et al.* 1983; Klienfeld 1979; Mohatt and Erikson 1981).

2.1.1 Two bilingual education classes in the United States

Their own study was carried out in two first-grade classes in a bilingual education programme for Mexican-American children in Chicago. The teachers and learners in both classes were Mexican-Americans and taught primarily in Spanish. The classes were positively evaluated by parents who opted for bilingual provision for their children even when their children qualified for monolingual provision in English in mainstream classes.

The success of these classes was partly due to the fact that both teachers had a teaching style that was significantly different from that of the Anglo teachers in mainstream classes. According to Cazden *et al.*, the teachers had a 'personalized style, a style characterized by *cariño* – a close and caring relationship' (1980: 67). The verbal and non-verbal features of this style were: use of Spanish pronouns and culturally specific terms of address which signalled closeness; frequent use of diminutives; regular reminders to the children that they should observe community norms of *respeto* (respect) and non-verbal expressions of *cariño*.

2.1.2 Bilingual support in two reception classes in Britain

In our study of reception classes here in the north west of England, the contrast between the interactional styles of the monolingual teachers and those of the bilingual classroom assistants was also striking. The bilingual assistants had a range of styles in their communicative repertoire and shifted between them depending on the kind of speech exchanges they were engaged in. In speech exchanges which were primarily learner-oriented, a close and caring relationship with the children was established. This was done not only by speaking in Panjabi, but also through pronoun choices and the use of terms of endearment, by referring to shared cultural knowledge and by demonstrating knowledge of the children's families and cultural values.

We found that there were age differences in the degree of closeness established with the children: in one of our two classes, the younger bilingual assistant employed the most intimate second person pronoun *tu* with the children while the older bilingual assistant used a slightly less intimate pronoun *tum* along with terms of endearment such as *beTe* (my child). The young bilingual assistant felt particularly close to the learners. She had brothers and sisters the same age and she herself had attended the same primary school and had been taught by people who were now her colleagues.

The children clearly responded positively to the interactional style of both the younger and older bilingual assistants. They reciprocated by addressing the bilingual assistants in Panjabi as 'sister' or 'auntie'. However, despite the cultural congruence between bilingual assistants and learners and despite the potential for exchanging cultural meanings in these mainstream classes, there was another crucial dimension to the social relations in the classes we observed: the asymmetrical social relations between bilingual assistants and monolingual class teachers. We could not overlook this. It severely constrained the work of the bilingual assistants and it clearly shaped the patterns of code-switching in different teaching/learning encounters.

2.2 Asymmetrical social relations in the classroom, in the school and beyond

The bilingual assistants who have been appointed in different schools and local authorities in Britain to work 'alongside' monolingual class teachers are invariably low-status staff and with few paths of professional development open to them. They often find themselves working in schools where there is, as yet, very little understanding among monolingual staff of the kind of linguistic or cultural contribution they can make to classroom practice.

In some of the schools we visited, the asymmetrical social relations between monolingual teachers and bilingual assistants that had already been created by educational policy decisions were being reproduced in the day-to-day life of the school: for example, in the way in which the role of the bilingual assistants was defined; in the amount of yard duty they were expected to do; in the extent to which they were involved in curriculum planning meetings. When bilingual assistants were involved in staff meetings, patterns of turn-taking and the use of names, titles and terms of address also served to position the bilingual assistants as low-status staff. In the classroom context, the monolingual class teacher was the main decision-maker. She took responsibility for assigning a participant role to the bilingual assistant from one teaching/learning event to another.

In many educational schemes for bilingual children from minority ethnic groups, adults who are speakers of minority languages find themselves acting as buffers between their local communities and the mainstream classroom. On the one hand, they are expected to be supportive and nurturing to young children from local minority communities as they make the social and cultural transition from home to school; on the other hand, they are expected to provide them with access to the curriculum and, in transitional bilingual schemes such as the one we have been investigating in the north west of England, they are expected to use the children's home language *so as to support their learning of English*. The transitional nature of provision for 'bilingual support' was clearly stated in local authority documents and was underpinned by the criteria used in allocating central government funding to support bilingual assistant schemes (Section 11 funding: for details see Bourne 1989).

In our view, the patterns of code-switching revealed in the transcripts of the bilingual events we observed and recorded need to be interpreted in this light. We found, for example, that the bilingual assistants oscillated between curriculum-oriented and learner-oriented talk. I will exemplify this with reference to one maths activity where the bilingual assistant was working with a small group of learners. She was reviewing concepts such as *circle, square* and *triangle*. She began by showing different shapes to the children and asking them what they were. She then asked them, one by one, to pick out a shape from the tray on the table. After this, she asked them to place the shapes on coloured paper, then to trace around the shapes and eventually cut them out and stick them onto A4-size white sheets to make geometric designs. Following Heath (1986), we classified the genre of classroom language use in the first part of this teaching/learning event as a 'label-quest' (1986: 167–8). In this part of the event, the bilingual assistant's main focus was on familiarising the children with the English labels for the geometric concepts she had in mind.

Building on the approach developed by Zentella (1981), we then looked at the pattern of code-switching across IRE exchanges. One pattern of code-switching predominated in the exchanges which occurred in this label-quest sequence:

INITIATION: Panjabi or Panjabi–English
RESPONSE: English
(FEEDBACK: English)

Where there was a code-switch in the utterance used by the bilingual assistant to initiate an exchange, it was most often a switch into English on a key item related to the topic of the teaching/learning event (e.g. shape, colour). This pattern of code-switching into English on single nouns or noun phrases related to the content of the activity recurred in all the label-quests we observed and recorded in this and other classrooms.

The bilingual assistant then went on to explain to the children how to do the tracing, cutting and pasting activity. She switched back into Panjabi. The children responded in Panjabi and their contributions were more spontaneous. Their utterances were much longer than the one-word utterances in the exchanges described above. The bilingual assistant's talk was more learner-oriented here. The change of footing from curriculum-oriented talk to learner-oriented talk was marked by a change in the bilingual discourse. In this and other events, the bilingual assistant clearly used code-switching as a resource for managing conflicting communicative demands; demands stemming from her dual role: as nurturer or 'auntie' on the one hand, and, on the other hand, as a bilingual classroom assistant attempting to ensure access to the curriculum for children in a transitional bilingual teaching/learning situation.

2.3 Concluding comments

We have now gained greater insights into the nature and significance of classroom code-switching through micro-level analyses grounded in ethnographic observation. Ethnographic approaches to the study of bilingual classroom interaction are now being developed in a number of different education settings. Yet, I would argue that we have as yet paid insufficient attention to the social dimensions of bilingual classroom discourse. I have illustrated this point by describing our work in an educational setting which is clearly characterised by asymmetrical relations of power between monolingual and bilingual teaching staff. To meet Fishman's (1977) challenge, I believe we need to develop more critical approaches to ethnographic work in the classroom and to our analyses of bilingual classroom discourse.We need to be able to show how code-switching in bilingual discourse is shaped by the social conditions operating in different types of classrooms and how differing views about the value and purpose of bilingual education are manifested in bilingual discourse practices. We also need to take account of the fact that the main dimensions of day-to-day life in bilingual and multilingual classrooms – curriculum organisation, pedagogy and social relations – are crucially shaped by social and political conditions beyond the classroom. An analysis of these intersecting influences is needed for different types of bilingual learning environment. It is only in this way we can build up a comparative account of what enables *and* constrains teachers and learners engaged in bilingual classroom communication.

Notes

[1] This work was carried out as part of an Educational Linguistic project at Lancaster University, entitled: 'Bilingual resources in primary classroom interaction'. It was funded by the Economic and Social Research Council for a three-year period from 1989 to 1992. My colleagues in the research team were: Mukul Saxena, David Barton and Roz Ivanic.

[2] This form of educational provision for bilingual learners in the early years of primary school has come to be known in the British context as 'bilingual support'. It amounts to the most minimal form of transitional bilingual education and, apart from occasional provision for 'community language teaching', it is the only form of bilingual provision available for bilingual learners in inner-city schools (Bourne 1989; Martin-Jones and Saxena, in press). Provision for bilingual support in the early years of primary education is now being developed by a large number of different local authorities. However, there are still very few guidelines available as to what bilingual support should entail in practice and there has been very little discussion among practitioners as to what role bilingual assistants should play or as to how class activities should be organised on a day-to-day basis.

[3] Fictitious name is given here to preserve confidentiality.

[4] Fictitious name to preserve confidentiality.

[5] The two Panjabi-speaking bilingual assistants in the classes we observed were of Pakistani origin and Urdu was already part of their communicative repertoire. However, they had both made efforts to learn some spoken Gujarati, the home language of some of the children in the class.

Bibliography

Alatis, J. E. (1980) ed. *Current issues in bilingual education: Georgetown University Round Table on Languages and Linguistics 1980.* Washington, D.C.: Georgetown University Press.

Au, K. H. and Jordan, C. (1981) Teaching reading to Hawaiian children: finding a culturally appropriate solution. In Trueba *et al.* (1981).

Auer, P. (1984) *Bilingual conversation.* Amsterdam: Benjamins.

(1990) A discussion paper on code alternation. In *Papers for the workshop on concepts, methodology and data.* (Held in Basel, 12–13 January 1990.) Strasbourg: European Science Foundation, 69–88.

Bourne, J. (1989) *Moving into the mainstream: LEA provision for bilingual pupils.* Windsor, Berks.: NFER-Nelson.

Cazden, C. B. (1988) *Classroom discourse: the language of teaching and learning.* Portsmouth, N.H.: Heinemann Educational Books.

Cazden, C. B., Carrasco, R., Maldonado-Guzman, A. A. and Erikson, F. (1980) The contribution of ethnographic research to bicultural bilingual education. In Alatis (1980).

Cazden, C. B., John, V. and Hymes, D. (1972) eds. *Functions of language in the classroom.* New York: Teachers College Press.

Dore, J. (1977) Children's illocutionary acts. In R. Freedle ed. *Discourse production and comprehension* I. Norwood, N.J.: Ablex.

Enright, D. S. (1984) The organisation of interaction in elementary classrooms. In Handscombe *et al.* (1984).

Erikson, F. and Mohatt, G. (1982) Cultural organization of participant structures in two classrooms of Indian students. In Spindler (1982).

Erikson, F., Cazden, C. B., Carrasco, R. and Maldonado-Guzman, A. (1983) *Social and cultural organisation of interaction in classrooms of bilingual children. Final report to the NIE.* (Cited in Cazden 1988.)

Fishman, J. A. (1977) The social science perspective. In *Bilingual education: current perspectives: social science.* Arlington, Va.: Center for Applied Linguistics.

Flanders, N. A. (1970) *Analysing teaching behaviour.* Reading, Mass.: Addison Wesley.

Gumperz, J. J. (1982) *Discourse strategies.* Cambridge University Press.

Guthrie, L. F. (1984) Contrasts in teachers' language use in a Chinese–English bilingual classroom. In Handscombe *et al.* (1984).

Handscombe, J., Orem, R. A. and Taylor, B. P. (1984) eds. *On TESOL 1983: the question of control.* Washington, D.C.: TESOL.

Heath, S. B. (1986) Sociocultural contexts of language development. In D. Holt ed., *Beyond language: social and cultural factors in schooling language minority students.* Los Angeles: Evaluation, Dissemination and Assessment Center, California State University.

Klienfeld, J. S. (1979) *Eskimo school on the Andreafsky.* New York: Praeger.

Legarreta, D. (1977) Language choice in bilingual classrooms. *TESOL Quarterly,* 1: 9–16.

(1979) The effect of program models on language acquisition by Spanish speaking children. *TESOL Quarterly*, 13: 521–34.

Lin, A. (1988) *Pedagogical and para-pedagogical levels of interaction in the classroom: a social interactional approach to the analysis of the code-switching behaviour of a bilingual teacher in an English language lesson*. Working Papers in Linguistics and Language Teaching, 11. University of Hong Kong Language Centre.

(1990) *Teaching in two tongues: language alternation in foreign language classrooms*. Research Report, 3. City Polytechnic of Hong Kong.

Martin-Jones, M. (1994) Code-switching, power asymmetries and the positioning of bilingual participants in classroom discourse. In D. Gorter, R. Boeschoten, P. Muysken, J. Nortier eds., *Proceedings of the Ljouwert/Leeuwarden Summer School on Code-Switching*. Ljouwert/Leeuwarden: Fryske Akademy.

Martin-Jones, M. and Saxena, M. (in press). Supporting bilingualism? Policies, power asymmetries and pedagogic practices. In J. Tollefson ed. *Language policy and language education: critical approaches*. Cambridge University Press.

Mehan, H. (1981) Ethnography of bilingual education. In Trueba *et al.* (1981).

Merritt, M. (1982) Distributing and directing attention in primary classrooms. In L. C. Wilkinson ed., *Communicating in the classroom*. New York: Academic Press.

Merritt, M., Cleghorn, A., Abagi, J. O. and Bunyi, G. (1992) Socializing multilingualism: determinants of code-switching in Kenyan primary classrooms. *The Journal of Multilingual and Multicultural Development*, 13 (1 & 2). (Special issues on 'Code-switching', ed. C. M. Eastman.)

Milk, R. (1981) An analysis of the functional allocation of Spanish and English in a bilingual classroom. *California Association for Bilingual Education: Research Journal*, 2 (2): 11–26.

(1982) Language use in bilingual classrooms: two case studies. In M. Hines and W. Rutherford eds., *On TESOL '81*. Washington, D.C.: Teachers of English to Speakers of Other Languages, 181–91.

Mohatt, G. and Erikson, F. (1981) Cultural differences in teaching styles in an Odawa school: a sociolinguistic approach. In Trueba *et al.* (1981).

Moll, L. E. (1981) The micro-ethnographic study of bilingual schooling. In. R. V. Padilla ed., *Ethnoperspectives in bilingual education research* III. Ipsilanti: Eastern Michigan University.

Moll, L. E., Diaz, E., Estrada, E. and Lopez, L. (1985) Making contexts: the social construction of lessons in two languages. In Saravia-Shore and Arvizu (1985).

Ovando, C. J. and Collier, V. P. (1985) *Bilingual and ESL classrooms: teaching in multicultural contexts*. New York: McGraw Hill Book Company.

Philips, S. (1972) Participant structures and communicative competence. In Cazden *et al.* (1972).

Ramirez, A. (1980) Language in bilingual classrooms. *NABE Journal*, 4 (3): 61–79.

Saravia-Shore, M. and Arvizu, S. (1985) eds. *Cross cultural and communicative competencies: ethnographies of educational programs for language minority students*. Washington, D.C.: Council on Anthropology and Education.

Sinclair, J. M. and Coulthard, R. M. (1975) *Towards an analysis of discourse: the English used by teachers and pupils*. Oxford University Press.

Spindler, G. D. (1982) ed. *Doing the ethnography of schooling: educational anthropology in action*. New York: Holt, Rinehart & Winston.

Townsend, D. R. (1974) A comparison of the classroom interaction patterns of bilingual early childhood teachers. Unpublished doctoral dissertation, University of Texas at Austin.

(1976) Bilingual interaction analysis: the development and status. In A. Simoes ed., *The bilingual child*. New York: Academic Press.

Townsend, D. and Zamora, G. (1975) Differing interaction patterns in bilingual classrooms. *Contemporary Education*, 46 (3): 196–202.

Trueba, H. T., Guthrie, G. P. and Au, K. H. (1981) eds. *Culture and the bilingual classroom: studies in classroom ethnography*. Rowley, Mass.: Newbury House.

Trueba, H. T. and Wright, P. (1981) A challenge for ethnographic researchers in bilingual settings: analyzing Spanish–English classroom interaction. *Journal of Multilingual and Multicultural Development*, 2: 243–57.

Wong Fillmore, L. (1980) Language learning through bilingual instruction. Unpublished mimeo. Berkeley: University of California.

Wong Fillmore, L. and Valadez, C. (1986) Teaching bilingual learners. In M. Wittrock ed., *Handbook of research on teaching: third edition*. New York: Macmillan Publishing Company, 648–85.

Ytsma, J. (1988) Bilingual classroom interaction in Friesland. In A. Holmen, E. Hansen, J. Gimbel and J. Normann Jorgensen eds., *Bilingualism and the individual*, Copenhagen Studies in Bilingualism, 4. Clevedon, Avon: Multilingual Matters.

Zentella, A. C. (1981) *Ta bien*, you could answer me *en cualquier idioma*: Puerto Rican codeswitching in bilingual classrooms. In R. Duran ed., *Latino language and communicative behavior*. Norwood, N. J.: Ablex Publishing Corporation, 109–32.

2

CODE-SWITCHING AND SOCIAL LIFE

6 THE PRAGMATICS OF CODE-SWITCHING: A SEQUENTIAL APPROACH

Peter Auer

1 Introduction

This paper will deal with code-switching in a specific sense. The perspective I want to take is an important one, but it does not exclude others.

Bilingualism (including multilingualism) is often thought of as multiple linguistic competences, i.e., as a mental disposition which is accessible only indirectly by the usual techniques of psycholinguistic research. In the mentalistic framework of generative grammar, bilingual competence is also accessible via the analysis of well-formed sentences involving two languages which may be treated as a window on the bilingual mind. Yet both the psycholinguist and the generative grammarian treat bilingualism as something which – like competence in general – is basically hidden underneath the skull and therefore invisible; it can be, and must be, made visible by psycholinguistic methods, or the methods of generative grammatical research. Beginning with the discussion of compound vs coordinate bilingualism in its psycholinguistic reformulation (see chapter 12, this volume), and up to the present generative work on grammatical constraints on code-switching (see chapter 9, this volume), there is an impressive amount of research which has been gathered from such a perspective.

Contrary to this tradition of research, I will be dealing here with bilingualism from the perspective of the conversationalist. For him or her, it has its foremost reality in the interactive exchanges between the members of a bilingual speech community (as well as between them and monolingual outsiders), by which they display to each other, and ascribe to each other, their bilingualism. According to this perspective, it is the task of the linguist not to discover by tests or other methods something which is basically concealed from the naive language user, but to reconstruct the social processes of displaying and ascribing bilingualism. As a feature of conversational (inter-)action, bilingualism provides specific resources not available to monolingual speakers for the constitution of socially meaningful verbal activities. The relationship between the use of two languages as a form-related property of one or more persons' speech and the conversational meaning of this speech is a relatively indirect and complicated one. It needs some theoretical background in order to be conceived properly, and it is this theoretical background which is the topic of this chapter. I will sketch a theory of conversational code-alternation which should be applicable to a wide range of conversational phenomena subsumed in the literature under such headings as code-switching, language choice, transfer/insertion etc., and to very different bilingual communities and settings. Such a theory of bilingual conversation obviously has to be complemented by another theory which explains who switches in a given community, why and when (cf. chapters 7 and 8, for such a micro/macro link). The resources available to bilingual conversationalists may be outlined independently, however, from their macro-social embedding. Needless to say, bilingual work on any concrete bilingual community has to refer both to micro and macro theories of code-alternation and to their interdependencies.

By reviewing some of the existing literature, and by referring to empirical work, it will (hopefully) become clear that any theory of conversational code-alternation is bound to fail if it does not take into account that the meaning of code-alternation depends in essential ways on its 'sequential environment'. This is given, in the first place, by the conversational turn immediately preceding it, to which code-alternation may respond in various ways. While the preceding verbal activities provide the contextual frame for a current utterance, the following utterance by a next participant reflects his or her interpretation of that preceding utterance. Therefore, following utterances are important cues for the analyst and for the first speaker as to if and how a first utterance has been understood. The sequentiality of code-alternation in the sense of this paper therefore refers both to preceding and subsequent utterances.

2 Preliminaries on definition and terminology

In view of the lack of a generally accepted terminology, it is necessary to define code-alternation in the specific sense in which the term is employed here, before entering into detailed discussion. *Code-alternation (used here as a cover term, i.e. hyperonym for code-switching and transfer) is defined as a relationship of contiguous juxtaposition of semiotic systems, such that the appropriate recipients of the resulting complex sign are in a position to interpret this juxtaposition as such.*

The criterion of contiguity excludes non-contiguous stretches of talk, for example, one occurring in the beginning, the other at the end of the conversation, or speaker X using language A on one occasion, and language B on another, from being analysed as instances of code-alternation. The criterion of juxtaposition implies that gradual transitions from one code into the other cannot be classified as code-alternation. Thus, a gradual transition from dialect into standard ('style-shifting') may be a very important interactional event, but it works differently from code-alternation and should not be confounded with it. The requirement that semiotic *systems* be juxtaposed excludes the possibility of single parameter changes being analysed as code-alternation. The most important of all the definitional criteria for code-alternation is that of its interpretative reality. It is the users of the signs who decide on their status. When we compare the speech of bilinguals with that of monolinguals in either of their languages, we notice a high number of 'marques transcodiques', 'qui renvoient d'une manière ou d'une autre à la rencontre de deux ou plusieurs systèmes linguistiques' (Lüdi 1987b: 2). Yet inside this very large domain of language-contact phenomena, it is necessary to draw a very basic distinction: that between contact phenomena classified as such by the linguist, and contact phenomena seen and used as such by the bilingual participants themselves. The question 'Do bilingual participants see and use it?' takes us from structural systems continually referring to each other, to the speakers. It implies the shift from a structural towards an interpretative approach to bilingualism.

3 Theories of the pragmatics of code-alternation

It is useful to start the discussion with two somewhat extreme theories of code-alternation which are (for very instructive reasons) bound to fail. The *first theory* of the conversational meaning of code-alternation is based on the assumption that *certain conversational activities prompt the usage of one language or the other qua activity type*. A particular activity type is seen as being linked to language B, such that in the environment of language A, code-alternation occurs. For instance, Fishman (1971) introduces the chapter on 'Interactional sociolinguistics' in his introductory book with an example which is reproduced here in part as data extract (1), between two Puerto Ricans:

(1)   [Boss has been dictating a letter to Mr Bolger to his secretary, Spanish in italics]
        Boss: . . . Sincerely, Louis Gonzalez
        Secretary: Do you have the enclosures for the letter, Mr Gonzalez?
        Boss: Oh yes, here they are.
        Secretary: Okay

Boss:	Ah, this man William Bolger got his organization to con-
	tribute a lot of money to the Puerto Rican parade. He's
	very much for it. *¿Tú fuiste a la parada?*
Secretary:	*Sí, yo fuí.*
Boss:	*¿Sí?*
Secretary:	*Uh huh.*
Boss:	*¿Y cómo te estuvo?*

[etc., continues in Spanish] (Fishman 1971: 37ff.)

Fishman recommends finding systematic ('emic') correlations between what he calls speech events and language choice in order to analyse code-switching as in the data extract: 'The first question that presents itself is whether one variety tends to be used (or used more often) in certain kinds of speech acts or events whereas the other tends to be used (or used more often) in others' (p. 41). He does not really apply this research strategy to his example, but it is easy to see that he would expect us to find some correlation between the speech event of an informal chat and Spanish on the one hand, and between a business transaction and English on the other.[1]

Note that in this approach, it is not the switching from one language into another which has meaning, but the association between speech activities and languages. Code-alternation is contingent on the juxtaposition of two activities associated with different languages. Had the 'boss' met his 'secretary' exclusively for the purpose of a chat, the whole interactive episode would have taken place in Spanish, but the usage of this language would have had the same social meaning, i.e., that of indexing a speech activity within the Spanish domain.

The weakness of this approach becomes apparent as soon as language choice is investigated empirically. In modern bilingual societies, the relationship between languages and speech activities is by no means unambiguous. Many speech activities are not tied to one particular language, and even among those which have a tendency to be realised more often in one language than in another, the correlation is never strong enough to predict language choice in more than a probabilistic way. (In Fishman's Puerto Rican case, it is certainly conceivable that the Puerto Rican boss might deal with his secretary in Spanish all the time; and he might well choose to use English even in talk about the Puerto Rican parade.)

Although the idea of Fishman and other scholars that specific speech activities are associated with specific languages receives some support from ritual language usage in 'stable' societies (as has been reported in a number of studies in the ethnography of communication), and although the associations between speech

activity and language are not completely free in 'mobile' bilingual societies or
speech communities either, this relationship is far more complex than such a
simple model would suggest (cf. di Luzio 1984). Many investigations have
shown that the mere fact of juxtaposing two codes can have a signalling value
of its own, independent of the direction of code-alternation; in such cases, it is
obviously impossible to explain the conversational meaning of code-alternation by
any kind of association between languages and speech activities. Striking evidence
for such a contrastive signalling value of language alternation comes from one of
the reportedly most frequent functions of code-alternation: the setting off of
reported speech against its surrounding conversational (often narrative) context.
Although one could think that the language of 'quoting is relatively predictable'
and that 'all one needs to know to predict the language in which most quotes will
be spoken is the language in which the original utterance was spoken' (as is indeed
contended by Gal 1979: 109), this is in fact not the case. Instead it is not unusual
for code-alternation to occur in cases where the language of reporting and the
inferrable language used by the original speaker diverge.[2] As an example, consider
the extract from an Italian–German bilingual conversation given in (2), where an
Italian student is talking about his quarrels with German classmates:

(2)   [report about German pupils in his class, Italian in italics]
        wenn ä Italiener kommt gell – sofort äh: *guardate*
        Ittakerstinker und so
        [*when Italians come you know – immediately (they say)* look *spaghetti*
        heads and so on (Auer 1984: 66)]

It is highly unlikely that the Germans would use an Italian phrase such as *guardate*
when insulting their Italian classmates. In such cases, the only function of code-
alternation is to provide a contrast between the conversational context of the quote
and the reported speech itself. As the speaker is already using German, this can
only be done by switching into Italian, at least for the beginning of the quote. Note
that the beginning of reported speech is not explicitly marked; more indirect
markers such as pausing and code-alternation fulfil this function.

A promising alternative approach to code-alternation might therefore consist of
analysing the signalling value of the juxtaposition of languages and deriving the
conversational meaning of code-alternation from it. This is quite different from
Fishman's approach, since no association between languages and speech activities
needs to be presupposed. Obviously, it requires a sequential account of language
choice, in which the language chosen for one speech activity must be seen against
the background of language choice in the preceding utterance. From this

perspective, the question is not what verbal activities are associated with one language or the other, but instead: in which activities do bilinguals tend to switch from one language into the other. In answering this question, researchers on code-alternation have developed elaborate typologies of code-switching. They seem to converge across bilingual communities on certain conversational loci in which switching is particularly frequent, such as:

(i) *reported speech*
(ii) *change of participant constellation*, particularly addressee selection – this includes the use of code-switching in order to include/exclude/marginalise co-participants or bystanders
(iii) *parentheses or side-comments*
(iv) *reiterations*, i.e. quasi-translations into the other language, for example for the purpose of putting emphasis on demands or requests, or for purposes of clarification, or for attracting attention, e.g. in the regulation of turn-taking (also called 'translations', 'repetitions' or 'recycling')
(v) *change of activity type*, also called 'mode shift' or 'role shift'
(vi) *topic shift*
(vii) *puns, language play, shift of 'key'*
(viii) *topicalisation, topic/comment structure.*

Although lists such as this one are useful because they demonstrate that some conversational loci are particularly susceptible to code-alternation, the mere listing of such loci is problematic, for a number of reasons.

First, the conversational categories used for the analysis are often ill-defined. Frequently, we get lists of conversational loci for code-alternation and examples, but no sequential analysis is carried out to demonstrate what exactly is meant, for example, by a 'change of activity type', or by 'reiteration'. A more in-depth sequential study of, for example, reiterations would make it clear that this category subsumes a number of very different conversational structures. What is lacking is the proper grounding of the categories employed in a theory of interaction.

Second, so-called typologies of code-alternation often confuse conversational structures, linguistic forms and functions of code-alternation. For instance, 'emphasis' may be a function of code-alternation, whereas 'reiteration' is a (group of) conversational structure(s). Reiteration may or may not serve the function of giving emphasis to a stretch of talk; both categories are on quite different levels. Or, to give another example: interjections and fillers in language A are often observed to be inserted in language B discourse. Yet 'interjection' and 'filler' are names for linguistic structures, their conversational status and their function are another issue. Or, a final example: mitigation and aggravation may be functions of code-alternation, but they are not conversational structures and therefore cannot be dealt with on a par with translations and repetitions (as attempted by Zentella 1981).

Third, lists of conversational loci for code-alternation, or typologies of functions, may give us an initial clue as to what is going on. There is every reason, however, to be sceptical about whether such listing will bring us closer to a theory of code-alternation, i.e., whether it can tell us anything about *why* code-alternation may have a conversational meaning or function. The list itself will hardly ever be a closed one, which shows that code-alternation is used in a creative fashion, and that it can have conversational meaning even if used in a particular conversational environment only once.

Fourth, and most important, the listing of conversational loci for code-alternation implies that code-alternation should have the same conversational status in both directions, i.e. from language A into B or vice versa. Now, although the conversational loci for alternation listed above may in fact be used for switching in both directions in one and the same speech community, the exact conversational meaning of these cases of alternation is often not identical. Consider a very simple example. Zentella (n.d.) lists among the types of code-switching, 'false start repairs' such as in (3):

(3)   *you could* – tú puede hacer eso . . .

         (Zentella n.d.)

Obviously, the speaker is correcting his or her language choice here. But why? The following explanations may be proposed: the 'false start repair' could mean that the speaker is accommodating to the recipient's language preference, or complying with the community norms for language choice, or that he or she is distancing him/herself symbolically from the recipient, or from the community norms, by choosing his/her own preferred language. In order to pinpoint the conversational meaning of such a case of code-alternation, we need to know about the 'episode-external' preferences of speakers for one language or the other, or about the community norms for that particular kind of interaction.

The following examples from the literature may show how the direction of conversational code-alternation enters into its interpretation, by virtue of being related to knowledge about the episode-external language preferences involved.

(i) Sebba and Wootton (1984) show on the basis of a careful sequential analysis that:

> participants in a conversation orientate to L[ondon] J[amaican] stretches embedded in a basically L[ondon] E[nglish] turn as having differential status from the adjacent LE material, providing the principal message content. On the other hand, LE stretches embedded within a basically LJ turn correspond to material of secondary importance, such as speakers' comments on thematically more important material, or diversions from the main theme of the turn, for instance those involving speaker-initiated insertion sequences. (p. 3)

Here, sequential analysis of code-alternation warrants an ascription of conversational meanings or functions to the varieties involved (foregrounding/ emphasis = London Jamaican; backgrounding = London English); in order to come to an interpretation of an individual instance of alternation, these meanings/functions (i.e., based on a linguistic–stylistic, yet extra-episodic, knowledge) have to be invoked.

(ii) In a study on one particular kind of reiteration, i.e. recycled first pair parts, I have shown (in Auer 1984b) that code-switching may occur on the recycled first pair part if the language chosen by the present speaker is not the 'unmarked' language of interaction between these participants, or if the co-participant is seen to have a preference for the other language. The extra-episodic knowledge necessary in order to interpret correctly the meaning of code-alternation is about language preference in particular speaker dyads.

(iii) In her study on Hungarian–German bilingualism in Oberwart, Austria, Gal (1979: 112ff.) observed that switching from Hungarian into German regularly occurred in a particular sequential position: it was used as a 'topper' in escalating angry arguments. Whenever a speaker switched into German, he or she marked the point of culmination of disagreement and hostility, 'a last word that was not outdone' (p. 117). She concludes from this and other conversational usages of switching into German that, according to the Oberwarters' conception of the languages in their repertoire, German connotes prestige, urban sophistication and authority, but also social distance. These attitudinal values of German are indexed and invoked by switching into this language in turn and contribute to its conversational meaning.

Let me summarise the argument so far. Up to now, two approaches to code-alternation which represent opposite extremes have been sketched and critically evaluated. According to the first, languages are said to be linked to verbal activities such that code-alternation is contingent on switching between two activities associated with different languages. According to the second, it is the juxtaposition of the two languages that constitutes the conversational meaning of code-alternation, but the direction of this alternation is irrelevant. As the discussion has shown, both approaches are empirically inadequate. In the typical bilingual speech community, the correlation between language and activity is not strong enough to make code-alternation predictable, but the direction of switching is nevertheless important for reconstructing its conversational meaning. How can this situation be accounted for?

4 The sequentiality of code-alternation

A framework for analysing code-alternation which is able to handle this kind of situation is available in the theory of contextualisation.[3] If we look upon code-alternation as a contextualisation cue, it is but one of an array of devices such as intonation, rhythm, gesture or posture which are used in the situated production and interpretation of language. Code-alternation works in many ways just like these other cues, a fact that calls for a uniform analysis. Treating code-alternation as a contextualisation cue also explains why the functions of this cue are often taken over by prosodic or gestural cues in monolingual conversation.

It is not possible to outline the theory of contextualisation more than super-ficially here. In very general terms, contextualisation comprises all those activities by participants which make relevant/maintain/revise/cancel some aspects of context which, in turn, is responsible for the interpretation of an utterance in its particular locus of occurrence. Such an aspect of context may be the larger activity participants are engaged in (the 'speech genre'), the small-scale activity (or 'speech act'), the mood (or 'key') in which this activity is performed, the topic, but also the participants' roles (the participant constellation, comprising 'speaker', 'recipient', 'bystander', etc.), the social relationship between participants, the relationship between a speaker and the information being conveyed via language ('modality'), etc., in short, just those aspects of context that have been found to be related to code-alternation (see above).

Contextualisation cues have the following characteristics.

(i) They do not have referential (decontextualised) meaning of the kind we find in lexical items. Instead, contextualisation cues and the interpretation of the activity are related by a process of *inferencing*, which is itself dependent on the context of its occurrence. The situated meaning of code-alternation therefore cannot be stated unless a sequential analysis is carried out. The same cue may receive a different interpretation on different occasions.

(ii) The way in which inferencing leads to contextual interpretation is twofold: by contrast or by inherent meaning potential. In the first, most simple, case, contextualisation cues establish contrasts and influence interpretation by punctuating the interaction. The mere fact of (usually abruptly) changing one (or more than one) formal characteristic of the interaction may be enough to prompt an inference about why such a thing has happened. In this process of inferencing, it is necessary to rely on information contained in the local context of the cue's occurrence. The only 'meaning' the cue has is (to paraphrase Jakobson's definition of the phoneme) to 'indicate otherness'. The direction of the change is irrelevant.

Yet, many contextualisation cues do more than that. Therefore, we have to distinguish a second case where contextualisation cues establish a contrast and thereby indicate that something new is going to come; but they also and at the same time restrict the number of possible plausible inferences as to what this might be. This is so because cues may have (received) an inherent meaning potential. This may be 'natural', e.g. when we observe a correlation between diminishing fundamental frequency on the one hand, and 'rest' or 'termination' on the other, which is exploited for marking unit closure (e.g. turn termination), or it may be conventionalised (as in the case of code-alternation).

(iii) Contextualisation cues often bundle together, e.g. there is a certain redundancy of coding which has specific interactional advantages. For the analyst, this redundancy provides methodological access to the conversational functions of one cue (e.g., code-alternation), since other cues supporting the same local interpretation can be used as 'external' evidence for the meaning of conversational code-alternation.

Code-alternation can and should be investigated on the conversational level as a contextualisation cue because it shares the above-mentioned features with other contextualisation cues. Yet code-alternation also has some characteristics of its own. For this reason, we need a specification of the contextualisation value of this cue, i.e., a theory of code-alternation.[4] According to my own approach to such a theory (see Auer 1984 and subsequent publications), the situated interpretation of code-alternation as a contextualisation cue is strongly related to sequential patterns of language choice. Four such patterns have to be distinguished.

A first pattern is that usually associated with conversational code-switching of the proto-typical case, such as in Fishman's example (1). In this case, a language-of-interaction (base language, unmarked language), A, has been established; at a certain point, speaker 1 switches to language B; this new language choice is accepted by speaker 2 as the new language-of-interaction so that beyond the switching point, only B is used. Schematically:

Pattern Ia: A1 A2 A1 A2//B1 B2 B1 B2

As a variant of this pattern, language alternation may occur within a single speaker's turn:

Pattern Ib: A1 A2 A1 A2 A1//B1 B2 B1 B2

The interpretation which code-alternation of this structural type usually receives is that of contextualising some feature of the conversation, e.g. a shift in topic, participant constellation, activity type, etc. It contributes to the organisation of discourse in that particular episode; for these types of switches, I use the term 'discourse-related code-switching'.

Another basic pattern looks like this:

Pattern IIa: A1 B2 A1 B2 A1 B2 A1 B2

Here, speaker 1 consistently uses one language but speaker 2 consistently uses another language. While such patterns of language choice have been reported for some bilingual communities (c. Gal 1979; Alvarez 1990), the more usual one is a variant of IIa:

Pattern IIb: A1 B2 A1 B2 A1//A2 A1 A2 A1

After a time of divergent language choice, one participant, 2, accepts the other's language, and the sequence continues with language A as the language-of-interaction. This pattern represents schematically what I call 'language negotiation'. It may occur at the beginning of an interactive episode or after a switching of type I.

Contrary to type I switching, type II tells us first something about speakers' 'preferences' for one language or the other, i.e., instead of redefining the discourse, it permits assessments of/by participants. I have therefore called this type of switching 'preference-related'; here, the term 'preference' must not be understood as a psychological disposition of the speaker, but rather in the more technical, conversation-analytic sense of an interactionally visible structure. The reasons for such a preference are an altogether different issue. By preference-related switching, a speaker may simply want to avoid the language in which he or she feels insecure and speak the one in which he or she has greater competence. Yet preference-related switching may also be due to a deliberate decision based on political considerations (see Heller, this volume).What surfaces in conversation will be the same sequential arrangement of language choices, interpreted differently in different social contexts.[5]

Up to now sequential patterns of language choice have been considered which start from the assumption that a speaker's turn, or at least its final part, is unambiguously in one language or the other; only in such a case is the recipient able to take up the present speaker's language choice. However, it is frequently observed that bilingual speakers keep language choice open by switching between languages within a turn in a way that makes it impossible to decide if language A or B is the 'base language'. The recipient of such a turn may continue in this mode (Pattern IIIa) or choose the language he or she thinks is appropriate or preferred (Pattern IIIb). The turn-internal switches that occur in such an ambiguous turn may have a conversational function, such as in the case of other-language reiterations for emphasis, or topic/comment switching (see below, p. 131); but the fact of keeping the language choice open also provides information about the speaker and his or her conceptualisation of the situation. Therefore, switching of this turn-internal type is often discourse-related and at the same time participant-related.

> *Pattern IIIa:*   AB1 AB2 AB1 AB2
> *Pattern IIIb:*   AB1//A2 A1 A2

Finally, code-alternation may occur in the middle of a speaker's turn without affecting language choice for the interaction at all. Such momentary lapses into the other language usually occur because a word or another structure in language B is inserted into a language A frame. The insertion has a predictable end; code-alternation defines a unit instead of a momentary departure from the language-of-interaction. Such a type of code-alternation I have called *transfer* (as opposed to code-switching).[6] Schematically, this pattern is represented as IV:

> *Pattern IV:*   A1[B1]A1

Transfer may be discourse- or participant-related. In the latter case, it may display a speaker's bilingual competence (for details, see Auer 1981).

The cross-cutting dichotomies of discourse- vs participant-related code-alternation on the one hand, and code-switching vs transfer on the other, provide a theory for the ways in which code-alternation may become meaningful as a contextualisation cue. This theory has been used empirically in a number of studies on Italian–German and Italian–(Canadian) English bilinguals (Auer 1983, 1984a, 1991), but also in partly refined versions in studies by Hannan (1986) and by Panese (1992) on (British) English/Italian data, by Alfonzetti (1992) on Italian standard/dialect data, and by Li (1994) on (British) English/Chinese data. Examples may be found in these publications and papers and will not be repeated here.

5 Code-alternation and language negotiation

What has been called discourse-related code-switching here (Pattern I) usually runs under the heading of conversational code-switching in the literature, and it has received much attention. On the other hand, matters of language choice for interactive episodes, processes of negotiation of a language-of-interaction between bilinguals, or patterns of language alternation due to a lack of competence (Pattern II, partly Pattern III) are usually not subsumed under conversational code-switching but considered to be either determined by societal macrostructures or by psycholinguistic factors. Thus, while discourse-related switching is analysed within conversational episodes and partly in conversation analytic terms, matters of language choice and language negotiation for an episode are relegated to ethnographic description.

In this section, it will be shown that it is not only discourse-related language alternation that must be given a conversational, sequential analysis, but other types of language alternation as well.[7] As examples, language negotiation and 'code-switching as an unmarked choice' will be discussed.

Why does language negotiation occur at all? The model underlying some approaches to code-alternation (including Blom and Gumperz's distinction between situational and metaphorical code-switching and Fishman's approach mentioned earlier, see above, pp. 117–18) seems to be that language choice is determined by situational parameters such as topic, participant roles or overall speech event. Within the situation defined by these parameters and determining language choice, deviations from the expected or unmarked language may occur for stylistic purposes; but conversational language negotiation has no place in such a conception.

There are at least two empirical problems with this approach (leaving aside theoretical problems concerning the notions of situation and context). First, in many if not all bilingual speech communities situational factors underspecify language choice, i.e. there are at least some situations in which language choice is open; the number of linguistically underspecified situations is particularly high in the 'new' bilingual communities that have come into being in Europe as a consequence of work migration. Here, language choice often ties up with individual histories of interaction in which patterns of language choice may have developed, or is simply a matter of individual preferences, which are, in turn, related to linguistic competences and personal linguistic biographies, as well as to complex matters of bi-cultural identity. The point is that these communities are too young and culturally unstable to have developed shared norms of language choice.

Second, there are many cases in which the situation is simply not defined unambiguously. In such a case, co-participants not only have the task of finding a language; they have to define the situation, among other things, by choosing a language. Carol Myers-Scotton has shown very convincingly for the African context how this can be done and how code-switching can be used in order to 'negotiate interpersonal relationships', instead of being determined by them (e.g., in Myers-Scotton 1990; Scotton 1988).

Due to undefined situations or non-determined language choices, processes of language negotiation occur and are open to conversation analytic treatment. Conversational sequences in which a base-language is negotiated have structural properties of their own. Consider the following examples, one from the Franco-Canadian context (4), the other from Galicia (5):

(4)   [at the reception of a hospital]
        01 Clerk: *Central Booking, may I help you?*
        02 Patient: Oui, allô?
        03 Clerk: Bureau de rendez-vous, est-ce que je peux vous aider?
        04   *May I help you?*
        05   (Silence)
        06   Est-ce que je peux vous aider?
        07   (Silence)
        08   Anglais ou français?
        09 Patient: *WHAT?*
        10 Clerk: *MAY I HELP YOU?*
        11   *Oh yes, yes, I'm sorry, I'm just a little deaf*
        (Heller 1982)

(5)   [informal conversation between three Galician men; A, an elementary
        school teacher, has given a lecture on the history of Galicia; R, the
        researcher, is known to study in the USA; he has been introduced to
        A by P, with whom he is acquainted personally]
        [after talk by A in Galician, with P as the primary addressee, A turns
        to R, introducing a new topic; there is a (discourse-related) switching
        into Spanish at this point; Spanish is marked by italics]
        01 A: [gazing at R., high] *y: qué tal el nivel de la*
        02   *Universidad/ es alto no?*
        03 R: si:
        04 A: *y qué qué haces? filología inglesa? o:*
        05 R: nom . . e:: . . linguüística . . pero estou interessado no

06   galego
07 A: ai, no galego/ *bueno y fuiste becado, becado para allá? o-*
08   *o-*
09 R: eh? si, bueno ali estou tamém trabalhando na universidade
10   e:, . . . despois derom-me umha beca pra vir aqui a galiza
11 A: ai, pra vir a galícia
12 R: (   ) . . . (e despois) marcho para alá
13 A: e e a- vas outra vez para alá
14   e [high] quê te- quê anos tes que estar ali
[etc., continues between A and R in Galician]

———

A: *annnd, what about the standards of the universities? They are high aren't they?*

R: yes.

A: *and what what are you studying? English Philology? or . . .*

R: no, uuh, linguistics, but I'm interested in Galician.

A: oh, in Galician. *So you went there with a scholarship? Or, or -*

R: uh? yes, well, there I'm also working in the university and later they gave me a grant to come here to Galiza.

A: oh, to come to Galicia

R: (   ) (and then) I'm going back there.

A: and and uh- you're going back there. So how many more years will you have to stay there?

[etc.]

(Alvarez 1990: 152f.)

In the first case, the clerk at the reception has the professional duty to accommodate to the client's preferred language, although he or she has to provide the first turn in the interaction. She does so by reformulating her English opening phrase in French after the client's French quasi-response in line 02. In the second case, there is an open clash between A's preference for Spanish and R's preference for Galician. In both cases, political and social considerations go into these preferences. The important point to make here, however, is that the politically, socially, or simply personally motivated preferences for one language or the other are made visible in conversational sequences of language negotiation, and are therefore amenable to sequential analysis. A closer look at such sequences of language negotiation does indeed reveal a number of structural features.

The Canadian example demonstrates one of them: an absence of response after first pair parts such as questions (see, for example, after lines 03, 04, 06) prompts first speakers' inferences, made visible through the repair type carried out by these speakers in order to locate and overcome the recipients' 'problem'. Whereas in monolingual inferences reiterations of first pair parts may lead to reformulations, or to speaking louder, locating 'problems' such as 'misunderstanding', 'not enough detail', or 'too soft', the foremost inference in the bilingual situation analysed by Heller is that of a wrong (inadequate) choice of language.

From the Galician example, we can learn how a language negotiation can be won. A starts to address the visitor from America in Spanish, although the latter has displayed at least passive competence of Galician in the prior discourse. R refuses to take up this language choice, insisting on Galician. There is a conflict over conversational language choice, which is 'won' by R; it is instructive to see how. For this, compare A's and R's language choice in responsive turns. A starts to yield in turns consisting of or containing repetitions, i.e. 07, 11, 13. R, on the contrary, sticks to Galician in his responsive turns (03, 05/6, 09/10). Now, it is a general feature of bilingual language negotiation (c. Auer 1983: 93ff.) that there is more pressure to accommodate to co-participant's language choice for turns or turn components with a high degree of cohesion with previous turns – such as reformulations, repairs and second pair parts – than in initiative turns or turn components, showing little cohesion with previous turn. R wins because he insists on 'his' language even in responsive turns; and he can be said to have won as soon as A uses Galician even for an initiative turn – such as the question in 14.

Language preference and language negotiation are also at play in Pattern III above, i.e., in *code-switching as an unmarked choice*. Scholars of code-switching from Labov (1977: 31) to Heller (1988a) and Scotton (1988) have suggested that frequent conversational code-alternation may be used for creating 'strategic ambiguity' (Heller) or because 'the speaker wishes more than one social identity to be salient in the current exchange' (Scotton). Code-alternation according to this pattern is given a participant-related meaning, indexing globally an ambiguous social situation. This is surely correct. However, it seems from the examples given for this type of alternation that the individual switches, although they are not 'socially meaningful', nevertheless may have individual discourse-related functions. Consider example (6):

(6)   [(Non-standard) Swahili–English–Lwidakho code-alternation.] A
       Luyia man is interviewing a Luyia woman who works in Nairobi as
       a nurse. They come from the same home area and he is a friend of her

husband. As a long-term resident of Nairobi, she now uses Swahili as her main language for informal interaction in Nairobi. [English in italics, Lwidakho underlined]

01	Int.:	unapenda kufanya kazi yako lini? Mchana au usiku?
02	Nurse:	*as I told you, I like my job,*
03		sina ubaguzi wo wote kuhusu wakati ninapofanya kazi.
04		*I enjoy working either during the day*
05		au usiku yote ni sawa kwangu.
06		Hata *family members* w-angu wamezoea mtindo huu.
07		*There is no quarrel at all.*
08		<u>Obubi bubulaho.</u>
09		Saa zengine kazi huwa nyingi sana na.
10		*There are other times when we just have light duty.*
11		<u>Valwale vanji,</u> *more work;*
12		<u>valwale vadi,</u> hazi kidogo.

01	Int.:	When do you like to work? Days or nights?
02	Nurse:	*As I told you, I like my job,*
03		I have no difficulty at all regarding when I do work.
04		*I enjoy working either during the day*
05		or at night, all is ok as far as I'm concerned.
06		Even my *family members* have gotten used to this plan.
07		*There is no quarrel at all.*
08		<u>There is no badness.</u>
09		Sometimes there is a lot of work and
10		*there are other times when we just have light duty.*
11		More patients, *more work;*
12		<u>fewer patients,</u> little work.

(Myers-Scotton (1990))

Surely, the interviewee here wants to leave language choice open; Swahili, English and Lwidakho are used one beside the other. However, the alternation between these three languages is not random. Instead, it seems quite clear that the speaker uses code-switching in order to structure her turn. Among the discourse-related functions of code-switching for this speaker are the following: (a) building up contrasts as in line 04 (English: 'during the day') vs line 05 (Swahili: 'at night'), or in line 09 (Swahili: 'times of hard work') vs line 10 (English: 'times of little work'), or in line 11 (English: 'more work') vs line 12 (Swahili: 'little work'); (b) for grammatically unmarked (asyndetic) 'if/then' structures as in line 11 (protasis: Lwidakho; apodosis: English) and line 12 (protasis: Lwidakho; apodosis: Swahili); (c) for reformulations for the purpose of giving emphasis to a statement, as in lines 07/08 (switching from English into Lwidakho). Leaving the language choice open therefore does not exclude the possibility of using code-alternation for discourse-related purposes.

6 Conclusion

I have tried to argue that between the grammar of code-alternation on the one hand, and its social meaning for the bilingual community at large on the other, there is a third domain that needs to be taken into account: that of the sequential embeddedness of code-alternation in conversation. This domain is relatively independent of the others. Its autonomy is given by the fact that the basic principles by which code-alternation is used in conversation as a meaningful semiotic resource can be stated independently of both the grammar and the macro-social context of code-alternation. Its autonomy is only relative, however, particularly with regard to the social meaning of code-alternation, because in a given bilingual speech community, the conversational patterns of code-alternation and indeed the local meaning given to an instance of code-alternation in a particular context will vary as a function of the status of the codes in the repertoire of the community.

Notes

[1] Other researchers have tried to find similar correlations, such as Sapiens (1982) for bilingual classroom interaction. See the critical summary of this research by Martin-Jones in chapter 5.

[2] See Gumperz 1982: 82; Auer 1984a: 319ff.; Alvarez 1990: ch. 4; Sebba and Wootton 1984.

[3] Cf. Gumperz 1982, 1990, 1992b, etc. For a theoretical summary, c. Auer (1992). Also c. Loke (1991) for an application of Gumperz's theory of contextualisation to code-alternation.

[4] Again, I can only give a very short summary here (for details, c.: Auer 1983, 1984a and b, 1987; for a summary: Auer 1988).

[5] Note that in a sequence of language choices such as IIb, switching recurs from one turn to the next following the dyadic pattern of a two-party conversation. Alternatively, if we focus on one speaker only, the shift of language in this person's speech occurs at the point where he or she 'yields' to the other party's preferred language (the point indicated by double slashes in IIb).

[6] Because of this term's unfortunate association with a certain theory of second language acquisition, it may be advisable to speak of 'insertion', rather than 'transfer'.

[7] Also c. del Coso-Calame et al. 1985; Nussbaum 1990; Auer 1981.

Bibliography

Alfonzetti, G. (1992) *Il discorso bilingue*. Milan: F. Angeli.

Alvarez, C. (1990) The institutionalization of Galician: linguistic practices, power, and ideology in public discourse. Ph.D. thesis, University of California at Berkeley.

Auer, P. (1981) Bilingualism as a members' concept: language choice and language alternation in their relation to lay assessments of competence. *Papiere des Sonderforschungsbereichs 99* (Universität Konstanz, Fachgruppe Sprachwissenschaft), 54.

(1983) Zweisprachige Konversationen. *Code-switching und Transfer bei italienischen Migrantenkindern in Konstanz. Papiere des Sonderforschungsbereichs 99* (Universität Konstanz, Fachgruppe Sprachwissenschaft), 79.

(1984a) *Bilingual conversation*. Amsterdam: Benjamins. (Revised and shortened English version of Auer 1983.)

(1984b) On the meaning of conversational code-switching. In Auer and di Luzio (1984), 87–108.

(1987) Le transfert comme stratégie conversationnelle dans le discours en 'L2'. In Lüdi (1987), 57–74.

(1988) A conversation analytic approach to codeswitching and transfer. In Heller (1988b), 187–214.

(1991) Italian in Toronto. A preliminary comparative report. *Multilingua*, 10: 403–40.

(1992) Instead of an introduction: on contextualizing language. In Auer and di Luzio (1992), 1–38.

Auer, P. and di Luzio, A. (1984) *Interpretive sociolinguistics*. Tübingen: Narr.

(1992) *Contextualising language*. Amsterdam: Benjamins.

Blom, J. P. and Gumperz, J. J. (1972) Social meaning in linguistic structures: code-switching in Norway. In J. J. Gumperz and D. Hymes eds., *Directions in sociolinguistics. The ethnography of communication*. New York: Holt, Rinehart & Winston, 407–34.

del Coso-Calame, F., de Pietro, J.-F. and Oesch-Serra, C. (1985) La compétence de communication bilingue. Etude fonctionnelle des code-switchings dans le discours de migrants espagnols et italiens à Neuchâtel (Suisse). In E. Gülich and T. Kotschi eds., *Grammatik, Konversation, Interaktion*. Tübingen: Max Niemeyer Verlag, 377–98.

di Luzio, A. (1984) On the meaning of language choice for the sociocultural identity of bilingual migrant children. In Auer and di Luzio (1984), 55–82.

Fishman, J. A. (1971) *Sociolinguistics*. Rowley, Mass.: Newbury.

Gal, S. (1979) *Language shift: social determinants of linguistic change in bilingual Austria*. New York: Academic Press.

Gumperz, J. J. (1982) *Discourse strategies*. Cambridge University Press.

(1992a) Contextualization and understanding. In A. Duranti and C. Goodwin eds., *Rethinking context*. New York: Cambridge University Press, 229–52.

(1992b) Further notes on contextualization. In Auer and di Luzio (1992).

Hannan, S. (1986) Using transfers: a conversation analytic approach to the study of transfers in Italian/English bilingual conversation. Unpublished MA thesis, University of York.

Heller, M. (1982) Negotiations of language choice in Montreal. In J. Gumperz ed., *Language and social identity*. Cambridge & New York: Cambridge University Press, 108–18.

(1988a) Strategic ambiguity: code-switching in the management of conflict. In Heller (1988b), 77–98.

(1988b) ed. *Code-switching: anthropological and sociolinguistic perspectives*. Berlin: Mouton de Gruyter.

Labov, W. (1977) *The unity of sociolinguistics*, Series B, 22. Linguistic Agency at the University of Trier.

Li, W. (1994) *Three generations, two languages, one family: language choice and language shift in a Chinese community in Britain*. Clevedon, Avon: Multilingual Matters.

Loke, K. (1991) Code-switching in children's play. In *Papers for the symposium on code-switching in bilingual studies: theory, significance and perspectives*. (Held in Barcelona, 21–23 March 1991.) Strasbourg: European Science Foundation, 287-318.

Lüdi, G. (1987a) ed. *Devenir bilingue – parler bilingue, Actes due 2e colloque sur le bilinguisme, Université de Neuchâtel, 20–22 Septembre 1984*. Tübingen: Max Niemeyer Verlag.

(1987b) Les marques transcodiques: regards nouveaux sur le bilinguisme. In Lüdi (1987a), 1–19.

Myers-Scotton, C. (1990) Intersections between social motivations and structural processing in code-switching. In *Papers for the workshop on constraints, conditions and models*. (Held in London, 27–29 September 1990.) Strasbourg: European Science Foundation, 57–82.

Nussbaum, L. (1990) Plurilingualism in a foreign language classroom in Catalonia. In *Papers for the workshop on impact and consequences/broader considerations*. (Held in Brussels.) Strasbourg: European Science Foundation, 141–64.

Panese, M. (1992) Il code-switching come strategia comunicativa: un indagine nella comunità italiana a Londra. In A. Sobrero ed., *Il dialetto nella conversazione*. Galatina: Congedo, 43–80.

Sapiens, A. (1982) The use of Spanish and English in a high school bilingual civics class. In. J. Amastae, L. Elias-Olivares eds., *Spanish in the United States: Sociolinguistic aspects*. New York: Cambridge University Press.

Scotton, C. M. (1988) Code-switching as indexical of social negotiations. In Heller (1988), 151–86.

Sebba, M. and Wootton, A. J. (1984) Conversational code-switching in London Jamaican. Unpublished manuscript, York University.

Zentella, A. C. (1981a) *Code-switching and interactions among Puerto Rican children.* Sociolinguistic Working Paper, 50, University of Texas at Austin.

(1981b) Hablamos los dos. We speak both. – Growing up bilingual in el Barrio. Unpublished Ph.D. thesis, University of Pennsylvania.

7 A SOCIAL NETWORK APPROACH TO CODE-SWITCHING: THE EXAMPLE OF A BILINGUAL COMMUNITY IN BRITAIN

Lesley Milroy and Li Wei

1 Introduction

The chapters collected in this volume illustrate a range of approaches to code-switching behaviour, some of which seem rather distant from the primarily social one which we shall present here. However, a coherent account of the social and situational context of code-switching behaviour is an important prerequisite even where the perspective of the researcher is not primarily social (for an example, see chapter 14, this volume). This chapter attempts to develop a coherent account of the relationship between code-switching and language choice by individual speakers, and of the relation of both to the broader social, economic and political context. The exposition is presented both in general terms which emphasise its applicability to a range of bilingual situations, and with specific reference to the example of the bilingual Chinese/English-speaking community in Tyneside, north-eastern England.

It is evident from the abundant research literature that a wealth of data and analyses of code-switching behaviour from many very different communities is readily available. What seems generally to be lacking is a coherent social framework within which to interpret these data and analyses. For example, Heller (1990) remarks that while John Gumperz, an important leader in the field, has always viewed code-switching as constitutive of social reality, he has perhaps been less successful in linking this interactional level with broader questions of social relations and social organisation. While Gumperz himself may not have intended to make this micro/macro link, it is important that those who develop his procedures should attempt to do so. Otherwise, insightful interactional-level analyses of data sets which cannot be compared with each other will continue to proliferate without any corresponding advance in understanding similarities and differences in the code-switching and language choice behaviours of different communities, or in explaining why rapid language shift is likely in a particular community.

136

Like Heller (1990), Woolard (1985), and Gal (1988, 1989), we take the starting point for any social or sociolinguistic model to be existing detailed sociolinguistic observations of code-switching behaviour. However, such everyday behaviour of social actors and larger-scale institutional analysis should be seen as related rather than as dissociated, as tends to be the case in the bilingualism literature (cf. the approaches of Fishman and Gumperz, which are generally considered quite separately). Giddens (1984) has developed a social theory based on the relationships between these two levels, commenting that 'the study of day-to-day life is integral to analysis of the reproduction of institutionalised practices' (1984: 282).

Any attempt to integrate micro- and macro-levels of analysis entails a consideration of patterns of *language choice* at the *community* (or even national) level, in conjunction with an analysis of *code-switching* at the *interactional* level. Myers-Scotton's (1986) remark that a model of code-choice needs to be in place before one can develop a model of code-switching is particularly relevant here, since it is important before attempting to account for code-switching behaviour to have some idea of how language choice is restricted for some speakers, or affected by social values assigned to community languages. For this reason, we shall have a good deal to say in this chapter about language choice although our focus is on code-switching.

The following sections are structured as follows. First, we shall outline relevant aspects of the concept of social network: then, relate the language-choice patterns of the community to its informal social structure; examine the reflection of these patterns in code-switching behaviour at the interactional level; and finally, we shall attempt to relate these observations to a wider social, political and economic framework.

2 The network concept

Social network analysis of the kind which is most relevant to sociolinguists was developed in the 1960s and 1970s by a group of mainly English social anthropologists. Personal social networks were generally seen as contextualised within a broader social framework, which was 'bracketed-off' to allow attention to be concentrated on developing less abstract modes of analysis which could account more immediately for the variable behaviour of individuals. However, it is important to remember that such bracketing-off is wholly methodological and does not reflect an ontological reality. While no-one claims that personal network structure is independent of the broader social framework which constantly constrains individual behaviour, a fundamental postulate of network analysis is that individuals create personal communities which provide them with a meaningful framework for solving the problems of their day-to-day existence (Mitchell 1986: 74). This kind of focus has made the social network approach a useful one for sociolinguists investigating relatively clearly definable communities like the Tyneside Chinese, as well as for researchers from other disciplines. For example, Riley *et al.* (1990) describe the application of network analysis in an international project encompassing communities in Sweden, West Germany, the United States and Wales, where the capacities of urban social networks to provide support for families are considered. Many of the methods developed by the research team for investigating and comparing social networks are of relevance to field sociolinguists (see Cochran *et al.* 1990). In the context of this chapter, the general assumption underlying our approach is that variation in the structure of different individuals' personal social networks will, for a number of reasons, systematically affect the way they use the two languages in the community repertoire.

A social network may be seen as a boundless web of ties which reaches out through a whole society, linking people to one another, however remotely. However, for practical reasons, social networks are generally 'anchored' to individuals, and analysis is effectively limited to between twenty and fifty individuals.

It is useful to dinstinguish between 'strong' and 'weak' ties of everyday life. In Belfast, a 'network strength scale' was devised to examine the relationship between strength of tie and variation in (monolingual) language behaviour (Milroy 1987: 139–43). However, since this scale was designed chiefly to examine the effect of *strong* ties contracted within a definable territory, it was not helpful in illuminating the network patterns contracted by the Tyneside Chinese, who were dispersed over a wide geographical area. The absence of a particular residential territory to which they could be identified as 'belonging' is the chief reason for the different approach described here.

To examine their network structure, we used the notions of 'exchange' and 'interactive' networks elaborated by Milardo (1988: 26–36). Exchange networks constitute persons such as kin and close friends with whom ego not only interacts routinely, but also exchanges direct aid, advice, criticism, and support; such ties may therefore be described as 'strong'. Interactive networks on the other hand consist of persons with whom ego interacts frequently and perhaps over prolonged periods of time, but on whom ego does not rely for personal favours and other material or symbolic resources; such ties may therefore be described as 'weak'. An example of an interactive tie would be that between a shop-owner and a customer. In addition to exchange and interactive ties, we identified a 'passive' type of network tie, which seemed particularly important to migrant families. Passive ties entail an absence of regular contact, but are valued by ego as a source of influence and moral support. Examples are physically distant relatives or friends.

Our basic procedure for comparative analysis of the 'strong tie' exchange network structures of persons in the Chinese community was to compile for each individual a list of twenty others who comprised significant daily contacts (cf. the procedure described by Mitchell (1986) in his study of the networks of homeless women in Manchester, England). Once these various 'networks' of twenty had been identified, contrasts between them were examined with respect to the extent of their ethnic and peer orientation. It is their ethnic orientation, expressed by an 'ethnic index' to represent the proportion of Chinese ties, which chiefly concerns us here. Ethnic indexes were also compiled for interactive and passive networks. For passive networks, the index was based on a figure of ten ties per individual, and for interactive networks, twenty or thirty. These differences in procedure for arriving at the three types of network index are not arbitrary. They reflect the abilities of persons to enumerate individuals with whom they have contracted different types of network tie (in the case of exchange and passive ties), and the capacity of the field-worker to make reasonably reliable observations (in the case of interactive ties).

Closeknit social networks consisting mainly of strong ties seem to have a particular capacity to maintain and even enforce local conventions and norms – including linguistic norms. Thus, network analysis offers a basis for understanding the social mechanisms that underlie this process of language maintenance, the converse of language shift. This is true whether we are looking at maintenance of a stigmatised urban vernacular in opposition to the publicly legitimised code, as in Belfast, or of an ethnic language. Migrant and other communities are not all equally successful in maintaining their community languages, and they also apparently vary in their inter-generational communication practices; for example the Panjabi and Bengali speakers in Newcastle do not seem to be experiencing such a sharp inter-generational disjunction as the Chinese community (Moffatt and Milroy 1992). We shall argue that network analysis can illuminate the social dynamics involved in this kind of inter-group difference.

It has sometimes been suggested that closeknit types of community network are nowadays marginal to urban life; for example, there is a large sociological literature on 'the stranger' and the marginal individual who is now often seen as typical of a modern city-dweller (Harman 1988). While this may reflect some kind of truth about urban life, it does not tell the whole story. Certainly the Italian American 'urban villagers' described by Gans (1962) or the closeknit Yorkshire mining communities described by Dennis, Henriques and Slaughter (1957) now seem less salient in American and British cites. However, such traditional working-class communities are apparently being replaced, in Europe and elsewhere, by similar types of community created by newer immigrants. Indeed, as Giddens (1989) points out, neighbourhoods involving close kinship and personal ties seem to be actually created by city life. Those who form part of urban ethnic communities such as the Newcastle Chinese gravitate to form ties with, and sometimes to live with, others from a similar linguistic or ethnic background. Such closeknit networks provide support while the community develops resources to integrate more fully into urban life (see chapter 2 for a full discussion of such migrant networks). Hence, for example, few of the Newcastle Chinese want their children to inherit their catering businesses, but prefer them to integrate into British society and train for higher-status employment.

The chief point we wish to emphasise here is that the type of closeknit network structure which seems to help maintain community languages is likely to be a product of modern city life rather than a residue of an earlier type of social organisation. In associating this level of social organisation with patterns of face-to-face interaction, we need to recall the role of such closeknit networks in renewing and maintaining local systems of norms and values within which discourse processes of the kind analysed by Gumperz (1982: 41–58) are understood and enacted. Indeed, language use is itself an excellent diagnostic of group collectivity.

3 The Chinese community

The Tyneside Chinese number between 5000 and 7000 persons, who are mostly bilingual in English and one of several Chinese languages for which we use the generic label 'Chinese'. Like other researchers who have worked with migrant communities, we are conscious of, and have tried to respond to, the need for a model of ongoing social and linguistic change, since code-switching and language-choice patterns need to be modelled very differently from those in well-established bilingual communities (Boeschoten 1990). We shall examine in this section the relationship between network structure and language-choice patterns in the bilingual Chinese community in Newcastle, before relating this analysis to code-switching behaviour at the interpersonal level.

Data collection procedures were ethnographic, to allow us to obtain a detailed and realistic picture of everyday patterns of language use by these bilingual speakers, and to uncover basic patterns of interaction and informal social organisation prior to a more systematic network analysis. Both linguistic and social information are derived chiefly from participant observation carried out in the field by Li Wei, who is himself bilingual in Chinese and English. Most of the linguistic data were collected during mealtimes, which provided a natural setting for inter-generational interaction. Two initial observations emerged from this participant observation, which were critical to a subsequent network analysis.

(i) The family is the primary unit of social organisation, having a clear internal authority structure. Like most Chinese migrant communities, the majority of the Tyneside Chinese earn their living from family-based catering businesses which rely almost exclusively on family labour. They thereby avoid high wages, overtime payments and other potential drains on resources. To provide service for the maximum number of potential customers, they do not live in identifiable settlements with a centralised authority structure. In this respect they contrast sharply with other linguistic minority communities in Britain, whose social organisation is less family-based and who cluster in specifiable urban areas. Generally speaking, Chinese caterers keep a low public profile and do not develop close personal ties with non-Chinese people. This dispersed settlement pattern and reliance on kin is important for subsequent network analysis.

(ii) Three groups were identifiable which are not always exactly isomorphic with the three generation cohorts of grandparents, parents and children:

(a) first-generation migrants;
(b) sponsored immigrants, who are either immediate kin of the first-generation migrants or have personal connections with people already established in this country;
(c) the British-born.

Subsequent analysis revealed that these groups contract quite different kinds of interpersonal network ties, which need to be interpreted within the framework of a social organisation which gives primacy to the family and an economic dependence on the catering trade, and it is the fact that these network-based groupings *partly* but *not entirely* correspond to social divisions based on gender, generation and occupation which gives the network concept its power to illuminate patterns of code-switching and language choice. Broadly speaking, the interpersonal networks of the three groups differ as follows.

Over the years, most *first-generation* migrants and those sponsored immigrants who are actively involved in the food trade have contracted network ties with *mainly Chinese* non-kin who are associated with their business and professional activities. However, the *sponsored immigrants*, mostly women and the elderly, more or less confine themselves to the *household* and *family*. *The British-born generation* differs from both these groups in having developed extensive network ties *outside the family* and often *outside the Chinese community* also. The educational level of this group is much higher than that of the others, and most British-born Chinese aspire to occupations other than the catering trade. Thus, the exchange networks of the economically active group, both men and women who belong mainly to the 'parent' generation cohort, are strongly Chinese-oriented but not restricted to kin, those of the economically less active adults are also Chinese-oriented but largely restricted to kin, while those of the British-born generation are less kin-oriented and less ethnically oriented than either of these groups.

We are now in a position to look at the linguistic consequences of these differing age-related social network types, drawing on analysis of a corpus of twenty-three hours of spontaneous conversation involving fifty-eight speakers in ten families. It was already clear from a period of participant observation that the language-choice patterns in the community corresponded to some extent to these groupings, varying from Chinese monolingualism in the 'grandparent' generation, through various proportions of Chinese–English bilingualism to the English-dominant bilingualism characteristic of the British-born Chinese. Tables 7.1 and 7.2 implicationally order the fifty-eight speakers (male and female listed separately) according to customary language choice with different addressees both within and outside the family, showing also the ethnic index associated with all three types of network. We have slightly adapted Gal's (1979) application of the implicational scale technique to examine both the social and stylistic dimensions of language choice, where speakers are ranked on the vertical axis and various interlocutor types on the horizontal axis. Those listed towards the top of the scale are speakers who use Chinese (C) on more occasions (i.e. with more interlocutor types), while those listed towards the bottom use more English (E). Interlocutors are also ranked according to the language choices of the vertically ranked speakers; those spoken to in Chinese by more speakers are listed towards the left, while those spoken to more in English are listed towards the right. Thus, the use of C with any particular interlocutor implies that C will be used with all interlocutors to the left of the scale, while if E is used with any interlocutor, it will be used with all interlocutors to the right. The use of both C and E to the same interlocutor will appear between the use of only C and the use of only E, and these are the situations where code-switching may (but not necessarily will) occur. Any choice that does not fit this pattern is considered 'unscalable'. Scalability is calculated as the percentage of cells that fit the scale model, and in both Table 7.1 and Table 7.2 is well in excess of the 85 per cent scalability which is normally considered to be a sufficient approximation to perfect scaling (Gal 1979; Fasold 1990).

Table 7.1 *Implicational scale for observed language choices by male speakers. (Scalability 98.2%)*

						Interlocutors											
A	B	C	a	b	c	1	2	3	4	5	6	7	8	9	10	11	12
25	6GP	73	20	100	10	—	C	C	—	C	C	C	C	C	C	C	C
1	1GP	66	20	100	10	—	C	C	—	C	C	C	C	—	C	C	C
45	9P	53	15	42	10	C	C	C	—	—	C	C	C	—	CE	CE	CE
10	3P	47	18	52	10	C	C	C	—	—	C	C	C	—	CE	CE	CE
5	2P	41	16	22	10	—	C	C	—	—	C	C	C	—	CE	CE	CE
26	6P	56	17	59	10	—	C	C	C	—	C	C	C	CE	CE	CE	CE
20	5P	37	17	19	10	C	C	C	—	—	C	C	C	CE	CE	CE	CE
53	10P	44	15	18	10	C	C	CE*	C	—	CE*	C	C	CE	CE	CE	CE
2	1P	35	16	18	10	—	C	C	C	—	C	CE	CE	—	CE	CE	CE
32	7P	49	12	49	10	C	C	C	—	—	CE	CE	CE	CE	CE	CE	CE
51	10GP	68	16	63	10	C	C	C	—	CE	CE	CE	CE	CE	CE	CE	CE
37	8GP	65	14	50	10	C	C	C	—	CE	CE	CE	CE	CE	CE	CE	CE
39	8P	44	14	11	10	C	C	C	CE	—	CE	CE	CE	CE	CE	CE	CE
15	4P	40	2	22	10	C	C	CE	—	—	CE	CE	CE	CE	CE	CE	CE
28	6C	22	1	32	6	—	C	CE	C*	CE	CE	CE	CE	CE	CE	CE	CE
47	9C	24	2	8	7	C	C	CE	—	CE	CE	CE	CE	—	CE	CE	CE
48	9C	22	3	0	9	C	C	CE	—	CE	CE	CE	CE	—	CE	CE	CE
12	3C	21	5	0	8	C	C	CE	—	CE	CE	CE	CE	—	CE	CE	CE
13	3C	19	0	0	8	C	C	CE	—	CE	CE	CE	CE	—	CE	CE	CE
49	9C	18	0	0	6	C	C	CE	—	CE	CE	CE	CE	—	CE	CE	CE
7	2C	15	2	0	6	—	C	CE	—	CE	CE	CE	CE	—	CE	CE	CE
8	2C	12	0	0	5	—	C	CE	—	CE	CE	CE	CE	—	CE	CE	CE
29	6C	17	0	9	5	—	CE	CE	C*	CE	CE	CE	CE	CE	CE	CE	CE
4	1C	10	0	0	4	—	CE	CE	C*	CE	CE	CE	CE	—	—	CE	CE
34	7C	18	0	0	5	C	C	CE	—	CE	CE	CE	CE	CE	CE	E	E
17	4C	11	1	0	6	C	C	CE	—	CE	CE	CE	CE	CE	—	E	E
43	8C	16	0	0	4	C	C	CE	CE	CE	CE	CE	CE	CE	—	E	E
55	10C	16	0	10	5	C	CE	CE	CE	CE	CE	CE	CE	CE	—	E	E
35	7C	15	0	0	3	C	CE	CE	—	CE	CE	CE	CE	CE	CE	E	E
22	5C	14	2	6	3	C	CE	CE	—	CE	CE	CE	CE	CE	—	E	E

A = speaker number; B = family membership (GP = grandparent; P = parent;
C = child; the numbers denote families 1–10); C = age; a = ethnic index of exchange network (total: 20 ties per speaker); b = ethnic index of interactive networks (percentage);
c = ethnic index of 'passive' networks (total 10 ties per speaker)
1 = grandparent, female; 2 = grandparent generation, female; 3 = grandparent generation, male; 4 = grandparent, male; 5 = parent, male; 6 = parent, female; 7 = parent generation, male; 8 = parent generation, female; 9 = child, female; 10 = child, male; 11 = child generation, male; 12 = child generation, female.
*These cells fail to conform to perfect scalability.

Table 7.2 *Implicational scale for observed language choices by female speakers. (Scalability 99.6%)*

										Interlocutors						
A	B	C	a	b	c	1	2	3	4	5	6	7	8	9	10	11	12
44	9GP	72	20	100	10	—	C	C	C	C	C	—	C	—	C	C	C
9	3GP	70	20	100	10	—	C	C	C	C	C	—	C	—	C	C	C
31	7GP	67	20	100	10	—	C	C	C	C	C	—	C	C	C	C	C
14	4GP	65	20	100	10	—	C	C	C	C	C	—	C	C	C	C	C
52	10GP	63	20	100	10	—	C	C	C	C	C	C	C	C	C	C	C
38	8GP	61	20	100	10	—	C	C	C	C	C	C	C	C	C	C	C
19	5GP	58	20	100	10	—	C	C	C	C	C	—	C	C	C	C	C
46	9P	50	18	41	10	C	C	C	—	C	C	—	C	—	CE	CE	CE
11	3P	46	20	54	10	C	C	C	—	C	C	—	C	—	CE	CE	CE
6	2P	38	20	20	10	—	C	C	—	C	C	—	C	—	CE	CE	CE
21	5P	35	20	65	10	C	C	C	—	C	C	—	C	CE	CE	CE	CE
3	1P	32	18	67	10	—	C	C	—	C	C	C	C	—	CE	CE	CE
27	6P	52	17	58	10	—	C	C	—	C	C	C	C	CE	CE	CE	CE
33	7P	42	15	50	10	C	C	C	—	C	C	—	CE	CE	CE	CE	CE
54	10P	45	18	11	10	C	C	C	—	C	C	CE	CE	CE	CE	CE	CE
16	4P	37	6	3	10	C	C	C	—	CE	CE	—	CE	CE	CE	CE	CE
40	8P	40	18	50	10	C	C	C	—	CE	CE	CE	CE	CE	CE	CE	CE
50	9C	22	2	58	8	C	C	CE	CE	CE	CE	—	CE	—	CE	CE	CE
56	10C	21	3	57	8	C	C	CE	CE	CE	CE	CE	CE	CE	CE	CE	CE
57	10C	18	2	0	5	C	C	CE	CE	CE	CE	CE	CE	CE	CE	CE	CE
41	8C	12	1	4	6	C	C	CE	CE	CE	CE	CE	CE	CE	CE	CE	CE
58	10C	12	1	8	4	C	C	CE	CE	CE	CE	CE	CE	CE	CE	CE	CE
42	8C	8	0	0	4	C	C	CE	CE	CE	CE	CE	CE	CE	CE	CE	CE
30	6C	20	1	12	7	—	CE	CE	CE	CE	CE	C*	CE	—	CE	CE	CE
18	4C	15	0	0	5	C	C	CE	CE	CE	CE	—	CE	—	CE	E	E
24	5C	9	1	6	4	C	C	CE	CE	CE	CE	—	CE	CE	CE	E	E
23	5C	11	0	0	3	C	CE	CE	CE	CE	CE	—	CE	CE	CE	E	E
36	7C	10	2	9	5	C	CE	CE	CE	CE	CE	—	CE	—	CE	E	E

A = speaker number; B = family membership (GP = grandparent; P = parent; C = child; the numbers denote families 1–10); C = age; a = ethnic index of exchange network (total: 20 ties per speaker); b = ethnic index of interactive networks (percentage); c = ethnic index of 'passive' networks (total 10 ties per speaker)

1 = grandparent, female; 2 = grandparent generation, female; 3 = grandparent generation, male; 4 = parent, female; 5 = parent generation, male; 6 = parent generation, female; 7 = grandparent, male; 8 = parent male; 9 = child, female; 10 = child, male; 11 = child generation, male; 12 = child generation, female.

The language-choice pattern of any individual speaker can be read across each row, while inter-speaker differences in language choice with particular interlocutors can be read down each column. The relationship between social networks and language-choice patterns is indicated by the ethnic indices associated with the three network types (exchange; interactive; 'passive'). Information on generation cohort and speaker age is provided in columns B and C.

On the horizontal axis, grandparents are listed at the far left and children at the far right, indicating that Chinese is generally used to grandparents and English to children. This addressee ranking largely corresponds with the speaker ranking on the vertical axis, where grandparents appear towards the top of the scales and children towards the bottom. Broadly speaking therefore, Chinese tends to be used by grandparents and to grandparents, while English tends to be used by children and to children. Both Chinese and English may be used by parents and to parents.

Gal (1979) suggests that it is through the association between language and interlocutor types of the kind shown here that languages acquire their social symbolism. For example, since in the Tyneside community Chinese is associated primarily with the grandparents, it may be described as the 'we code' for older speakers; English on the other hand, which is associated chiefly with British-born children, may be regarded as their 'we code'. Note that even this tentative generalisation, which takes some account of the inter-generational change in patterns of language use, rejects any assumption that the ethnic language of the community is the 'we code' and the language of the majority the 'they code'.

Closer examination of the implicational scales reveals however that the interaction between the social and stylistic dimensions of language choice needs a more sophisticated analysis than this, since not all speakers of the same generation share the same language-choice patterns, some being ranked either higher or lower than most other members of their generation on the vertical scale. For instance, speakers 51 and 37 (from families 10 and 8, aged 68 and 65 respectively) are ranked much lower than the other grandparents in Table 7.1 and lower even than some of the parents, indicating that they use relatively more English. Furthermore, those who are listed at the extreme bottom of the scales are not always the youngest speakers in the child generation; for example, speakers 23 and 36 at the bottom of Table 7.2 are in fact older than speakers 42 and 24. The social network variable is important precisely because such variations in language-choice patterns cannot be accounted for *entirely* by the variables of age and generation.

Relative to other members of the grandparent generation, speakers 51 and 37 have fewer ethnic ties in their networks, and relative to other members of the child generation those listed at the bottom of the scales have even fewer Chinese contacts. In other words, these 'anomalous' speakers seem to have contracted personal social network ties rather different from those typical of members of their peer generation.

Interestingly however, inter-speaker variations of this kind are closely associated with interlocutor types, in that speakers with different network patterns adopt different language-choice patterns with particular interlocutors. For example, while speakers of the parent generation who have relatively more Chinese-oriented networks use Chinese for communication between spouses, those with relatively fewer Chinese ties may use both Chinese and English with this addressee type (compare for example, speakers 32 and 2, listed in Table 7.1). Similarly, while all children use Chinese with grandparents (especially female grandparents), and both Chinese and English with parents, some (but not all) use only English with their peers.

Attempts to infer the social symbolism of Chinese and English by identifying the generations with which they are associated are therefore too simplistic. Tables 7.1 and 7.2 suggest that particular languages are associated with particular groups of speakers who have contracted similar types of social network but, although different network types are plainly associated with age and generation (and to a lesser extent gender), they also vary between individuals despite these associations. Thus, social network can account for patterns of language choice more economically than the other, related, variables, in that it illuminates the behaviour of apparently anomalous individuals as well as that of speakers who fall into the expected groups. Most strikingly, the network variable is a more accurate predictor of language choice than that of generation, with which it is closely associated but not isomorphic. Li (1994) reports the results of an initial statistical analysis (using analysis of variance and rank order correlation procedures) which explores more systematically relationships between variables of gender, generation and age, as suggested by the language-choice patterns which emerge from Tables 7.1 and 7.2.

4 Network-specific conversational code-switching patterns

The implicational scales presented in Tables 7.1 and 7.2 not only illuminate the interaction between inter- and intra-speaker linguistic variation but also locate specifically the contexts (indicated by a CE pattern) where *conversational code-*

switching is likely to occur. In this section, we shall explore more systematically the interactional patterns associated with conversational use of the two community languages, focussing on the outcome of the language-choice patterns described above at the level of everyday interactional behaviour.

Extracts (1) and (2) are discussed by Pong (1991) as typical of the different kinds of language-mixing behaviour of the child and the parent generations. Note however that the fluent code-switching of the bilingual teenagers in (1) indicates a language choice pattern which is rather less English-oriented than that of the speakers listed at the very bottom of the scales. The parents in (2) regard themselves as monolingual Chinese speakers, and the only English words they use are the borrowings 'football hooligan' and 'pub' (for a discussion of the distinction between borrowing and code-switching, see Poplack and Sankoff (1984)).

(1)   Fieldworker: Gem nei dei dou m wui hao leu wen go ying guog yen
                       zou peng yeo ne wo (So you won't consider having an
                       English girlfriend)
        Anthony: Zou peng yeo wui, **but not a wife**. (Yes friends, but not
                       a wife)

        . . . .

        Anthony: Yeo hou do yeo **contact**. (We have many contacts)
        George: **We always have opportunities** heu xig kei ta dei fong
                       gao wui di yen. Ngo dei xi xi dou **keep in contact**. (We
                       always have opportunities to get to know people from
                       other churches. We always keep in contact)
                       (Pong 1991: 24)

(2)   Father: Bed guo, Ying Guog di heo seng zeo kuai di la. Bin dou yeo
                   Ying Guog gem do *football hooligan*. (But the teenagers in
                   Britain are very badly behaved. Where else can you find so
                   many football hooligans?)
        Mother: Ni dou di heo seng zung yi yem zeo. So yi ngo m bei di zei
                   neu heu *pub* ga. (The teenagers here like to drink. That's
                   why I never allow my children to go to pubs)
                   (Pong 1991: 99)

These two extracts illustrate contrasting inter-generational patterns of conversational behaviour which partly derive from the language-choice patterns described in the preceding sections. To a very large extent these patterns are associated not only with the different socialisation patterns described above, but with differing levels of ability in the two community languages. However, inter-generational differences in the way the two languages are used in conversation are often subtle, and seem to be better analysed as *socially symbolic discourse behaviours* rather than as following from these community-level social variables or from individual language competence in any obvious way. We shall examine this dimension of code-switching behaviour within a general *conversation analysis* framework (cf. Auer, this volume). Briefly, this involves searching the data for recurrent sequential patterns, which are then interpreted with reference both to the observable behaviour of participants, and to generalisations derived inductively from previously observed conversational corpora (see Levinson 1982; Atkinson and Heritage 1984). Using this general framework, we shall look in this section at how speakers alternate their two languages in conversation as a procedure for the organisation of preference marking, repairs, and insertion sequences. Examples (3)–(5) involve inter-generational communication between parents and children, while the participants in (6)–(9) are same-generation peers.

4.1 Preference marking

Consider first the following conversational sequences where a micropause is indicated by a full stop within parentheses, and the duration of longer pauses is indicated in seconds, also within parentheses. Simultaneous speech is enclosed within square brackets, as are translations.

(3)   (Dinner table talk between mother A and daughter B)
        A: Oy-m-oy faan a? A Ying a?
        [Want or not rice?]
        B: (No response)
        A: Chaaufaan a. Oy-m-oy?
        [Fried rice.   Want or not?]
        B: (2.0) I'll have some shrimps.
        A: Mut-ye? (.) Chaaufaan a.
        [What?]   [Fried rice.]
        B: Hai a.
        [OK.]

In (3), a mother, speaking Cantonese throughout, offers her daughter rice. The child first delays her response to the offer, and then in English requests an alternative to rice. Her final acceptance is in Cantonese.

In (4), B, a boy of twelve, is playing with a computer in the living-room. A is his mother.

(4)   A: Finished homework?
          (2.0)
       A: Steven, yiu mo wan sue?
              [want to review (your) lessons]
       B: (1.5) I've finished.

In this extract, B does not respond to his mother's question. She then switches to Cantonese for a further question, which B apparently understands as an indirect request to review his lessons. His response is marked by a pause as 'dispreferred' and his language choice contrasts with that of his mother. In both (3) and (4) dispreferred responses seem to be marked by code-switching to a contrasting language, as well as by the more usual pause.

A rather clear example of this pattern can be seen in (5), where A is the mother, B, her nine-year-old daughter, and C her twelve-year old son:

(5)   A: Who want some? [Crispy a.]
       B: [Yes.]
       A: Yiu me?
          [Want some?]
       B: Hai a.
          [Yes.]
       (A handing over some spring rolls to B)
       A: (To C) Want some, John?
       C: Ngaw m yiu.
          [I don't want.]
       A: M yiu a? Crispy la.
          [Don't want]
       C: (Shaking head) mm

In this sequence, B twice accepts A's offer of spring rolls, twice using the same language as A (English and Cantonese respectively) for this preferred response. However, when C declines A's offer we find a pattern similar to the one which is evident in (3) and (4). After a short pause, C selects a language different from the language used for the first pair part; A uses English for the offer whereas C uses Cantonese for the refusal. This example supports Auer's argument that the contrast is more socially meaningful than the actual choice of language. Switches marking dispreferred responses can be in either direction.

Dispreferred responses in monolingual English conversations (e.g. refusals and disagreements as opposed to acceptances and agreements) are generally marked by various structural complexities including pauses before delivery, 'prefaces' such as 'but' and 'well', token agreements, appreciations and apologies (see further Levinson 1983: 334–5). Sequences (3), (4) and (5) suggest that contrasting choices of language, with the second part speaker choosing a language different from the first part speaker, can be used to mark dispreference in bilingual conversation in much the same way as a wide range of markedness features in monolingual conversation. In fact, Auer (1991) argues that code-switching is the most significant discourse marker in bilingual conversations in the sense that marked language choices are more noticeable than other discourse markers (see also Lavandera 1978; Gumperz 1982). It is perhaps for this reason that code-switching may even replace some language-specific dispreference markers. For example, although we have shown that pauses accompany code-switching in this conversational context, we find that in our corpus English discourse markers such as 'well' and 'but' do not.

A general pattern which emerges from these examples and many others in the corpus is that code-switching to mark dispreferred second parts occurs chiefly in *inter-generational conversation*. Furthermore, it is usually *children* who use English to mark their dispreferred responses to the Chinese first pair parts of their parents or grandparents (although this is not invariably the case, as can be seen in (5) above). Code-switching seldom seems to be used to mark dispreference in conversations between speakers of the same generation, and where it is, the language direction of the switch is less predictable. The emergence of a general pattern of this kind lends support to the point made earlier, that the association between conversation structure and language choice varies between speakers. Thus, in order to understand the social and discourse meaning of code-switching, we need to relate specific interactional strategies to the more general patterns of language choice and language ability at the inter-speaker (or community) level.

4.2 Repair

Consider now the following three sequences, which involve older speakers. A and B are both women in their early forties.

(6)   A: . . . koei hai yisaang.

[He's a doctor.]

B: Is he?

A: Yichin (.) hai Hong Kong.

   [Before]   [In Hong Kong.]

In (6), B's utterance, in a language contrastive with that of A's preceding utterance, initiates a self-repair by A, prompting her to specify more accurately that the man mentioned in her first turn was formerly a doctor in Hong Kong, but is not currently a doctor in Britain.

In (7), where A and B again are both women, A in her forties and B in her mid-twenties, B similarly marks a repair initiator with a contrasting choice of language. Here she queries the accuracy of A's assertion that the person she is trying to contact on the telephone will ring in a short time.

(7)   A: Da m do. Koeige telephone gonggan. Koei dang yatjan joi da.

          [Can't get through. Her telephone is engaged. She'll ring again in

          a short while.]

      B: She ring?

      A: Hai a, ngaw da.

         [Yes, I'll ring.]

In (8) A, a woman in her late thirties initiates a subsequent other-repair by B, a man in his late twenties. Again the repair initiator is marked by a contrasting choice of language as in the previous two examples.

(8)   A: He's a [ku:] . . . (.) I don't know how to say (.)

         send message (.) Nay ji-m-ji a?

              [Do you know?]

      B: Oh, courier.

      A: Yes, courier.

Researchers have frequently observed that code-switching can serve such functions as word-finding, self-editing (with or without discernible errors), repetition, emphasis, clarification, confirmation, and so forth. All these uses are parts of a more general repair procedure, examples of which we have illustrated. Although they are difficult to analyse quantitatively because of the multifunctional nature of specific conversational contributions, the association between code-switching and repair is a common one in our corpus. Furthermore, this association seems to be generation-specific in that it is characteristic of adult but not of child bilingual speakers.

The role of code-switching in organising discourse can be seen also in conversation sequences which do not fit the adjacency pairs structure; it is to these sequences that we now turn.

4.3 Presequences

Not all conversational sequences can be analysed as paired sets of utterances or as chained to the preceding and following utterances in a linear fashion, as illustrated by our examples so far. The first utterance in (9) is an example of the first part of a 'pre-sequence', a type of conversational structure which prefigures or clears the ground for a later interactional episode. Presequences simultaneously mark the boundary of two such episodes (Levinson, 1983), and our data suggest that this boundary is often marked by code-switching. In (9), A is talking with his (female) cousin B, about one of their friends who has been ill. Both speakers are in their twenties:

(9)   A: Did you see Kim yesterday?
       B: Yeah.
       A: Mou mat si . . .
          [It's not serious . . .]
       B: Yau di tautung je, Mou mat si ge.
          [(She) only has a little head-ache. It's nothing serious.]
       A: Ngaw jing yiu man nay.
          [I was just about to ask you.]

A's first utterance is a question checking the precondition for his subsequent enquiry about their friend's health. After B confirms that she is in a position to provide this information, A embarks upon his intended enquiry. The boundary between presequence and target sequence is marked here by code-switching, while in monolingual discourse, presequences are often marked prosodically or phonologically in various ways (Levinson 1983: 345ff.).

In this section we have cited examples to illustrate some of the conversational patterns marked by code-switching which recur in our corpus, and we have suggested that code-switching might plausibly be viewed as fulfilling some specifiable conversational functions. Probably because of the contrasting language preferences of the children on the one hand and the parents and grandparents on the other, it seems to be particularly common in inter-generational communication, as illustrated by examples (3)–(5). In addition to the functions of preference marking, marking of repairs and presequence boundary marking illustrated by the full set of examples, code-switching seems to be used to regulate turn-taking in various ways (see Li 1994). As we have hinted, the adoption by individuals of one or another of these discourse strategies seems to a considerable extent to be generation and network-specific. For example, parents and grandparents seem generally not to code-switch during peer conversations except to mark self-repairs, as illustrated by (6)–(8). However, they sometimes switch from Chinese to English when they are addressing children, particularly to mark turn allocation and repair initiators. On the other hand, children (and the British-born generation generally) tend to use English with their peers, and to switch to Chinese to mark pre- and embedded sequences, as illustrated by (9). However, we have the tendency of this generation to mark dispreferred responses by switching from Chinese to English.

These inter-generational differences in code-switching practices might be described as interactional reflexes of the network- and generation-specific language-choice preferences in the Tyneside Chinese community. Although they can sometimes be related to practical constraints arising from the language preferences and language abilities of different subgroups, many code-switching practices such as those exemplified in (3)–(8) cannot easily be related to such constraints, and are better interpreted as network-specific strategies of a socially symbolic kind (Gumperz 1982: 71).

5 Social network and the broader social framework

As well as relating interactional and community levels of analysis, network structure can relate to social, economic and political structure. The main point we need to make here is that the various network types discussed in this chapter do not constitute themselves in a socially arbitrary fashion. Particularly, the characteristic occupational preferences of the economically active Chinese largely determine the nature of the ties which they contract with others. Similarly, the mainly kin-oriented ties which the economically dependent adults contract are a natural consequence of the Chinese family system. The British-born generation, for their part, by attending school and participating in life outside the community will contract ties with non-Chinese peers.

A coherent theory of language choice and code-switching needs to make explicit the relationship between community networks – 'frames' within which language choice takes place – and large-scale social and economic structure. As Gal (1988) points out, the success, persistence and precise form of the 'opposition' to mainstream values symbolised by minority language maintenance depends not upon community-internal linguistic or interactional factors, but upon the relation of the group to the national economy and to like groups in other cities or states; we need both a socio-political and interactional level of analysis. The outcome in terms of language (or dialect) survival or shift in Belfast may be different from that in Paris or Copenhagen; in Catalonia different from Gascony. It will be constrained by local variations in political, economic and social structure.

What we seem to need is a *social* (as opposed to a sociolinguistic) theory which can associate these network patterns with specifiable subgroups which in turn emerge from larger-scale social, economic and political processes. One useful integrated analysis is proposed by Giddens (1984), but the *life-modes* theory of the Danish anthropologist Thomas Højrup, which is grounded firmly in systematic ethnographic work, is particularly helpful. Offering an analysis which is designed to be generally applicable to Western Europe but which allows for local, historically contingent differences in social and economic systems, Højrup proposes a division of the population into subgroups which are described in terms of three life-modes. These life-modes are seen as both social and cultural, as necessary and inevitable constituents of the social structure as a whole which spring from economic systems of production and consumption. Thus, like social network types, they are not socially or culturally arbitrary, but are the effect of 'fundamental societal structures which split the population into fundamentally different life-modes' (Højrup 1983: 47). The precise way in which they split the population will however vary from state to state, depending on local political and economic systems. Højrup's analysis focusses on the differing ideological orientation of the three subgroups to work, leisure and family, and from the point of view of this research, the distinction between Life-mode 1, the life-mode of the self-employed, and Life-mode 2, that of ordinary wage-earner is particularly important. The life-mode of a different kind of wage-earner, the high-powered Life-mode 3 executive, is quite different from either.

A closeknit family-centred network with a strong solidarity ideology and little distinction between work and leisure activities is characteristic of the self-employed. Conversely, wage-earners will be embedded in less kin-oriented and generally looser-knit networks. This analysis, to which we cannot do justice here, converges with our own in that different network types seem to form in response to the conditions associated with different life-modes. We would predict a more Chinese-oriented pattern of language choice by speakers who are embedded in closeknit networks, and would expect such a personal network structure to be related to life-mode. Indeed this seems to be the case. For example, two speakers in our sample are a married couple who are employed by a local computer company. They interact on a daily basis with English-speakers, retaining contact with other Chinese only for a short time on Sundays, the traditional community meeting-day. Their command of English is very much better than other economically active Chinese. Højrup does not see the life-mode of the self-employed as a relic of an earlier period but as highly efficient and competitive, given its flexibility of operation and the commitment of the producers. He uses the Danish fishing industry as an example, but his description applies equally well to the Newcastle Chinese family catering businesses.

6 Conclusion

While we have used the Tyneside Chinese community to illustrate a social network perspective of code-switching and language choice, the analysis presented in this chapter is intended to be of more general application. We have argued that network analysis can illuminate our understanding of patterns of code-switching and language choice for three reasons.

First, while network interacts with a number of other social variables such as generation, gender, and occupation, it is capable of accounting more generally than any other single variable for patterns of code-switching language choice. Second, it can also deal in a principled way with the bilingual behaviour of 'anomalous' individuals whose language patterns are unlike those of their peers, in that they can be shown to have contracted different types of personal network structure. Third, a network analysis can, we have suggested, form an important component in an integrated social theory of language choice. It links the community with the interactional level in focussing on everyday behaviour of social actors, and we have examined in this chapter some generation- and network-specific conversational patterns. The link with the economic and sociopolitical level derives from the observation that networks seem to form not arbitrarily but in response to social and economic pressures. We briefly examined this latter link in terms of Højrup's life-modes analysis.

The research on the Tyneside Chinese community reported here is still in progress, and the next step is the development of a statistical model to show more precisely how extralinguistic variables such as generation, gender and occupation interact with network in affecting the bilingual behaviour of individual speakers.

Note

The research described in this paper is partly supported by two grants from the Economic and Social Research Council (numbers R000 221074; R000 232956).

Bibliography

Atkinson, M. and Heritage, J. (1984) eds. *Structures of social action*. Cambridge University Press.

Auer, P. (1991) Bilingualism in/as social action: a sequential approach to code-switching. *Papers for the symposium on code-switching in bilingual studies: theory, significance and perspectives* II. (Held in Barcelona, 21–23 March 1991.) Strasbourg: European Science Foundation.

Boeschoten, H. (1990) Asymmetrical code-switching in immigrant communities. In *Papers for the workshop on constraints, conditions and models*. (Held in London, 27–29 September 1990.) Strasbourg: European Science Foundation, 85–100.

Cochran, M., Larner, M., Riley, D., Gunnarsson, M. and Henderson, C. R. (1990) eds., *Extending families*. Cambridge University Press.

Dennis, N., Henriques, F. M. and Slaughter, C. (1957) *Coal is our life*. London: Eyre and Spottiswoode.

Fasold, R. (1990) *The sociolinguistics of language*. Oxford: Basil Blackwell.

Gal, S. (1979) *Language shift: social determinants of linguistic change in bilingual Austria*. New York: Academic Press.

(1988) The political economy of code choice. In Heller (1988), 245–63.

(1989) Language and political economy. *Annual Review of Anthropology*, 18: 345–67.

Gans, H. J. (1962) *The urban villagers: group and class in the life of Italian-Americans* (2nd edn). New York: Free Press.

Giddens, A. (1984) *The constitution of society*. Cambridge: Polity Press.

(1989) *Sociology*. Cambridge: Polity Press.

Gumperz, J. J. (1982) *Discourse strategies*. Cambridge University Press.

Harman, L. D. (1988) *The modern stranger: on language and membership*. Berlin: Mouton de Gruyter.

Heller, M. (1988) ed. *Code-switching: anthropological and sociolinguistic perspectives*. Berlin: Mouton de Gruyter.

(1990) The politics of codeswitching: processes and consequences of ethnic mobilisation. Paper presented at the third workshop of the European Science Foundation Network on Code-switching and Language Contact, Brussels.

Højrup, T. (1983) The concept of life-mode: a form-specifying mode of analysis applied to contemporary western Europe. *Ethnologia Scandinavica*, 1–50.

Lavandera, B. (1978) The variable component in bilingual performance. In J. Alatis ed., *International dimensions of bilingual education*. Washington, D.C.: Georgetown University Press, 391–411.

Levinson, S. (1983) *Pragmatics*. Cambridge University Press.

Li, W. (1994) *Three generations, two languages, one family: language choice and language shift in a Chinese community in Britain*. Clevedon, Avon: Multilingual Matters.

Li, Wei, Milroy, L. and Pong Sin Ching (1992) A two step sociolinguistic analysis of code-switching and language choice: the example of a bilingual Chinese community in Britain. *International Journal of Applied Linguistics*, 2 (1): 63–86.

Milardo, R. M. (1988) Families and social networks: an overview of theory and methodology. In Milardo ed., *Families and social networks*. Newbury Park, Calif.: Sage, 13–47.

Milroy, L. (1987) *Language and social networks* (2nd edn). Oxford: Basil Blackwell.

Mitchell, J. C. (1986) Network procedures. In D. Frick *et al.* eds., *The quality of urban life*. Berlin: Mouton de Gruyter, 73–92.

Moffatt, S. and Milroy, L. (1992) Panjabi/English language alternation in the classroom in the early school years. *Multilingua*, 11 (4): 355–84.

Myers-Scotton, C. (1986) Diglossia and code-switching. In J. Fishman *et al.* eds., *The Fergusonian impact*. Berlin: Mouton de Gruyter, II, 403–17.

Pong Sin Ching (1991) Intergenerational variation in language choice patterns in a Chinese community in Britain. Unpublished M. Phil. thesis, University of Newcastle upon Tyne.

Poplack, S. and Sankoff, D. (1984) Borrowing: the synchrony of integration. *Linguistics*, 22, 99–135.

Riley, D., Cochran, M., Henderson, C. R., Gunnarsson, L. and Larner, M. (1990) Settings and methods. In Cochran *et al.* (1990).

Wirth, L. (1938) Urbanism as a way of life. *American Journal of Sociology*, 44 (1): 1–24.

Woolard, K. (1985) Language variation and cultural hegemony: toward an integration of sociolinguistic and social theory. *American Ethnologist*, 12: 738–48.

8   CODE-SWITCHING AND THE POLITICS OF LANGUAGE

Monica Heller

It's not always how you play the game, it's how you use the rules[1]

1 Introduction

In 1977, the government of the province of Quebec passed Bill 101, a law to affirm and support French as the official and dominant language of the province. This law was a key element in Francophones' strategy to overcome two centuries of domination by English-speakers, and it touched on many domains, notably government, education and the workplace. Among other things, it required practitioners of certain professions (such as pharmacy, nursing, engineering) to demonstrate adequate knowledge of French in order to be licensed to practice. For some, this meant passing tests of French proficiency created and administered by the government.

In 1978, an English-speaking gentleman arrived at the office where these tests were administered and presented himself at the front desk, where the receptionist was chatting in French with a co-worker. He asked the receptionist, 'Could you tell me where the French test is?' The receptionist responded in French, 'Pardon?' The man repeated his request in English, 'Could you tell me where the French test is?' The receptionist asked, 'En français?' The man replied, 'I have the right to be addressed in English by the government of Quebec according to Bill 101.' The receptionist turned to her colleague and asked, 'Qu'est-ce qu'il dit?' ('What's he saying?'). In the end, both parties won: the man got his information without having to speak French, and the receptionist was able to show him the right direction without having to speak English.

In this encounter, as in so many others in Quebec (then, and still today), it is possible to see that the struggle between speakers of French and speakers of English is waged not only in the legislature, but also in face-to-face interactions. Indeed, the politics of language permeate not only interactions in the kinds of institutional settings where language is closely and obviously linked to ethnic

158

interests (as in the above example), but also many others which occur regularly in daily life.

The purpose of this chapter is to discuss ways in which the study of code-switching is relevant to the politics of language, by which I mean the ways in which language practices are bound up in the creation, exercise, maintenance or change of relations of power. I am principally concerned here to set out a theoretical framework which situates the study of code-switching within the larger agenda of the study of the politics of language, and which is intended to be useful in framing future research.[2]

I will argue in this chapter that the study of code-switching illuminates language politics only to the extent that it is situated in the broader study of language practices. Code-switching has to be seen as an interactional moment whose significance can only become apparent when linked to other instances of language use. In the first part of the chapter I will develop the theoretical framework which elaborates this view. In this vein, I use code-switching in an extended sense, to refer not only to instances of inter-sentential switching, but also to less structurally integrated instances of language alternation or language choice.

The second part of the chapter focusses on the kinds of questions that can be addressed within that framework, drawing on my own work in Canada.[3] In particular, it will address questions related to: (i) the linguistic resources available to speakers as a consequence both of their own position in the local speech economy and of the nature of the local speech economy as emergent from international networks and social, political and economic relations; and (ii) the ways in which relations of power can be transformed through language practices which draw on those resources.

In this framework language is seen as related to power in two ways. First, it is part of processes of social action and interaction, part of the ways in which people do things, get things, influence others, and so on. Second, language itself thereby becomes a resource which can be more or less valuable, according to the extent that the mastery of ways of using language is tied to the ability to gain access to, and exercise, power.

2 Code-switching, repertoires and resources

Code-switching becomes available as a resource for the exercise of, or resistance to, power by virtue of its place in the repertoires of individual speakers, on the one hand, and of its position with respect to other forms of language practices in circulation, on the other. This view hinges on a notion of code-switching as a means of drawing on symbolic resources and deploying them in order to gain or deny access to other resources, symbolic or material. It builds both on Bourdieu's concepts of symbolic capital and symbolic marketplaces, and Gumperz's concepts of speech economies and verbal repertoires (Bourdieu 1977, 1982; Gumperz 1982).

I will use Bourdieu's concepts in the following way. I take code-switching as a means of calling into play specific forms of linguistic and cultural knowledge, forms which conventionally possess certain kinds of value. That value is linked to the extent to which those forms facilitate access to situations where other kinds of symbolic and material resources are distributed, resources which themselves have value based on the prevailing modes of organisation of social life in the community (and who controls them). Certainly some resources have a concrete, functional basis to their value (like food); but most are related in more indirect ways to the methods people have of calculating honour, or status or prestige. Their value is in any case a function of processes of power and solidarity, that is, on the one hand, the means to mobilise and allocate resources, and, on the other, the ability to mobilise other people in the name of common concerns which are held to override both what the members of a group might have in common with others and any differences which may exist among them. Solidarity can thus be bound up in the development of ties and cultural practices which help members of an elite to maintain their position of power, or in the development of relations and practices which help members of a subordinate group cope with, or resist, their condition of subordination.

Groups which control valued resources (of whatever kind) also control the 'marketplace' (in Bourdieu's terms) in which they are exchanged, the set of social relations in which the value of resources is defined and resources themselves are exchanged. Beyond sheer force, such marketplaces operate through hegemonic practices, through symbolic domination, through convincing participants that the values and modes of operation of the marketplace are immutable and universal. In the terms of the metaphor of power as game with which I began, specific groups set the rules of the game by which resources can be distributed. In other words, it is necessary to display appropriate linguistic and cultural knowledge in order to gain access to the game, and playing it well requires in turn mastery of the kinds of linguistic and cultural knowledge which constitute its rules. Buying into the game means buying into the rules, it means accepting them as routine, as normal, indeed as universal, rather than as conventions set up by dominant groups in order to place themselves in the privileged position of regulating access to the resources they control. Bourdieu has insisted over and over again that it is precisely through appearing not to wield power that dominant groups wield it most effectively (Bourdieu 1982; Gal 1989).

These notions tie into those of Gumperz in a number of ways. First, both Bourdieu and Gumperz have noticed that linguistic and cultural capital are not equally distributed in any given community, despite the fact that all members of the community might share (at least along some dimensions) the same scale of values, that is, they all might agree on the fact that it is the capital (and other resources associated with it) concentrated in the hands of one group that is what is really valuable in life. In Gumperz's terms, forms of language are distributed unequally across a speech community. Individual members have verbal repertoires which draw on part, but rarely all, of the forms in circulation. Further, it is this unequal distribution as well as the way in which unequally distributed resources are deployed which drives the operation of the marketplace, and hence the reproduction of relations of power. Only some members of a population are in a position to decide what will count as appropriate behaviour in situations where resources are distributed and to evaluate performances there; normally, it is the symbolic capital which dominant groups already possess which is the key to participation and success in the situations they control. As Gumperz and others have shown, an inability to bring to bear appropriate conventions of behaviour on key situations in daily life where crucial decisions about one's access to resources are decided (a job interview, an exam., a courtroom trial, etc.) can result in the systematic exclusion of segments of the population from the resources distributed there.

In order to understand the value that code-switching has as a practice, then, it is essential to understand the broader game in which code-switching is merely one set of possible moves. In order to explain code-switching's occurrence, it is equally necessary to grasp the nature of individual repertoires, that is, to understand why it is available as a resource to some and not to others. Similarly, it is necessary to understand how it can be that code-switching as a practice can emerge in specific communities at specific historical moments, and not at others, and how it can either persist or fade away.

Code-switching is thus a form of language practice in which individuals draw on their linguistic resources to accomplish conversational purposes; those resources have value in the terms of the various existing marketplaces. In other terms, those resources constitute the basis of strategies, like code-switching, for playing the game of social life. Language practices are inherently political insofar as they are among the ways individuals have at their disposal of gaining access to the production, distribution and consumption of symbolic and material resources, that is, insofar as language forms part of processes of power.

However, as noted above, linguistic resources are among the symbolic resources which are, generally speaking, not equitably distributed in society. Some people, by virtue of their social position, have access to more- or less-highly valued forms of language, and are more or less able to control the value accorded to linguistic resources in society in general. Equally, to the extent that more than one market is available (or that more than one game can be played), people will have differential access to those games or markets.

Woolard (1985) has pointed out that Bourdieu's notion of marketplace is restrictive in that it assumes a single dominant marketplace. One can argue that Gumperz's notion of speech economy encounters the same conceptual problem. In addition, both suffer from the assumption that marketplaces, or speech economies, are somehow bounded, that it is possible to identify where their limits are. Much recent ethnographic work has pointed to the necessity of rethinking these dimensions of the notions involved.

Woolard's work in Catalonia has addressed the problem of the unified marketplace by showing how different sources of power (economic vs politico-legal) can form the basis of alternative marketplaces, where the different forms of language in circulation (in this case, most relevantly Castilian and Catalan) have different value (Woolard 1985, 1989). My own work in Quebec and Ontario (Heller 1989a, b; Heller 1994; Heller and Lévy 1992a, b) has shown the same kinds of tensions to be operating there, in that marketplaces can splinter and individuals can adopt a variety of strategies in the face of difficult and changing conditions depending on both the resources to which they have access and their individual calculations of strategies which they perceive to be in their best interests. This has notably been the case for the relationship between the historically English-dominated private sector, the new basis of Francophone power in the public sector and Francophones' use of that power-base to gain entry into the private sector. Some individuals find themselves involved simultaneously in social arenas reflecting different 'moments' in this historical transition, such as Franco-Ontarian women married to Anglophone men at a time when Anglophone domination was clear, but who, having raised a family, re-enter the workforce to find that their once-stigmatised French has new value. The new opportunities opened up for them in this way also raise a number of difficult questions, including how to cope with linguistic insecurity constructed through years of subordination and language transfer and how to re-define marital and parental relations in which ethnolinguistic relations of domination no longer so completely overlap gender relations of inequality.

Thus, a number of different scenarios may exist: a community may be dominated by one marketplace, by one game with one set of rules regarding the use and value of the resources circulating there. People have to deal with that situation as well as they can; I will return in the following section to what some possibilities might be. Alternatively, it might be possible to play more than one game at a time; this too will be taken up in the next section. For our purposes now, what is important to recognise is that games are mutable and potentially multiple, as are the nature and value of the resources that are at once at issue there and simultaneously the means of access to further resources.

Empirical work has dealt less successfully with the second problem mentioned, that is, with the impossibility of identifying clear boundaries or limits to the games or markets involved. The most promising leads are emerging through various forms of network analysis, which recognise that social processes emerge from sets of interactional experiences which tie together both people and the conditions of their lives. One dimension of networks is therefore the ties which exist among individuals (as mediated by their participation in social institutions; cf. Milroy 1987; Milroy and Milroy 1992).

Giddens (1979, 1984) and Cicourel (1980) have pointed to other dimensions of networks, which are equally important. Giddens refers to these ties as existing both in space and in time. For him, a central element of social process concerns the ties which exist among events or experiences. Interactions, in his view, have both intended and unintended consequences which affect the lives of participants, as well as the lives of others who may not have been present, across time. Equally, they can best be understood when they are linked to other forms of social interaction which may be concurrent, but geographically removed. To give a simple example, I may receive a telephone call from a colleague at another university requesting a reference for a former student who has applied for a job there. That telephone conversation is tied to past interactions I and my colleagues have had with that candidate as well as to future possibilities that she might actually end up teaching at that university; they in turn, are also undoubtedly linked to interactions which may be occurring simultaneously, for example, exchanges between students and faculty at that university which may inform the hiring committee's ideas about the kind of candidate they want to recruit in order to meet current student needs. They are also linked in broader ways to other interactions and institutionalised processes: how, say, students who are members of minority groups become qualified for and interested in training and subsequent employment in post-secondary institutions. Marcus (1986) and Gal (1989) have pointed to the necessity in particular of understanding the global economic processes in which interactions are embedded: the kind of conversation I have with my colleague, indeed the possibility of having it at all, is bound up in political and economic relations which increasingly tie us to the rest of the world, but in specific, concrete and historically conditioned ways.

In this vein, Cicourel and Giddens have also focussed on how such interactions are shaped by social institutions whose functioning is far beyond the control of any small subset of individuals, and which emerge through a variety of forms of interaction, not merely the face-to-face. The complex relations we build through family, school, law, medicine and the like occur also through text as well as talk, through visual as well as verbal means, and so on.

Perhaps most importantly, Giddens and Cicourel have also drawn attention to the ways in which social processes at once shape, and are shaped by, social interaction. Marketplaces, games, speech economies may exist, and act, in Giddens's terms, as constraints on the possibilities open to any given individual; but they are also products of interaction. Individuals can use the resources they have available to them strategically, to play the game, but more importantly, to use the rules, and, indeed, even to change them. Social process is thus both constraint and possibility, obstacle and opportunity.

The conceptual and methodological challenge posed by such arguments is to be able to identify the linkages which we think exist, and beyond that, to discover the significance of the social processes which are constituted there. If we want to understand how code-switching is linked to relations of power, it is therefore not enough to examine instances of code-switching in specific interactions. It becomes necessary to discover both what the consequences (intended and unintended) of code-switching might be for individuals, and also how code-switching is tied to all the interactions which occur where code-switching does not.

Yet herein lies precisely the reason why code-switching is so compelling as a means of discussing power. For the analyst, it acts as a flag, it signals that here, in this interaction, people are drawing on their linguistic resources in some way which will have an effect both on them and on others. They are using language to take action in a complex world, to react to their experience and to create it anew. (For further discussion, see Heller 1992.)

3 Code-switching and the politics of language use

The framework outlined above makes it possible to use the study of code-switching in certain specific ways in order to shed light on how language use is bound up in the creation, maintenance or change of relations of power. In this section, I will briefly outline what some relevant questions might be, and how some recent work addresses them. Code-switching is clearly a means of drawing on a variety of linguistic resources in the course of a single interaction. The questions it raises are linked both to what speakers are trying to do through code-switching and to what makes it possible to attempt what they are attempting.

In this section, I want to focus both on different ways of dominating and on different ways of coping with conditions of subordination, principally by examining individual and collective strategies which may involve moves towards unified, or, on the contrary, multiple alternative marketplaces. While I will not, in the space available, be able to cover all possible logical or ethnographically demonstrated combinations, I do want to set up a framework which might help us situate current research and guide us in specific directions for further work. My goal, then, is the more modest one of pointing to some ways in which the study of code-switching can form part of a broader understanding of the politics of language use.

One framework that I find useful is drawn from the work of Barth (1969). While Barth did not specifically discuss language practices, his work on the relationship between ethnic boundaries and material and symbolic resources is illuminating. There are three sets of concepts that may be useful in understanding how language can play a role in the unfolding of that relationship.

First, Barth pointed out that ethnic relations depend on a differential distribution of access to and control over resources, or what he termed 'ecological niches'. That distribution, however, can vary along two dimensions, namely, it may be complementary (groups occupy different niches) or competitive (groups vie for control over the same niche), and it may be equal or unequal (the resources controlled and the ability to control them may be differentially valued or differentially effective).

One category of ethnic relations includes, then, contact between groups each of which controls different, complementary, but equally valued resources. However, different and unequal economic relations are more commonly represented in the literature. Gal (1979), McDonald (1990) and Dorian (1981) all provide examples of marginal groups (Hungarians, Bretons, Gaelic-speaking Scots) engaged in farming and/or fishing who come into contact with other, more powerful groups (speakers of German, French and English, respectively) as the latter expand their industrial activities into (from their perspective) more remote areas.

Competitive and equal relations characterise to a certain extent the relationship between the French and the Flemish in Belgium, or the French and the English in Canada, as illustrated, for example, by Quebec companies in which English-speakers retain power due to their accumulated knowledge and current links to

North America, while Francophones seek to compete on the same terrain but from the different power-base of recent political mobilisation through the public sector (Heller 1989a).

Finally, competitive and unequal relations obtain between Francophones and Anglophones elsewhere in Canada, or between the Welsh- and English-speaking urbanised middle classes of Wales (cf. Williams 1987). While groups compete for the same resources of industrialised, capitalist society, they usually do not do so from an equal position of strength.

Second, Barth discussed the ways in which processes of domination are tied to stability or change in ecological niches. Under conditions of stability, the issue becomes one of how dominant groups maintain their position of power, and of how subordinated groups, and individual members of those groups, cope with those conditions of subordination. Under conditions of ecological change, however, the issue becomes how individuals and groups cope with conditions of change beyond their control, or how they set off conditions of change themselves. It is also possible to take another angle on this set of problems, and ask what it is that makes for conditions of stability or change.

Third, Barth focussed more narrowly on the strategies disadvantaged social actors adopt, either individually or collectively. In particular, attention centred on instances in which members of one group possess resources of low value, or no longer have access to any resources at all (say, due to some radical ecological imbalance). These strategies can be seen as falling into two broad categories: what the members of that group do when they decide that their best bet is to go after the resources of another group, which would correspond to a collective mobilisation with the goal of creating an alternative marketplace, and what they do when they decide that their best bet is to develop an alternative resource base of their own (but which might include a role as brokers). In either case, strategies can be individual or collective: the first category would include individual assimilation or collective incorporation, or potentially individual takeovers and redefinitions of positions of power within the target group as well as collective mobilisation for similar takeovers; while the second would comprise individual or collective brokerage roles, as well as individual pioneering or collective mobilisation for the creation of alternative marketplaces.

In any of these cases, it is clear that language represents one set of potentially valuable resources, specifically insofar as it is bound up with processes of getting access to, and controlling production of, other valuable material and symbolic resources. Code-switching is one way in which it is possible to manipulate valuable linguistic resources, and indeed to manipulate the definition of their value.

That is, in order for code-switching to have any meaning at all, it must draw on resources which are somewhere separate, either in the lives of individuals or in their distribution in a network of individuals who are otherwise linked. In other words, there has to be some kind of separation somewhere in the various kinds of linkages explored above, whether these are links between people or events, across time or space. Here I am referring to the meaning of code-switching as a communicative practice, and not to the meaning of specific switches.

4 Language practices, code-switching and strategies for power and solidarity

In what follows, I will examine some of the strategies outlined above, in order to provide some examples of the complex interaction between the constraints imposed by social structure and human agency, in terms of the discussion in section 2. In particular, I will focus on the way in which language practices, including code-switching, can become salient means for achieving social, economic and political goals.[4]

I will focus here on the relations of power between Francophones and Anglophones in Canada. The history of these relations is such that it is possible to find examples of the ways in which language played a role in the exercise of domination, and in coping with, or resistance to, that domination on the part of members of the subordinate group, including strategies of assimilation, brokerage and collective mobilisation. Central dynamics have included the increasing integration of Francophones into national and international networks and markets, and a playing-off of political power against power emergent in the economic realm. In this respect, over the course of time, one can see elements of what I described earlier as being cases of unequal and complementary as well as of unequal and competitive relations. One can even see glimmerings of relations which might be described as equal and competitive.

For much of the course of English–French relations, at least until the Francophone mobilisation beginning in the 1960s, in day-to-day terms, domination was exercised through the imposition of British social and cultural practices in sectors of contact between groups, most notably through the imposition of English as the language of public and inter-group private communication. This linguistic domination worked insofar as members of other groups were unable ever to learn to speak English well enough to truly master the game or to get themselves taken seriously as English-speakers (in Bourdieu's terms, to produce the legitimate discourse, or to become legitimate speakers). It also rested on the use of bilingual brokers (generally native speakers of French) who could mediate between Anglophone bosses, for example, and their Francophone workers. It was here, in such circumstances, that one found code-switching practices, which took their significance precisely from their location in the relations of power between Francophones and Anglophones. (Little is known about the practices of the old Francophone elite, which played an important brokerage role as well.)

For most members of subordinate groups, however, the issue became one of coping with conditions of subordination. Until Francophones became increasingly integrated into national markets as a result of industrialisation and other economic shifts after the Second World War, French was principally important in locally circumscribed arenas where certain kinds of resources were circulated, resources which were only valued by the minority and often because they were resources which helped individuals cope with the conditions of their lives. They included, and to this day for Francophones who remain locked in certain subordinate economic niches continue to include, the products of subsistence practices, but also symbolic resources such as emotional support.

We saw this clearly in discussions with some Francophone women in northern Ontario, women who came from families which were part of the industrial workforce and/or engaged in lumbering or (mainly subsistence) farming, and structurally excluded from avenues of social mobility. English in this milieu is clearly a path to social mobility; indeed, social mobility is next to impossible without it. As part of a strategy of upward mobility, these women had in fact married Anglophones. At the same time, French is the language of home and of friendship. Marie, for example, is a Francophone woman married to an Anglophone and living in Sudbury, a town in northern Ontario with a Francophone population of about 30 per cent, most of them working-class. She values English and uses it extensively. However, she, along with many others in her situation, has a strong support network of female kin and friends with whom she speaks French or, more accurately, what some call 'bilingue' and others, including Marie, call 'mélangé' ['mixed'], that is, an English–French code-switching variety. These are the people she turns to when she needs to talk about marital problems or problems with the children (problems which often take on ethnic as well as purely interpersonal dimensions). For example, Marie says, 'Quand on se rencontre on va parler puis ça vient toujours sur ce sujet-là, tu sais, les hommes (rires), et puis on pense pas mal toutes pareil comme tu sais' ['When we meet we'll talk and it always comes to that subject, you know, men (laughter), and we all think pretty much the same like you know']. Later, she says, about these same conversations with her female friends, 'Comme je te dis on va de une à l'autre tu sais . . . puis je te dis c'est bien mélangé . . . ça vient naturel, on sonne pas tellement intelligent, mais en tout cas' ('like I'm telling you we go from one to the other you know . . . and I tell you it's really mixed . . . it comes naturally, we don't sound so bright, but anyway']. In this case, the practice of code-switching among Marie and her friends has to be read as a means by which subordinate Francophones make sense of their position of powerlessness both as Francophones and as women. Through these practices they are able to create and retain vital support networks which enable them to survive the consequences of otherwise playing the game according to the rules set by Anglophones.

In other cases, some individual members of subordinate groups do attempt assimilation, for example through intermarriage, but in any case certainly through language learning. Nadine is a Francophone woman who was brought up in monolingual towns of southern Ontario. She still understands but no longer speaks French, and passes for an Anglophone. Louis, on the other hand, is a Francophone living in Montreal, who had managed to obtain a low management position in a large national brewery owned and operated by an Anglophone family. For most of his career he had to work in English, but he never mastered English well enough to pass as an Anglophone, and never rose very high in the organisation (although he did carve out an important niche for himself as a broker between the Anglophone monolingual bosses and the Francophone monolingual factory workers). In these cases, code-switching may be part of a process of eventually successful assimilation (seen at the level of individuals as a process of language learning or collectively as one of language shift), or alternatively it may be part of a process of assimilation blocked by strong power relations in which code-switching functions to mediate between unequal groups. Louis's inexpert English, for example, marks him as someone who has lived all his life on the edge of both groups, without being able to gain the access to Anglophone networks with which mastery of English is associated.

Finally, groups may react to their conditions of subordination by mobilising, either to take over the dominant group's resources, or to create alternative markets of their own. Native groups in Canada, for example, are currently debating which of these strategies to adopt: some argue that it is best to return to the land, to re-invest in the value of traditional subsistence practices and ways of life. Others argue that it is too late, that the aboriginal population is already too integrated into national and international networks to withdraw, and that it is therefore better to seek exclusive control of some of those resources in that unified marketplace, and hence some measure of possibility of defining the rules of the game to their own advantage. Francophone mobilisation in Canada has certainly taken that route: the goal is to gain access to global networks and globally valued economic resources, but without having to become Anglophones to do so. In these cases, code-switching may be a means of re-defining conventions of language choice as part of a process of re-defining relations of power. In the late 1970s in Quebec, Anglophone domination of public life was exercised in part through the prevailing convention of using English in public encounters. Francophones wishing to contest those relations of power could do so by contesting conventions of language choice. The more radical resisters made radical choices, insisting on unilingual French in place of unilingual English. Others attenuated their strategy through code-switching practices which allowed for subtler negotiations towards the same end.

More attention has been given in the literature to strategies of domination, resistance and mobilisation than to strategies adopted by formerly dominant groups in the face of successful mobilisation. Nonetheless, one can expect a number of different strategies to emerge. A recent article in a Canadian news-magazine gave a revealing survey of Anglophone responses to Francophone mobilisation in Quebec (Tombs 1991). These responses include: (i) emigration: rather than learning French in order to cope with the new conditions of the marketplace, some Anglophones take their linguistic capital to a market where it retains its value; (ii) promotion of national bilingualism: by preserving a concept of a unified bilingual marketplace, English retains its value through its link to the rest of Canada, while not claiming pre-eminence over French; (iii) accommodation: acceptance of a de-valued status for English and of an augmented value for formerly stigmatised French; (iv) assimilation: rejection of any further use for English; (v) promotion of Anglophone rights: acceptance of a re-defined marketplace as limited to Quebec, but development of an Anglophone niche within that market; and (vi) development of a niche as bilingual brokers between monolingual Francophones in Quebec and monolingual Anglophones in the rest of North America.

Depending on the strategy adopted, code-switching may or may not make sense or be effective. One would imagine that those who leave, or, on the contrary, stay but in order to vigorously promote Anglophone rights, would be the most likely to adopt monolingual language practices. Those who advocate accommodation would probably speak French to Francophones, but would be likely to code-switch among themselves, as presumably would brokers. Those who advocate national bilingualism might adopt code-switching practices in a wide variety of situations. Depending on one's social position, it may or may not be possible to adopt any one of these strategies, with the mastery of specific kinds of linguistic resources that each entails. Those who have had access to French (through intermarriage, education, work opportunities, etc.) might be less likely to move; it certainly strikes me as no coincidence that the example of brokerage cited by Tombs concerned a man of Irish origin, since the Irish and the French have historically had close (although sometimes conflictive) relations through shared class background and shared religion (and possibly shared interests in symbolic opposition to people of English origin).

The preceding examples also illustrate the methodological importance of seeing code-switching as an interactional moment with links in both time and space to other forms of social interaction, and with consequences for social actors. Yet it is equally important to grasp the significance of the nature of the interaction, for not all interactions have equal weight. As Gumperz (1982) and others have pointed out, the interactions which take place in the important social institutions of our society carry more weight than others.

Thus what code-switching does is to flag to the analyst a moment, a locale, a piece of social process where somehow at least two sets of symbolic and material resources are at issue for the participants. It is as a result a point of entry into understanding the nature and significance of those resources for the different groups of people involved in their production, allocation and consumption, and hence into the nature of the relationship among those groups. It is one way, among others, for people to draw on their linguistic resources to create and deal with the relations of power which frame their lives.

5 Conclusion

In this chapter I have tried to set out a framework for exploring ways in which language practices are bound up in relations of power. I have argued in particular that it is difficult to understand the significance of any given language practice, such as code-switching, without grasping its relationship to other language practices in individual repertoires and in collective speech economies. More importantly, it is essential to link those practices to the ideologies which legitimate the unequal distribution of resources and the value accorded them, and to the real-world consequences they have for people's lives. In particular, it is possible to see in language practices the tension between power and solidarity, and hence ways in which power is maintained or may be successfully resisted or overturned.

In attempting to understand such important processes through an analysis of code-switching, we have in fact had to call into question the distinctions we were making between 'micro' levels of social interaction and 'macro' levels of social processes. If we can use code-switching to understand processes like power and solidarity, it is because code-switching shows us how specific interactions are mediated through social institutions and linked across time and space to other interactions, through their intended and unintended consequences. If we translate the language of 'macro' and 'micro' into the language of constraint and possibility, or, to use Giddens's terms, 'structure' and 'agency', then we can see both how the linguistic resources at issue in any given interaction flow from a particular (and often institutionalised) arrangement of such resources and the way in which individuals are positioned to exploit them, and how the exploitation of those resources in particular ways has consequences for the possibilities which open up in front of social actors (present or absent).

Such a view has particular methodological implications. If one takes as one's point of departure an attempt to understand language as political, then there are at least two ways into the problem. One is to chart out the speech economy and individual repertoires, the institutions and networks and the links between inter-actions, which characterise daily life in whatever locale one has chosen to focus on. In this approach, one discovers the extent to which language varieties are sepa-rated, or, on the contrary, overlap in the ways which lead to code-switching. One can then explain that, in terms of the strategies adopted for gaining or maintain-ing access to resources and of the conditions which render certain strategies feasible or sensible for different people.

A second approach is to take specific language practices and the patterns of their occurrence as a signal that some question of unequal distribution of resources, some form of the process that is the development and exercise of (or resistance to) power, is relevant here, at this moment, in this situation. One can then follow the variety of paths which stem from that interaction: its links to other interactions of similar type, to other interactions participants have elsewhere and in the future, to interactions involving others but which have consequences for these participants or for the shape of this kind of interaction, and so on.

The systematic use of both these approaches is necessary in order to accumulate the kind of ethnographic material on which theory-building relies. Through such ethnographic studies it is possible to understand on the one hand the conditions which allow certain kinds of strategies, and hence certain kinds of language practices, to emerge, and, on the other, the ways in which certain kinds of prac-tices lead to specific consequences in terms of relations of power among groups and members of groups.

Notes

1 From the song 'Love Played a Game' (Bryant, Peebles and Hodges); A. Peebles, 'I'm Gonna Tear Your Playhouse Down', 1985 (Los Angeles, Cream/Hi Records, Inc.).

2 While the paper is devoted to the politics of language use in everyday life, I also intend it to be applicable to the more institutionalised forms that such issues can take, in the form of language policy. In using the term 'language policy' I mean the ways in which governments or para-governmental organisations seek to contribute to the politics of language through conventionalised and institutionalised language practices or statements of preference regarding those practices. Language policies are therefore particular manifestations of the politics of language.

3 Excellent studies have, of course, been carried out in Europe and elsewhere. See, for example, Gal 1979, 1987; Hewitt 1989; McDonald 1990; Rampton 1991; Williams 1987; Mérida and Prudent 1984; Lafont 1977; and Woolard 1985, 1989. The focus on Canada is motivated by my own experience and knowledge. The data I draw on are from research projects funded by the Government of Quebec and the Social Sciences and Humanities Research Council of Canada, whose support I gratefully acknowledge. I am also grateful to the other authors in this volume, and especially to Lesley Milroy, for insightful comments on an earlier version of this paper.

4 Much of this discussion draws on Heller 1982, 1989a, 1992, 1994 and Heller and Lévy 1992a, b.

Bibliography

Barth, F. (1969) ed., *Ethnic groups and boundaries*. Boston: Little, Brown.

Bourdieu, P. (1977) L'économie des échanges linguistiques. *Langue Française*, 34: 17–34.

(1982) *Ce que parler veut dire*. Paris: Fayard.

Cicourel, A. (1980) Three models of discourse analysis: the role of social structure. *Discourse Process*, 3: 101–32.

Dorian, N. C. (1981) *Language death: the life cycle of a Scottish Gaelic dialect*. Philadelphia: University of Pennsylvania Press.

Gal, S. (1979) *Language shift: social determinants of linguistic change in bilingual Austria*. New York: Academic Press.

(1987) Code-switching and consciousness on the European periphery. *American Ethnologist*, 14 (4): 637–53.

(1989) Language and political economy. *Annual Review of Anthropology*, 18: 345–67.

Giddens, A. (1979) *Central problems in social theory*. Berkeley: University of California Press.

(1984) *The constitution of society*. Cambridge: Polity Press.

Gumperz, J. J. (1982) *Discourse strategies*. Cambridge University Press.

Heller, M. (1982) Negotiations of language choice in Montreal. In J. Gumperz ed., *Language and social identity*. Cambridge and New York: Cambridge University Press, 108–18.

(1989a) Aspects sociolinguistiques de la francisation d'une entreprise privée. *Sociologie et Sociétés* 21 (2): 115–28.

(1989b) Communicative resources and local configurations: an exploration of language contact processes. *Multilingua*, 8 (4): 357–96.

(1992) The politics of codeswitching and language choice. *Journal of Multilingual and Multicultural Development*, 13 (1, 2): 123–42.

(1994) *Crosswords: language, education and ethnicity in French Ontario*. Berlin: Mouton de Gruyter.

Heller, M. and Lévy, L. (1992a) Mixed marriages: life on the linguistic frontier. *Multilingua*, 11 (1): 11–43.

(1992b) La femme franco-ontarienne en situation de mariage mixte: féminité et ethnicité. *Recherches Féministes*, 5 (1): 59–82.

Hewitt, R. (1989) Creole in the classroom: political grammars and educational vocabularies. In R. Grillo ed., *Social anthropology and the politics of language*. London: Routledge, 126–44.

Lafont, R. (1977) A propos de l'enquête sur la diglossie: l'intercesseur de la norme. *Lengas*, 1: 31–9.

Marcus, G. (1986) Contemporary problems of ethnography in the modern world system. In J. Clifford and G. Marcus eds., *Writing culture*. Berkeley and Los Angeles: University of California Press, 165–93.

McDonald, M. (1990) *We are not French*. London: Routledge.

Mérida, G.-J. and Prudent, L.-F. (1984) . . . an langaj kréyol dimi panaché . . . : interlecte et dynamique conversationnelle. *Langages*, 74: 31–46.

Milroy, L. (1987) *Language and social networks* (2nd edn). Oxford: Basil Blackwell.

Milroy, L. and Milroy, J. (1992) Social network and social class: towards an integrated sociolinguistic model. *Language in Society*, 21 (1): 1–26.

Rampton, M. B. H. (1991) Interracial Panjabi in a British adolescent peer group. *Language in Society*, 20 (3): 391–422.

Tombs, G. (1991) Entre l'exaspération et l'exode. *L'Actualité*, 15 November 1991, 49–54.

Widmer, J. (1989) Statut des langues dans une administration plurilingue. In B. Py and R. Jeanneret eds., *Minorisation linguistique et interactions. Actes du symposium de Neuchâtel, Septembre 1987*. Geneva: Droz, 115–21.

Williams, G. (1987) Bilingualism, class dialect and social reproduction. *International Journal of the Sociology of Language*, 66: 85–98.

Woolard, K. (1985) Language variation and cultural hegemony: toward an integration of sociolinguistic and social theory. *American Ethnologist*, 12: 738–48.

(1989) *Double talk: bilingualism and the politics of ethnicity in Catalonia*. Stanford University Press.

3

GRAMMATICAL CONSTRAINTS IN CODE-SWITCHING

9 CODE-SWITCHING AND GRAMMATICAL THEORY

Pieter Muysken

In the last fifteen years, a large number of studies have appeared in which specific cases of intra-sentential code-switching were analysed from a grammatical perspective, involving a variety of language pairs, social settings and speaker types. It was found that code-switching is a quite normal and widespread form of bilingual interaction, requiring a great deal of bilingual competence. In individual cases, intra-sentential code-switching is not distributed randomly in the sentence, but rather it occurs at specific points.

Where much less agreement was reached is with respect to general properties of the process. Various 'constraints' and 'models' regulating intra-sentential code-switching (the type most interesting from the grammatical perspective) have been proposed and tested, with the result that some cases appear to fall under one constraint, and others under another. This is by itself unsatisfactory. We do not know in any systematic way how different the models proposed are, neither intrinsically nor in their predictions. It should be mentioned at this point that many of the studies do not make the constraints or models very explicit, limiting themselves to descriptive statements. Therefore, an account is needed of the grammatical notions relevant to code-switching. These notions can then be used both to characterise specific instances of intra-sentential switching and to relate the various proposals in the literature to each other.

I will organise this chapter around five main questions:

(i) to what extent is code-switching seen as alternational and symmetrical (and hence involving properties of both languages involved) or insertional (and hence primarily governed by features of one dominant language)?

(ii) to what extent are restrictions on the code-switching process seen as absolute or relative?

(iii) to what extent is the relevant syntactic representation of the switch point seen as involving syntactic dependency?

(iv) to what extent are sentential and lexical phenomena seen in the same perspective?

(v) to what extent does equivalence between patterns or elements of the languages involved play a role, and how should this equivalence be characterised?

Before treating these five questions one by one, it is important to discuss further the relation between grammatical theory and code-switching. There are at least two connections between the two. First, I think this type of research is crucial for linguistics as a scientific discipline. What makes code-switching so special that it warrants relatively complex and time-consuming, hence costly, research is the following: one of the crucial questions in modern linguistics is the division of labour between the lexicon and the grammar of a language. To what extent do we rely on properties of individual words, when we produce and comprehend utterances, and to what extent on general rules of the language we speak? Related to this question – and for many researchers the same question phrased differently – is the following: can we reduce the differences between languages to lexical differences? If so, all that is specific about a language is its lexicon, and the lexicon plays a very major role in sentence production and comprehension. In the latter case, we should note, there *are* no rules specific to the language we speak, independent of lexical items. This complicated cluster of questions has produced much research and a so far inconclusive debate in the linguistic literature. I think the study of code-switching and language contact can uniquely contribute to elucidating and perhaps ultimately resolving these issues. When sentences are built up with items drawn from two lexicons, we can see to what extent the sentence patterns derive from the interaction between these two lexicons.

Second, the sociolinguistic study of code-switching cannot proceed without a solid, theoretically based 'structural analysis'. To understand which cases are of the same type, and which are different, to see which patterns are exceptional or marked and which are not, to be able to do quantitative research, for all this we need to know what the structural features of the patterns are. The present chapter discusses some of the descriptive tools that can be used for the analysis.

Clearly we should aim for universal explanations when looking for grammatical constraints. Much recent research into code-switching constraints is characterised by an attempt to relate two observations: (a) in different contact situations different switch patterns are found; (b) the differences are related, at least in part, to typological characteristics of the languages involved.

We can imagine two approaches to account for this.

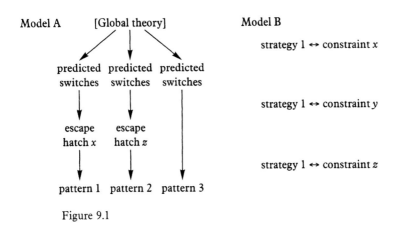

Figure 9.1

(A) A model that believes there is a general set of constraints on code-switching, constituted, for example, by structural equivalence (Poplack 1980, this volume), or government (DiSciullo, Muysken and Singh 1986), or a matrix language/ embedded language asymmetry (Myers-Scotton 1993b, this volume). In model A, the assumption is that the global theory makes a more limited set of switch sites available in specific instances than would be desirable. In those cases, escape hatches are needed, making additional switch sites possible.

(B) In model B, implicit in at least some of the recent work by Poplack and associates, different switching strategies occur – flagging, constituent insertion, etc. – governed by constraints specific to those strategies. There is no specific relation between linguistic properties of the languages involved and the choice of the strategy. What unifies both approaches is that both end up with a series of different language-mixing patterns or strategies.

In my view, it is methodologically desirable to aim for approach A, for three reasons. First, A makes a unified account possible. Second, in B it is not clear why in a given situation one strategy is preferred over another. Third, in the absence of a global theory, the relation between specific strategies and constraints remains unclear.

Model B has advantages over A if it turns out that the choice of a specific switching or mixing pattern is not motivated by structural considerations, and a combination of both models is called for if it is only partially motivated by structural considerations.

Keeping these observations in mind, we will now consider the five principal issues in the grammatical analysis of code-switching.

1 Is code-switching alternational or insertional?

Other authors might come up with a different general picture, but one could say that there are two dominant approaches to intra-sentential code-switching: those in terms of the *alternation* of the languages involved in the switch, and those in terms of a single-language matrix structure into which *insertion* of a constituent from another language takes place. Under this latter view we can conceive of the process of code-switching as something akin to borrowing: the insertion of an alien lexical or phrasal category into a given structure. The difference would simply be the size and type of element inserted, e.g. noun in borrowing vs noun phrase in code-switching.

It is clear there is alternation between codes in, for example, inter-sentential switching, and insertion with single borrowed elements. The question is whether we can establish objectively which process we are dealing with in the other cases. Some criteria:

(i) when several constituents in a row are switched, which together do *not* form a constituent, alternation is more likely – otherwise we would have to assume multiple contiguous insertions; conversely, when the switched elements are all single, well-defined constituents, e.g. noun phrases or prepositional phrases, insertion is a plausible option.

(ii) when the switched element is at the periphery of an utterance, alternation is a clear possibility; conversely, when the switched string is preceded *and* followed by material from the other language, insertion may be more plausible, particularly if the surrounding material is grammatically linked in some kind of structure.

(iii) longer stretches of other-language material are more likely to be alternations.

The modality of these criteria makes it clear that there will be many undecidable cases. Is a subject in language A followed by a verb phrase in language B a case of alternation, of subject insertion, or of verb phrase insertion? For many language pairs the order of subject and verb phrase will be identical, so the clause as a whole may not belong to one language.

Consider a few examples:

(1)   Yo anduve *in a state of shock* pa dos días.

'I walked in a state of shock for two days.' (Pfaff 1979: 297)

Here the temporal expression *pa dos días* is clearly related to the verb *anduve*. Similarly:

(2)   es una *little box* asina y ya viene . . .

       [It is a little box like this and it comes already . . .] (Lance 1975: 145)

Here the post-nominal determiner *asina* is clearly related to the article *una*.

However, there is not always such a relation. A few cases to illustrate this include:

(3)   [A] Right to 104th Street [B] *donde tenía una casa* [C] which were furnished rooms.

       [Right to 104th Street where I had a house which were furnished rooms.] (Sankoff and Poplack 1981: 35)

Here the Spanish fragment (B) modifies *Street* in (A) and the second English stretch (C) modifies *casa* ('house') in (B). Clearly the English fragments (A) and (C) are not syntactically related. Similarly:

(4)   [A] Why make Carol *sentarse atras [B] pa'que* everybody has to move [C] *pa'que se salga.*

       [Why make Carol sit at the back so that everybody has to move so that she can get out.] (Poplack 1980: 589)

Here the sentence fragment (B) is a complement to (A), and (C) is a complement to (B). Notice that the first Spanish fragment here contains both a verb phrase, *sentarse atras*, and purposive complementiser, *pa'que*. Neither between the English fragments nor between the Spanish ones is there a particular grammatical relation. A final example:

(5)   [A] *Se me hace que* [B] I have to respect her [C] *porque 'ta* . . . older.

       [It appears to me that I have to respect her because [she] is . . . older.]

       (Lance 1975: 143)

Again, (B) is a complement to (A), and (C) modifies (B). Notice that *porque 'ta* (because [she] is) does not form a unique constituent, excluding other elements – in this case 'older'.

   It is clear that this type of data cannot be handled very well in a model which takes insertion into a matrix and a dependency relation between matrix and inserted material as its primes. Rather, the type of data has led to the idea that order equivalence across the switch point is what constrains code-mixing here.

1.1 Determining the base-language

In those cases where it is reasonable to assume that there is a base-language (also termed: matrix language) in a code-switched sentence, as in insertion models (e.g. Myers-Scotton 1993b, this volume), how do we determine which one it is? The answer to this question is in part empirical, in part theoretical in nature.

A discourse-oriented way of determining the base-language is: the language of the conversation. A statistical answer would be: the language in which most words or morphemes are uttered. A psycholinguistic answer could be: the language in which the speaker is most proficient. None of these answers is particularly satisfactory from the point of view of grammatical analysis. From that perspective, two types of answers have been given. In a model that attaches great importance to a parsing procedure from left to right, the first word or set of words in the sentence determines the base-language (such a model is reported on in Joshi 1985), triggering a set of analytic rules. Whatever insights this yields, care should be taken that switched left-peripheral interjections, exclamatives or adverbial adjuncts are not taken as the first element. These elements do not in any way determine the structure of the rest of the sentence.

In a structurally oriented model, some element or set of elements determines the base-language: often the main verb, which is the semantic kernel of the sentence, assigning the different semantic roles and determining the state or event expressed by the clause, is taken to determine the base-language. Plausible though adoption of the main verb as determining the base-language may be, in many languages there is a strategy to incorporate alien verbs, e.g. through agglutinative prefixes, as in Swahili, or through an auxiliary verb such as 'do', as in Hindi. In these cases, taking that borrowed verb as determining the base-language is clearly not correct. In the Matrix Language Frame model proposed by Myers-Scotton, the grammatical morphemes have to be from the base-language.

In the perspective of the government model (DiSciullo *et al.* 1986; see section 3), there need not be a single base or matrix language for the clause. Still, there is a notion of base or matrix present in that model: each governing element (e.g. verb, preposition, auxiliary) creates a matrix structure. If the chain of government were unbroken, the highest element in the tree would determine the language for the whole tree; this would often be the inflection on the finite verb, as in the theory proposed by Klavans (1985) and taken up by Treffers-Daller (1991). In subordinate clauses, this would be the complementiser.

1.2 Function and content morphemes

In much of the literature on code-switching, and particularly in insertional models, the distinction between function and content morphemes plays an important role (Joshi 1985; Myers-Scotton, this volume). There is no single valid criterion for distinguishing these two classes: rather, different sub-classes can be distinguished on the basis of at least four different criteria. A first one is 'open' versus 'closed' class. Nouns and verbs typically belong to open classes, pronouns typically to closed ones. Adjectives in many languages form an open class, but in some a small closed one. There is often only a limited number of co-ordinating conjunctions and adpositions in a language, but equally often elements could still be added to these categories.

A more precise criterion would therefore be whether a given closed class is *paradigmatically* organised, i.e., whether the elements in it are defined in opposition to each other (present vs past, singular vs plural, definite vs indefinite etc.). Pronoun and tense systems particularly tend to be tightly organised paradigmatically.

A third criterion may be *role in structuring the clause*. Some elements, such as subordinating conjunctions and agreement and tense markers, play a central role in the clause; others, such as diminutive markers and degree adverbs, a more peripheral role.

Finally, an important distinction is that between *bound* and *free* morphemes. In many, but not all, languages – e.g. the Northwest Coast Amerindian languages form an exception – the bound morphemes are function elements.

Given these different criteria different sub-classes can be distinguished in the categorial systems of various languages, in a way that needs to be made more precise. The same holds for the role these sub-classes play in theories of switching. The Matrix Language Frame model rests on the assumption that code-switched sentences have one base-language, or matrix language. This matrix language determines the order of the elements in mixed constituents and provides the 'system morphemes' (function morphemes) in such constituents.

2 Absolute or relative restrictions

Many models propose principles ruling out certain types of switch, but what is the nature of the predictions made? Poplack (1980), working in the variationist framework, proposes general constraints which are supposed to hold for the majority of cases. DiSciullo *et al.* (1986) make absolute, all-or-nothing, claims. In more recent work exploring the implications of the theory of government for code-switching, however – e.g. Treffers-Daller (1991) – a probabilistic perspective is taken. Rather than just trying to predict which switches are disallowed, an attempt is made to establish which kinds of switches are the more frequent ones. Sankoff and Poplack (1981) explored this direction as well, but interpreted the results as showing that there were no fundamental differences in probability for any switch site, and did not return to it in later work. Myers-Scotton (1993a) proposes to account for the unmarked cases of code-switching, allowing the socially marked cases to fail the predictions made.

At the present stage my own bent is towards probabilitistic statements. Absolute constraints, that could be invalidated by as few as one counterexample, are less appropriate for performance data, particularly data which arise from quite complex factors, not all of which are always under control. Just making a general statement about which type of switch is not likely to occur, as in the Poplack (1980) paper, misses the point that some types of switches are less frequent than others, within a given corpus.

Statements in terms of markedness as a yes/no factor, as in the work of Myers-Scotton (this volume, and the references cited there), seem somewhat unsatisfactory to me, for three reasons: (i) it is hard to argue for the (un)markedness of any single instance of switching; (ii) so far there is little indication that the patterns of code-switching in communities where code-switching is not a discourse mode are highly unusual; (iii) suppose the restrictions on code-switching are in part due to factors determined by our grammatical competence. Then we should look to what extent rules of our grammar are violated in stylistically marked registers of the monolingual speech mode. The answer is: not a great deal. There are specific stylistically marked syntactical patterns, but they do not depart from our grammar as a whole in significant ways. Hence there is no immediate reason to expect socially marked code-switching to do so.

I want to stress here that it is as important to consider the non-occurring switches as the ones that do occur. In which places in the sentence do we find that speakers refrain from switching? From the perspective of structural analysis these would correspond to the starred examples in a Chomskyan article, and from that of Labovian sociolinguistics, to the non-application cases. Nortier (1990: 124–40), for instance, shows that in her corpus there are switches at every conceivable juncture in the sentence (although not always equally frequently), but this has not been demonstrated for other cases of switching.

A very complicated issue concerns the relation between qualitative structural and quantitative distributional analysis. Since intuitions about code-switching are not always reliable (and we do not know when they are and when they are not), and psycholinguistic experimental techniques to study grammatical factors in code-switching are not yet well developed, we have to work with natural speech data. Since we do not know how the grammar and the lexicon interact with other psychological faculties to produce actual speech, we clearly cannot ignore phenomena such as frequency of occurrence and regularity. This would lead us to take the frequent types of switches as the main body of evidence, and to consider the infrequent ones as possibly fluke phenomena, performance errors and the like (*pace* the need to consider non-occurring switches).

Two (possibly related) complications arise, however. First, frequency may result from the conventionalisation of a certain type of switch, rather than from a crucial grammatical factor. Second, we do not yet know enough about the relation between frequency distributions of specific grammatical patterns in monolingual speech data and properties of the grammar to handle frequency in bilingual data with any assurance.

3 Head/dependent relations: the syntactic government model

In some perspectives on code-switching the relation between a lexical element and its syntactic environment plays an important role, e.g. Bentahila and Davies (1983) and DiSciullo *et al.* (1986). The idea behind these perspectives is that a lexical item will often require specific other elements in its environment, and this requirement may be language-specific and can be formulated in terms of the head–complement relations of X-bar theory.

The traditional assumption behind X-bar theory is that syntactic constituents are endocentric, i.e., that their properties derive from those of their head. Thus a noun phrase inherits many of its features from the head noun; the internal constituency of a verb phrase in terms of number of objects, etc., derives from the properties of the verb. Another way of saying this is that the head noun or head verb project their features in the phrase, but not beyond it. The central notions involved here are exploited in the code-switching literature under the government constraint: not only the categorial and semantic features of a lexical head are projected in the constituent, but also its language index.

The relation between a head and its syntactic environment is thus circumscribed by the relation of government. For code-switching the government constraint was formalised in DiSciullo *et al.* (1986) as follows:

(6) $\star$ [$X^p\ Y^p$] , where X governs Y, and p and q are language indices

The nodes in a tree must dominate elements drawn from the same language when there is a government relation holding between them. In this formalisation the notion of government was taken willy-nilly from Chomsky (1981), where the general structural dependence on a syntactic head within a maximal projection was meant, e.g. between *see* and *THE BOOK* or between *on* and *THE BENCH* in *did you see THE BOOK* and *on THE BENCH*.

For the purposes of the government constraint, this notion was inappropriate in two ways. First, the class of governors included not only content words (such as verbs and prepositions) but also functional categories such as inflection, the complementiser, etc. Thus the frequent switches between, for example, the inflected verb and the subject or between the complementiser and the clause were ruled out. In spite of the theoretical appeal of this constraint and of its empirical success, it has the drawback that it must explain why the following government relations fall outside the constraint:

(7)   between INFL and the subject:
       Les canadiens[f] *scrivono* 'c'[i.]
       'The Canadians write "c".'

(8)   between Det/Q and N:
       a. Io posso fare i[i] *cheques*[f.]
          'I can make [out] the checks.'
       b. Mettava tanto[i] *maquillage*[f] sulla faccia[i.]
          'She put so much make up on her face.'
          (DiSciullo *et al.* 1986: 13–15)

(9)   between V and Adv:
       Uno no podía comer carne[s] *every day*[e.]
       [We couldn't eat meat every day.] (Sankoff and Poplack 1981: 27)

For (7) there was no real explanation. (8) was explained by assuming that government is minimal and that minor categories mark the phrase they are contained in by their index without governing their complement (not in accordance with Aoun and Sportiche 1983). The assumption that government is minimal, i.e. holding only on the level of V ' (the minimal verb phrase), was meant to explain (9) as well.

Second, the domain of government was too large, including in principle the whole maximal projection. Thus switches between determiners or quantifiers and the noun they modify or between the verb and a locational adverb are predicted to be ungrammatical as well, again contrary to the evidence. For this reason the government constraint was modified in Muysken (1990):

(10)   *$[X^p \ Y^q]$, where X L-marks Y, and p and q are language indices
(1990: 124)

L-marking is a more restricted notion of lexical government by a non-function word under thematic marking. The domain of lexical dependency is a proper subdomain of the domain of structural dependency: government, in exactly the right way. L-marking corresponds to the notion of government in the grammatical tradition. The notion of L-marking has the theoretical attraction that the language indices needed to account for the possible patterns are induced from the lexicon. In this revised view code-switching is possible where the chain of local dependencies resulting from L-marking is broken. If we assume that INFL does not L-mark (to account for (7)), that determiners and quantifiers are heads (hence determiner phrase, quantifier phrase) but not L-markers (so that the switches in (8) are not excluded), and that V does not L-mark time adverbs (as in (9)), then it accounts for the cases listed.

Even in this more limited form the government constraint is simply too strong, whatever its initial appeal. Counterexamples abound, for example in Nortier (1990), where the government constraint is explicitly tested on data from Moroccan Dutch–Arabic switching. Verbal and prepositional object noun phrases are often in a different language from their governing verb or preposition. Crucial counterexamples include (with the number of incidences in Nortier's corpus given in parentheses):

(11)   [a]   žib li-ya *een glas water of zo*.   (7)
                'Get for-me a glass of water or so.'
        [b]   anaka-ndir *intercultureel werk*.   (14)
                'I I-am-doing intercultural work.'
        [c]   wellit *huisman*.   (10)
                'I-became "houseman".' (Nortier 1990: 131)

We get seven cases of switching between indirect and direct object (11a), no less than fourteen cases of switching between verb and direct object (11b), and ten cases involving a predicate after a copula-type verb, (11c). I should also mention the occurrence of ninety-seven switches of object noun phrases involving a single noun.

The data in (11) are particularly damaging since switching between subject and verb is, if anything, less frequent in Nortier's corpus than switching between object and verb. We also find fifteen cases where a Dutch noun phrase is the complement of a Moroccan Arabic preposition, as in (12).

(12)   [a]   u dewwezna f- *zelfde tijd*
                and we-spent in same time
         [b]   ka-yxxes bezzaf dyal *generaties voorbijgaan*
                it-must much of generations pass   (Nortier 1990: 139)

These data clearly show that the government constraint, even in the revised form of Muysken (1990), cannot be maintained. The distribution of switched noun phrases is much wider than predicted. A way to salvage what is valuable in the government constraint is presented in section 5 below. What is valuable in it is that it predicts in a general way that the looser the syntagmatic relation is in a sentence, the easier it is to switch. This prediction is borne out by all available data.

It may be worthwhile to discuss the relation between government models and the model elaborated by Myers-Scotton (1993b). Both models share the idea of an asymmetry between a matrix and an embedded language. For the purpose of the discussion let us call the matrix language the governing language. Where the two models differ is in what counts as a governor. While the government model, particularly in its later versions, specifically excluded functional elements from being relevant governors in terms of code-switching constraints, as outlined above, the Myers-Scotton models are focussed on functional elements as governors for code-switching. It is fair to say that this latter option must be much closer to the truth.

4 Similarities between sentential and lexical phenomena

In many situations of intense language contact, a number of phenomena involving 'mixing' are going on at the same time: lexical borrowing, code-switching, interference, calquing, relexification, semantic borrowing, L1 transfer in L2 learning, possibly convergence. It is not always possible to decide beforehand what is what and therefore it is important to depart from a set of clear cases, abstracting away from the others, and setting up models which will divide, perhaps artificially, the domain of study into distinct sets of phenomena (e.g. borrowing and code-switching, or syntactic convergence and code-switching).

This procedure of abstraction will be justified if it is possible in the next stage of research either to unify the initially separate domains at a higher level of abstraction or to make strong empirical claims about the properties of the distinct sets of data, allowing one to subsequently classify the unclear cases. Thus it appears that at present the general contours of the phenomenon of lexical borrowing are becoming firmly established; this will allow us to separate it from phenomena such as calquing, if these are indeed systematic.

4.1 The borderline between borrowing and switching

Code-switching is the use of two languages in one clause or utterance. As such code-switching is different from lexical borrowing, which involves the incorporation of lexical elements from one language in the lexicon of another language. Here I will try to deal with this distinction in somewhat more precise terms; the notions of word, and the above-word and below-word levels, play a central role.

Code-switching can be conceived of as involving words with different language indices, marked with p and q subscripts here, inserted into a phrase structure (13), where the brackets labelled S mark the clause level, while lexical borrowing can be conceived of as involving formatives (F) inserted into an alien word structure (14) (the word structure is alien because it behaves externally like an element from the host language):

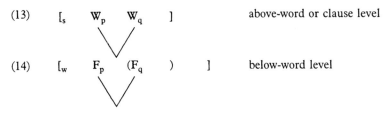

(13) $[_s$ W_p W_q $]$ above-word or clause level

(14) $[_w$ F_p $(F_q$ $)$ $]$ below-word level

Here the brackets labelled W mark the word level. I will use the term sub-lexical for mixing below the level of insertion of a word into a syntactic tree; and the term supra-lexical for mixing at the level of insertion into a tree and in the syntactic projection of a word. Thus a word can be inserted into a syntactic tree as, say, English, even though some of its components are French. This conception has several interesting results.

There are two dimensions to what I will pre-theoretically call lexical interference (both code-switching and borrowing): (a) whether a particular case occurs at the supra-lexical or sub-lexical level, in the sense just described; and (b) whether it involves being listed (DiSciullo and Williams 1989) or not.

The dimension of listedness refers to the degree to which a particular element or structure is part of a memorised list, which has gained acceptance within a particular speech community. We can arrange linguistic elements on a scale running from essentially creative to essentially reproductive.

Jackendoff (1975) and others have pointed out, of course, that these two dimensions are not entirely separate. The sub-lexical mode is primarily reproductive (listed), the supra-lexical, syntactic mode primarily creative. Nonetheless, there are many languages, for example polysynthetic and agglutinative languages, in which processes of word-formation can be highly creative. Similarly, there are aspects of phrase structure, most clearly in idioms and collocations, which are to some extent reproductive. For this reason, it is better to see these dimensions as separate.

When we look at linguistic interference in terms of these dimensions, the following picture emerges:

(15)   not-listed   listed

supra-lexical   code-switching (a)   conventionalised code-switch-
                                       ing (b)
sub-lexical   nonce loans (c)   established loans (d)

Most code-switchings are of course spontaneously formed in discourse, (a). There is recent evidence, however, in work of Poplack and Sankoff, that certain patterns of switching are more frequent in one speech community, other patterns in another speech community (the language pair involved being the same). In this case one might speak of conventionalised code-switching, (b).

The phenomenon of nonce loans, (c), was first described by Haugen (1950) and has recently been taken up in work of Poplack and Sankoff (see also Poplack and Meechan, this volume); elements are borrowed on the spur of the moment, without yet having any status in the receiving speech community. Finally, established loans, (d), are a familiar phenomenon.

Taking this set of distinctions into account, we can now turn to the problem that has dominated the field in recent years: the demarcation between borrowing and code-switching. In Poplack and Sankoff (1984), which summarises much earlier work, the following distinctions were listed between code-switching and borrowing:

(16)   borrowing   code-switching

no more than one word   +   −
adaptation: phonological   ±/+   ±/−
             morphological   +   −
             syntactic   +   −

frequent use	+	–
replaces own word	+	–
recognised as own word	+	–
semantic change	+	–

Notice that we can identify the phenomena associated with lexical borrowing with those associated with ordinary morphological derivation. It has often been noted that lexical borrowing, in contrast with code-switching, involves gradual semantic specialisation over time, blurring of morpheme boundaries, lexical unpredictability, etc. These strikingly resemble the properties of derivational morphology. Both can be viewed as the consequences of lexicalisation typical of sub-lexical structures. Code-switching has the ordinary, supra-lexical, productive properties of syntax.

Much of the recent and very productive work in generative morphology, however, is based on the premise that there is a common set of formal principles to morphological and syntactic structure, such as headedness, government, etc., independent of the phenomenon of lexicalisation. Similarly, we may explore the possibility that parallel constraints govern borrowing and code-switching.

4.2 Morphological typology

Morphological typology plays a role in code-switching as far as we consider the type of word-internal mixing involved in morphologically integrated borrowing as a type of code-switching. Here I will illustrate the issues involved in trying to unify the grammatical constraints on borrowing with those on code-mixing, in terms of the notion of local coherence imposed by language indices. Code-mixing can be conceived of as involving words with different language indices inserted into a phrase structure tree, while lexical borrowing can be conceived of as involving formatives inserted into an alien word structure. Following the general notions of government or L-marking elaborated above, borrowing is predicted to be easier when the components of a word are more loosely connected, as in agglutinative or compounding morphology.

The unified perspective adopted here allows us to link the ways in which elements are borrowed to the morphological typology of languages. Several cases come to mind. In Hindi and other languages of the Indian subcontinent it is possible to form complex verbs by appending a semantically neutral verb 'do' to a content word. This morphological possibility makes it extremely easy to borrow verbs:

(17)   *onti* kare
         [to hunt]   SRANAN
         bewijs kare
         [to prove]   SRANAN/DUTCH BORROWING

These examples are from Surinam Hindustani (Kishna 1979). The verb *kare* 'do' is the morphological head of the construction, and assigns its Hindustani language index to the whole verb, without internally imposing lexical restrictions ('L-marking' in the framework of Chomsky 1986) on the alien element (Muysken 1993). Similar constructions are found in examples from Tamil (Sankoff *et al.* 1990) and from Navaho (Canfield 1980). In the analysis proposed here, these cases are made possible because the auxiliary verb does not L-mark, i.e. does not specifically select, its complement.

A second case involves highly agglutinative languages. In these languages elements can easily be incorporated and can receive affixes productively. Consider a Finnish example:

(18)   Misis K. oli housekeeper-*iina*
         Mrs. K. was   [essive case]
         [Mrs. K. was the housekeeper]   (Poplack *et al.* 1987: 38)

There is L-marking on the phrasal level, which is unproblematic because the noun is Finnish externally, but there is no L-marking between the case affix and the noun.

We predict that fusional languages are highly resistant to borrowing, since there the shapes of the formatives are highly interdependent. This prediction is borne out. In fusional languages we see the typical noun/verb asymmetries in borrowability most clearly: nouns, which can generally occur uninflected, are frequently borrowed, while verbs rarely are.

5 Equivalence

In much work on language contact, at least since Weinreich (1953), and including, for example, the tradition of contrastive grammar research, the notion of equivalence plays an important role. The guiding assumption is that equivalence between the grammars of two languages facilitates bilingual usage, be it second language learning, lexical borrowing, or code-switching.

There can be equivalence of categories (lexical elements, phonemes, phrase structure nodes, morpho-syntactic features) or of relations between categories, in structuralist terms. The latter are either syntagmatic (e.g. word-order or agreement rules) or paradigmatic (equivalent oppositions).

5.1 Categorial equivalence

Here I will consider just word-order equivalence and categorial equivalence. Word order equivalence is a sub-case of categorial equivalence, under the government theory, since the rightward governing verb is not directly equivalent to a leftward governing verb, just like a postposition (governing leftward) is not immediately perceived as the categorial equivalent of a preposition (governing rightward). In the Sankoff and Poplack (1981) and Sankoff and Mainville (1986) formalisations there is the preliminary idealisation of categorial equivalence: there is assumed to be a match between both the terminal and the non-terminal nodes in the syntactic tree of the languages involved in the switch. It has been pointed out before that this idealisation is unwarranted; in fact there is no exact match between categories in different languages. Well-documented problem areas in categorial equivalence include clitic versus non-clitic pronouns, types of determiners and demonstratives, and types of auxiliary elements.

We may need to conceive of equivalence not only as a grammatical notion, but also from a psycholinguistic perspective. This allows us to treat processes of code-switching in diachronic and sociolinguistic terms. Assume that one bilingual speech community does not recognise the categories from different languages as equivalent, and another one does. This will have immediate impact on code-switching patterns, of course. We can think then of the recognition of categorial equivalence as the first step in the process of syntactic convergence. A category often recognised as equivalent may be 'noun', and frequently also 'noun phrase' will be recognised as such, whereas conjunctions are perhaps less likely to be interpreted as equivalent. In addition, phonological and morphological factors (e.g. similar paradigms) may be involved in furthering the recognition of equivalence.

5.2 Word order equivalence

The word order equivalence constraint was given an informal formulation in Poplack (1980) – switching is only possible at points where the order of linguistic elements in both languages is the same – and was then formalised in Sankoff and Poplack (1981) and in Sankoff and Mainville (1986). In the latter work the following formalisation of the constraint is presented:

Given a 'set E of immediate descendants of the node directly above the two constituents', then 'the symbol for any nodes in E to the left of the boundary between the two constituents must precede the symbols for all nodes in E to the right of the boundary, in the right side string of the two rules from the two grammars'. (Sankoff and Mainville 1986: 6)

Thus the formal definition of the word order equivalence constraint is in terms of the immediate daughters of a given phrase structure node. The precise definition of word order equivalence is crucial, as can be seen when we compare Dutch and English word order in the light of the equivalence constraint (Adelmeijer 1991). In simple main clauses, surface strings are similar:

(19)   Mary eats apples./Marie eet appels.

In informal linear terms a switch would be allowed at every point, then, in these sentences. Notice, however, that many grammarians, adhering to different theoretical models, assign rather different structures to these sentences. In some Government and Binding analyses, for instance, the English verb *eats* occupies the auxiliary position, and the Dutch verb has been moved into the complementiser position (e.g. Koster 1978). The English subject is in its canonical position, while the Dutch subject has been moved into sentence-initial position. A switch between subject and verb would not be possible under the more formal configurational definition in terms of sister nodes.

The opposite result is found when we take main clauses with a fronted adverbial. In English this element will precede the subject, while in Dutch it will occur in pre-verbal first position instead of the subject:

(20)   Now Mary eats an apple./Nu eet Marie een appel.

Under a purely linear conception of equivalence, a switch would not be allowed after *now/nu*; the element following differs in both languages: the subject in English, the finite verb in Dutch. Under the more formal conception of equivalence in terms of sister constituents, there is equivalence between the clausal constituents following the fronted adverbial, and hence switching would be allowed.

One of the conceptual problems with the notion of word order equivalence is that the order of elements in the sentence is expressed in phrase structure configurations, but results from the interaction of a number of independent principles (see particularly the work of Stowell (1981), Travis (1984) and Koopman (1984)). Some of these principles include:

(21)   directionality of government (Case, Theta)
        [NP V], * [V NP] under leftward government
        [P NP], * [NP P] under rightward government

(22)   adjacency or other locality conditions on government
        [V NP X], * [V X NP], since case assignment is local

(23)   iconicity
        [E1 E2], * [E2 E1], where E1 and E2 are coordinate events and E1
        preceded E2 in time

(24)   Considerations of given/new, functional sentence perspective, topic/
        comment, etc.
        [given information   new information]

(25)   prosodic considerations
        [short constituent   long constituent]

Now with respect to these principles (and undoubtedly there are more), two things may be said. First, they do not form a natural class, and derive from different components of linguistic theory in the wide sense. Second, only the first two are likely to be language specific, generally speaking, and hence pertinent to the equivalence constraint. Notice now that (21) and (22) are directly determined by government.

Thus a formulation of the equivalence constraint that realistically covers word order differences involves the notion of government. The constraint at the intersection of the earlier approaches may then be formulated as:

(26)   * [Xp, Yq], where X L-marks Y, p and q are language indices, and
        there is no equivalence between the category Y in one language and
        the category Y in the other language involved.

To see what this means we must return to the issue of equivalence. The linear notion of equivalence would translate in this framework as Xp governing leftward or rightward.

6 Conclusion

A more general way of approaching equivalence in code-switching research is through the notion of neutrality. If we take a strong system-oriented view and conceive of the juxtaposition of material from different languages in one utterance as theoretically problematic – when the grammar of each single language is viewed as a system *où tout se tient* [everything holds together], in Saussure's terms – then we can imagine there to be various strategies to make mixing, juxtaposition, less offensive. In other words, code-switching is impossible in principle, but there are numerous ways that this fundamental impossibility can be circumvented. Something that should be ruled by the very coherence imposed by the sentence seen as syntagmatic unit, is made possible in any of four ways, thus neutralising the system conflict:

(i) switching is possible when there is no tight relation (e.g. of government) holding between two elements, so-called paratactic switching;

(ii) switching is possible under equivalence;

(iii) switching is possible when the switched element is morphologically encapsulated, shielded off by a functional element from the matrix language;

(iv) switching is possible when at the point of the switch a word could belong to either language, the case of the homophonous diamorph (e.g. *in* in English, German or Dutch).

The loose, associative, style of this survey of grammatical notions relevant to the analysis of code-switching is not accidental. It reflects my perception of the present state of the field as characterised by pluralism and the growing recognition that various mechanisms may play a role in different code-switching situations.

Bibliography

Adelmeijer, L. (1991) The level of code-switching. Unpublished MA thesis in Linguistics, University of Amsterdam.

Aoun, J. and Sportiche, D. (1993) On the formal theory of government. *The Linguistic Review*, 2: 211–36.

Bentahila, A. and Davies, E. E. (1983) The syntax of Arabic–French code-switching. *Lingua*, 59: 301–30.

Canfield, K. (1980) Navaho–English code-mixing. *Anthropological Linguistics*, 22: 218–20.

Chomsky, N. (1981) *Lectures on government and binding*. Dordrecht: Foris.

(1986) *Barriers*. Cambridge, Mass.: MIT Press.

DiSciullo, A.-M., Muysken, P. and Singh, R. (1986) Government and code-mixing. *Journal of Linguistics*, 22: 1–24.

DiSciullo, A.-M. and Williams, E. (1989) *On the definition of word*. Cambridge, Mass.: MIT Press.

Haugen, E. (1950) The analysis of linguistic borrowing. *Language*, 26: 210–31.

Jackendoff, R. (1975) Morphological and semantic regularities in the lexicon. *Language*, 51: 639–71.

Joshi, A. K. (1985) Processing of sentences with intrasentential code-switching. In D. R. Dowty, L. Karttunen, A. M. Zwicky eds., *Natural language parsing*. Cambridge University Press, 190–205.

Kishna, S. (1979) Lexicale interferentie in het Sarnami. Unpublished MA thesis in Linguistics, University of Amsterdam.

Klavans, J. E. (1983) The syntax of code-switching: Spanish and English. In L. D. King and C. A. Matey eds., *Selected papers from the 13th Linguistic Symposium on Romance languages*. Chapel Hill, N.C.: 213–31.

Koopman, H. (1984) *The syntax of verbs*. Dordrecht: Foris.

Koster, J. (1978) *Locality principles in syntax*. Dordrecht: Foris.

Lance, D. M. (1975) Spanish–English code-switching. In E. Hernández-Chavez, A. Cohen, A. F. Beltramo eds., *El lenguaje de los chicanos*. Arlington, Va.: Center for Applied Linguistics, 138–53.

Muysken, P. (1990) A unified theory of local coherence in grammar contact. In P. H. Nelde ed., *Confli(c)t*, ABLA Papers, 14. Brussels: ABLA, 123–8.

(1993) Grammatical constraints on code-switching. The case of Indic mixed compounds. Presented at the ESF Pavia Summer School on Code-Switching and Language Contact.

Myers-Scotton, C. (1993a) *Social motivations for code-switching. Evidence from Africa*. Oxford: Clarendon Press.

(1993b) *Duelling languages: grammatical structure in code-switching*. Oxford: Clarendon Press.

Nortier, J. M. (1990) *Dutch–Moroccan Arabic code-switching among young Moroccans in the Netherlands*. Dordrecht: Foris.

Pfaff, C. W. (1979) Constraints on language mixing: intrasentential code-switching and borrowing in Spanish/English. *Language*, 55: 291–318.

Poplack, S. (1980) Sometimes I'll start a sentence in Spanish Y TERMINO EN ESPAÑOL: toward a typology of code-switching. *Linguistics*, 18: 581–618. Also in J. Amastae, L. Elias-Olivares (1982) eds. *Spanish in the United States, sociolinguistic aspects*. Cambridge University Press, 230–63.

Poplack, S. and Sankoff, D. (1984) Borrowing: the synchrony of integration. *Linguistics*, 22: 99–136.

Poplack, S., Wheeler, S. and Westwood, A. (1987) Distinguishing language contact phenomena: evidence from Finnish–English bilingualism. In P. Lilius, M. Saari eds., *The Nordic Languages and Modern Linguistics*, 6. (Proceedings of the Sixth International Conference of Nordic and General Linguistics in Helsinki, 18–22 August 1986.) 33–56. Also in K. Hyltenstam, L. K. Obler (1989) eds., *Bilingualism across the lifespan. Aspects of acquisition, maturity and loss*. Cambridge University Press, 132–54.

Sankoff, D. and Poplack, S. (1981) A formal grammar for code-switching. *Papers in Linguistics: International Journal of Human Communication*, 14 (1): 3–46.

Sankoff, D. and Mainville, S. (1986) Code-switching of context-free grammars. Ms. Université de Montréal.

Sankoff, D., Poplack, S. and Vanniarajan, S. (1990) The case of the nonce loan in Tamil. *Language Variation and Change*, 2: 71–101.

Sankoff, D., Poplack, S. and Wheeler, D. (1988) Code-switching in two communities.

Stowell, T. (1981) The origins of phrase structure. Unpublished doctoral dissertation, MIT.

Travis, L. (1984) Determinants of word order. Unpublished doctoral dissertation, MIT.

Treffers-Daller, J. (1991) French–Dutch language mixture in Brussels. Unpublished Ph.D. thesis, University of Amsterdam.

Weinreich, U. (1953) *Languages in contact*. The Hague: Mouton.

10 PATTERNS OF LANGUAGE MIXTURE: NOMINAL STRUCTURE IN WOLOF-FRENCH AND FONGBE-FRENCH BILINGUAL DISCOURSE

Shana Poplack and Marjory Meechan

1 Introduction

A primary goal of any study of language mixture is to determine the properties of the internal grammars of bilinguals. Specifically, what grammar is utilised at the point where languages meet? Do speakers operate with a single base grammar which is on occasion overlaid with lexical items from another language or are different grammars activated at different times? If the latter is the case, what structural principles govern their juxtaposition? In this chapter, we demonstrate how the variationist method yields straightforward answers to these questions and further, assert that it is the only method which can irrefutably do so.

Empirical studies of bilingual performance data have revealed that the utterance-internal combination of elements from more than one grammar may surface in a number of different forms, some of which are illustrated in (1), where French-origin items (italicised) alternate with Wolof items.

(1)   **amoon**   **naa fi**   **nak**   **benn** *copine* **koo**   **xam ni daf ma**
         have+PAST I   LOC CONJ IND   friend   that+you know that she me
         *attacher***woon** *début*   *d' année mais*   **sama** *idées* **yooyoo**
         attach+PAST beginning   of year   but   POSS ideas DEM
         tax   **ba** **leegi mu jappantewoon ak**   **man,** *c'est que* **moom**
         cause that now she dispute+past with me   it's that she
         féministe **la**   *quoi* **ta man** *je défendais*   *des*   *idées* **yoo**
         feminist it's   what so me I defend+PAST IND ideas that+you
         xamenta ni   **gəm**   **mu**   **ma ko**   **sax.**
         know   that believe   PRO   I   PRO ADV
         [I even had a girlfriend here at the beginning of the year, but my ideas made her fight with me. It's that she was a feminist while I defended ideas that I didn't even believe.] (Wolof 4: 242: Spkr 3)[1]

These include code-switching and lexical borrowing on the community and individual level. As discussed in Poplack (1990), 'code-switching' may be defined as the juxtaposition of sentences or sentence fragments, each of which is internally consistent with the morphological and syntactic (and optionally, phonological) rules of its lexifier language. Intra-sentential switching may occur freely at 'equivalence sites', i.e. points around which constituent order in the two languages is homologous. In some language-specific contexts, 'constituent insertion' may also occur. Here the internal structure of the constituent is determined by the grammar of the lexifier language, and its placement is determined by the language of the sentence into which it is inserted. 'Borrowing' is the *adaptation* of lexical material to the morphological and syntactic (and usually, phonological) patterns of the recipient language. Established 'loanwords' (which typically show full linguistic integration, native-language synonym displacement, and widespread diffusion, even among recipient-language monolinguals) differ from 'nonce borrowings' only insofar as the latter need not satisfy the diffusion requirement. Borrowed forms of both types are generally indistinguishable from their native-language counterparts at all but the etymological (and variably, phonological) level.

The identification and analysis of code-switching and borrowing are the focus of much current controversy. Some researchers argue that these language contact phenomena should be distinguished, (e.g. Boeschoten 1990; Eliasson 1989, 1990; Muysken 1987; Poplack 1990; Poplack *et al*. 1988b; Sankoff *et al*. 1990), though consensus has yet to be reached on which surface manifestations should be classed in which category. Others contend that code-switching and borrowing are either undifferentiated by the bilingual speaker or operationally indistinguishable (Bentahila and Davies 1991; Myers-Scotton 1993; Treffers-Daller 1991) and should not be considered distinct entities.

The crux of the problem resides in the status of *lone* L_b incorporations into otherwise L_a discourse, a phenomenon that, ironically enough, constitutes the richest portion of any bilingual corpus systematically studied. In this chapter we provide an empirical test of whether they are best treated as code-switches or borrowings, making use of the variationist approach to language contact and data from natural bilingual discourse involving French and two languages of the Niger-Congo family, Wolof and Fongbe. The principles of the variationist framework as they relate to the study of language contact have been detailed in Poplack (1990) (cf. also Poplack *et al*. 1987 and Sankoff *et al*. 1990). The most important for present purposes include the focus on spontaneous speech data of skilled bilinguals, the empirical analysis of all of the relevant data, and, of particular concern here, circumscription of the variable context, or defining the object of study.

Our approach involves using the facts of variability to determine the language membership of ambiguous items, such as the lone French-origin nouns in otherwise Wolof discourse (e.g. *copine, idées, féministe*) in (1). Adumbrated in Sankoff *et al.* (1990), where variable rates of case-marking were compared in this same connection in English-origin and native Tamil nouns, here we expand the exercise to take account of the *patterning* of variability. By making a detailed assessment of the distribution of modifier usage on lone French-origin nouns in otherwise Wolof and Fongbe contexts and systematically comparing it with that of their lexical counterparts in each of the languages in contact as well as in unambiguous, multiword code-switches (e.g. *Je défendais des idées* in (1)) between them, we establish whether the different linguistic contexts we have isolated can be correlated with distinct patterns of noun modification.

This enables us to compare details of structure too specific to be due to coincidence or universals. In the case that interests us here, for example, if lone French-origin nouns in otherwise Wolof/Fongbe[2] discourse show the detailed patterns of noun modifier usage of monolingual Wolof/Fongbe nouns, but none of the patterns of French nouns in monolingual French discourse, the interpretation must be that their structure is that of Wolof/Fongbe and not that of French, regardless of the etymology of the noun. This means that they are being treated grammatically as if they were *borrowed* into Wolof/Fongbe and not *code-switched* into French.

The method is equally amenable to testing other claims, though these are not the major focus of this paper. If, for example, no one category of other-language material can be associated with any particular grammar (Bentahila and Davies 1991; Treffers-Daller 1991), then both lone French-origin nouns and longer stretches will be shown to pattern identically.[3] If, on the other hand, the mixed-language material is the product of a grammar distinct from either of the grammars making up the language pair (resulting, for example, in a 'suspension of syntax' (Muysken 1987: 37) see also Boeschoten (1990)), then the data will be revealed to pattern with neither the monolingual French nor the monolingual Wolof/Fongbe nouns. Comparison of the patterning of the bilingual and monolingual NP in Wolof–French and Fongbe–French bilingual discourse will enable us to assess these claims. The NP is a particularly fruitful locus for this type of study because, as has been found elsewhere (e.g. Berk-Seligson 1986; Poplack 1980; Poplack *et al.* 1988b; Treffers-Daller 1991), the bulk of the French-origin material in these data is found in this context. It also provides a nice illustration of our method, since both Wolof and Fongbe are isolating languages, with no nominal morphology to speak of, and spoken French provides little potential for overt morphological marking here as well. These facts obviate the morphological criterion for loanword integration, making the status of a lone French-origin noun like *copine* in (1) particularly difficult to assess. We therefore appeal to the syntax of nouns and NPs, focussing on their variable distribution across modification structures. In interpreting the results we rely, as is standard in variation research, on *relative* proportions rather than relations of all or nothing.

2 Data and method

2.1 Data

2.1.1 The corpora

A recurrent criticism of early quantitative analyses of stuctural constraints on code-switching is that they dealt with languages which were typologically similar, such that there were relatively few structural incompatibilities for speakers to cope with in switching among them (Eliasson 1989; Muysken 1991; Poplack *et al.* 1987). As part of our ongoing quest to elucidate the constraints on language mixing in typologically distinct language pairs (Naït M'Barek and Sankoff 1988; Poplack *et al.* 1987; Sankoff *et al.* n.d.; Sankoff *et al.* 1990), we focus in this chapter on the intraclausal combination of French with either of two African languages that differ typologically from French and each other.

Bilingual data sets were collected for each language pair, using standard variationist methodology and social network techniques, under sociolinguistic conditions propitious to the spontaneous use of both contact languages. The Wolof–French materials were gathered by a highly educated and proficiently bilingual speaker during informal in-group conversations with nine members of his social network. All of the informants, recent immigrants to Canada, range in age from twenty-nine to forty-seven, are fluent speakers of Wolof and French, having received secondary education or more in French before leaving Senegal. All but one currently reside in Montreal, where, with the exception of two students, most are employed in the service sector.

The Fongbe–French materials were recorded in Cotonou, Bénin, among a sample of twenty bilingual Béninois, stratified according to age and educational level. The four retained for this study, all ethnically Fon, are between eighteen and twenty-five, reflecting the average age of Cotonou residents. Three are currently students and one works as a mechanic. At the time of the interview, all had received between seven and eighteen years of formal instruction in French.

Data collection methodology and conditions for use of French were comparable across corpora. In particular, though these speakers were all born and raised in Africa, they were educated entirely in French, and may be said to have had extensive contacts with that language. The resulting corpora contain copious manifestations of the language contact phenomena of interest to us here.

2.1.2 The bilingual corpus

From the tape-recorded conversations, every utterance, broadly defined, in which both French and Wolof/Fongbe co-occurred, was transcribed into *Concorder*, a concordance application for the MacIntosh (Rand and Patera 1992). This constitutes the bilingual corpora on which the analyses reported below are based. From this corpus, every noun was extracted, regardless of language (Wolof, Fongbe or French) or context (monolingual or those in which both Wolof/Fongbe and French co-occur within or at the boundary of the NP).[4] This gave a total of 2,646 lone nouns and 121 longer stretches (Table 10.1).

Table 10.1 *Distribution of the data by corpus*

Corpus	Wolof–French			Fongbe–French		
Context	French	Wolof		French	Fongbe	
Language of noun:	French	French	Wolof	French	French	Fongbe
Lone nouns	403	583	265	231	608	556
Multiword fragments		75			44	

As our principal goal is to determine the status of *lone* lexical items in otherwise Wolof/Fongbe discourse – whether code-switches or borrowings – we first classified the nouns to enable us to address this question.

Wolof/Fongbe nouns in otherwise Wolof/Fongbe contexts, underlined in (2) and (3), and French nouns in otherwise French contexts, underlined in (4), form the monolingual contextual categories.

(2)   **nga nara takk <u>jabar</u> dem ci   <u>sǝriñ</u>   mu listixaaral   la.**
you want marry woman go   PREP marabout he look+CAUS you
[You want to marry a woman, you go to a marabout who goes to see her for you.] (Wolof 2: 558: Spkr 02)

(3)   **ní ǹ jró ná ɖà   <u>wɔ́</u> mɔ́   ɔ́   ǹ nɔ̀   zé   sìn   ɖó**
If I want FUT prepare dough example TOP I HAB carry water LOC
<u>àdò</u>   jì.
hearth on
[If I want to make dough, for example, I carry water to the hearth.]
(Fongbe 1: 5: Spkr 01)

(4)   *parce que la **langue** c'est la   **clé** de la   **civilisation.***
because   DEF language it's   DEF key of DEF civilisation
[Because language is the key to civilisation.] (Fongbe 4: 1108: Spkr 04)

A third category comprises the contentious forms, lone French-origin nouns in otherwise Wolof/Fongbe contexts, underlined in examples (5) and (6).[5] A noun was considered to fall into this category if:

(i) It was bordered on both sides by Wolof/Fongbe material, as in (5).

(5)   **ní à   *exagerer* ɖò   <u>*soleil*</u> mɛ̀ ça *peut entraîner la*   *maladie.***
if you overdo   LOC sun in that can cause   DEF sickness
[If you overdo it in the sun, that can cause sickness.] (Fongbe 2: 634: Spkr 02)

(ii) It is bordered on only one side by Wolof/Fongbe material, provided it appears in clause-initial or clause-final position, as in (6).

(6)   *et   puis* CL/*science* xlέ   mǐ gbèɖé ɖɔ̀ <u>*tonnerre*</u> hù   mɛ̀   ɖòkpó.
and then   science shows us never that thunder kills person one
[And science has never shown that thunder killed one person.]
(Fongbe 3: 780: Spkr 03)

These restrictions effectively limit our study to intraclausal contexts.[6]

We compare these with still another category of data composed of nouns internal to French multiword fragments embedded within a clause involving an NP, as in configuration IV in Table 10.2[7] and examples (7) and (8).

(7)   *elle parle français mais des fois*   day   def ay ‖ *mots en anglais*
she speak French but   sometimes AUX do IND words in English
au   milieu.
PREP middle
[She speaks French but sometimes puts English words in the middle.]
(Wolof 2: 525: Spkr 02)

(8)   àlì   lέ   ɔ́   ‖ *stade suprême de dégradation* yĕ   ɖè.

street PLU DEF   state supreme of degradation they LOC

[The streets are in a supreme state of degradation.]

(Fongbe 3: 240: Spkr 03)

Table 10.2 summarises the way the nominal constructions in our data were classified. Included in this study are only those fragments where the language boundary impinges on the NP, either within or immediately prior to it. Although postnominal and post-NP position are of greater interest for our purposes (Table 10.3) since they often constitute a conflict site for code-switching under equivalence, it is notable that only one unambiguous switch involving determiners occurred here. The data in this position thus have no bearing on language mixture in the modification structures of interest to us, and so do not figure in the calculations in Tables 10.4 and 10.5.

Table 10.2 *Classification of nominal constructions*

| # | Language configuration | | | |
	Preceding context	Noun	Following context	Classification
I	Wolof/Fongbe	Wolof/Fongbe	Wolof/Fongbe	Monolingual Wolof/Fongbe
II	French	French	French	Monolingual French
III	Wolof/Fongbe	French	Wolof/Fongbe	French-origin in Wolof/Fongbe context
IV	Wolof/Fongbe	French	French	French multiword fragments

2.2 Coding and analysis

2.2.1 NP structure in monolingual and bilingual discourse

Wolof features a mixed NP structure, with most nominal modifiers following the noun, as in (9), although indefinite articles, most possessives and some adjectives may precede (Gamble 1963; Grelier 1970; Ka 1994; Njie 1982; Rambaud 1963; Samb 1983) – see Table 10.3.[8]

(9)   **yeen <u>ay   borom   kər   yi</u>,   maa ngi   <u>seen   ganaaw</u>**
you IND proprietor house DEF I   AUX POSS back
lu   ngeen ma sant ma def ko.
what you   me ask I   do PRO
[You're the bosses, I'm lower than you, I'll do whatever you ask.]
(Wolof 1: 953: Spkr 01)

In Fongbe, on the other hand, the NP is strictly left-headed. All modifiers follow the noun, as in (10), with the exception of numerals, which precede (Akoha 1980; Brousseau and Lumsden 1990).

(10)   **<u>xwé   ḍàxó ḍòkpó gbè</u> ázɔ̃   ná   hán ǎ.**
house big   a   in   work FUT lack NEG
[In a big house there is no lack of work.] (Fongbe 6: 66: Spkr 08)

Like Wolof, French features a mixed NP structure with determiners and some adjectives preceding the noun and most adjectives and relative clauses following, as in (11) (Grevisse 1986).

(11)   *il y a   <u>différents types de wolof</u>.* **Boo   nekk e**
there are different kinds of Wolof if+you be   PRT
à Paris, ñoom ils   ont   <u>un   wolof américanisé</u>.
in Paris they they have IND Wolof Americanised
[There are different kinds of Wolof. If you're in Paris, they have an Americanised Wolof.] (Wolof 1: 633: Spkr 01)

Table 10.3 summarises the monolingual rules for nominal modifier placement in each of Wolof, Fongbe and French.

Table 10.3 *Comparison of noun modifier positions in Wolof, Fongbe and French*

Language	Position 2	Position 1	N O U N	Position 1	Position 2	Position 3
Wolof	Indefinite	Adjective Numeral		X	Definite	Rel/PP
French	Indefinite Definite	Adjective Numeral		Adjective	X	Rel/PP
Fongbe	X	Numeral		Adjective	Indefinite Definite	Rel/PP

Focussing on sites of structural equivalence and contrast, we first note that relative clauses and prepositional phrases occur postnominally in each of the languages. The boundaries between the noun and these constructions thus qualify as equivalence sites for intraclausal code-switching. Similarly, both French and Wolof allow prenominal modification with indefinite articles, numerals and some adjectives; the sites between the noun and these modifiers are also equivalence sites for code-switching. Where Wolof and French differ is with respect to definite article and attributive adjective placement. French requires prenominal determiners and Wolof definite articles must be postposed. As for adjectives, while French allows both pre- and postnominal placement, in Wolof, the only position directly adjacent to the noun is prenominal.[9]

Shared structure is even more sharply limited in the French/Fongbe pair. With the exception of relative clauses, prepositional phrases and numerals, only the boundary between noun and postnominal adjective emerges as an equivalence site here, although even this is more of a virtual than an actual slot, since Fongbe speakers canonically express adjectival modification by means of adjectival verbs (Meechan and Poplack 1993). In addition, though not shown in Table 10.3 due to the impossibility of unambiguously assessing the position of its (null) modifiers, Wolof and Fongbe differ from French quantitatively, if not qualitatively, in their preference for bare nouns. This extremely common option is used in a wide range of contexts in both African languages, including: contexts with universal or generic reference as in (12), partitive expressions, focus constructions and negations as in (13), noun–noun modification expressions in Fongbe [sín] and [tòn], or Wolof [u], as in (14), in certain verb + noun constructions as in (15).

(12)   mǐ ɖɛ̆   ɖĕ   ká   ɖò   *afrique* fí dìn   ɔ̀,   jɔ́nhɔ́n ɖè ǎ.
        we other REL MOD LOC Africa be now TOP   wind   be NEG
        [For those of us who are here in Africa now, there is no cold.]
        (Fongbe 1: 795: Spkr 01)

(13)   jotu   ñu   dərəm rek.
        receive+NEG they penny ADV
        [They didn't receive a penny.] (Wolof 2: 923: Spkr 02)

(14)   *mais* yow boo   nekk e   ci   biir u tubab   rek anh!
        but   you if you be   PRT PREP inside of french   ADV argh
        [But you, if you only live among the white people, argh!]
        (Wolof 1: 572: Spkr 01)

(15)   é nɔ́   ɖó   xὲsín nú mì *trop.*
         it MOD make fear   for me too much
         [That scares me.] (Fongbe 2: 88: Spkr 02)

The undetermined noun in French, though attested, is highly limited, being largely restricted to a few constructions such as copula + certain predicate nominals, as in (16), nominal apposition, 'N *de* N' modification structures and a few lexicalised cases such as *avoir faim,* and *avoir peur.*

(16)   *il   est Ø créateur de l'   univers.*
         He is   creator   of DEF universe
         [He is the creator of the universe.] (Fongbe 4: 957: Spkr 04)

Given the condition of equivalence on intraclausal code-switching (Poplack 1980), according to which (unambiguous) switching is free to occur only between sentence elements that are normally ordered in the same way by the monolingual grammars in contact, and the fact that borrowing involves the grammatical structure of one language only, with the other playing a solely etymological role, the facts depicted in Table 10.3 can be predicted to affect patterns of language mixture in these language pairs as follows: multiword fragments should figure at sites where both members of the language pair feature the same modification structures. Lone French-origin nouns should take the noun modification structures of the language into which they are incorporated if many or most are borrowings, and should take the noun modification structures of French if they are switches. In what follows, we assess which of these hypotheses best accounts for the data, using variationist methodology.

2.2.2 Coding procedures

Each noun in each corpus, regardless of language or context, was coded for the type of modification structure in which it occurred. We isolated four main types: (i) overt indefinite article, (ii) overt definite article, (iii) no article but other modifier (e.g. demonstrative, possessive, focus marker, interrogative, numeral, relative clause) and (iv) no modification at all.

The set of Wolof definite articles *Ci/Ca* [the] were coded as definite, and *Cenn* [one] and *ay* [some], as indefinite.[10] In Fongbe, definite reference is marked by (or otherwise coincides with) the topic marker, 'ɔ́, and indefinite reference is marked by (or coincides with) the existential, 'ɖè'. In what follows, we coded (and shall refer to for convenience) the topic marker 'ɓ' as definite, and the existential as indefinite.[11] The French determiners *le/la/les* [the] were coded as definite, *un/une* [one, a], *du/des* [some] and partitives, as indefinite. The remaining overt modification structures were similarly coded according to category (e.g. possessive, demonstrative, relative clause, adjective, etc.). These modifiers occurred relatively rarely in each of the languages. In what follows, we refer to them as 'other modification'.[12]

In addition, we coded French multiword fragments according to whether they occurred at equivalence sites,[13] as established in Table 10.3.

2.3 The analysis

For each language involved in the study, we first calculated the proportion of nouns in each modification context out of the total number of nouns in that category. The distribution of modifiers across the nouns in each data set was then systematically compared in pairwise fashion with that of every other data set. Thus patterns of nominal modification in lone French-origin nouns in Wolof/ Fongbe contexts were compared with their counterparts in each of the corresponding monolingual contexts (French nouns in French contexts and Wolof/Fongbe nouns in Wolof/Fongbe contexts). This is illustrated in Figure 10.1. The results of these comparisons were then analysed by means of χ^2 analysis[14] to determine which data sets differed from each other and whether the differences were statistically significant.

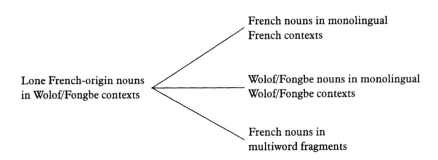

Figure 10.1 Three-way comparison of the distribution of nominal modification

3 Results

Figure 10.2 displays graphically the relative proportions of mixed nominal construction types in the data. In both corpora, the lone French-origin nouns form the overwhelming majority of the data.

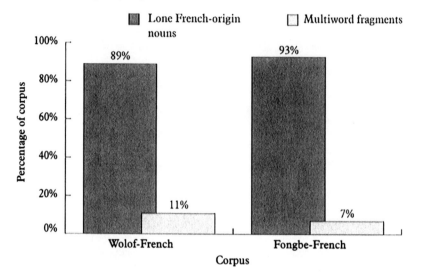

Figure 10.2 Distribution of mixed constructions involving French nouns in Wolof-French and Fongbe-French bilingual discourse

3.1 Wolof–French

3.1.1 Lone French-origin nouns

We now examine noun modification patterns on (monolingual) Wolof nouns in Wolof contexts and compare them to (monolingual) French nouns in French contexts. Figure 10.3 reveals that French nouns are typically modified with overt determiners, mostly definites, and to a lesser extent, indefinites as in (17).

(17) **_le   petit pays_**   _que nous avons, c'est pas   mettre_
      DEF little country that we   have,   it's NEG put

      un   petit fonctionnaire ñu   saacc xaalis bi.
      IND little official   they steal money DEF

      [The little country that we have, it's not a question of putting in a little official who steals money.] (Wolof 2: 318–24: Spkr 01)

In Wolof, on the other hand, the majority of nouns either surface bare, as in
(18), or with some other form of modification (e.g. the possessive *seen* in (9)).
These differences are statistically significant, indicating that (monolingual)
French differs from (monolingual) Wolof with regard to nominal modification.

(18)   **mooy nguur u negar.**

it's   power of black

[It's the power of the black.] (Wolof 1: 953: Spkr 01)

How do these patterns compare with noun modification usage for lone French-
origin nouns in otherwise Wolof contexts? If they pattern like their French counterparts in monolingual contexts, this will be evidence that they are *switches* into
French, whereas if they pattern like Wolof nouns, they can be inferred to have
been *borrowed*.

The distribution of lone French-origin nouns in otherwise Wolof contexts
across the four categories of Wolof noun modification is also depicted in Figure
10.3. These nouns may be seen to pattern almost identically with Wolof nouns in
monolingual Wolof contexts: like them, they co-occur with overt Wolof definite
articles about a third of the time. Another 24% surface bare (vs 30% for Wolof),
and 31% (27% for Wolof) appear with some other form of modification. These
latter two rates are significantly higher than those characterising monolingual
French nouns, but roughly the same as those characterising monolingual Wolof
nouns.

Only with indefinites do lone French-origin nouns show more overt marks than
their monolingual Wolof counterparts (15% French-origin vs 7% Wolof); a dif-

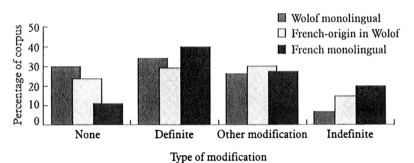

Figure 10.3 Patterns of noun modification on lone French-origin nouns in
otherwise Wolof contexts, as compared with monolingual Wolof and
French nouns (based on tables A and B in the appendix)

ference that is statistically significant. How can this result be interpreted? Recall that Wolof definite articles (Table 10.3) are postposed to the noun. Wolof indefinite markers, however, are preposed, making them structurally equivalent to the French indefinite construction. It is precisely in the indefinite context that we observe a reversal in distribution. Here, rates of overt determiner expression for lone French-origin nouns are significantly *higher* than those for monolingual Wolof nouns, patterning instead with their French counterparts, albeit at a lower rate. We hypothesise that this intermediate status is due to the inclusion among the lone French-origin nouns modified by Wolof indefinite articles of some (single-word) code-switches at the equivalence site between (preposed) indefinite article and noun. This suggestion is bolstered by the other evidence in Figure 10.3 that lone French-origin nouns in *non-equivalent* definite and zero modification structures pattern like monolingual Wolof, but not like French, nouns.

In the category of 'other modification', French-origin nouns also pattern like Wolof nouns in monolingual contexts. However, and this points up the necessity of extending the comparison to *both* contact languages, our method revealed these modifiers to pattern like their monolingual French counterparts as well. This is because these two languages coincidentally share virtually the same usage patterns for each of the modifiers in this category.[15] Therefore, patterns of 'other modification' are silent with regard to our hypothesis. This is an important caveat, because all too often, other-language material is erroneously classified without ever having determined its relationship to *each* of the languages in contact.

We have reviewed a number of lines of evidence suggesting that the lone French-origin nouns in otherwise Wolof contexts are acting as Wolof lexical items, i.e. as borrowings. However, a crucial element of the comparison remains unexplored. We now examine the behaviour of nominal elements in multiword French fragments to verify that not only do lone French-origin items pattern like Wolof nouns but also that they do *not* pattern like code-switches.

3.1.2 Multiword fragments

Pre-NP position is widely cited as a favourable locus for code-switching (Berk-Seligson 1986; Poplack 1980; Treffers-Daller 1991). In Wolof–French bilingual discourse, a total of seventy-five multiword fragments, as in the underlined portion in (19), occurred in this position, constituting 12% of mixed constructions involving nouns.

(19) *des fois*   **da**   **nga y**   xool   0pt > || *un film avec des*
sometimes AUX you ASP watch   a film with IND
sous-titres en français.
subtitles   in French
[Sometimes you watch a film with subtitles in French.]
(Wolof 1: 319: Spkr 01)

What are the characteristics of these French stretches? Table 10.4 displays the distribution of modification on French nouns within French multiword fragments in Wolof–French bilingual discourse.

Table 10.4 *Distribution of modification on French nouns within French multiword fragments in Wolof–French bilingual discourse*

Language of modifier:	French	Wolof	Unknown	Total	
Marker:	N	N	N	N	%
Definite	18	3	0	21	28%
Indefinite	15	11	0	26	35%
None	0	0	9	9	12%
Other modification	18	1	0	19	25%
Total N	51	15	9	75	

We first note that the overwhelming majority of nominal switches (63%) feature an overt determiner, whereas less than half of the lone French-origin nouns in Wolof discourse which we have characterised as borrowings do (cf. Figure 10.3). Most of the switches occur in the context of an indefinite article. We have already observed that this constitutes one of the few equivalence sites for intraclausal code-switching involving nouns. The indefinite articles surface in either language, as in (19) and (20), i.e. the switch may (and does) occur either before or after the indefinite determiner.

(20) **da**   **nga y**   xaar **ba**   *élections* **yi**   bɔggɔ des **ay**   *six mois*
AUX you ASP wait until elections DEF want   stay ART six months
yooyu rek   **nga ñibbi**   *quoi.*
DEM ADV you return eh
[You wait until there's only six months left for elections and then you return, eh.] (Wolof 2: 52: Spkr 02)

In contrast, almost all of the definite determiners in multiword fragments are lexicalised in French only, as in (21). Here, the switch boundary is located *before* the full NP, and not within it.

(21)   **am   na *parents* yoo   xam   nak   leegi dañuy   jɔnd ‖**
        have it parents that+you know CONJ now AUX+they buy
        le   dictionnaire de rap-là pour au moins **mɔn   a   jeli**
        DEF dictionary of RAP for   at least   be able PREP understand
        boys   yi.
        young the
        [There are some parents who buy that rap dictionary to at least be able to understand the young people.] (Wolof 3: 837: Spkr 04)

This result is also as would be expected if a principle like equivalence were constraining code-switching, since the boundary between noun and French or Wolof definite article is a conflict site for code-switching under equivalence.

Additional evidence comes from the distribution of bare nouns in the French multiword fragments. Unlike the case of the lone French-origin nouns, where 24% of all noun modification structures featured bare nouns (Figure 10.3), very few of the noun phrases in multiword fragments lack an overt determiner (12%). We return to this finding below.

A final observation concerns the structural status of these multiword fragments in the discourse. A full 80% occur at points in the discourse where the syntax is simultaneously compatible with both Wolof and French grammars. This is in further contrast with the lone French-origin nouns in Wolof discourse, which occurred overwhelmingly in Wolof, but not French, constructions.

3.1.3 Multiword fragments at non-equivalence sites

What of the minority (N = 15) of multiword fragments that do not appear at equivalence sites? We now review their characteristics. Fourteen nominal constructions occurred at points compatible with Wolof but not French syntax, divided (roughly equally) between noun + adjectival modification structures, as in (22), and 'N *de* N' modification structures, as in (23). Upon closer examination, it appears that these structures in fact display many of the characteristics of loanwords. What are these characteristics?

(22)   *oui oui* <u>*même âge*</u> **bi**   **la.**
        yes yes same age DEF FOC
        [Yes, yes, it's the same age.] (Wolof 3: 413: Spkr 01)

(23)   **fexeel**   **ba**   **nekk ci**   <u>*tête de liste*</u>   **bi**   **rek.**
        try+IMP until be   PREP head of the list DEF ADV
        [Try to be only at the head of the list.] (Wolof 2: 33: Spkr 02)

For one thing, most of these nominal constructions, regardless of type, feature undetermined nouns. In this they resemble the borrowed lone French-origin nouns, while differing from the multiword fragments that *do* appear at equivalence sites. In the latter context, only one NP in a multiword fragment contained a bare noun, appearing, parenthetically, in one of the rare equivalence sites in which a null determiner is permissible in French as well, given in (24).

(24)   **ba** ‖ <u>*midi*</u> *jusqu'au soir*   **di**   **na** *défiler deux cents,*   *deux cents*
        from noon until   night AUX it pass by two hundred two hundred
        sénégalais différents.
        senegalese different
        [From noon 'til night you are going to see two hundred, two hundred different Senegalese pass by.] (Wolof 1: 665: Spkr 01)

Second, like the borrowed French nouns in otherwise Wolof contexts, they are completely embedded in Wolof discourse; unlike the multiword fragments involving French NPs, French lexical items do not continue beyond the boundaries of the NP.

Moreover, the 'N *de* N' constructions virtually all consist of frozen or idiomatic expressions functioning as compounds, e.g. *langue de cuisine* [broken language], *conditions de vie* [living conditions], *tête de liste* [head of the list], most likely incorporated unanalysed into Wolof. With one exception, the remaining nouns are all modified by two adjectives independently found to have been borrowed in these data: *même* [same], as in (22) and *vrai* [real]. If *vrai* and *même* are loanwords, they constitute a Wolof context by the criterion invoked in footnote 5 above; the French-origin nouns they modify should therefore actually be classed among the lone French-origin nouns studied in section 3.1.1.

However, perhaps the most important evidence that these fifteen nominal constructions are borrowed and not switched comes from their patterns of adjective placement. Seven of the French-origin nominal constructions in Wolof–French bilingual discourse consisted of a noun + attributive adjective. As detailed elsewhere (Meechan and Poplack 1993), French tends to postpose noun-modifying adjectives to their head, a pattern which is borne out in the French spoken by the Wolof–French bilinguals in our sample (ibid.). It is thus striking that in all but one of the attributive adjective constructions in the data, the adjectives are *preposed* to the head.

Why should this be? The answer resides in the structure of the recipient language. Prenominal adjectives are optional in Wolof, while directly postposed adjectives are strictly excluded.[16] The most logical explanation for the adjectival modification patterns of these nominal constructions is that they have been borrowed into Wolof.

As a final test of this hypothesis, we compare modification patterns for the nominal constructions occurring at non-equivalence sites with those occurring at equivalence sites. Recall that the crucial differences between Wolof and French involve lack of an overt article, prevalent in the former but rare in the latter, and overt indefinite determination, rare in the former, but prevalent in the latter. Strikingly, it is precisely here that the reversal in patterns of nouns occurring at equivalence and non-equivalence sites is most apparent. The nouns at non-equivalence sites pattern like monolingual Wolof nouns, confirming that they are being treated as borrowings, while the nouns at equivalence sites pattern like monolingual French nouns, exactly as would be expected of code-switches. This is bolstered by the finding that indefinite determination occurs disproportionately more among French nominal constructions occurring at equivalence sites. We have already noted that this is due to the fact that French and Wolof coincide in prenominal placement of indefinites, a fact which facilitates code-switching between them at this site.

On the basis of the preceding analyses, we are now in a position to identify the fifteen nominal constructions at non-equivalence sites as borrowings. When we remove them from the calculations in Table 10.4, we find that *all* but one of the (unambiguous) prenominal switches occur at equivalence sites. Thus, in Wolof–French bilingual discourse, the problem of non-equivalence presented by the NP is resolved, i.e. the boundary between Wolof discourse and a French NP is constructed perfectly.[17]

Summarising, the variationist method has revealed not only quantitative, but also qualitative differences between the two major categories of mixed nominal constructions we have examined thus far. The lone French–origin nouns are modified according to Wolof, not French, patterns of (overt and zero) modification and appear overwhelmingly in Wolof, not French, syntactic structures. At the same time their patterning differs significantly from that of French nouns both in monolingual French discourse and in multiword fragments.

Having previously laid to rest the possibility that these results could be due to coincidence, since monolingual French determination structures were shown (Figure 10.3) to differ significantly from those of Wolof, we may now conclude that in these contexts most of the lone French-origin nouns in Wolof contexts are functioning, for all intents and purposes, like monolingual Wolof nouns, i.e. as borrowings.[18]

The method also reveals that the multiword French fragments in fact represent two classes of materials. One shows the internal structure of Wolof (as well as French), but appears at syntactic boundaries compatible with Wolof only. We have reviewed a number of lines of evidence arguing that these too are borrowings, largely frozen expressions which are fortuitously multiword fragments. The other shows the modification structure of monolingual French but not Wolof NPs, while appearing overwhelmingly at syntactic boundaries compatible with *both* French and Wolof, rather than with Wolof alone, i.e. at equivalence sites. Using the same line of reasoning employed earlier, we conclude that these fragments are French, not only etymologically but also grammatically; i.e. they are code-switches. The structural distinction between the categories of code-switching and borrowing is perhaps most eloquently illustrated by one of our Wolof informants, who, within the same discourse, first switches (25), then borrows (26), the French noun *égalité* [equality].

(25)   **sunu** *idées* **yu   ñu am   rek,   xam   nga ay** ‖ *égalité,   fraternité,*
        POSS ideas that we have ADV know you IND equality, fraternity
        égalité   entre   hommes et   femmes.
        equality between men   and women
        [Our ideas that we have, you know, equality, fraternity, equality between men and women.] (Wolof 4: 230: Spkr 3)

(26)   **ma ñəw   fii,   degg** *affaire* **u** *égalité* **ay** *hommes*
        I   come LOC understand thing of equality IND men
        ak *femmes* **yooyu.**
        and women DEM
        [When I came here, I heard about the equality thing between men and women.]
        (Wolof 4: 238: Spkr 3)

3.2 Fongbe–French

3.2.1 Lone French-origin nouns in otherwise Fongbe discourse

As in the Wolof case, the overwhelming majority of mixed discourse involving nominal constructions consists here too of lone French-origin nouns in an otherwise Fongbe context, accounting for a full 93% of mixed NPs in the data (Figure 10.2). As previously, we compare their distribution across different categories of noun modification with that of two corpora of Fongbe and French nouns in their respective monolingual contexts.

The comparison will prove particularly instructive, since NP structure differs considerably from Wolof to Fongbe, as indicated in Table 10.3. Given that determination patterns in the (monolingual) French spoken in the two communities are basically the same (showing more definite than indefinite and more overt than no determination; cf. Figures 10.3 and 10.4), any differences in their treatment of French-origin material in bilingual discourse may more readily be attributed to the structure of the recipient language.

We mentioned above that virtually all Fongbe noun modifiers are postposed, as in (27), making the NP structure of the language almost totally non-equivalent to that of French.

(27)   **gbὲ   ɔ́**   **é ɖò nùkɔ̀n yì wὲ ɖò**   *plan* **ɖé   lέ**   **jí,**
            world DEF it be before go it's LOC plan IND PLU on

      ɖò gŭɖò   yì wὲ ɖò *plan* **ɖé   lέ**   **jí.**
      be behind go it's on plan IND PLU on

      [The world goes forward from some points of view and backward from other points of view.] (Fongbe 3: 1128: Spkr 03)

In addition to these structural differences, Figure 10.4 shows that there are statistically significant differences between the two languages in *rate* of modifier usage. Most important of these is the fact that Fongbe nouns tend *not* to co-occur with overt determiners like their French counterparts, surfacing instead as bare nouns. We now compare noun modification usage in lone French-origin nouns in otherwise Fongbe contexts.

It is immediately apparent from Figure 10.4 that lone French-origin nouns in otherwise Fongbe contexts pattern with monolingual Fongbe nouns, as was observed in Wolof. They too co-occur with each of the four categories of modification at nearly the same rates. The only exception is again the category of 'other modification'. This time, the lone French-origin nouns show significantly higher

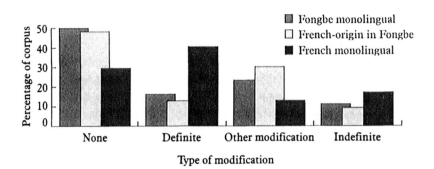

Figure 10.4 Patterns of modification on lone French-origin nouns in otherwise Fongbe contexts, as compared with monolingual Fongbe and French nouns (based on tables C and D in the appendix)

rates of these modifiers. Interestingly, analysis reveals that this apparent discrepancy is derived from the behaviour of possessive marking, and is explicable thus: the disproportionate number of possessive markers in the lone French-origin nouns is paralleled by a disproportion in lexical types. Once the data are normalised according to type, it becomes evident that both native Fongbe and lone French-origin nouns co-occur with possessive markers at approximately the same rate.

Not only do the lone French-origin nouns pattern with their Fongbe counterparts, they differ massively from monolingual French nouns: for example, they take definite markers only 16% of the time as opposed to 40% of the time in monolingual French; they take indefinite markers only 9% of the time, as compared with 17% in monolingual French. If these nouns were more than only etymologically French, their lexical requirements with respect to determiners should come from French. Hence, the co-occurrence patterns of such nouns with determiners, regardless of the language of the latter, should mirror those of French. If they are functioning as Fongbe nouns, even for the nonce, they have no such restrictions. The only plausible explanation for the pattern in Figure 10.4 is that the lone French-origin nouns have been borrowed into Fongbe. We now turn to an examination of the multiword fragments.

3.2.2 Multiword fragments

Forty-four multiword fragments involving the NP were initially identified in these data, as in (28).

(28)   ázɔ̌   ɖò tò   mì tɔ́n   mɛ̀ có   mì nɔ́   ɖò
work be country we POSS in however we HAB say
ǹ nyí ‖*diplômé   sans   emploi   diplômé   sans   emploi.*
I be   graduate without employment graduate without employment
[There is work in our country; however, we say 'I am an unemployed
graduate, an unemployed graduate'.] (Fongbe 3: 1396: Spkr 03)

This figure, constituting no more than 7% of the mixed tokens involving nouns
(Figure 10.2) is remarkably meagre given the widely attested favoured status of
nominal elements in code-switching (e.g. Berk-Seligson 1986; Poplack 1980;
Poplack et al. 1988b; Treffers-Daller 1991).

What are the characteristics of these multiword fragments? In examining the
distribution of modification of French nouns within multiword French fragments
in Fongbe–French bilingual discourse with regard to the familiar categories of
modification (Table 10.5), we observe that the patterns differ both from those of
monolingual French in showing few overt determiners, and from those of monolingual Fongbe and lone French-origin nouns in otherwise Fongbe contexts in
showing a disproportionate amount of 'other' modification. Moreover, a full 68%
of them occur at non-equivalence sites, an inordinately large proportion as compared to Wolof, where virtually none of the multiword fragments occurred at such
sites.[19] Let us examine these switches in more detail.

Table 10.5 *Distribution of modification on French nouns within multiword French fragments in Fongbe–French bilingual discourse*

Language of determiner:	French	Fongbe	Unknown	Total	
Marker:	%	%	%	N	%
Definite	2	3	0	5	11%
Indefinite	1	2	0	3	7%
None	0	0	11	11	25%
Other modification	25	0	0	25	57%
Total N	28	5	11	44	

Closer inspection reveals that these multiword French nominal constructions
constitute a category distinct from the constructions already identified as code-
switches and borrowings. They have the following distinguishing characteristics.

(i) They virtually always consist of one of three modification structures: noun and adjectival as in (29), numeral and noun as in (30) or 'N *de* N' as in (31), explaining their elevated rate of 'other modification'.

(29)   énέ   ɔ́   *conséquences sociales* wὲ nyí *chômage*   mὲ
       DEM DEF consequences social   it's be unemployment people
       lέ   tɔ̀n.
       PLU POSS
       [These are the social consequences of unemployment.]
       (Fongbe 3: 135: Spkr 03)

(30)   hwé   nέ   nú   ɔ́   ǹ ná   ɖò *quatorze ans* ɖó   wὲ
       moment DEM while TOP I FUT be fourteen years have be
       [At that time, I was fourteen years old.] (Fongbe 1: 611: Spkr 01)

(31)   yé   ɖóná yí   *autorisation*   ɖé   mais *autorisation   de*
       they must take authorisation whatever but authorisation of
       principe   wὲ.
       principle it's
       [They must get permission, but it's token permission.]
       (Fongbe 4: 161: Spkr 04)

(ii) Most of them lack an overt determiner.

(iii) They are completely embedded in Fongbe discourse, insofar as French lexical items do not continue beyond the boundaries of the NP.

They differ substantially from other switches that have been empirically studied on at least three counts: their grammatical (here, determiner) structure differs from that of their lexifier language, their internal constituency is highly limited and the return to Fongbe takes place immediately after the NP.[20] Yet (in contrast with the superficially similar nominal constructions identified as borrowings in the Wolof corpus), our method provides evidence precluding so identifying these constructions. Recall that borrowing canonically consists of single content words or frozen expressions. Some of these NPs, on the other hand, are so complex as to render any appeal to borrowing forced at best, as seen in (8).

Even where the NP consists of no more than Noun + Adj, the resulting groupings are productive, as in (32), rather than idiomatic or frozen.

(32)   *ou bien* é nyɔ́   hú   *mimétisme inconscient.*
       or well it be good COMP mimicry unconscious
       [Or else, it's better than unconscious mimicry.]
       (Fongbe 3: 1446: Spkr 03)

In addition, the adjectives feature French morphology where applicable, agreeing in gender with their head, as in (33) and (34).

(33)   à   ɖòná ɖó   *formation précise* có   bó   yì   *aventure.*
you must have training   precise before and go adventure
[You must have precise training before going on an adventure.]
(Fongbe 4: 303: Spkr 04)

(34)   à   kà   ɖóná ɖó   *objectif précis*   à   ɖònă ɖó   *programme.*
you MOD must have objective precise   you must have programme
[You must have a precise objective, you must have a programme.]
(Fongbe 4: 319: Spkr 04)

The French nominal constructions in French multiword fragments in fact correspond to the 'constituent insertions' identified by Sankoff and Naït M'Barek (1990). To qualify as a constituent insertion according to their definition, the French constituent should be embedded in Fongbe syntax while retaining the internal structure of French. In fact, most of these French nominal constructions (including more than half of those classed under 'other modification') lack an overt determiner. We assume that these are *Fongbe* structures, since bare nouns are vastly preferred in that language, whereas monolingual French nouns display a distinct tendency to co-occur with overt determiners (Figure 10.4).

Of course, in their tendency to surface bare, the constituent insertions resemble not only monolingual Fongbe nouns, but also the lone French-origin nouns in otherwise Fongbe contexts shown in section 3.2.1 to pattern like the former. Can we infer, using the same logic as previously, that the French nouns are also indistinguishable from the longer stretches? To do so, it will be necessary to demonstrate that their internal constituencies are also comparable.

As a methodological caveat, we note that the only way to determine the internal structure of a lone lexical item is through analysis of its morphological structure. We remarked earlier that Fongbe is an isolating language, featuring virtually no overt morphology on the noun. Moreover, the few potential loci for productive morphological marking of nouns (e.g. irregular plurals and gender) rarely ever occurred in our French data. Indeed, the impossibility of assessing morphological integration in these language pairs was the original motivation for the present comparative study of modification structures. We therefore focus on the internal structure of the constituent insertions, as in Table 10.6, and compare it, where possible, with what we know of monolingual Fongbe, taken from Meechan and Poplack (1993).

Table 10.6 *Internal structure of French constituents inserted in Fongbe–French bilingual discourse*

Structure of NP	N	%
Noun + adj.	17	39%
Adj. + noun	4	9%
Numeral + noun	10	23%
Noun *de* noun	9	20%
Other structures	4	9%
[(Fr Det) + Noun + (Det)]		
	44	

Table 10.6 shows that approximately half of the constituent insertions contain an attributive adjective, most featuring Noun + Adj order. This is the canonical pattern of adjectival expression, in both 'standard' French and the (monolingual) French of these speakers. Recall that in Fongbe, though direct noun modification using Noun + Adj order is theoretically permissible (section 2.2.1), this option is rarely used. In a study of adjectival modification among sixteen of the speakers constituting the Fongbe–French speaker sample corpus (ibid.), only two adjective types occurred in monolingual Fongbe direct noun modification structures. The canonical method of adjectival expression in Fongbe is via adjectival verbs in predicative position. We conclude that the internal structure of the constituent insertions is that of French.[21]

4 Discussion and conclusions

The variationist method has revealed that lone French–origin nouns in otherwise Wolof and Fongbe discourse pattern like monolingual Wolof and Fongbe nouns with regard to their modification structures. At the same time they have been shown to pattern, where the structure of the language pair allows this to be established, *differently* from French nouns in both French monolingual contexts and in multiword fragments. Given the definition of borrowing in section 1, we are now in a position to conclude that the lone French-origin nouns are *borrowings* into Wolof and Fongbe, whether nonce or established.

The multiword fragments in this study, though surprisingly rare in both corpora, were revealed by our method to comprise three classes of materials. The first, characteristic of Wolof–French bilingual discourse, shows the internal structure of French, but not Wolof, and occurs overwhelmingly at equivalence sites, i.e. syntactic boundaries that are homologous in both French and Wolof. These correspond to the elements we have defined (section 1), as code-switches under equivalence. The small class of apparent exceptions in the Wolof–French corpus, though similar in surface form, were revealed, by the same comparative analysis of their distribution and internal structure, to pattern like Wolof, and not like French, i.e. like borrowings. The third class, characteristic of Fongbe–French bilingual discourse, features the internal constituency of French, but occurs at syntactic boundaries compatible with Fongbe. These correspond to the elements we have identified as constituent insertions.

Both types of (multiword) switches to French pattern internally with the (monolingual) lexifier language. Switches under equivalence occur at points around which the word order of the languages involved in the switch is homologous; constituent insertions, in contrast, need only respect the word order of the language into which they are inserted. Given the surface similarities among these classes of multiword fragments, we stress that neither their characteristics nor the distinctions between them could have been uncovered without reference to the quantitative details of their internal and external *patterning*, as revealed by the variationist method.

We have made no operational attempt to distinguish between nonce borrowings and established loans in this paper, because there is ample evidence that there is no difference between them with regard to their syntactic integration into the recipient language (Poplack *et al.* 1988a; Poplack *et al.* 1988b).[22] In any event, their exact status in no way impinges on the inescapable finding, confirming those in Poplack *et al.* (1987) and Sankoff *et al.* (1990), that lone other-language-origin nouns behave *differently* from multiword fragments, regardless of whether the latter can be identified as code-switches under equivalence, as in the Wolof case, or constituent insertions, as in the Fongbe case. This is the most compelling evidence that these results of language contact must be distinguished for the purposes of constructing a theory of constraints on either of their structures.

How can the preference for constituent insertion in Fongbe–French bilingual discourse be explained? This may well be a community strategy, comparable to the preference for flagged code-switching between English and French in Ottawa-Hull (Poplack 1985), as was found by Sankoff and Naït M'Barek (1990) in comparing language mixture in two communities of fluent Arabic–French bilinguals. We suggest that the explanation may be (at least in part) structural.

There are basically no equivalence sites for intraclausal switching between Fongbe and French in the vicinity of the noun.[23] It is reasonable to inquire why use of French is not then simply restricted to borrowing, with long stretches eschewed altogether. In a sense, it is. Constituent insertion is exceedingly rare, not accounting for more than 5% of all mixed structures involving nouns (Figure 10.2). Indeed, although insertion has sometimes been proposed as a general model for language mixture (e.g. Rivas 1981; Joshi 1985; Myers-Scotton 1993), we note that, in contrast to equivalence-based switching, in the languages in which it has been identified empirically, its scope of application is highly limited. In the Moroccan Arabic–French discourse studied by Sankoff and Naït M'Barek (1990), only the determiner phrase (DP) (Abney 1987) is affected, in Tamil–English (Sankoff *et al.* 1990), only quotative clauses are involved and in the Fongbe–French case studied here, only a complement of DP is involved. Clearly, constituent insertion is not exploited by bilinguals in a wholesale manner, but rather involves only some constituents on a situation- and language-specific basis.

Now constituent insertion imposes weaker constraints on the languages involved than switching under equivalence. While it too requires that the internal grammaticality of the switched fragment be preserved, for its placement it need only refer to the word order of the language into which it is inserted. The only possibilities for (and sites of) switching under equivalence in Fongbe–French bilingual discourse are in numeric determination structures and in the small set of French constructions which admit null determiners. We may speculate that, depending on the structure of the languages at their disposal, speakers will opt to relax one of the requirements of the equivalence constraint rather than refrain from code-switching completely, albeit for a limited class of constituents. Strong support in favour of this suggestion comes from comparison with Wolof, where the structural conflict with French is only partial. In contrast to Fongbe, *all* of the French multiword fragments that could unambiguously be identified as code-switches within the Wolof DP occurred at the equivalence site between indefinite articles and nouns. We may thus infer that only where the grammar provides no other option do compromises with equivalence occur.

Whether or not this suggestion accounts for the (sporadic) use of constituent insertion among the Fongbe–French bilinguals in this study in no way detracts from the major findings of this study. These are as follows: other-language multiword fragments functioning as code-switches are distinct from lone other-language items, most of which are borrowings, in their patterning and their distribution. Therefore borrowings, whether nonce or established, not only can but must be distinguished from code-switches, of the types discussed here or others, in any attempt to construct a theory of the behaviour of either. Models which fail to do so necessarily run the risk of concealing important structural distinctions.

APPENDIX

Table A. *Patterns of modification on Wolof nouns in Wolof contexts and French nouns in French contexts*

Language of noun and its context	Wolof		French		Stats.	
Marker:	N	%	N	%	χ^2	sig
Definite	94	35%	164	41%	1.84	
Indefinite	19	7%	80	20%	20.37	√
None	80	30%	45	11%	38.03	√
Other modification	72	27%	114	28%	.10	
Total N	265		403			

Table B. *Patterns of modification on lone French-origin nouns in an otherwise Wolof context, as compared with monolingual Wolof and French nouns*

Language of context	French		Wolof			
Language of noun:	French		French		Wolof	
Marker:	N	%	χ^2	sig	χ^2	sig
Definite	173	30%	12.84	√	2.84	
Indefinite	90	15%	3.25		11.18	√
None	142	24%	26.98	√	3.21	
Other modification	179	31%	.67		1.09	
Total N	583★					

★This total is not 584 because one token had both Cenn and Ci.

Table C. *Patterns of modification on Fongbe nouns in Fongbe contexts and French nouns in French contexts*

Language of noun and its context	Fongbe		French		Stats.	
Marker:	N	%	N	%	χ^2	sig
Definite	89	16%	93	40%	53.99	√
Indefinite	60	11%	39	17%	5.51	√
None	278	50%	68	29%	28.00	√
Other modification	129	23%	31	13%	9.64	√
Total N	556		231			

Table D. *Patterns of modification on lone French-origin nouns in otherwise Fongbe contexts as compared with monolingual French and Fongbe nouns*

Language of context	French				Fongbe		
Language of noun	French				French		Fongbe
Marker:	N	%	χ^2	sig	χ^2	sig	
Definite	80	13%	81.48	$\sqrt{}$	1.64		
Indefinite	53	9%	11.73	$\sqrt{}$	1.31		
None	293	48%	24.08	$\sqrt{}$	.19		
Other modification	182	30%	24.10	$\sqrt{}$	6.62	$\sqrt{}$	
Total N	608						

Notes

We gratefully acknowledge the support of the Social Sciences and Humanities Research Council of Canada in the form of grants #410-90-0336 and #410-93-0464 to Poplack and #752-92-0380 to Meechan for the work on which this chapter is based. The Wolof and Fongbe data were collected and transcribed respectively by Moussa Ndiaye and Comlan Tossa, who also participated in designing and implementing the coding protocol. We thank David Sankoff and Pieter Muysken for comments and critiques that substantially improved this work. A preliminary version of this paper was presented at NWAVE 22.

[1] Each example is identified by corpus (Wolof or Fongbe), cassette number, line number on the transcript and speaker number, in that order. The data show phonological variability which is not necessarily represented in the orthography. Examples are glossed, where possible, with the corresponding English lexical item rather than grammatical labels. Where the exact English correlate was not clear, or to clearly identify determination types recognised by this study, grammatical markers were glossed with the following codes: 1sg = first person singular, 2sg = second person singular, 3sg = third person singular, 1pl = first person plural, 2pl = second person plural, 3pl = third person plural, ADJ = adjective (pre- = prenominal, post- = postnominal), ADV = adverb, ART = article, ASP = aspect marker, AUX = auxiliary, CAUS = causative marker, CL = clause, COND = conditional marker, CONJ = conjunction, DEF = definite marker, DEM = demonstrative, EMP = emphatic, FOC = focus, FUT = future marker, GEN = genitive, HAB = habitual marker, IMP = imperative, IND = indefinite, LOC = locative, MOD = modal, NEG = negation, PAST = past tense, PLU = plural, POSS = possessive, PREP = preposition or postposition, PRO = pronoun, PRT = particle, REF = reflexive, REL = relator/relative, SUBJ = subjunctive, TOP = topic marker. Translation of discourse particles in this and ensuing examples is approximate.

[2] Reference to the African languages as Wolof/Fongbe here and elsewhere in this chapter is conventional only and in no way implies that they may be equated in any sense other than in their relationship to French in the mixed constructions examined here.

[3] If the lone nouns are more appropriately construed as code-switches, as predicted by, among others, the Matrix Language Frame (MLF) Model (Myers-Scotton 1993), our coding system should also reveal no systematic distinction between our categories of lone French-origin nouns and multiword fragments. This is because most, if not all, of the lone French-origin nouns (identified as code-switches in the MLF model) would be expected to follow the 'matrix language' (ML) grammar, as would some (unknown) proportion of the multiword fragments. Since our category of multiword fragments comprises both Myers-Scotton's 'embedded language' (EL) 'islands' and ML+EL constituents, each of which is predicted to behave differently, no coherent pattern of noun modification *systematically* relating the lone nouns to the multiword fragments should emerge.

[4] Proper nouns, which often behave idiosyncratically with respect to determination, along with nouns that are ambiguous as to language origin, were excluded from the study.

5 Wolof/Fongbe contexts, on occasion, include French-origin verbs independently found to have been borrowed into Wolof/Fongbe, as in the following example:

> **fokk naa moom moo   la   *envoyerwoon lettre* bi   *quoi.***
> think I   him   FOC+he you send+past   letter DEF what
> [I think it's him that had sent you the letter eh.]
> (Wolof 3: 1442: Spkr 1)

[6] Conjunctions like *mais* and *parce que* were considered extraclausal for these purposes and so did not play a role in determining the language of the clause.

[7] There is no theoretical reason for limiting the study to French multiword fragments; these simply constituted the overwhelming majority of the available data.

[8] Although no Wolof adjectives actually appeared prenominally in the corpus, we note that the structural position exists (Grelier 1970).

[9] Adjectival modification in Wolof is canonically expressed through a (postposed) relative clause, as in the example below, taken from Meechan and Poplack (1993).

> **jabar   bu   yem,   nga ko məna takk.**
> woman REL be ordinary you pro can   marry
> [You can (only) marry an ordinary woman.] (Wolof 3: 1274: Spkr 04)

[10] Wolof determiners are formed by attaching a class-marking consonant C (e.g. [b], [j], etc.) to the root morpheme. [y] indicates plural. Only one singular determiner of the form aC appeared in these data (in a frozen form).

[11] The functional and structural status of the Fongbe article is ambiguous. As our informant was unable to reliably distinguish the topic function from the defi-

nite reference function, when the marker ɔ̀ was not syntactically disambigu-
ated as to function, we simply coded nouns modified with it as definite. As will
be seen, even if some of the items we coded as definite are in fact, topic markers
(assuming the distinction between them is meaningful), this would only
strengthen our findings.

12 The χ^2 test for significance requires that each category contain a minimal
number of tokens, necessitating that other modification categories be col-
lapsed.

13 Lone French-origin nouns showed no variability, insofar as all occurred at the
syntactic boundaries required by the language into which they were incorporated. Some of these may of course have coincided with French syntactic boundaries, thereby rendering these boundaries equivalence sites, but this is
fortuitous.

14

$$\chi^2 = \sum_{i=1}^{2} \frac{(\chi_i - n_i\hat{\theta})}{n_i\hat{\theta}(1 - \hat{\theta})}$$

where $\frac{x_1}{n_1}$ and $\frac{x_2}{n_2}$ are the proportions of the marker in question in French and
Wolof/Fongbe and

$$\hat{\theta} = \frac{x_1 + x_2}{n_1 + n_2}.$$

Significance was set at the .05 level.

15 The one apparent counterexample, involving more possessive marking in
monolingual Wolof nouns, was revealed to be semantically, rather than structurally, motivated.

16 Note that even the one example featuring N + Adj. order admits an analysis
based on Wolof syntax. The adjective involved (*québécois*) is identical with its
corresponding noun, making the structure ambiguous with the permissible
Wolof N (*u*) N modification construction.

17 The only exception involves the following example which, parenthetically,
constitutes the only palindromic switch structure (cf. Sankoff *et al.* 1990) in
the data.

> *le   terme technique* **nga   y   *utiliser   plus   que   euh   l'   anglais***
> DEF term   technical   you   ASP   use   more   than   uh   DEF   English
> ***courant* bi.**
> everday DEF
> [It's technical terms that you use more than uh- everyday English.]
> (Wolof 4: 146: Spkr 04)

18 Some of them (e.g. those modified with indefinite determiners) may well be
single-word code-switches. This does not affect our point which is simply that
these cases are ambiguous as to status and therefore shed no light on the
structure of code-switching.

19 Note that we adopt a stricter version of equivalence here than that defined in
section 1. According to the latter, switches violating the equivalence constraint
would fall to 52%.

[20] Making use of the additional argument that they tend *not* to occur at equivalence sites would be circular in this context, since this is the issue at hand.

[21] The numeral + noun and 'N *de* N' constructions shed no light on this issue as their structures are coincidentally homologous in both members of the language pair.

[22] The results of this study may be added to the accumulating body of evidence supporting this claim.

[23] This difficulty may be exacerbated by the possibility that Fongbe may, in fact, lack a category of determiners comparable to French, thereby compounding structural non-equivalence with categorial non-equivalence. Resolution of this issue must await a typological analysis of Fongbe nominal structure.

Bibliography

Abney, S. (1987) The English noun phrase in its sentential aspects. Unpublished Ph.D. dissertation. Cambridge, Mass.: MIT Press.

Akoha, A. B. (1980) *Quelques éléments d'une grammaire du fon-gbè: nominal et syntagme nominal.* Thesis for 'le doctorat de troisième cycle'. Université de Paris III.

Bentahila, A. and Davies, E. E. (1991) Constraints on code-switching: a look beyond grammar. In *Papers for the symposium on code-switching in bilingual studies: theory, significance and perspectives.* (Held in Barcelona, 21–23 March 1991.) Strasbourg: European Science Foundation, 369–405.

Berk-Seligson, S. (1986) Linguistic constraints on intrasentential code-switching: a study of Spanish/Hebrew bilingualism. *Language in Society,* 15: 313–48.

Boeschoten, H. (1990) Asymmetrical code-switching in immigrant communities. In *Papers for the workshop on constraints, conditions and models.* (Held in London, 27–29 September 1990.) Strasbourg: European Science Foundation, 85–100.

Brousseau, A.-M. and Lumsden, J. (1990) Nominal structures in Fongbe. In C. Lefebvre ed., *La genèse du créole haïtien: un cas particulier d'investigation sur la forme de la grammaire universelle. Études syntaxiques, phonologiques et lexicales.* Université du Québec à Montréal, 1–32.

Eliasson, S. (1989) English–Maori language contact: code-switching and the free morpheme constraint. *Reports from Uppsala University Department of Linguistics,* 18: 1–28.

(1990) Models and constraints in code-switching theory. In *Papers for the workshop on constraints, conditions and models.* (Held in London, 27–29 September 1990.) Strasbourg: European Science Foundation, 17–55.

Gamble, D. P. (1963) Elementary Wolof grammar. In G. Manessy and S. Sauvageot eds., *Wolof et Serer: études de phonétique et de grammaire descriptive.* Dakar: Publications de la Section de Langues et Littératures, 131–61.

Grelier, S. (1970) *Essai de comparaison morpho-syntaxique de l'anglais, du wolof et du français.* Dakar: Centre de Linguistique Appliquée de Dakar.

Grevisse, M. (1986) *Le bon usage* (12th edn). Paris: Duculot.

Joshi, A. K. (1985) Processing of sentences with intrasentential code-switching. In D. R. Dowty, L. Karttunen, A. M. Zwicky eds., *Natural language processing: psychological computational and theoretical perspectives.* Cambridge University Press, 109–205.

Ka, O. (1994) *Wolof phonology and morphology.* Lanham, Md.: University Press of America.

Meechan, M. and Poplack, S. (1993) Orphan categories and adjectival expression: a comparative study of Wolof–French and Fongbe–French bilingual discourse. Manuscript, University of Ottawa.

Muysken, P. (1987) Neutrality in code mixing. In *Eigen en vreemd: identiteit en ontlening in taal, literatuur en beeldende kunst: handelingen van het 39ste Nederlands Filologencongres, Vrije Universiteit, Amsterdam, 18–19 December, 1986.* Amsterdam: VU Uitgeverij, 359–73.

  (1991) Needed: a comparative approach. In *Papers for the Symposium on Code-switching in Bilingual Studies: theory, significance and perspectives.* (Held in Barcelona, 21–23 March 1991.) Strasbourg: European Science Foundation, 253–72.

Myers-Scotton, C. (1993) *Duelling languages: grammatical structure in code-switching.* Oxford: Clarendon Press.

Naït M'Barek, M. and Sankoff, D. (1988) Le discours mixte arabe/français: des emprunts ou alternances de langue? *Canadian Journal of Linguistics/Revue Canadienne de Linguistique,* 33 (2): 143–54.

Njie, C. M. (1982) *Description syntaxique du Wolof de Gambie.* Dakar: Les Nouvelles Éditions Africaines.

Poplack, S. (1980) Sometimes I'll start a sentence in Spanish Y TERMINO EN ESPAÑOL: toward a typology of code-switching. *Linguistics,* 18: 581–618. Also in J. Amastae, L. Elías-Olivares (1982) eds., *Spanish in the United States. Sociolinguistic aspects.* Cambridge University Press, 230–63.

  (1985) Contrasting patterns of code-switching in two communities. In H. J. Warkentyne ed., *Methods V: Papers from the Fifth International Conference on Methods in Dialectology.* University of Victoria Press, 363–86.

  (1990) Variation theory and language contact: concept, methods and data. In *Papers for the workshop on concepts, methodology and data.* (Held in Basel, 12–13 January 1990.) Strasbourg: European Science Foundation, 33–66. Also in D. Preston (1993) ed., *American dialect research: an anthology celebrating the 100th anniversary of the American Dialect Society.* Amsterdam: Benjamins, 251–86.

Poplack, S., Clément, R., Miller, C., Trudel-Maggiore, M. and Purcell, K. (1988a) Peut-on entendre l'intégration d'un emprunt? Paper presented at NWAVE 17, November 1988, Université de Montréal.

Poplack, S., Sankoff, D. and Miller, C. (1988b) The social correlates and linguistic processes of lexical borrowing and assimilation. *Linguistics,* 26: 47–104.

Poplack, S., Wheeler, S. and Westwood, A. (1987) Distinguishing language contact phenomena: evidence from Finnish–English bilingualism. In P. Lilius, M. Saari eds., *The Nordic languages and modern linguistics,* 6. (Proceedings of the Sixth International Conference of Nordic and General Linguistics in Helsinki, 18–22 August 1986.) 33–56. Also in K. Hyltenstam, L. K. Obler

(1989) eds., *Bilingualism across the lifespan. Aspects of acquisition, maturity and loss*. Cambridge University Press, 132–54.

Rambaud, J. B. (1963) De la détermination en wolof. In G. Manessy and S. Sauvageot eds., *Wolof et Serer: études de phonétique et de grammaire descriptive*. Dakar: Publications de la Section de Langes et Littératures, 11–23.

Rand, D. and Patera, T. (1992) Concorder. Version 1.1S. Montreal: Centre de recherches mathématiques.

Rivas, A. (1981) *On the application of transformations to bilingual sentences*. Amherst: University of Massachusetts, Department of Spanish and Portuguese.

Samb, A. (1983) *Initiation à la grammaire Wolof*. Dakar: Institut Fondamental d'Afrique Noire.

Sankoff, D., Monpetit, C. and Dupont, M. (n.d.) Issues in bilingual syntax: Tagalog–English code-switching and borrowing. Manuscript, Université de Montréal.

Sankoff, D. and Naït M'Barek, M. (1990) Dramatically contrasting language mixture strategies in two communities of fluent Arabic–French bilinguals. Paper presented at NWAVE 19, October 1990, University of Pennsylvania.

Sankoff, D., Poplack, S. and Vanniarajan, S. (1990) The case of the nonce loan in Tamil. *Language Variation and Change*, 2: 71–101.

Treffers-Daller, J. (1991) Towards a uniform approach to code-switching and borrowing. In *Papers for the workshop on constraints, conditions and models*. (Held in London, 27–29 September 1990.) Strasbourg: European Science Foundation, 259–77.

11 A LEXICALLY BASED MODEL OF CODE-SWITCHING

Carol Myers-Scotton

1 Introduction

Although the first students of code-switching (CS) focussed on its social functions and were largely sociolinguists, soon a structural question – where in a sentence might a speaker switch from one linguistic variety to another – caught the attention of more researchers. These now included not only sociolinguists, but also syntacticians and psycholinguists. The first of these looked to the surface structure of sentences for clues about constraints on switching. For example, many concentrated on the extent to which like constituents matched in word order across the languages involved in CS (e.g. Lipski 1977; Pfaff 1979; Poplack 1981; Sridhar and Sridhar 1980). Others pointed to surface category memberships, arguing that switches were not possible involving certain categories, such as pronominal clitics (Timm 1975) or any bound morphemes (Poplack 1981). Still others suggested that the size of the constituent had something to do with its switchability (e.g. Gumperz 1982). The common feature of such structural constraints was that while they described CS phenomena in a specific data set, they had no independent motivation relating them to other findings or to theories about the nature of linguistic structures. Possibly for this reason, when subsequent researchers examined other data, they found many counterexamples to the earlier claims (e.g. Bokamba 1988; Romaine 1989).

This emphasis on only descriptive adequacy changed in the mid-1980s as some researchers sought explanations for CS configurations within current syntactic or psycholinguistic theories. Some researchers with specialisations in syntax motivated their CS constraints with the 'government conditions' posited for monolingual data within a Government and Binding framework (see Chomsky 1981). For example, DiSciullo, Muysken and Singh (1986) argued that switching was impossible within a maximal projection. However, many counterexamples to such constraints have been cited as well (see Pandit 1990; Myers-Scotton 1993b). Others, beginning with Joshi 1985, paid special attention to psycholinguistic models (see Garrett 1975, 1990) which posit that open- and closed-class items are retrieved at different stages in language production (see also Petersen 1988; Kamwangamalu 1989; Myers-Scotton and Azuma 1990; Azuma 1991).

Finally, while discounting the importance of surface level equivalences, other researchers emphasised more abstract level equivalences to account for switchability. By implication, such researchers motivated their hypotheses with the lexially based subcategorisation restrictions found increasingly in syntactic theories. One of the first to do this, Bentahila and Davies (1983), cited clashes between languages regarding subcategorisation for specific syntactic structures (e.g. whether a specific verb is subcategorised for a finite complement in one language, but an infinitival complement in another language) as an explanation of instances where CS does not occur. Later, Azuma (1991) referred to similar clashes in subcategorisation (e.g. does a specific verb take a direct object in one language but a prepositional phrase in another language?). From a related point of view, Muysken (1991) spoke of 'categorial equivalence' across languages as a constraint on CS (e.g. does one language use predicate adjectives while another language uses stative verbs to convey the same types of concepts?).

Meanwhile, given the counterexamples cited to various proposed constraints on CS and the apparent variation in the type of CS patterns existing in the world, some researchers questioned whether generally applicable constraints on CS exist at all, even for data drawn from only a single language pair (see Clyne 1987; Romaine 1989). Others (e.g. Bentahila and Davies 1992) continued to stress the influence of social and psychological variables on switching patterns.

Against this backdrop, this chapter sketches my approach to intra-sentential CS as contained in the Matrix Language Frame model (hereafter MLF model).[1] The proposition supported is that intra-sentential CS is governed by a set of abstract principles which seem to apply to CS data sets across different communities and therefore are apparently cognitively based.

I begin by stating the basic premise of the MLF model and comparing it briefly with earlier approaches. A discussion of how to identify a Matrix Language in CS utterances follows; it is the dominant language in structuring intra-sentential CS constituents. I then detail the three hypotheses structuring the model and provide examples from different CS data sets which support these hypotheses. This discussion includes an explication of the distinction between system and content morphemes, a distinction crucial to testing the hypotheses. I conclude with some implications of the model for other types of bilingual speech production and for syntactic and psycholinguistic theories.

2 MLF model: the basic premise

The heart of the MLF model is the claim that two interrelated hierarchies direct the structuring of sentences containing CS. These are:

(a) the Matrix Language vs Embedded Language hierarchy. Of the two or more languages involved in CS, one plays the more dominant role. It is labelled the Matrix Language (hereafter the ML), with the other language(s) labelled the Embedded Language(s) (hereafter the EL(s)).

(b) the system vs content morpheme hierarchy. The terms 'system' and 'content' morpheme will be discussed in more detail shortly; here, suffice it to say that function words and inflectional affixes are prototypical system morphemes while noun and verb stems are prototypical content morphemes. System morphemes are important because they build constituent frames, and only one source of system morphemes can control constituent frame formation at one point in time. It is the ML which always 'wins out' in frame control for mixed constituents, supplying system morphemes. The EL may only supply content morphemes in mixed constituents (and, occasionally, 'syntactically irrelevant' system morphemes which typically only appear attached to EL content morphemes). In addition, 'EL islands', constituents well-formed in the EL (composed of both EL content and system morphemes) also occur in intra-sentential CS. As will become clearer, EL material is always thought of as having been inserted in an ML frame. Thus, the MLF model views intra-sentential CS specifically as a Complement Phrase (CP) or 'sentence bar' containing at least one constituent with morphemes from two or more languages; in addition, the CP can contain EL islands, as well as ML islands (constituents entirely in the ML). The ML vs EL distinction is relevant to the CP because its grammatical frame comes from the ML.

3 Comparisons with earlier approaches

In focussing on what happens during language production, the MLF model departs from the earlier work discussed above. Generally, this work dealt with either equivalences in surface word order or the effect of hierarchies in phrase structure trees (e.g. the relationship between a head and its maximal projection). However, the MLF model claims that the explanation for surface CS configurations (and their phrase structure relationships) lies in language production processes which are lexically based. That is, directions 'calling' grammatical structures are contained in *lemmas*, abstract entries in a speaker's mental lexicon (see Levelt 1989). Lemmas include all the non-phonological aspects of an item's lexical information.[2]

Which lemmas are activated depends on decisions made at the most abstract level of production, the conceptual level. In CS, based partially on informational aspects of the message which the speaker wishes to convey, the competition over which language will supply the lemmas to be activated is decided. In addition, in either monolingual or bilingual speech, the *form* of the utterance depends on both pragmatic and socio-pragmatic considerations. They have to do with whatever intentionality the utterance will convey, in addition to its explicature. Messages of intentionality arise from the form which an utterance takes; form includes the medium or language in force. Intentionality carried in an utterance's form may convey additional messages expanding on the referential intent of the utterance; these are pragmatic messages. Or the utterance's form may convey intentions of a socio-psychological nature; these are socio-pragmatic messages. In CS, it seems clear that the source language of particular lemmas conveys such intentional meaning; that is, there is a 'message' in code choice in CS (see Myers-Scotton 1993a).

Clearly, the production system recognises the source of lemmas, for when lemmas send instructions to the formulator (a sort of morphosyntactic control central), language-specific morphosyntactic frames result. That is, the formulator activates only those morphosyntactic procedures which were called by the active lemmas, and it inhibits other procedures. Thus the surface configuration of lexemes in a morphosyntactic frame is the net result of lemma selection at abstract levels. (See Figure 11.1.)

While the MLF model is one of few production-based CS models, it still builds on earlier work. First, the claim of differential participation of the ML and EL in CS utterances is at least implicit in several earlier treatments (e.g. Sridhar and Sridhar 1980; Nishimura 1986), as well as explicit in Joshi 1985 (although not fully developed). More recently, others have begun to consider this distinction (e.g. Nortier 1990; Muysken, this volume). And many others recognised, if only in passing, that the difference in status of open- and closed-class morphemes affects their potential for being produced in the EL. Further, like Joshi's and Azuma's work (cited above), the MLF model is partially motivated by psycholinguistic models of language production which are based on speech-error data. Finally, claims I will make regarding necessary congruency are reminiscent of earlier work on subcategorisation, although the MLF model seeks to make general claims about congruency, rather than ones specific to a language pair or category.

Conceptual level:	Speaker's intentions regarding referential information and pragmatic and socio-pragmatic messages
Functional level:	Select lemmas from mental lexicon (congruent with intentions)
	Lemmas send directions to the formulator (regarding morpho-syntactic procedures)
	(Result: basic sentential frame is set)
Positional level:	Select phonological representations
	(Result: lexemes are realised)
	Direct positioning of lexemes

Figure 11.1

4 Defining the ML

Because the ML plays the main role in setting the sentence frame when CS arises, its identification is important. Since the reason to identify the ML at all is to predict structural constraints, its definition must be independent of its structural role. That is, for example, identifying the ML as the language of the finite verb or of its inflections, in effect, obviates the point of identifying the ML. The ML is defined *in order to predict* the source of the morphosyntactic frame; of course this includes verb inflections.

As I argue elsewhere (Myers-Scotton 1993b, 1993c), selection of the ML has a sociolinguistic basis, even though this selection has structural consequences. While important, psycholinguistic considerations are less crucial. True, the speaker must be relatively proficient in the ML, since it will supply the morpho-syntactic frame of mixed constituents; yet, there are clear cases where the speaker's first language is the EL, *not* the ML.[3]

Three criteria, applied in concert, define the ML.

(i) The sociolinguistic basis of the ML is clear since the ML is the language which is the more unmarked (in terms of its socio-psychological associations) for the interaction type in which the CS occurs. Often the ML will be the language most associated with solidarity-building functions for the speakers.

(ii) Speaker judgments also point toward the ML. Kamwangamalu and Lee (1991) provide empirical evidence that persons engaged in CS can identify which language is the ML.

(iii) The relative frequency of morphemes from the participating languages is also a good indicator: the ML is the language providing relatively more morphemes for the relevant interaction type than the other language(s) used in the same conversation. A discourse sample of at least two sentences (within the same turn or across speakers) is a minimum.[4]

Assignment of the ML is a dynamic matter. Even though sociolinguistic and psycholinguistic criteria are not amenable to measurement, in general, a major change in their content means a change in the assignment of ML status. For example, within the same interaction, the ML can change when there is an adjustment in situational factors (e.g. a new topic, an added participant). Within a community, the ML can change over time, especially when there are realignments of socio-psychological values because such realignments may trigger a language shift. For a variety of reasons, even when a shift is only in progress, the target language of the shift becomes the likely candidate to take over, at least for some interactions, as the ML during CS.

5 The ML hypothesis of the MLF model

I turn now to the first of the three hypotheses of the MLF model which are relevant to this paper, the ML Hypothesis. The MLF model views the frame of any sentence as a set of structural specifications. Frame construction is driven by those lemmas in the mental lexicon activated by directions from the conceptual level. Lemmas, which are tagged for a specific language, include in their content directions to the formulator regarding the morphosyntactic procedures to be activated in language production.

The purpose of the ML Hypothesis is to explain what goes into the frame-building of mixed CS constituents (i.e. composed of morphemes from both the ML and EL). Within the model, these mixed constituents are also called ML + EL constituents.

The ML Hypothesis is motivated by two lines of research within psycholinguistics. First, motivation comes from those psycholinguistic models of language production (e.g. Garrett 1975, 1990; Levelt 1989; Bock 1991) which posit a two-step process in sentence production. While details differ from one model to another, generally these models suggest that the retrieval process is different for open- vs closed-class elements (roughly similar to content vs system morphemes). The premise that not all morphemes are treated the same in language production suggests an explanation for CS configurations.[5]

For example, Garrett (1990) argues that, in contrast with open-class elements, closed-class elements are accessed separately as part of the morphosyntactic planning frame. Some of the evidence leading to such hypotheses comes from monolingual speech-error data. In speech errors the typical pattern is this: when content morphemes 'exchange places' in a sentence, function words or inflections typically stay in their original slots and do not 'exchange' with their heads. For example, see (1) in which the plural suffix 'remains in place' while its 'correct' head (*song*) is misplaced; also note that in (2) the past tense suffix does not 'move' with its head (*flood*):

(1)   We'll sit around *the song* and sing *fires*.
        (Target: we'll sit around the fire and sing songs.)
        (Garrett 1990: 159)

(2)   The *flood* was *roaded*.
        (Target: the road was flooded.)
        (Stemberger 1985: 162)

Second, the ML Hypothesis is based on the idea that, of the languages in bilingual speech production, one is more activated than the other(s) (Green 1986). Empirical support for this idea is the finding of a 'base-language effect' in experimental studies of the word-recognition processes of bilinguals; that is, the first reaction of subjects (in word-recognition tasks) is to assign a new word to the 'base' language of the context, not the 'guest' language (see Grosjean 1988).

These claims and findings offer motivation for the ML Hypothesis, which states that two factors pattern together in mixed CS constituents: dominant language status (i.e. Matrix Language status) and the supplying of those morphemes which make up the constituent's frame. Stated formally, the hypothesis is this:

The ML determines the morphosyntax of ML + EL constituents.

From this, two testable principles follow. Examples supporting these principles are given below.

(i) The Morpheme Order Principle: surface morpheme order will be that of the ML in ML + EL constituents.

(ii) The System Morpheme Principle: all 'syntactically or externally relevant' system morphemes come only from the ML in ML + EL constituents.

Any system morpheme is considered 'syntactically relevant' only if it takes part in agreement relationships external to its own head (see example (8) below where this point is clarified).

Obviously, in order to test this principle, a clear distinction between system and content morphemes is required. What follows is such an explication under the MLF model (see Myers-Scotton 1993b).

6 Distinguishing content and system morphemes

First, from a functional perspective, system morphemes include those categories of lexical items sharing a general deictic function; that is, they 'point directly', meaning their values are locally determined. For example, Demonstrative is such a category or variable because it represents a class of variants whose values are context-specific. Stated more formally, any lexical item belonging to a syntactic category which involves *quantification across variables* is a system morpheme. This means that syntactic categories which are system morphemes (e.g. Demonstrative) are classes of individuals or events, and specific system morphemes are the specific individuals or events (e.g. *this*, *that*, in English). Within the MLF model, system morphemes are characterised as [+Quantification] or [+Q].

Prototypical syntactic categories which are [+Q] are those involving specification across individuals, such as quantifiers, determiners and possessive adjectives. [+Q] is also a property of inflectional categories which express person, gender or case. However, quantification may also apply across events (see Dowty 1979). Thus, [+Q] may also be considered a property of other categories, such as tense and adverbs expressing intensity or time (e.g. *very*, *soon*) but not adverbs derived from adjectives (e.g. *brightly*). In sum, any lexical item which is a member of a syntactic category which can be specified as [+Q] is a system morpheme.

Second, remaining syntactic categories necessarily have the feature [−Q]. The MLF model classifies them for one of the two features relating thematic roles to the predicate argument structure of a constituent. Thematic roles (also called theta-roles), of course, refer to the semantic relationship between verbs and their arguments. For example, transitive verbs typically assign the theta-roles of agent and patient to their arguments. Information about this relationship is part of the lemma entry of the verb (i.e. its entry in the mental lexicon).

The two features related to theta roles are 'theta-role assigner' and 'theta-role receiver'. Plus settings for either of these features are associated with content morphemes, but not with system morphemes. Ouhalla (1989: 10–11) reaches a similar conclusion when he observes that 'functional categories lack thematic grids' and 'substantives have thematic grids'.[6] Since they assign theta-roles, most verbs and some prepositions will be content morphemes. Some verbs or prepositions, however, have the reading [-theta-role assigner]; therefore, they are system morphemes. Among verbs, these are the copula and the *do* of '*do* constructions' (exemplified below). Also, some prepositions are system morphemes (e.g. the possessive *of* in English as in *book of John*). Such prepositions only assign case while prepositions which are content morphemes assign both case and theta-roles (e.g. *beside*).

In addition, nouns, pronouns and descriptive adjectives are potential content morphemes by virtue of the relevance of the feature 'theta-role receiver' to their classification. (Note that those other categories included under the category NP are not considered since they have already been assigned as system morphemes, based on their association with the feature [+Q].)

The claim that nouns and descriptive adjectives are content morphemes seems non-controversial since they typically receive theta-roles. In addition, those pronouns which receive theta-roles also are content morphemes; these are the free-form pronouns except the dummy pronouns (*it* and *there* in English). Dummy pronouns and clitic pronouns (i.e. morphologically attached pronouns) do not qualify as theta-role receivers. Regarding clitics, Jake (1994) argues that the form of clitics is structurally determined by either overt arguments (i.e. nouns or free-form pronouns governing the clitic appear in addition to the clitic) or null arguments (i.e. only the clitic appears). It is these nouns and pronouns, not the clitics, which are theta-role receivers. Thus, because clitics (and also agreement morphology) are not directly associated with a theta-role receiving argument, these categories are system morphemes.

Finally, some categories qualify as content morphemes because of their discourse-level roles. At this level, they signal such semantic content as REASON and MANNER (see Talmy 1985). These include subordinating conjunctions (e.g. *because, but*) and possibly some complementisers. More study of complementisers is needed, however. Note that classifying these categories as content morphemes modifies the discussion in Myers-Scotton 1993b. (Refer to Figure 11.2 for full details.) How to treat sentential complementisers (e.g. *that* in English) remains a problem. They are easily borrowed (like content morphemes) but they behave in most (not all) CS data sets as if they were system morphemes (see Myers-Scotton 1993b: 129–32).

7 Examples supporting the ML hypothesis

Some of the examples of this chapter come from my own field-work in Nairobi, Kenya. Other examples are taken from the general CS literature. Only space restrictions limit the number and variety of examples cited, since all known examples, with a very few clear exceptions, support all the hypotheses of the MLF model. Examples (3) through (9) show the preeminence of the ML over the EL in setting the frame for ML + EL constituents, whether for ML

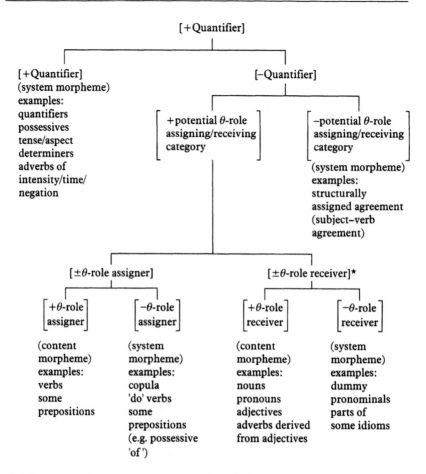

* Discourse-level content morphemes not included.

Figure 11.2

morpheme order or for ML system morphemes. In the MLF model, 'constituent' is used to refer to any group of morphemes showing structural dependency relations (i.e. hierarchical relations). Since strings in sentences show hierarchical relations, it should be no surprise that what is identified as one ML + EL constituent may well be part of a larger ML + EL constituent.

Note that ML + EL constituents typically consist of singly occurring EL morphemes embedded in a frame of any number of ML morphemes.[7] Some others (Sankoff et al. 1990) argue that many of the singly occurring EL morphemes which are identified here as CS forms are 'nonce borrowings'. The MLF model relates CS and borrowing as processes and CS forms and borrowed forms as states (i.e. surface forms): both CS forms and borrowed forms show the morphosyntax of the ML (see Myers-Scotton 1992b and 1993b for a full discussion). For example, in (3) the borrowed form *party* and the CS forms *corner*, *time* and *movements* are equally integrated into the ML morphosyntax. Therefore, the model argues there is no motivation for a category such as 'nonce borrowings'.

(3)　　　... Wewe katika hiyo *party* nzima hukuona msichana kasoro Rose
　　　　　tu? Wewe ulikuwa umejikunja kwa *corner*

　　　　　u-　　na-　　-m-　　*time* tu. Unamuangalia *movements*

　　　　　2S-NON-PAST- OBJ 3S time just　　　　　　movements

　　　　　y-ake　　　z-olé ...

　　　　　CL.9-POSS CL.10-all[8]

　　　　　'... In that whole party you didn't see [another] girl, just Rose? You
　　　　　just put yourself in a corner and "timed" her. You were watching all
　　　　　her movements ...'
　　　　　(Swahili–English #16 Myers-Scotton 1993b: 86–7)

Swahili can be established as the ML of the discourse for all Swahili–English examples cited here. Consider *u-na-m-time* literally 'you-NON-PAST-her-time' ['you were timing her']. Note that the tense prefix and the object prefix precede the verb stem, according to Swahili specifications, even though they are affixes of an English verb stem. Second, note *movements yake zote* literally 'θ-movements CL.9-her CL.10-all' ['all her movements'].[9] The head-first word order of Swahili, not the head-last order of English for NPs, is followed. Just as important, the Swahili modifiers follow Swahili modifier order, with the possessive adjective preceding the quantifier.[10]

(4)　　　Noch schlimmer, wenne de *client recalé* wurd am *permis* weje de *panne d'essence*.
　　　　　'Even worse, when the learner is failed in the test because of the empty tank [referring to a driving test].'
　　　　　(Alsatian/French Gardner-Chloros 1991: 152)

All indications are that Alsatian is the ML in this conversational turn. Note that the French verb precedes the Alsatian auxiliary *wurd* in accordance with Alsatian syntactic specifications. In the French equivalent (*est recalé* [is failed]) the order is reversed.

In order to falsify the Morpheme Order Principle, one would have to find examples, such as (5a), in which the modifier *mbili* [two] precedes its head, *plate*. That is, the morpheme order would have to be that of English, the EL in this case. Nothing like it occurs in Swahili–English data studied to date. Conversely, there are many actual examples such as (5b) in the data studied (i.e. with EL head nouns taking ML morpheme order for their modifiers).

(5a)   *Anakula mbili *plate* . . .
(5b)   Anakula *plate* mbili . . .
        'He eats two plates . . . '
        (Swahili–English #6 Myers-Scotton 1993b: 86)

Thus, whether a certain morpheme order is acceptable in a mixed CS constituent depends on only one factor: is this the ML order for such a constituent? Failure to recognise this fact is behind earlier puzzlement as to why bilinguals rejected certain test sentences. That is, the reason a sentence such as *I went to the house chiquita* (Pfaff 1979: 307) is unacceptable in Spanish–English CS is not that the order of modifiers does not match in Spanish and English, as Poplack's Equivalence Constraint suggests. Rather, the reason is that the ML here is apparently English, and in English modifiers typically precede, not follow, head nouns. That is *chiquita* is out of place in an ML frame.

Examples (6) through (9) support the System Morpheme Principle, which calls for all relevant system morphemes to come from the ML in mixed constituents. The principle is so stated that any of three strategies meet its specifications. They are:

(i) example (6): all system morphemes which are required by ML well-formedness conditions appear in the constituent and all come from the ML.

(ii) example (7): as long as it has no syntactic relations outside of its head (i.e. it is not externally relevant), an EL system morpheme may accompany an EL content morpheme (e.g. an inflection marking plurality), if the ML system morpheme performing the same function also appears.

(iii) examples (8) and (9): stems may be accessed as 'bare forms'; that is, they do not show the system morphemes required by ML well-formedness conditions.

(6)   . . . Unaanza ku-*behave* kama watu wa huko
                INFIN-
         wa- -na-   -vyo-   -behave
         3PL NON-PAST MANNER
         ' . . . You being to behave as people of there behave.'
         (Swahili–English #6 Myers-Scotton 1993b: 103)

Note that in this example all of the verbal inflections come from Swahili, the ML. Since inflections are system morphemes, the fact they come only from the ML in mixed constituents supports the System Morpheme Principle. In example (3) we saw that the possessive adjective (*yake* [her]) and the quantifier (*zote* [all]) in the NP *movements yake zote* [all her movements] both came from Swahili, the ML, not English, the EL. Again, the discussion above and Figure 11.2 indicate how both of these categories are analysed as system morphemes.

Other CS researchers report similar findings regarding system morphemes; that is, they come from the ML, not the EL, in mixed constituents. For example, in discussing mixed NPs in CS utterances in Brussels, Belgium, for which Brussels Dutch is the apparent ML, Treffers-Daller (1991: 197) states, 'Almost all [French] attributive adjectives receive normal Dutch inflection.' Also, in writing about Turkish–Dutch mixed constituents produced by Turkish immigrants in the Netherlands (with Turkish as the apparent ML), Boeschoten (1990: 89) states that the full range of Turkish inflections is represented, but 'Dutch articles and plurals never occur and are rejected by bilinguals . . . '.

(7)   . . . a-ka-ndi-*waste*-er-a *time* yangu, ma-*chance-s* a-cho a-aka-per-a . . .
        CL.6-
        ' . . . You have wasted my time and those chances are gone . . . '
        (Shona–English Crawhall 1990)

In this case, the interest is specifically with *ma-chance-s* since it shows 'double morphology' (see Myers-Scotton 1993b). That is, the system morpheme marking plurality is duplicated, with both the English suffix (-*s*) and the Shona class six prefix (*ma-*). However, Shona is the ML here and only the Shona prefix is 'externally active' (i.e. with syntactic relationships outside its head). The external relevance of *ma-* is clear since it controls class six agreements on the following demonstrative (*a-cho*, 'CL.6-those') and for the pronominal clitic on the verb stem (*a-aka-per-a* [they are gone]).

(8)   had *uitkering*
        'this unemployment benefit'
        (Moroccan Arabic–Dutch Nortier 1990: 199)

In this case, Moroccan Arabic is the ML. The noun from the EL (Dutch) is a 'bare form' because it does not show the definite article (in addition to the demonstrative *had* [this]) which Arabic requires in such an NP.

'Bare forms' do not violate the System Morpheme Principle since the principle does not require that ML system morphemes be present, but only that if any externally relevant system morphemes are present, they must come from the ML. However, 'bare forms' are a problem for the MLF model. For some reason having to do with lack of congruence between the ML and the EL, 'bare forms' are EL-content morphemes which manage to slip through the frame-building step without receiving ML system morphemes. See Myers-Scotton and Jake (forthcoming) for some tentative explanations.

(9)   Turker alsa, *klant*-lar   *wegjagen* yap-iyor
                   customer-PL chase   do-PROG
        'If he were to take Turks, he chases away customers.'
        (Turkish–Dutch Boeschoten 1990: 90)

Example (9) shows a special type of a mixed constituent, seemingly designed to make up for the fact that its main verb is a 'bare form'. This constituent is a '*do* construction', consisting of an EL verb stem with no inflections and an ML *do* verb inflected with system morphemes from the ML. Such *do* constructions occur in many, but not all, of the CS language pairs studied to date, from Japanese/English (Azuma 1991) to Panjabi–English (Romaine 1989) to Shona/English (Myers-Scotton 1993b).

In (9) above, the Dutch noun *klant* [customer] takes a Turkish plural suffix. This follows the predictions of the System Morpheme Principle. To falsify the principle, one would have to produce examples where 'externally relevant' system morphemes come from the EL; that is, in this case, a Dutch plural morpheme would have to appear in place of the Turkish system morpheme.

8 Further hypotheses of the MLF model

In addition to the ML Hypothesis, the other main hypotheses of the MLF model are the Blocking Hypothesis and the EL Island Trigger Hypothesis.

8.1 The ML Blocking Hypothesis

While content morphemes in ML + EL constituents may come from either the ML or the EL, not all EL content morphemes are acceptable. This hypothesis predicts which EL content morphemes may appear in ML + EL constituents. It follows:

> A Blocking Filter blocks an EL content morpheme *not congruent with its corresponding ML morpheme*.

'Congruency' is defined as a match between the EL content morpheme and the ML content morpheme in two ways. First, if its counterpart in the ML is a system morpheme, there is no match at all. For example, if a pronoun in the EL is a free form and a theta-role receiver and therefore is a content morpheme, but its match in the ML is a pronominal clitic and therefore not a theta-role receiver, then the EL morpheme – even though it is a content morpheme – may not appear in a mixed constituent; see example (10). Second, an EL content morpheme must match its ML counterpart in terms of its subcategorisation features. These features specifically refer to theta roles (their assignment in the case of verbs and prepositions and their reception in the case of nouns, descriptive adjectives and pronouns); see example (11). Research to date indicates that congruence at two levels must be considered, the Lexical–Conceptual Level and the Predicate–Argument Level. How these are relevant is currently being studied (Myers-Scotton and Jake, forthcoming). Indications are that not only sentence-level considerations are important; congruence at the discourse level also must be considered.

Examples (10) and (11) illustrate some instances.

(10)   *You didn't have to worry* que *somebody* te iba a tirar con cerveza o una

             COMP   you

       botella *or something like that.*

       'You didn't have to worry that somebody was going to throw beer or a bottle at you or something like that.'

       (Spanish–English Poplack 1981: 170)

There are several EL islands (from English) in this sentence, but the interest now is in the ML + EL constituent, *que somebody te iba a tirar con cerveza o una botella.* This analysis assumes that Spanish is the ML. The English content morpheme *somebody* (as an existential pronoun, it is a content morpheme, not a quantifier selecting an individual) can occur because it is congruent with a Spanish counterpart, which is also a content morpheme. However, English *you* is blocked by the Blocking Hypothesis; that is, even though it too is also a content morpheme in English, it could not have occurred instead of Spanish *te* because of lack of congruency between the two morphemes. The Spanish equivalent of *you* is best considered a pronominal clitic which does not receive a theta-role (English *you* does receive a theta-role); therefore, *te* is a system morpheme while English *you* is a content morpheme.

(11)   *She* wa, *took her a month to come home* yo.

        TOPICALISER   EMPHATIC

        'Talking about her, [it] took her a month to come home, you know.'

        (Japanese–English Nishimura 1986: 136)

Nishimura states that Japanese is the ML in (11), even though this particular sentence contains a long EL island in English.[11] The EL pronoun (*she*), an emphatic here, encodes the discourse thematic role TOPIC, and occurs with the Japanese topicaliser *wa* (a system morpheme). *She* can occur because it is congruent with a Japanese emphatic pronoun, since both are content morphemes.

To falsify the Blocking Hypothesis, an EL content morpheme, for which there is no congruent ML content morpheme, would have to occur in an ML + EL constituent. For example, consider the possible occurrence of the English preposition *in* in a mixed constituent when Swahili is the ML in Swahili–English CS. Since *in* is a theta-role assigner (i.e. it assigns a locative role in the PP (prepositional phrase) which it heads), it is a content morpheme. Yet, *in* does not have a Swahili counterpart (since in Swahili the verb assigns a locative role to nouns via the suffix -*ni*). Thus, it is predicted *in* may not occur in mixed Swahili–English constituents, and there are no such instances in the data studied. (Note that *in* may occur in an EL island, since a motivation for EL islands is that they make possible EL lexemes prohibited in mixed constituents.)

To summarise the model to this point, the ML Hypothesis in conjunction with the Blocking Hypothesis has these results: (i) the main structural components of the ML (as well as many content morphemes) come from the ML; (ii) EL content morphemes may be inserted in ML + EL constituents if they are congruent with an ML content morpheme.

While it is true this means that ML + EL constituents are produced under directions from both ML and EL lemmas, ML lemmas are in charge of constituent formulation. Examination of the resulting constituents shows this is so in two ways: (i) the morphosyntactic frame is from the ML, and (ii) EL lexemes appearing do so according to the Predicate–Argument Structure requirements contained in ML lemmas. EL lemmas do 'call' these EL content lexemes, but these lemmas may only be activated in mixed constituents if they are sufficiently congruent with ML counterparts at the Lexical–Conceptual Level. Other yet to be identified features may be relevant, too.

If no EL lemmas are involved at all, then the language production formulator produces another type of constituent, the ML island. While they are like ML + EL constituents in being well-formed according to ML specifications, ML islands differ from ML + EL constituents because they include only ML morphemes.

As will become clear in the next section, the only way to realise either (i) an EL content morpheme when the match between an EL lemma and an ML lemma is too limited, or (ii) an EL system morpheme (except through 'double morphology' as discussed above) is to do so in an EL island. EL islands occur when only EL lemmas are selected from the mental lexicon.

8.2 The EL Island Trigger Hypothesis

This hypothesis is a corollary to both the ML Hypothesis and the Blocking Hypothesis in that it predicts those configurations in which EL morphemes which violate those hypotheses may appear. These are EL islands, grammatically well-formed constituents entirely in the EL. The EL Island Trigger Hypothesis follows:

> Activating EL lemmas triggers the formulator in the production system to inhibit ML morphosyntactic procedures and accept EL procedures so that the current constituent surfaces as an EL island.

For all three types of the constituents appearing in sentences showing CS (i.e. ML + EL constituents, ML islands, and EL islands), the *origination process* is the same. At the conceptual level, what counts as a decision is made to encode a concept with a lemma or lemmas from one language rather than the other. As implied above, decisions resulting in CS (i.e. decisions away from a monolingual discourse in the ML or the EL) would seem to be largely pragmatically or socio-pragmatically based. That is, the act of CS conveys some type of intentionality in addition to referential information.

When the decision at the conceptual level is to activate an EL lemma (excepting those supporting an EL lexeme which has a congruent ML counterpart), the only way to do it is to produce an EL island. Thus, it is now the EL which is sending directions to the formulator for activating morphosyntactic procedures, and an EL island results. (Refer to Figure 11.1 again.)

There is another hypothesis for how EL islands are produced. A 'misfiring' may occur. That is, the formulator somehow accesses an EL system morpheme during frame-building rather than the ML morpheme called for by the ML procedures which had been active. As Green (1994) notes, 'There is evidence from slips of the tongue within the same language that speakers can sometimes entertain more than one way of formulating an idea.'

What types of constituents occur as EL islands? While many EL islands are obligatory (i.e. they contain EL system morphemes or follow EL morpheme order), optional EL islands also occur. Many of the obligatory EL islands in my Swahili–English corpus (N = 121) do begin with EL quantifiers which are of course system morphemes (e.g. *some problems*). Many optional EL islands seem to be either formulaic (e.g. *c'est à dire* or its English counterpart *that is to say*) or adjuncts rather than verb complements. Many optional EL islands in the Swahili–English corpus are time adjuncts (e.g. *last night*). While it seems that any constituent may be an ML island (and they occur very frequently), most optional EL islands carry a low functional load and are structurally peripheral.

Also, EL islands *within* ML + EL constituents are possible and may even be quite frequent in some data sets (see Myers-Scotton 1993b: 151–4). French islands of DET + N within larger ML + EL constituents for which Arabic is the ML are found in Bentahila and Davies 1992.

EL islands require the same type of systematic study given until now only to ML + EL constituents. As a beginning, their distribution needs systematic analysis. For example, it seems that the central arguments of the sentence are rarely in optional EL islands. Treffers-Daller (1991) also refers to the peripheral nature of EL islands in general in her Brussels Dutch–French corpus.

Even more important to investigate further is the relationship of ML dominance to EL island formation. There is some evidence that, even while EL islands are well-formed in the EL, the structural choice between EL alternatives is under influence from the ML (Myers-Scotton 1994). Further, one could argue that obligatory EL islands only result because their material is incongruent with ML framing specifications. In this sense, they are under ML control.

The following examples illustrate EL islands typical of the 121 EL islands occurring in the Nairobi corpus of Swahili–English CS. As noted above, many islands begin with system morphemes as do the islands in (12) and (13).

(12)   . . . Ni-ka-maliza *all the clothing*.
        ' . . . And I've finished [washing] all the clothing.'
        (Swahili–English #39 Myers-Scotton 1993b: 80)

(13)   Tu-na-m-let-e-a *our brother* wa Thika.
        'We are taking [it] to our brother of Thika.'
        (Swahili–English #6 Myers-Scotton 1993b: 141)

(14)   Hata siyo mwezi jana. I-li-kuwa *early this month*.
        'Not even last month. It was early this month.'
        (Swahili–English #36 Myers-Scotton 1993b: 147)

Notice how the EL Island Trigger Hypothesis strengthens the overall model by restricting the occurrence of EL material in intrasentential CS. It does this in two ways: first, it states when EL material *must* surface as an EL island, and it only allows such islands as meet EL conditions for well-formed constituents. That is, EL islands are more than simply a sequence of two or more EL morphemes. Second, since well-formedness conditions call for constituents showing internal structural dependencies, singly occurring CS forms cannot be EL islands. If such forms (single EL lexemes) are to occur at all, they must occur in mixed constituents where they must meet the specifications set for these constituents by the ML Hypothesis and the Blocking Hypothesis.

9 Conclusion

This chapter has shown how the MLF model accounts for intra-sentential CS data. Its overall argument can be characterised under three headings.

(i) The model sees CS utterances as arising in two ways, neither of which has anything to do with surface level 'switching'. (a) For ML + EL constituents, CS configurations arise through an 'insertion process'. That is, ML content morphemes or EL content morphemes are simply inserted into constituents entirely prepared by ML morphosyntactic procedures. Only those EL content morphemes meeting certain ML lemma specifications are inserted. (Fused units of an EL stem + affix, as discussed above under 'double morphology', are analysed as single content morphemes by ML framing procedures.) ML islands are produced when, for whatever reason, no EL lemmas (which support EL content morphemes) are activated; thus, ML procedures are in control of frame-building for both ML islands and ML + EL constituents. (b) EL islands arise when there is a *switching of procedures* (initiated at the conceptual and lemma levels) from those of the ML to those of the EL.

(ii) Just as other naturally occurring linguistic data, CS is governed by structural principles of well-formedness; that is, possible combinations can be predicted. Further, the same basic principles structuring CS utterances apply generally across speech communities. These principles are 'pre-syntactic' in the sense that they are lexically based and realised at an abstract level in decisions to activate lemmas tagged for specific languages which, in turn, send directions to the formulator (the 'control-central' in language production). CS data and the provisions of the model constitute tests for the ability of current syntactic and psycholinguistic theories to accommodate such cross-linguistic data, and for specific claims for monolingual data. For example, Jake (1994) uses CS data to argue against the analysis of Pronoun as a unitary functional category. Also, if the principles governing CS apply universally as it is argued here, it is likely that the same principles apply to other types of bilingual speech production (e.g. second language acquisition, pidgin/creole development), although how they are played out will differ, given the different sociolinguistic and psycholinguistic accompaniments of different language contact phenomena (see Myers-Scotton 1995).

(iii) Still, these claims do not mean that the social profiles of communities and the socio-psychological motivations of speakers are incidental in CS. First, the very designation of the ML obviously depends on the prevailing psycholinguistic and sociolinguistic factors which will be specific to each community. Second, the *performance* of CS need not be the same everywhere. While the MLF model predicts only a limited set of options, which permissible patterns are preferred may be a function of the specific psycho-sociolinguistic profiles of the communities, or of the individual speakers involved (Myers-Scotton 1993a, 1993c).

APPENDIX

Symbols and Abbreviations

2, 3	2nd, 3rd person
*	not grammatically acceptable
CL	class
COMP	complementiser
CP	complement phrase
CS	code-switching
EL	embedded language
INFIN	infinitive
IP	projection of INFL (simple sentence)
IP INFL	(inflectional) phrase
ML	matrix language
N	number
NON-PAST	non-past tense
NON-PRES	non-present tense
OBJ	object
PL	plural
POSS	possessive
PROG	progressive
Q	quantification
S	singular

Notes

1 I gratefully acknowledge support for African field work under a Fulbright Research Grant (1983) and a Social Science Research Council Grant (1988), supplemented by a University of South Carolina Grant. My writings on the social motivations of CS include: Scotton 1986, 1988a, 1988b; Myers-Scotton 1993a and 1993c. My main treatments on structural constraints include: Scotton 1988b; Myers-Scotton 1992a, 1992b, 1993b, 1993c, 1994a and 1994b. ESF working papers are Myers-Scotton 1990 and 1991.

2 Levelt also refers to phonological 'pointers' which are involved in the surface-level realisation of lexemes.

3 Such examples as the following can be multiplied: a first-language speaker of English, who also speaks Dutch but at a less fluent level, is married to a Dutch woman; they live in Amsterdam and engage in CS in home conversations for which Dutch, not English, is the ML.

4 The frequency criterion has two riders. (i) The ML can only be identified for sentences containing CS material if such sentences are studied within a larger corpus. Ideally, any frequency count should refer to an entire converssation; but how large the corpus must be is unresolved. (ii) Any morpheme count must not include cultural borrowings from the EL (words for objects and concepts new to the ML culture). The interaction type may be such as to stimulate the use of many such borrowings (e.g. scientific discourse). For some speakers, EL cultural borrowings are established loanwords in the ML; therefore, there is as much reason to count them as ML morphemes as there is as EL morphemes.

5 Evidence from certain types of aphasia also shows differences in the loss of system morphemes vs content morphemes (Zurif 1990).

6 Ouhalla's interest in functional categories (similar, but not identical, to system morphemes) is different from mine. He argues for their importance in explaining the structural representation of given constructions and the grammatical processes which they may undergo. He also explains variation in structural representations across languages in terms of cross-linguistic differences in the selectional properties of certain functional categories.

7 There are four cases in the Nairobi corpus of two-lexeme noun phrases from the EL in ML + EL constituents and conforming to ML order (e.g. *Kulikiwa na table long* [there was a long table]). Most multiple-lexeme phrases from the EL are EL islands.

8 Noun classes in Bantu languages are traditionally numbered by Bantuists.

9 The noun *movements* is analysed as showing the zero allomorph of the noun class prefix for class ten.

10 The agreements in this example are non-standard, since they are governed by one noun but come from two different classes.

11 The ML + EL constituent is the larger clausal IP, which includes the VP *took her a month to come home* as an internal EL island, which is framed by a null pronoun from Japanese (-theta-role receiver] and the particle *yo*. To interpret

English as the ML in this sentence is not possible, because then this VP would have to be well-formed in English; but it lacks a sentential subject.

Bibliography

Azuma, S. (1991) Two level processing hypothesis in speech production: evidence from intrasentential code-switching. In *Proceedings of Annual Conference 27*. Chicago Linguistic Society.

Bentahila, A. and Davies, E. E. (1983) The syntax of Arabic–French code-switching. *Lingua*, 59: 301–30.

(1992) Code-switching and language dominance. In R. J. Harris ed., *Cognitive processes in bilinguals*. Amsterdam: Elsevier, 443–58.

Bock, J. K. (1992) A sketchbook of production problems. *Journal of Psycholinguistic Research*, 20: 141–60.

Boeschoten, H. (1990) Asymmetrical code-switching in immigrant communities. In *Papers for the workshop on constraints, conditions and models*. (Held in London, 27–29 September 1990.) Strasbourg: European Science Foundation, 85–100.

Bokamba, E. (1988) Code-mixing, language variation, and linguistic theory: evidence from Bantu languages. *Lingua*, 76: 21–62.

Chomsky, N. (1981) *Lectures on government and binding*. Dordrecht: Foris.

Clyne, M. G. (1987) Constraints on code-switching: how universal are they? *Linguistics*, 25: 739–64.

Crawhall, N. (1990) Unpublished Shona–English data.

DiSciullo, A.-M., Muysken, P. and Singh, R. (1986) Government and code-mixing. *Journal of Linguistics*, 22: 1–24.

Dowty, D. (1979) *Word meaning and Montague grammar*. Dordrecht: Reidel.

Gardner-Chloros, P. (1991) *Language selection and switching in Strasbourg*. Oxford: Clarendon Press.

Garrett, M. F. (1975) The analysis of sentence production. In G. Bower ed., *Psychology of learning and motivation* IX. New York: Academic Press, 133–77.

(1990) Sentence processing. In D. Osherson and H. Lasnik eds., *An invitation to cognitive science*. Cambridge, Mass.: MIT Press, 133–75.

Green, D. W. (1986) Control, activation and resource: a framework and a model for the control of speech in bilinguals. *Brain and Language*, 27: 210–23.

(1994) Personal communication.

Grosjean, F. (1988) Exploring the recognition of guest words in bilingual speech. *Language and Cognitive Processes*, 3: 233–74.

Gumperz, J. J. (1982) Conversational code-switching. In his *Discourse strategies*. Cambridge University Press, 55–99.

Jake, J. L. (1994) Intrasentential codeswitching and pronouns: on the categorial status of functional elements. *Linguistics*, 32: 271–98.

Joshi, A. K. (1985) Processing of sentences with intrasentential code-switching. In D. R. Dowty, L. Karttunen, A. M. Zwicky eds., *Natural language parsing*. Cambridge University Press, 190–205.

Kamwangamalu, N. (1989) Some morphosyntactic aspects of French/English-Bantu code-mixing. In B. Music *et al.* eds., *Parasession on language contact. Meeting of the Chicago Linguistic Society (1989).* Chicago: Linguistic Society, 157–70.

Kamwangamalu, N. and Lee, C. L. (1991) 'Mixers' and 'mixing': English across cultures. *World Englishes,* 10: 247–61.

Levelt, W. J. M. (1989) *Speaking: from intention to articulation.* Cambridge, Mass.: MIT Press.

Lipski, J. (1977) Code-switching and the problem of bilingual competence. In M. Paradis ed., *Aspects of bilingualism.* Columbia, S.C.: Hornbeam Press, 250–63.

Muysken, P. (1991) Needed: a comparative approach. In *Papers for the Symposium on Code-switching in Bilingual Studies: theory, significance and perspectives.* (Held in Barcelona, 21–23 March 1991.) Strasbourg: European Science Foundation, 253–72.

Myers-Scotton, C. (1990) Intersections between social motivations and structural processing in code-switching. In *Papers for the workshop on constraints, conditions and models.* (Held in London, 27–29 September 1990.) Strasbourg: European Science Foundation, 57–82.

(1991) Whither code-switching? Prospects for cross-field collaboration: production-based models of code-switching. In *Papers for the Symposium on Code-switching in Bilingual Studies: theory, significance and perspectives* I. (Held in Barcelona, 22–23 March 1991.) Strasbourg: European Science Foundation, 207–31.

(1992a) Constructing the frame in intrasentential codeswitching. *Multilingua,* 11: 101–27.

(1992b) Comparing codeswitching and borrowing. *Journal of Multilingual and Multicultural Development,* 13 (1–2): 19–39.

(1993a) *Social motivations for codeswitching: evidence from Africa.* Oxford: Clarendon Press.

(1993b) *Duelling languages: grammatical structure in code-switching.* Oxford: Clarendon Press.

(1993c) Common and uncommon ground: social and structural factors in codeswitching. *Language in Society,* 22: 475–503.

(1994) (forthcoming) Language processing and the mental lexicon in bilinguals. In R. Dirven and J. Vanparys eds., *New approaches to the lexicon, selected papers from the 18th LAUD Symposium on the Lexicon.* Frankfurt: Peter Lang.

(1995) (forthcoming) 'Matrix language choice' and 'morpheme sorting' as possible structural strategies in pidgin/creole formation. In A. Spears and D. Winford eds., *Pidgins and creoles: structure and status.* Amsterdam: Benjamins.

Myers-Scotton, C. and Azuma, S. (1990) A frame-based process model of code-switching. In M. Ziolkowski, K. Deaton, M. Noske eds., *Proceedings from the 26th Regional Conference.* Chicago Linguistic Society, 307–21.

Myers-Scotton, C. and Jake, J. L. (forthcoming) Matching lemmas: a model of bilingual language competence/production. Submitted for publication.

Nishimura, M. (1986) Intrasentential code-switching: the case of language assignment. In J. Vaid ed., *Language processing in bilinguals: psycholinguistic and neuropsychological perspectives.* Hillsdale, N. J.: Lawrence Erlbaum, 123–43.

Nortier, J. M. (1990) *Dutch–Moroccan Arabic code-switching among young Moroccans in the Netherlands*. Dordrecht: Foris.

Ouhalla, J. (1989) *Functional categories and parametric variation*. London: Routledge.

Pandit, I. (1990) Grammaticality in code-switching. In R. Jacobson ed., *Codeswitching as a worldwide phenomenon*. New York: Peter Lang, 33–69.

Petersen, J. (1988) Word-internal code-switching constraints in a child's grammar. *Linguistics*, 26: 479–93.

Pfaff, C. W. (1979) Constraints on language mixing: intrasentential code-switching and borrowing in Spanish/English. *Language*, 55: 291–318.

Poplack, S. (1981) Syntactic structure and social function in code-switching. In R. P. Duran ed., *Latino language and communicative behavior*. Norwood, N.J.: Ablex, 169–84.

Romaine, S. (1989) *Bilingualism*, Language in Society 13. Oxford: Basil Blackwell.

Sankoff, D., Poplack, S. and Vanniarajan, S. (1990) The case of the nonce loan in Tamil. *Language Variation and Change*, 2: 71–101.

Scotton, C. M. (1986) Diglossia and codeswitching. In J. A. Fishman *et al.* eds., *The Fergusonian impact* II. Berlin: Mouton de Gruyter, 403–15.

(1988a) Codeswitching as indexical of social negotiations. In M. Heller ed., *Codeswitching: anthropological and sociolinguistic perspectives*. Berlin: Mouton de Gruyter, 151–86.

(1988b) Code-switching and types of multilingual communities. In P. Lowenberg ed., *Language spread and language policy, Georgetown Roundtable on Languages and Linguistics '87*. Washington, D.C.: Georgetown University Press, 61–82.

Sridhar, S. N. and Sridhar, K. (1980) The syntax and psycholinguistics of bilingual code-mixing. *Canadian Journal of Psychology*, 34: 407–16.

Stemberger, J. P. (1985) An interactive activation model of language production. In A. W. Ellis ed., *Progress in the psychology of language*. Norwood: Erlbaum, 143–86.

Talmy, L. (1985) Lexicalization patterns: semantic structure in lexical forms. In Timothy Shopen ed., *Language typology and syntactic description* III. Cambridge University Press, 57–149.

Timm, L. A. (1975) Spanish–English code-switching: *el porqué y how-not-to*. *Romance Philology*, 28: 473–82.

Treffers-Daller, J. (1991) French–Dutch language mixture in Brussels. Unpublished Ph.D. thesis, University of Amsterdam.

Zurif, E. B. (1990) Language and the brain. In D. Osheron and H. Lasnik eds., *An invitation to cognitive science* I. Cambridge, Mass.: MIT Press, 177–98.

4

CODE-SWITCHING IN BILINGUAL DEVELOPMENT AND PROCESSING

12 A PSYCHOLINGUISTIC APPROACH TO CODE-SWITCHING: THE RECOGNITION OF GUEST WORDS BY BILINGUALS

François Grosjean

1 Introduction

Code-switching has received considerable attention in recent years from linguists and sociolinguists, and it is no surprise, therefore, that researchers in the other fields of linguistics, such as psycholinguistics and neurolinguistics, should show interest in the phenomenon (see Harris 1992 and Vaid 1986, for recent edited books covering these areas). In what follows, we will first briefly review past work in the psycholinguistics of bilingualism and show how the language mode a bilingual is in when communicating (the monolingual mode or the bilingual mode) needs to be taken into account when studying language processing. We will then focus on a particular aspect of perception and comprehension in the bilingual language mode: the lexical access of code-switches and borrowings. We will describe a number of studies aimed at getting a better understanding of this process and will end with a model of guest word recognition. Before proceeding, though, it is important that we say a few words on how we view the bilingual person.

We will call 'bilingual' those people who use two, or more, languages (or dialects) in their everyday lives. Bilinguals are not the sum of two complete or incomplete monolinguals but have a unique and specific linguistic configuration. They have developed competencies in their languages to the extent required by their needs and those of the environment. They normally use their languages – separately or together – for different purposes, in different domains of life, with different people. Because the needs and uses of the languages are usually quite different, bilinguals are rarely equally or completely fluent in their languages. Levels of fluency in a language will depend on the need for that language and will be domain-specific, hence the 'fossilised' competencies of many bilinguals in their different languages. As the environment changes and the needs for particular skills also change, so will the bilingual's competence in these various language skills. New situations, new environments, new interlocutors will involve new linguistic needs and will therefore change the language configuration of the person involved.

With this 'holistic' view of the bilingual in mind, we will now address the issue of the psycholinguistics of bilingualism and, in particular, of mixed language processing.

2 Psycholinguistics and bilingualism

The basic aim of experimental psycholinguistics, which has concentrated to a large extent on monolinguals, is to study the perception, comprehension, production and memorising of language, be it spoken language, written language or sign language. The psycholinguist attempts to describe and to model the operations that take place during the on-line processing of language, that is, from the moment an utterance is heard or seen by the receptors (ears, eyes) to the moment its internal representation is computed and stored, and, in production, the operations that occur between the moment there is an intention to communicate and the actual output of the utterance, be it spoken, written or signed. In recent years, considerable advances have been made in understanding the underlying processes that allow the production and perception of language. New paradigms have been developed, different linguistic theories have been presented, converging evidence has been obtained from several types of population (children, adults, aphasics, etc.) and new models have replaced old ones. (For a review of the field, see Foss 1988; Garman 1990; Garnham 1985; Levelt 1989; Osherson 1990; Singer 1990; Tartter 1986, among others.)

The psycholinguistics of bilingualism also attempts to describe and explain the operations that take place during language processing but concentrates on people who know and use two or more languages. Until recently the emphasis has been put on the independence of the languages (how does the bilingual keep the two languages separate; does the bilingual have one or two lexicons?) to the detriment of issues such as the on-line processing of language, be it in a monolingual language mode or in a bilingual language mode (see next section). Much research was conducted, for example, on the co-ordinate–compound–subordinate distinction. Despite its inherent appeal, no amount of experimentation has brought conclusive evidence that bilinguals can be classified as co-ordinate, compound or subordinate. (See Grosjean 1982, for a review of studies in this domain.)

Another area of considerable investigation has been whether bilinguals possess one or two internal lexicons. Proponents of the one-lexicon view (also referred to as interdependent storage) state that linguistic information is stored in a single semantic system. Words from both languages are organised in one large lexicon, but each word is 'tagged' to indicate the language it belongs to. Other researchers have claimed that bilinguals have two lexicons (the independent storage view), and that the information acquired in one language is available in the other only through a translation process. Again, despite a large number of studies, no clear-cut results have been found. In fact, it has been proposed recently that bilinguals have *three* stores, one conceptual store corresponding to the bilingual's knowledge of the world and two language stores, one for each language (Paradis 1980, 1989). Considerable work has addressed the issue of the bilingual lexicon recently (see, for example, Schreuder and Weltens 1993).

A third issue of interest has been the ability of bilinguals to keep their two languages separate. Researchers have postulated the existence of a language switch which allows bilinguals to gate out the language not in use, and experimental studies have been conducted to find evidence for this proposal. The results obtained have been inconclusive or, to say the least, questionable, and currently it is felt that no switch, be it psycholinguistic or neurolinguistic, exists in bilinguals. Rather, it has been proposed that bilinguals are probably using various activation and deactivation procedures to keep their languages separate in the monolingual mode and to make them interact in the bilingual mode (Paradis 1980, 1989; see also section 3 of this chapter).

Now that it is generally accepted that the bilingual is not two monolinguals in one person, but a unique speaker–hearer using one language, the other language, or both together depending on the interlocutor, situation, topic, etc., current psycholinguistic research is trying to understand the processing of language in the bilingual's different language modes. In what follows we examine these modes, define a number of terms and then review some of the recent work on the on-line processing of code-switches and borrowings.

3 The bilingual's language modes

We propose that in their everyday lives, bilinguals find themselves at various points along a situational continuum which induce a particular language mode. At one end of the continuum, bilinguals are in a totally monolingual language mode: they are speaking (or writing) to monolingual speakers of either language A or of language B and therefore have to restrict themselves to just one language (A or B). At the other end of the continuum, they are with bilinguals who share their two languages (A and B) and with whom they normally mix languages (code-switch and borrow); they are here in a bilingual language mode. Hereafter we will refer to the two end points of the continuum when speaking of language modes, but we should keep in mind that intermediary levels exist between the two. We should note also that bilinguals differ among themselves as to the extent they travel along the continuum; some rarely find themselves at the bilingual end (purists, language teachers, etc.) whereas others rarely leave this end (bilinguals who live in tight-knit bilingual communities where a form of mixed language is one of the language norms).

In the monolingual language mode, bilinguals adopt the language of their monolingual interlocutor(s) and deactivate, as best they can, the other language. Bilinguals who manage to do this totally and, in addition, who speak the other language fluently and have no foreign accent in it, will often 'pass' as monolinguals. In fact, deactivation is rarely total and this is clearly seen in the interferences bilinguals produce. An 'interference' is a speaker-specific deviation from the language being spoken due to the influence of the other 'deactivated' language. Interferences can occur at all levels of language (phonological, lexical, syntactic, semantic, pragmatic) and in all modalities (spoken or written language). They are usually of two kinds: 'static interferences' which reflect permanent traces of one language on the other (such as a permanent accent, the meaning extensions of particular words, specific syntactic structures, etc.), and 'dynamic interferences', which are the ephemeral intrusions of the second language (as in the case of the accidental slip on the stress pattern of a word due to the stress rules of the other language, the momentary use of a syntactic structure taken from the language not being spoken, etc.). To these between-language deviations, one needs to add within-language deviations (see Grosjean 1982) such as overgeneralisations, simplifications and hypercorrections which can occur when a language is mastered only to a certain level of proficiency. Of course, any speaker, whatever the language (or languages), and whatever the language mode, will make production errors such as slips of the tongue and false starts and will hesitate when speaking. We should note, finally, that putting a bilingual in a monolingual language mode allows one to study interferences (and other types of deviations) more easily but that these also occur in the bilingual language mode, along with code-switches and borrowings.

In the bilingual language mode, both languages are activated. Bilinguals usually choose a base-language to use with their interlocutor (that is, a main language of interaction) but can, within the same interaction, decide to switch base languages if the situation, topic, interlocutor, function of the interaction, etc. requires it. We will use the terms 'language choice' for the 'decision' that is taken as to the base-language to be used and 'language switch' for the shift from one base-language to the other. Once a particular base-language has been chosen (even if only momentarily), the bilingual can bring in the other language depending on a number of factors which we will not review here. This general operation, which we can label 'language mixing', is often made up of two different processes: code-switching and borrowing. 'Code-switching' is shifting (switching) completely to the other language for a word, a phrase, a sentence, etc. 'Borrowing' is taking a word or short expression from the other language and (usually phonologically or morphologically) adapting it to the base-language. It can also refer to taking the meaning component of a word or expression and grafting it onto a word or series of words in the base-language, but in this case it may be that the underlying processes at work are quite different from those involved in code-switching and outright borrowing. One needs to distinguish an 'idiosyncratic loan' (which we have called a 'speech borrowing' and which Poplack and Sankoff (1984) refer to as a 'nonce borrowing') from a word which has become part of a language community's vocabulary and which monolinguals also use (what we refer to as a 'language borrowing'). In our experimental research, we are only interested in the former type of borrowing. We should note, also, that the line is very fine between rapid language switching (as defined above) and code-switching, and between code-switching for a very short segment and borrowing.

Any discussion of the concepts of language contact will have to address each of the categories listed above even if in the end it is decided to regroup them into a global category. It is important, however, not to regroup categories too quickly, as in the case of interferences (and within-language deviations) and code-switches and borrowings. Until the 1960s, the literature had a tendency to label all language contact phenomena observed in bilingual production as interference (see Weinreich 1953); more recently, due to extensive research on code-switching, traces of language contact have often been packaged under the general term of 'code-switching'. We propose that at the level of the bilingual's underlying linguistic systems and of the psycholinguistic processes that take place during the perception, comprehension and production of language, we may be dealing with different phenomena which, on the surface, may at times appear to be identical. Thus, 'baving' (from the French verb *baver* [to dribble]), produced in an English monolingual language mode, is most probably the result of the deactivated language intruding (in a static or a dynamic manner) onto the language being spoken (an interference, therefore), whereas in a bilingual language mode, it is either an interference or the normal access of a word in the less activated lexicon and its integration into the base language (a borrowing). To obtain a better grasp of the concepts that apply to language contact, we will need much more research into the structure and organisation of the bilingual's language systems, as well as into the processing mechanisms involved in the production and perception of language when bilinguals are in various language modes.

As concerns language processing in bilinguals, it is clear that a psycholinguistic model of bilinguals will have to account for the perception and production of language in the different language modes. It will have to describe the ways in which bilinguals in the monolingual mode differ from monolinguals in terms of perception and production processes, and it will have to explain the actual interaction of the two languages during processing in the bilingual mode. In what follows, we will leave aside processing in the monolingual mode (certainly the mode which has received the most attention from researchers) and will concentrate on the bilingual language mode. Here we will study one aspect of language perception and comprehension – the lexical access of code-switches and borrowings – and will propose a model to account for the recognition of guest words in bilingual speech.

4 Lexical access in the bilingual language mode

In recent years, a great deal of research has been conducted on lexical access in monolinguals. We know, for example, that certain properties of words affect their recognition: their frequency of use, their length, their phonotactic configuration, their uniqueness point (i.e. the point in the left-to-right phonotactic configuration at which the word diverges from other words), their lexical neighbourhood. We also know that when words are presented in context, their lexical properties interact with various sources of knowledge (linguistic rules, knowledge of the world, discourse, etc.) to speed up or slow down the recognition process (see Frauenfelder and Tyler 1987, for a review). The exact nature of the 'interaction' between the properties of the words and the sources of knowledge remains to be described adequately, and the controversy concerning the moment at which 'top-down' information enters the lexical access process has yet to be resolved (Forster 1976; Marslen-Wilson 1987; McClelland and Elman 1986; Swinney 1982). However, one conclusion that emerges from this research is that recognising a word may not be a simple mapping between its acoustic–phonetic properties and its entry in the mental lexicon (although see Klatt 1979). Instead, it may well be a rather complex process that involves various narrowing-in and monitoring stages, correcting strategies, post-access decision stages, and even look-ahead and look-back operations (Grosjean 1985a; Grosjean and Gee 1987; McClelland and Elman 1986).

Word recognition in bilinguals has received much less attention, especially when it concerns the access of code-switches and borrowings. The literature most closely related to this latter question dates back a number of years and examines the perception and production of language mixtures, most of them ungrammatical (Kolers 1966; Macnamara and Kushnir 1971; Neufeld 1973; etc.). In a first exploratory study, Soares and Grosjean (1984) investigated the lexical access of base-language words and code-switched words by means of the Phoneme Triggered Lexical Decision task (Blank 1980). English–Portuguese bilingual subjects were presented with sentences and were asked to listen for a word or a nonword within them which began with a pre-specified phoneme. Once this word (or nonword) was found, the subjects had to indicate as quickly as possible whether the item was a real word or not. English monolingual subjects were run on the English sentences only, whereas bilingual subjects were tested on three separate sets of sentences (English, Portuguese and code-switched). Before each set, every effort was made to induce the appropriate language mode: English, Portuguese or bilingual.

Two main findings emerged from this study. The first was that although bilinguals accessed real words in English as quickly as English monolinguals, they were substantially slower at responding to nonwords. This finding provided additional evidence for the residual activation of the other language when the bilingual is in a monolingual language mode (Altenberg and Cairns 1983; Obler and Albert 1978). Soares and Grosjean hypothesised that a nonword triggers a complete search of the base-language lexicon (or an activation of the lexicon, depending on the access theory one espouses) which is then immediately followed by at least a partial search (or activation) of the other, less active, lexicon, and this before the stimulus is classified as a nonword. Hence the longer reaction times.

The second finding was that bilinguals took longer to access code-switched words in the bilingual language mode than they did base-language words in the monolingual language mode. Although at first this was accounted for by suggesting that bilinguals always search the base-language lexicon before the less activated lexicon, in a later paper Grosjean and Soares (1986) suggested that a number of factors could account for the delay, irrespective of the access strategy. Cross-language coarticulation, delay or absence of certain segmental and suprasegmental language switches in the speaker's production, base-language context and the listener's tendency to assimilate ambiguous items during the perception of code-switches could all explain why some code-switches (and for that matter, borrowings) take time to access in the appropriate lexicon.

Subsequently, the importance of the base-language context was investigated in depth by means of a categorical perception paradigm (Bürki-Cohen, Grosjean and Miller 1989). French–English bilinguals identified stimuli from computer-edited series that ranged from an English to a French word. It was found that the base-language had a contrastive effect on the perception of a code-switched word when the end points of the between-language series were strongly marked phonetically as English and French respectively. However, when the end points of the series were less marked phonetically, no effect of the base-language was found. (This latter finding is currently being re-examined.) Thus, the results provided evidence that the perception of a code-switched word is influenced by the base-language context in which it occurs and, moreover, that the nature of the effect probably depends on the acoustic–phonetic characteristics of the code-switched words.

In a more recent study (Grosjean 1988), an attempt was made to track down a number of additional factors which could account for the time it takes to recognise guest words, that is code-switches and borrowings. It was assumed that the bilingual has two lexicons which are interconnected in some way, and that guest words are stored, and therefore have to be accessed during bilingual speech, in the less activated lexicon. This exploration revolved around the role of two variables: a structural or 'word type' variable, and an output or 'language phonetics' variable. Concerning word type, we asked the following questions: first, would guest words that are marked phonotactically as belonging to the guest language lexicon (e.g. in a French sentence, the words 'slash', 'blot', 'drop', which we called Type 1 words) be recognised sooner and with more ease than words not marked in this way? Second, would guest words that belong solely to the guest-language lexicon (we called these Type 2 words; e.g. 'feed' or 'lean') be easier to process than words that do not belong to just one lexicon? Third, would guest words that have near homophones in the base language (Type 3 words; e.g. 'pick', 'pique', 'knot', 'note', 'sit', 'cite') be recognised with more difficulty than other guest-language words? As for the second variable, the language phonetics of the word (i.e. the language it is pronounced in), we asked the following question: would guest words which retain a phonetic cue as to which lexicon they belong to be easier to process than words which are integrated phonetically and morphologically into the base language? In other words, would code-switched words, which normally retain a phonetic cue as to the lexicon they are a part of, be accessed more easily than borrowings which are usually integrated into the base language, and hence have lost some of the cues pertaining to their lexicon of origin?

The guest words, all of them English verbs, were embedded in the French segment 'Il faudrait qu'on . . . ' which was then followed by an appropriate noun phrase (e.g. 'Il faudrait qu'on *knot* les deux cordes'). The sentences were recorded by a French–English bilingual with no apparent accent in either language. Then, by means of computer editing, a series of segments of increasing duration were gated starting with 'Il faudrait qu'on' and going all the way to the end of the sentence (Grosjean 1980). Bilingual subjects (French–English) listened to the segments and, after each presentation, were asked to guess the verb being presented, to give a confidence rating and to finish off the sentence. In the data analysis we examined the isolation point of each word, that is, that point (defined as the percentage of the way through a word) at which each subject correctly guessed the stimulus word and did not subsequently change his or her guess, as well as the erroneous candidates proposed prior to the isolation point.

The results confirmed the importance of the two variables under study. First, words that are marked phonotactically as belonging to the guest language only (e.g. 'slash', 'blot') were identified sooner than words not marked in this way. Subjects needed 66% of Type 1 words to identify them as opposed to 78% for Type 2 words. Second, words that belong solely to the guest lexicon (Type 1 and 2 words) were recognised sooner than words that do not belong to just one lexicon (Type 3): 97% of Type 1 words and 92% of Type 2 words were identified before their ending whereas only 43% of Type 3 words fell into this category. Third, words in the guest-language lexicon that have close homophones in the base language (Type 3 words) were processed with more difficulty than other guest-language words: 37% of the Type 3 words were isolated after their acoustic offset but before the end of the sentence, and a full 20% were never identified at all. We noted a great deal of variability in the results of Type 3 words. Some were isolated before their offset, others after their offset and some never at all. We hypothesised that this could be explained by the 'frequency pull' of the guest words (i.e. the English items) as compared to their base-language counterparts (the French words). If a guest word is more frequent than its base-language homophone (e.g. 'pick' as compared to 'pique'), then the former will be identified quickly. However, if the guest word is less frequent (e.g. 'knot' vs 'note'), then the listener is 'directed', as it were, towards the base-language item and the guest word is identified later or never at all. The hypothesis proved correct: a high correlation (0.77) was found between word frequency and isolation point; the stronger the pull towards the base-language homophones, the later the isolation point of the guest words.

As concerns the output variable, it appeared from the data that the way a guest word is said (that is, as a code-switch or as a borrowing) affects more the narrowing-in process that leads to word identification than the actual point in time at which the word is identified. We found that, during the selection phase, the proportion of guest-language candidates was greater for code-switches than for borrowings. We also noted that strong language phonetic cues (such as those of a plosive or a lateral) strongly activated either the English or the French lexicon, depending on the phonetics of the guest word, and thus affected the language of the candidates proposed. Thus, when guest words that began with /t/ or /l/ were said as code-switches, listeners invariably proposed English candidates, whereas when they were said as borrowings (in French, therefore), they wrote down French candidates. It was only at the fourth or fifth gate of the borrowings (that is, some way into the word itself) that listeners realised that no word with that beginning existed in the French lexicon and that they started proposing English candidates. Finally, we found that the candidates proposed for Type 3 words were quite different depending on whether they were said as borrowings or as code-switches. In the former case, subjects invariably chose the base-language homophone 'pique' for 'pick', 'note' for 'knot') but, in the latter case, only 16% fell into this category. The majority (71% of the candidates for Type 3 code-switches) involved the addition, omission or substitution of one or more phonemes (e.g. 'set' proposed for 'sit', 'fourre' for 'fool', 'coure' for 'cool', etc.). This indicated the very real difficulties subjects had with items in which the language phonetics activated one lexicon (in this case, the English one) but the base-language context and the presence of a near homophone in that language activated the other (the French lexicon).

In summary, the study showed not only that the recognition of guest words in bilingual mixed speech is a highly complex process but that certain factors play a role in the access of the lexicons during mixed speech: the phonotactics of the guest word, the presence or absence of a base-language homophone, the frequency of the latter and the language phonetics of the guest word.

5 A model of guest word recognition

A model of guest word recognition will have to account for the general effects that have been found in studies of word recognition in monolinguals as well as the effects that are specific to bilingual language processing. Among the general effects we find the following.

(i) Low-frequency words take more time to recognise than high-frequency words.

(ii) Words are not always recognised from left to right, from onset to offset.

(iii) When words presented in isolation are recognised from onset to offset, recognition occurs close to the word's uniqueness point.

(iv) Words in continuous speech are not always recognised one word at a time, i.e. two words can be recognised simultaneously, or a later-occurring word can be recognised before an earlier-occurring word.

(v) The syntactic, semantic and pragmatic contexts of the sentence in which a word occurs affect its recognition.

(vi) Various sources of knowledge, such as the listener's knowledge of the world, and of the rules of the language, also affect the word's recognition.

In addition to these general effects, a model for bilinguals will need to capture the effects that are emerging from research on guest word recognition. Among these we find the following.

(i) The base-language effect. When a guest word is presented in a base language context, and only its very beginning has been heard, the candidates proposed are invariably members of the base-language lexicon.

(ii) The phonotactic effect. Words marked phonotactically as belonging to the guest language only (e.g. Type 1 words in the 1988 study) are recognised sooner and with more ease than words not marked in this way.

(iii) The single lexicon effect. Words that belong solely to the guest lexicon (e.g. Types 1 and 2 words in the 1988 study) are recognised sooner and with more ease than words that do not belong to just one lexicon.

(iv) The base-language homophone effect. Words in the guest-language lexicon that have close homophones in the base language (e.g. Type 3 words) are processed with more difficulty than other guest-language words.

(v) The language phonetics effect. (a) During the narrowing-in stage preceding the isolation of a word, the proportion of guest-language candidates is affected by the language phonetics of the word. (b) Strong language phonetic cues will activate the lexicon that contains words characterised by these cues, and thus affect the language of the candidates proposed and, at times, the final isolation point of the appropriate candidates (as for words with cross-language homophones). (c) Cross-language homophones pronounced in the base language (e.g. Type 3 borrowings in the 1988 study) are isolated later than when they are pronounced in the guest language (e.g. Type 3 code-switches), and the nature of the candidates prior to isolation are quite different for the two versions of the words.

(vi) The frequency effect for cross-language homophones. The ease with which a guest-language homophone is identified depends on the 'frequency pull' of that word as compared to that of its base-language homophone.

Although most existing models of monolingual spoken word recognition can be modified to account for word recognition during mixed speech processing, the type of model that may have the most promise is an interactive activation model, such as the TRACE model proposed by McClelland and Elman (1986). According to this model, language processing takes place through the excitatory and inhibitory interactions of a large number of processing units, each working continuously to update its own activation on the basis of the activation of other units to which it is connected. In TRACE, the units are organised in three levels: features, phonemes and words. Throughout the course of processing, each unit is continually receiving input from other units, continually updating its activation on the basis of these inputs and, if it is over threshold, it is continually sending excitatory and inhibitory signals to other units. Connections between levels are bidirectional and there is no between-level inhibition (inhibition only exists within one level, between units that are inconsistent with one another). Although neither word-frequency nor context effects are at present accounted for by the model, these can be built in quite easily, according to the authors: word frequency can be accommodated in terms of variation in the resting activation level of word units, and contextual influences can be thought of as supplying activation to word units from even higher levels of processing.

How could this interactive activation view of word recognition be modified in order to accommodate language processing in bilinguals, be it in a monolingual or in a bilingual language mode? First, we will assume that bilinguals have two language networks (features, phonemes, syllables, words, etc.) which are both independent and interconnected. They are independent in the sense that they allow a bilingual to speak just one language; they are interconnected in the sense that the monolingual speech of bilinguals often shows the active interference of the language not in use, and that bilinguals can code-switch and borrow quite readily when they speak to other bilinguals. This view has long been defended by Paradis (1981, 1986, 1989), who proposes that both languages are stored in identical ways in a single extended system, though elements of each language, because they normally appear only in different contents, form separate networks of connections, and thus a subsystem within a larger system. According to him, bilinguals have two subsets of neural connections, one for each language (each can be activated or inhibited independently because of the strong associations between elements), while at the same time they possess one larger set from which they are able to draw elements of either language at any time. Another assumption that can be made is that, in the monolingual language mode, one language network is strongly activated while the other is activated very weakly; the resting activation level of the units of this other network is therefore very low.

The main characteristics of the model, which deals primarily with lexical access in the bilingual mode, are the following.

(i) Both language networks (features, phonemes, syllables, words, etc.) are activated but the base-language network is more strongly activated (this accounts for the base-language effect). The resting activation level of the language that is not being used as the base language (i.e. the guest-language network) can be increased or decreased depending on the amount of language mixing (code-switching, borrowing) that occurs during the interaction.

(ii) The activation of a unit in a network and of its 'counterpart' in the other depends on their degree of similarity. Thus, for example, if English /b/ is activated, French /b/ will also be activated (to some extent, at least) as the consonants in the two languages are quite similar. On the other hand, the activation of English word initial /p/ will lead to a much lower level of activation of French word initial /p/, as the two consonants are quite different. When English /r/ is activated, its French counterpart should receive very little activation (apart from some possible top-down lexicon activation due to the fact that the two sounds have the same orthography). Cross-language activation of 'counterpart' units concerns phonemes but also other types of units (features, words, etc.).

(iii) The activation of units (or of a combination of units, such as consonant clusters) that are specific to one language increases the overall activation of that language network and thus speeds up the recognition of words in that language (this accounts for the phonotactic and the language phonetics effects).

(iv) The activation of words that are specific to just one language increases the overall activation of that network and thus speeds up the recognition of the words from that language (this accounts for the single lexicon effect of Type 1 and 2 words).

(v) The activation of words that are similar in the two lexicons will normally slow down the recognition of guest-language words (this explains the cross-language homophone effect). However, the frequency pull of cross-language homophones (reflected in their different resting activation levels), and the language phonetics of the input, will interact with the recognition process of guest words to speed up or slow down their access (this accounts for the word-frequency and language phonetics effects of Type 3 words).

Much work will need to be done to refine this interactive activation view of the recognition of words in bilinguals. In particular, we need to think about which connections – between and within language networks – are inhibitory and which are excitatory. As we learn more about such models in general, and as more experiments on bilingual mixed speech are conducted, changes will be made to this model. What is encouraging is that such a view does away with the switch or monitor mechanism that has been proposed by a number of researchers (Macnamara 1967; Obler and Albert 1978) but rightly criticised by Paradis (1980, 1989). According to the proponents of the switch or monitor mechanism, its role is to tell the processing system which language is being spoken so as to direct the incoming signal to the processors of the appropriate language. The evidence for this mechanism is mainly based on studies which have shown that it takes bilinguals more time to process mixed speech than monolingual speech. However, this evidence is both insubstantial and indirect. It is not because bilinguals may process code-switches more slowly than base-language words, that one can conclude that there is a language switch/monitor involved in the processing; the delay could be due to numerous other factors (see Grosjean and Soares 1986). In addition, the proponents of the mechanism do not address pertinent questions such as: is the switch/monitor an essential part of language processing or does it 'fall out' of the processing? If the former, at what stage does it come in – during the acoustic-to-phonetic mapping of the speech sounds or after this mapping? The data and the model we have presented do not prove the absence of a language switch or monitor, they simply show that the processing system can do without it, and that language decisions (e.g., was that word English or French?) can simply emerge from the process. Having heard a particular sound, syllable or word, we can then make the metalinguistic statement that language X or language Y is being spoken. That the system needs to make this decision in order to process the incoming signal is highly unlikely.

It is clear that the lexical access of code-switched words and borrowings is both variable and complex. Only further research involving the use of different language pairs, paradigms, materials and procedures will allow us to better understand the operations which underlie the lexical access of these words.

6 Conclusion

The psycholinguistics of language processing in bilinguals is still very much in its infancy. In the years to come it will have to explain in what way bilinguals in the monolingual mode are similar to, and in what way they are different from, monolinguals during speech perception, word recognition, syntactic and semantic processing and memorising, as well as in the processes involved in language production. In the bilingual mode, the challenge for the psycholinguist will be to account for how mixed language processing takes place so rapidly and so efficiently, despite as we now know, the need for many intricate underlying operations.

Acknowledgments

The preparation of this chapter was supported by a grant from the Swiss National Science Foundation (12-33582.92). The author would like to thank the two editors for their helpful comments on earlier versions of the manuscript.

Bibliography

Altenberg, E. and Cairns, H. (1983) The effects of phonotactic constraints on lexical processing in bilingual and monolingual subjects. *Journal of Verbal Learning and Verbal Behavior*, 22: 174–88.

Blank, M. (1980) Measuring lexical access during sentence processing. *Perception and Psychophysics*, 28: 1–8.

Bürki-Cohen, J., Grosjean, F. and Miller, J. (1989) Base language effects on word identification in bilingual speech: evidence from categorical perception experiments. *Language and Speech*, 32: 355–71.

Forster, K. (1976) Accessing the mental lexicon. In R. Wales and E. Walker eds., *New approaches to language mechanism*. Amsterdam: North-Holland, 257–87.

Foss, D. (1988) Experimental psycholinguistics. *Annual Review of Psychology*, 39: 301–48.

Frauenfelder, U. and Tyler, L. (1987) eds., *Spoken word recognition*. Cambridge, Mass.: MIT Press.

Garman, M. (1990) *Psycholinguistics*. Cambridge University Press.

Garnham, A. (1985) *Psycholinguistics*. London: Methuen.

Grosjean, F. (1980) Spoken word recognition processes and the gating paradigm. *Perception and Psychophysics*, 28: 267–83.

  (1982) *Life with two languages. An introduction to bilingualism*. Cambridge, Mass.: Harvard University Press.

(1985a) The recognition of words after their acoustic offset: evidence and implications. *Perception and Psychophysics*, 38: 299–310.

(1985b) The bilingual as a competent but specific speaker–hearer. *Journal of Multilingual and Multicultural Development*, 6: 467–77.

(1988) Exploring the recognition of guest words in bilingual speech. *Language and Cognitive Processes*, 3: 233–74.

Grosjean, F. and Gee, J. (1987) Prosodic structure and spoken word recognition. *Cognition*, 25: 135–55.

Grosjean, F. and Soares, C. (1986) Processing mixed language: some preliminary findings. In Vaid (1986), 145–79.

Harris, R. (1992) ed. *Cognitive processing in bilinguals*. Amsterdam: Elsevier.

Klatt, D. (1979) Speech perception: a model of acoustic–phonetic analysis and lexical access. *Journal of Phonetics*, 7: 279–312.

Kolers, P. (1966) Reading and talking bilingually. *American Journal of Psychology*, 3: 357–76.

Levelt, W. J. M. (1989) *Speaking: from intention to articulation*. Cambridge, Mass.: MIT Press.

Macnamara, J. (1967) The bilingual's linguistic performance: a psychological overview. *Journal of Social Issues*, 23: 59–77.

Macnamara, J. and Kushnir, S. (1971) Linguistic independence of bilinguals: the input switch. *Journal of Verbal Learning and Verbal Behavior*, 10: 480–7.

Marslen-Wilson, W. (1987) Functional parallelism in spoken word-recognition. *Cognition*, 25: 71–102.

McClelland, J. and Elman, J. (1986) The TRACE model of speech perception. *Cognitive Psychology*, 18: 1–86.

Neufeld, G. (1973) The bilingual's lexical store. *Working Papers on Bilingualism*, 1: 35–65.

Obler, L. K. and Albert, M. (1978) A monitor system for bilingual language processing. In M. Paradis ed. *Aspects of bilingualism*. Columbia, S. C.: Hornbeam Press, 105–13.

Osherson, D. (1990) ed. *An invitation to cognitive science: language*. Cambridge, Mass.: MIT Press.

Paradis, M. (1980) The language switch in bilinguals: psycholinguistic and neuro-linguistic perspectives. In P. Nelde ed. *Languages in contact and conflict*. Weisbaden: Franz Steiner Verlag, 501–6.

(1981) Contributions of neurolinguistics to the theory of bilingualism. In R. Herbert ed. *Applications of linguistic theory in the human sciences*. Department of Linguistics, Michigan State University, 180–211.

(1986) Bilingualism. In *International encyclopedia of education*. Oxford: Pergamon Press, 489–93.

(1989) Bilingual and polyglot aphasia. In F. Boller, J. Grafman eds., *Handbook of neuropsychology* II. Amsterdam: Elsevier Science Publishers, 117–40.

Poplack, S. and Sankoff, D. (1984) Borrowing: the synchrony of integration. *Linguistics*, 22: 99–135.

Schreuder, R. and Weltens, B. (1993) eds. *The bilingual lexicon*. Amsterdam: John Benjamins.

Singer, M. (1990) *Psychology of language*. Hillsdale, N. J.: Lawrence Erlbaum.

Soares, C. and Grosjean, F. (1984) Bilinguals in a monolingual and a bilingual speech mode: the effect of lexical access. *Memory and Cognition*, 12: 380–6.

Swinney, D. (1982) The structure and time-course of information interaction during speech comprehension: lexical segmentation, access and interpretation. In J. Mehler, E. Walker, M. Garrett, eds. *Perspectives on mental representations*. Hillsdale, N.J.: Lawrence Erlbaum, 307–12.

Tartter, V. (1986) *Language processes*. New York: Holt, Rinehart & Winston.

Vaid, J. (1986) ed. *Language processing in bilinguals: psycholinguistic and neuropsychological perspectives*. Hillsdale, N.J.: Lawrence Erlbaum.

Weinreich, U. (1953) *Languages in contact*. The Hague: Mouton.

13 CODE-SWITCHING IN BILINGUAL FIRST LANGUAGE ACQUISITION

Regina Köppe and Jürgen M. Meisel

1 Introduction

Extensive research over the last twenty years on language contact phenomena and especially in the domain of code-switching has led investigators to agree that bilingual code-switching can be characterised as being governed by grammatical as well as pragmatic constraints. However, up to now, the development of such formal and functional principles during the course of the linguistic development of bilingual children has not been studied to a larger extent.

With respect to pragmatics, we still know little about how and when the bilingual child discovers that the use of both languages in its environment is governed by social and pragmatic rules. As far as the acquisition of grammatical constraints is concerned, we are facing theoretical as well as empirical problems. On the one hand, the debate on the formulation of universal grammatical constraints on code-switching is still very much open, concerning cross-linguistic validity as well as the specific formulation within grammatical theory. On the other hand, we cannot examine the acquisition of grammatical constraints on code-switching without taking into account the linguistic development of the child in both languages.

In what follows, we will briefly summarise the knowledge currently available on these issues. We will then present a number of findings from our research based on the analysis of bilingual children living in a German community, who acquire German and French simultaneously. We will also try to contribute to a clearer classification and explanation of bilingual children's mixed utterances. Finally, we will point to some open questions which require further research.

2 Terminology and definitions

In view of the enormous variety of terminological distinctions and labels which one finds in the literature on code-switching, and in order to contribute to the

276

clarification of the underlying concepts, we will briefly explain the terminology used in this chapter. A distinction which researchers have frequently left unclear – and which is extremely important for any analysis of mixed speech from an acquisitional perspective – is that between surface phenomena and their underlying causes.

To begin with, we restrict the term 'bilingual first language acquisition' to individuals who acquire two (or more) languages simultaneously, i.e. who are exposed to both languages from early on – before age 3;0[1] (McLaughlin 1984: 73).

With regard to the linguistic performance of bilinguals, the term '(language) mixing' refers to any utterance or conversation containing features of both languages (Meisel 1989, 1994a), irrespective of the reasons which cause this to happen.

The term 'code-switching', more specifically, is used in the almost commonly accepted sense to describe a certain skill of the bilingual speaker that requires pragmatic and grammatical competence in both languages. With respect to pragmatic competence, code-switching refers to the ability to select the language according to external factors like the particular interlocutor, the situational context, the topic of conversation, etc. Concerning grammatical competence, adequate code-switching requires that switches within one sentence observe specific grammatical constraints.

It may, of course, be the case that the bilingual speaker, when using both languages in the same utterance or conversation, violates syntactic or pragmatic constraints on code-switching established by the language use of his bilingual community. This kind of violation will be called 'code-mixing'. It has often been claimed (see Volterra and Taeschner 1978; Redlinger and Park 1980) that young children's code-mixing can at least partly be explained as a failure in separating the two linguistic systems on the level of grammatical competence, a phenomenon which we will call 'fusion'. As has been argued in Meisel (1989), the assumption that fusion is in fact a common phenomenon in bilingual language development still lacks empirical evidence. In any case, for our argumentation it will suffice to assume that early code-mixing can simply be accounted for by the lack of knowledge of these constraints.[2] In other words, it may be a performance phenomenon although we do not want to exclude the possibility that fusion may indeed occur. In addition, we want to point out that involuntarily triggered switches which are often corrected afterwards are not regarded as code-mixing.

Finally, let us add that one has to distinguish the phenomena just mentioned from 'borrowing', where elements from one language are '[integrated] phonologically and morphologically into the base language' (Grosjean 1982: 129), although the distinction may not always be clear-cut (see Muysken, this volume; Pfaff 1979: 295–6; Gardner-Chloros 1987: 102).

3 Acquisition of code-switching – a review of the literature

Even though many authors working on bilingual first language acquisition have noted anecdotal observations concerning the occurrence of code-switching, there exist only a very few systematic analyses of code-switching from a developmental perspective (e.g. Oksaar 1976, 1978; Vihman 1984, 1985). For this reason, our brief summary will mainly refer to longitudinal studies on bilingual language acquisition, which typically concern a linguistic environment where each person speaks one language or where, at least, extensive use of code-switching as a speech mode cannot be observed.

3.1 Pragmatic functions of code-switching

Turning now to the acquisition of the pragmatic functions of code-switching, two major types of switching, which are acquired successively, can be distinguished. The first type, which we will call 'language choice', refers to the ability to select the appropriate language as base language of the conversation according to the interlocutor, the topic of the conversation or the situational context. It is generally agreed that the practice of determining language choice according to situational factors is established quite early. The language spoken by the interlocutor seems to be the first and most important factor for language choice. From around the age of two years onwards, bilingual children appear to stick closely to the well-known principle 'une personne – une langue' (Ronjat 1913: 94), as they adequately switch languages according to the interlocutor (see Bergman 1976; Clyne 1987b; Fantini 1985; Kielhöfer and Jonekeit 1983; Saunders 1988; Taeschner 1983; Vihman 1985; and others). The fact that most children raised bilingually in an otherwise monolingual community apparently experience what Arnberg (1987: 72) calls a 'language shock', i.e. the fact that most people only understand one of their languages, seems to reinforce the development of those interpersonal distinctions and to contribute to the awareness of the child's own bilingualism. In consequence, self-corrections in cases when the child addresses someone in the wrong language are observed quite early: Vihman (1985: 313) notes the age of 2;0 and Taeschner (1983: 171) the age of 2;6.

Note that, in the course of the child's language development, the factor 'interlocutor' may become increasingly complex: especially with bilingual interlocutors,[3] the child has to find out whether the interlocutor expects to be addressed in only one language, or whether he accepts the use of both languages.[4]

The only case of language choice that is not guided by the interlocutor is reported by Fantini (1985: 73), whose son switched languages according to the topic of the conversation at the age of ten years.

In contrast to language choice, which is used during interactions with monolingual as well as with bilingual interlocutors, other uses of code-switching require a bilingual hearer, i.e. switches that convey specific social or pragmatic information such as metalinguistic comments, quoting someone in his own language, playing with both languages, etc. Such switches roughly correspond to what has been called 'conversational switching' (in contrast to language choice as 'situational switching', see Blom and Gumperz 1972; Gumperz 1976).

For instance, Saunders (1988) and Fantini (1985) report that, from the age of 2;0 onwards, their children began to repeat their own utterances in both languages in order to attract both their parents' attention or in order to assure that the content of their utterance was understood. This behaviour can easily be explained by the fact that, at least at the beginning of language development, parents normally understand utterances of both languages and react even when addressed in the 'wrong' language.

As a consequence of their increasing bilingual awareness during their third year, children begin to comment on their own language use and to ask their parents for translations (see Clyne 1987b; Taeschner 1983). This is reported as early as age 2;2 by Kielhöfer and Jonekeit (1983: 45). Note that such metalinguistic awareness clearly indicates separation of the two languages and also the child's ability to switch, both of which nevertheless are present earlier than the child's bilingual awareness.

At the same age, i.e. from the age of 2;3 onwards (Saunders 1988: 70), first uses of both languages in role-play can be observed. Note that toys or animals may also be regarded as bilingual interlocutors and involved in translation games or role-play (ibid.: 72ff.).

Fantini (1985: 69) reports that his son began to quote other people's utterances in the original language at the age of 3;5. According to Kielhöfer (1987: 143f.), at the age of 4;1, a French–German bilingual boy used code-switching, in reporting a conversation, to mark his own utterances in contrast to those of other speakers, which he translated.

Finally, from the age of approximately 4;0 onwards, some bilingual children are reported to use 'marked language choice' (Fantini 1985: 66ff.) as a stylistic means of expression, in order to amuse or to tease the hearer or even to exclude a third person from the conversation.

With respect to language development, we would like to point out that switching according to the interlocutor as well as rhetorical repetitions or role-play, which can be observed as early as the age of 2;0 do not necessarily involve intra-sentential switching. Switching serving more complex functions, on the other hand, which is used from approximately 3;0 onwards, is more likely to be intra-sentential. In other words, intra-sentential switches may be acquired later not only because they are conceptually more complex, but also because they require syntactic knowledge that might not be available at the age of 2;0. In the next section, we will address the question of grammatical development in greater detail.

3.2 Syntactic aspects of language mixing

Studies on early language mixing are concerned primarily with the question of language separation, and, frequently, a high mixing rate in early stages is assumed to indicate fusion of the two language systems on the level of grammatical competence (see Volterra and Taeschner 1978; Redlinger and Park 1980, and others). However, authors like Bergman (1976) and Lindholm and Padilla (1978) report that the mixing rate, even in the early stages, is very low. In any case, such counts, whether they show increasing or decreasing mixing rates, have to be interpreted very carefully. It is necessary to relate mixing rates to qualitative aspects (which categories are mixed; what are the structural conditions for switching; how far developed is the child's grammatical competence, etc.), and to pragmatic–functional considerations (are the mixes conscious; do they respect functional/social rules of languages use; is the addressee bilingual or monolingual; does the mixed item represent a 'culturally bound' expression that cannot be translated, and so on).

Note that the distinction between different categories of words which are mixed may help us to distinguish code-mixing from code-switching in early child language. Vihman (1985) notes that early mixing of isolated lexical items mostly concerns what she calls, not quite appropriately, 'function words', including all categories except nouns, verbs and adjectives, whereas later on, mixing mostly consists of single noun switches. Interestingly enough, the predominance of nouns (and of NPs, in general) has been reported in studies on adult code-switching and in studies on child bilingualism, alike. Poplack (1980) reports in her study on Spanish–English code-switching that single nouns and object noun phrases (switched with a frequency of 9.5% and 7.6%, respectively) were more likely to be mixed intra-sententially than verbs (1%) or verb phrases (2.2%), for example. Consequently, the switch point Det/N (19%) occurred far more often than switching between subject NP and VP (3%). These findings seem to be corroborated by studies on the mixed speech of bilingual children. Lindholm and Padilla (1978) find in their cross-sectional study on Spanish–English bilingual children (age 2;10–6;2) that single nouns accounted for 75% of the mixes found in their data. Redlinger and Park (1880) and Taeschner (1983) also found that nouns are mixed far more often than other constituents.[5] However, as Veh (1990) observes, these figures do not take into account development aspects. If, for example, the claim advanced by Vihman turns out to be right, early code-mixing of 'function words' should decrease as soon as grammatical constraints on code-switching are acquired, so that only later mixes should be classified as code-switching.

Turning now to the question of the syntactic regularities of sentence-internal language mixing, one of the most important findings is that researchers have proceeded from category- and language-specific constraints (e.g. Timm 1975; Gumperz 1976; Pfaff 1979) to the formulation of more general constraints like Poplack's (1980: 585f; this volume) Free Morpheme Constraint and Equivalence Constraint.

More recently, attempts to describe formal regularities of intra-sentential code-switching by means of few universal principles have been formulated within the framework of generative grammar (see Woolford 1983; Joshi 1985, and others; see also Muysken, this volume). For instance, DiSciullo, Muysken and Singh's 'government constraint' tries to capture the fact that switching mainly occurs at phrase boundaries or between a specifier and the head of a projection (DiSciullo, Muysken and Singh 1986: 21).

A common feature shared by the principles and constraints cited thus far is that all of them have to admit the existence of counterexamples, i.e. some data or pairs of languages where the given constraint appears not to be valid. However, given the facts that in most studies, nouns are far more often mixed than finite verbs, and, in addition, that mixing seems not to occur, or only very rarely, between constituents which are contained in the INFL phrase (e.g. between negation and finite verb, between finite and nonfinite verb or between subject clitic and finite verb), we may tentatively conclude that what is called in recent terminology 'functional heads' (which correspond to the function words in Muysken, this volume), and especially the verbal functional category INFL, seem to strongly constrain code-switching. Nouns and noun phrases, on the other hand, do not seem to present major obstacles for code-switching.

Let us assume that we are right in hypothesising that functional categories play a crucial role in constraining code-switching. Any attempt to adequately formulate these constraints will depend on a well-developed theory of functional categories as well as on the correct definition of 'government', etc. Yet it is also reasonable to assume that our current understanding of these grammatical notions is still not comprehensive. As a consequence, adequate explanatory formulations of grammatical constraints on code-switching are probably not yet possible. Yet our theoretical insights are of a nature which should allow us to arrive at good approximations of explanatory adequacy.

In addition to theoretical problems with formulating universally adequate grammatical constraints on code-switching, research concerned with the acquisition of those constraints faces a further problem: this issue cannot be analysed without taking into account the general development of syntax in both languages. This is, in fact, an important point which is overlooked in most of the available studies. Although this may appear to be trivial, we would like to stress that one first needs to determine by which age children may be said to use a syntactic mode of language processing, as opposed to a pragmatic mode (see Givón 1979), before one may reasonably search for grammatical constraints.

One of the few studies that have addressed the question of syntactic constraints on children's language-mixing is the cross-sectional study by McClure (1981) who analysed the mixed speech of Spanish–English bilingual children (aged from three to fifteen years). McClure cites a number of examples of sentences violating most of the constraints proposed by Timm (1975) and Gumperz (1976). It should be pointed out, however, that she does not present further information as to the frequency of such violations, nor does she mention the age of the children producing them. At any rate, even McClure did not find examples of switching between pronominal subjects and finite verbs or between finite verbs and objects.

Vihman (1984) observes two examples of violations of the equivalence constraint in the speech of one of her two children. Yet, given the limited number of these counterexamples, one has to ask to what extent such violations may count as evidence against a proposed grammatical constraint or against its acquisition at a given age. As will be shown in the analysis of our own data, it is by far more striking that in the overwhelming majority of cases, grammatical constraints on code-switching are in fact respected. One should at least consider the possibility that part of the apparent 'counterexamples' might be performance errors.

4 The DUFDE study

Some of the issues and questions raised have been investigated by ourselves and by other members of the research group, DUFDE.[6] In this research project, the simultaneous acquisition of German and French by thirteen children of pre-school age is studied longitudinally. The children are videotaped every second week while interacting freely in play situations with two researchers, one speaking only French with the child, the other consistently sticking to German. The recordings last for approximately sixty minutes each, half in German and half in French. At least one recording per month is transcribed and analysed; the transcriptions contain both linguistic and nonlinguistic interactions and the relevant contexts. For more details concerning population, design and methodology of the study, see Schlyter (1990) and Köppe (1994).

In what follows, we want to present some of the results obtained by two studies concerning pragmatic (Köppe 1990) and syntactic (Veh 1990) aspects of the mixed speech of two children, Annika (A) and Ivar (Iv). Ivar was 1;3 and Annika was 1;4 at the beginning of the data collection period. Both children are growing up in middle-class families in Hamburg, Germany. French is the native language of both mothers, the fathers' first language is German. Each parent uses his or her respective native tongue when communicating with the children. Annika's parents speak German with each other, while Ivar's parents use French as the language of communication. For both children, French initially appears to be the dominant input language, and during this period it is also the language preferred by the children.

Annika, a girl, is the first child. Her mother, a French and Malagasy bilingual herself, stayed home to take care of Annika until the child was 4;0. Annika's younger brother was born when she was 2;9. From the age of 2;11 onwards, she spent weekday mornings in a German daycare centre. She speaks French with her mother, with French friends in Germany and during stays in France or Madagascar (approximately six weeks every year). Initially, both languages seem to have been equally well developed, but after age 2;6, German began to be the more dominant language.

Ivar, a boy, is also the first-born child. His younger brother was born when he was 4;2. Ivar's mother takes him to France to see his grandparents and other relatives about twice a year. She also makes efforts to ensure that he has sufficient opportunities to speak French by maintaining contact with French-speaking friends in Hamburg. Up to the age of 4;0, Ivar was cared for by a German sitter three times a week. Beginning at the age of 3;0, he also began participating in a

German-speaking playgroup; from 4;0 until 4;9 he attended a French kindergarten three to four times a week. Ivar's two languages have always been well in balance, except for a short period at age 2;3, when, according to our analyses, his French was weaker.

Ivar's mixed speech has been analysed from 1;05,24 to 5;01,22 for syntactic aspects and from 2;05,07 to 5;01,22 for pragmatic aspects. Annika's speech was analysed for syntactic aspects from the first recording onwards (1;04,12) up to the age of 4;03,24, while the pragmatic analysis began at the age of 2;0,10.

During the recordings, the interviewers are supposed to keep languages strictly separated, and the communication situation is defined by the adult as monolingual. In the given setting, we thus expected that code-switching would occur less often than in a bilingual situation, and that its use would be motivated primarily by situational factors like language choice according to the interlocutor. For instance, the child may switch because he does not accept playing with only one of the interviewers and tries to integrate both into the game. Other occasions for code-switching are interactions with the child's parents who sometimes interrupt the recordings. Formally, we expected that inter-sentential switching would predominate, as situational switching normally does not require changing of the interlocutor in mid-sentence.

We would like to emphasise that the recording situation, in spite of giving few occasions for code-switching, may facilitate the task of analysing the children's mixed speech: in a situation where the child is expected to speak only one of his languages, the child's motivations for early mixing as well as the external factors that might be guiding the child's language choice should be easier to determine.

It should also be noted that this kind of data can be used for quantitative analyses only in a limited sense as there are recordings without any kind of language alternation as well as recordings with many switches. It thus follows that, at least for the pragmatic analysis, we have to rely primarily on qualitative differences in switching behaviour.

5 Acquisition of functions and constraints – empirical results

5.1 Pragmatic functions of code-switching

It is particularly important to take into account not only the interacting adult's expectations of language choice, but also the child's perspective. Thus, if the child's utterances, at an early stage of development, do not correspond to the regularities of switching in use in its linguistic environment, we might certainly conclude that the child has not yet acquired these rules. Nevertheless, we should also be aware of the possibility that the child has developed his own rules of language choice which do not necessarily coincide with those of his environment. For instance, the child may define the situation as bilingual, as representatives of both languages are present, or switches may be triggered by the presence of the mother in the room, etc. Moreover, with increasing age, the child will observe that his interlocutors are not truly monolingual, as he may hear the German assistant converse in French with the child's mother, or both assistants speaking German to each other, etc.

Turning now to the data, we find that both children select the appropriate language with each person from 1;4 to 1;5 onwards. The very first examples of code-switching concern cases where the children are addressed by another person and answer to the respective language. Such switches occur from 2;5 onwards in Ivar's data and from 2;0 onwards in Annika's data (see Figures 13.1 and 13.2).

(1)   (Ivar 2;07,17)[7]

      Iv: (to G): oh der kann nich fahr(en) der auto
           [oh this one can't move the car]
      F: qu'est-ce qu'elle a fait l'auto la voiture?
           [what has it done the auto the car?]
      Iv: *peut peut pas rouler*
           [*can can not move*]

First self-initiated switches, i.e. when the child addresses someone without being asked to do so, occur at the age of 2;8 for Ivar and 2;0 for Annika. Early self-initiated switches mainly consist of short utterances like deictic elements (*da/ là* [*there*]) and imperatives like *guck/regarde* [*look*], serving to show or to explain something to the person who does not take part in the game.

(2)   (Ivar 2;11,21)

      F: et comment est-ce qu'il va partir à Paris?
           [how will he go to Paris?]
      Iv: avec- avec le avec-
           [with- with the with-]
      Iv (to G): *will weggehen*
           [*(I) want to leave*]

It is important to observe that language choice is nearly error-free when it is initiated by the child itself. Moreover, none of the (few) switching errors can be

Ivar

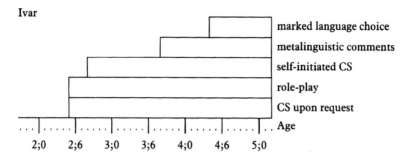

Figure 13.1 Functions of code-switching

Annika

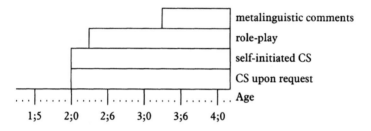

Figure 13.2 Functions of code-switching

attributed to a lack of knowledge of switching regularities. Instead, they can be explained as simple performance errors which are quickly corrected:

(3)   (Ivar 2;09,18)
        G: frag sie doch mal 'was ißt du denn gern?'
                [why don't you ask her: 'what do you like to eat?']
        Iv (to F): eh, brot? *du pain? de pain?*
                [eh, bread? *bread? bread?*]
        F: hein? quoi?
                [hem? what?]
        Iv: nee n-no de pain? comme manger?
                [*no* no bread? to eat?]

Even in those cases where switching does not only consist of short remarks to the other interviewer, but where the child – mostly Ivar – interacts with both interviewers, switching quickly between languages and translating, very few errors occurred. A kind of triggered error, called 'blocked switching' by Saunders (1988:

89) occurs several times in translation situations. In (4), Ivar only repeats the German question to the French interviewer instead of translating it.

(4)   (Ivar 3;08,29)
          G: ja frag sie doch mal ob sie mit ins uni-restaurant mitkommt
                      [yes ask her if she wants to come with us to the university
                      restaurant]
          Iv (to F): willst du mit, uni im restaurant kommen?
                      [do you want to come with us to the university restaurant?]
                      [. . .]
          F: hein?
                      [hem?]
          G: Marie-France versteht dich doch so nicht
                      [Marie-France doesn't understand you this way]
          Iv: nö
                      [no]
          Iv (to F): willst du mit im uni res-
                      [do you want to come with us to the unversity res-]
          [Ivar interrupts his utterance and begins to laugh]
          Iv (to G): wie heißt das französisch ein uni-restaurant?
                      [how does one say in French a university restaurant?]

With regard to Annika, we may add that not only does she correct her errors, but she also adopts different strategies in order to avoid errors or to avoid the use of the wrong language. Not only at earlier stages of language development, but as far as the age of 3;7, switches into French are introduced by simple utterances like proper names or deictic elements. Also, she simplifies the content of her utterances, or she tries to communicate only non-verbally, and she changes the addressee in mid-sentence if she does not know how to continue in the language used initially:

(5)   (Annika 3;07,13)
          G (to M): Annika hat uns gerade erzählt daß sie selber der osterhase ist
                      [Annika has just told us that she is the easter bunny herself]
          M (to A): c'est quoi?
                      [why?]
          A (to M): *parce que-*
                      [*because-*]
          [Annika hesitates]

A (to G):   *wir machen die eier*
            [*we paint the eggs*]

In contrast to the frequent instances of language choice, few switches serving different functions could be observed. In spite of the scarcity of such examples (Ivar: twelve cases throughout the observation period; Annika: seven), they emerge in the same order of functions for both children, and the ages at which such switches occur coincide with what is reported in the literature.

First instances of role-play occurred at the age of 2;6 for Ivar and at 2;3 for Annika. In example 6, Ivar leaves the room in order to buy something to eat. As in everyday life, this happens in German. Coming back to the French interviewer, Ivar switches back to French.

(6)   (Ivar 2;08,15)
        F: oui on veut manger
                  [yes we want to eat]
        [Ivar leaves the room and pretends to buy something]
        Iv: *so ham wir/hier sieben mark, so*
                  [*so we have/here seven marks*]
        Iv (to F): *on va- on va manger*
                  [*we are- we are going to eat*]

According to notes taken by the children's parents, Ivar and Annika began at roughly the same age (about 2;5) to ask for translations or to make metalinguistic comments. During the recordings, however, this function only occurred more than a year later, at age 3;8 for Ivar and at age 3;5 for Annika.

(7)   (Annika 3;07,13)
        A (to M): mais maintenant comment ça s'appelle encore *vorlesen?*
                  [but now how does one say again for *to read?*]
        M: qu'est-ce que tu veux savoir?
                  [what do you want to know?]
        A: *vorlesen*
                  [*to read*]
        M: lire
                  [to read]

Finally, from age 4;4 onwards, Ivar uses marked language choice in order to create funny effects by playing with the two languages or even to exclude a person from the conversation. This can be seen in example 8, where he speaks German with his mother, but switches back to French to let the French assistant know that he does not care whether or not she understands what he is saying in German. Annika does not use switching for this purpose.

(8)   (Ivar 4;04,14)

Iv (to M):   böse kleine männchen und dann ham sie a(ber) bestimmt angst

[wicked little men and then they surely are afraid]

F: moi j'comprends pas, oui mais ça c'est de l'allemand dis donc

[I don't understand, yes but that's German]

M: elle comprend pas Marie-Claude, tu sais

[Marie-Claude doesn't understand, you know]

Iv (to M):   *ça fait rien*

[*that doesn't matter*]

5.2 Syntactic constraints on code-switching

In this section, we will mostly refer to the results of two studies by Veh (1990) and Meisel 1994a concerning syntactic aspects of the intra-sentential mixing of Ivar and Annika.

In the data of both children, a high mixing rate could be observed from the beginning of the recordings onwards, which, at the ages of 2;05,07 for Ivar and 2;0,17 for Annika, decreases quickly and then generally does not rise above 3% from 2;07,17 (Ivar) and 2;0,17 (Annika) onwards. Moreover, many recordings do not contain any mixing at all. This generally concerns the German part of the recording.

With respect to the frequency of specific syntactic categories, Veh (1990) notes a change again around the age of 2;5 in Ivar's data. Whereas nouns (and NPs) are mixed throughout the whole period of investigation, 'function words' – as defined by Vihman (1985), i.e. mostly diectic expressions (*da/là* [there], *das/ça* [this]), negative (*nein/non* [no]) and affirmative particles (*ja/oui* [yes]) and adverbials (*noch/encore* [more]) – are mixed primarily up to 2;3. From 2;4 onwards, the number of mixed 'function words' decreases constantly, and mixing of lexical categories like nouns and some verbs (the latter are mixed only up to the age of 2;6) predominates. Our analysis shows that the same development can be observed in Annika's data, the change between mixing of so-called 'function words' and mixing of lexical categories occurring around the age of 2;0.

In sum, the findings by Vihman (1985) are corroborated in the data of both children: early mixing primarily concerns what she calls 'function words' and is substituted later by mixing of lexical categories, mostly nouns.

Turning now to the question of whether the children's use of switching conforms to syntactic constraints or not, Veh (1990) notes that at earlier stages of development, the exact sentential position of a switch is difficult to determine as long as the children omit obligatory elements of the sentence. Consequently, if the child's utterances apparently violate certain syntactic constraints on code-switching, we have to determine whether it is the constraint that is not yet acquired by the child, or whether the child's grammar simply lacks the necessary elements to which the constraint applies. This is to say that we also have to ask from what age we can assume that the child is indeed using grammatical means of organising language and, consequently, from what age it is justified to analyse the observed facts in terms of syntactic constraints.

Recent studies of language development, for example, Radford (1990), argue that early child grammars consist exclusively of lexical categories, lacking functional categories like INFL and COMP; for a discussion of these hypotheses, see the contributions in Meisel (1994a). Others have argued that early child language is not organised by means of grammatical principles at all. The most recent version of this theory is developed by Bickerton (1990) who distinguishes 'protolanguage' (non-grammatical speech) from language proper, the onset of the latter occurring around age 2;0. Let us assume, with regard to the following discussion, that children use grammar, in the technical sense of term, only after they have access to functional categories, e.g. INFL.

The predictions one can make on the basis of these assumptions suggest that before the development of functional categories, bilingual children's code-switching will not be guided by syntactic principles at all. If we can corroborate this, observing that syntactic constraints are respected as soon as functional categories are developed, this will in turn constitute strong evidence in favour of the claim that adult code-switching is indeed guided by grammatical principles. In effect, not only recent constraints like DiSciullo, Muysken and Singh's government constraint (1986), but also most of the earlier constraints proposed by investigators like Timm (1975), Gumperz (1976) and others, could be reformulated in accordance with more recent insights into grammatical development, including those referring to the importance of categories like INFL and its projection, IP (see also Muysken, this volume).

As for the empirical evidence available, Veh (1990) could observe, once again, important changes in Ivar's data around the age of 2;4 to 2;5. Concerning the sentential position of switches, she notes that, up to the age of 2;4, most of the mixes concern sentences with omitted elements and that those mixes can occur between all kinds of constituents (deictic elements, nouns, adjectives, verbs, adverbs, interjections, negative and affirmative particles, etc.). Some switch points seem to be preferred during this first stage, namely switches between deictic elements and nouns (9, 10), nouns and nouns (11) and verbs and nouns (12 and 13).

(9)   (1;11,17)   *ça ça* sonne
                   [*this this* sun]

(10)   (2;00,02)   das *bateau*
                   [this *ship*]

(11)   (2;00,29)   *nounours* sand
                   [*teddy bear* sand]

(12)   (2,04,09)   *tombé* berg
                   [*fallen* mountain]

(13)   (2;04,09)   sent *füße*
                   [smells *feet*]

Veh nevertheless points out that this preference cannot be accounted for in terms of 'syntactic constraints'; rather, it reflects the high frequency of those categories in Ivar's speech as well as the frequent omission of obligatory elements like determiners and finite verbs. Concerning full sentences, (few) examples of violations of specific syntactic constraints generally also occur only during this first stage of Ivar's development, before age 2;5. For instance, we find some switches between finite and nonfinite verbs (14) or between personal pronoun and finite verb (15). Interestingly enough, Veh encountered no switches between negation and finite verb, and violations of the free morpheme constraint occurred only up to the age of 2;5 (16).

(14)   (2;00,29)   nounours il a *reit*é
                   [teddy bear he has *rid*den]

(15)   (2;00,29)   das *dort* ne?
                   [this *sleeps*, right?]

(16)   (2;04,09)   deddy *rë*sucht
                   [teddy bear seeks *again*]

During the second stage, beginning at the age of 2;5, there is no more mixing in sentences with omission of elements, and Ivar's intra-sentential mixing is mostly reduced to the insertion of single nouns or switching between determiners and nouns in the object NP.[8]

(17)   (3;01,02)   moi je va à la *küche*
                       [me I goes to the *kitchen*]

Note that this qualitative change occurs exactly at the point when, according to Meisel (1990), the functional category INFL appears in Ivar's grammar in both languages.

With respect to Annika's data, Veh notes that almost no qualitative developments could be observed, with the exception of the first occurrence of switching between determiner and noun in object NPs at the age of 2;6. From then on, as in Ivar's data, this switch point is the most frequent one. Note also that, in contrast to Ivar's development, where switching within sentences with omitted elements could be attributed to the incomplete development of syntax until 2;5, Annika uses this switching type throughout the whole period of investigation, and Veh also finds some violations of syntactic constraints at a later age:

(18)   (4;03,24)   il a *gewonnen*
                       [he *has won*]

(19)   (3;07,02)   ça c'est Daniel*s*
                       [this is Daniel'*s*]

It would be premature to conclude that Annika has not yet acquired syntactic regularities of code-switching at the age of four years. Köppe (1990) and Veh (1990) argue that Annika's switching behaviour, differing from that of Ivar in crucial ways, can be accounted for by specific communication strategies. In addition, these cases might also be regarded as simple performance errors since they are extremely infrequent.

As will be apparent from the preceding analysis, there are good reasons to assume that early mixing can be differentiated formally and functionally from code-switching.

Ivar's data clearly show that the acquisition of grammatical constraints on code-switching is related to the development of syntax in general. On the basis of quantitative as well as qualitative changes, two stages could be distinguished. The first stage, formally characterised by the absence of the functional category

INFL, shows high mixing rates of 'function words'. Also, we observe that mixing appears not to be constrained syntactically, nor does it follow any obvious pragmatic motivation. Meisel (1994a) emphasises that, for most of these 'function words', the children know and use the two corresponding items in both languages, so that their substitution in utterances of the other language cannot be explained by vocabulary needs. At around the age of 2;5, mixing rates quickly decrease, and we observe no more mixing of 'function words'. In addition, syntactic constraints on code-switching are rarely violated, and mixing primarily consists of the insertion of single nouns. With respect to pragmatic functions of code-switching, remember that the first example of situational code-switching also occurred at the age of 2;5.

Vihman's hypothesis (1985) is thus corroborated by the data, and we assume that the emergence of the category INFL in Ivar's grammar around the age of 2;5 (Meisel 1990) largely accounts for the passage from the first to the second stage.

In Annika's data, we find roughly the same development, i.e. mixing rates decrease at 2;0, and she begins to proceed from mixing of function words to switching of single nouns as well as to acquire pragmatic regularities of code-switching at the same age. Even if her switches do not appear to observe grammatical constraints as clearly as those of Ivar,[9] it appears to be far more important that her normal language use indeed exhibits pragmatic as well as grammatical regularities from very early on, as has already been mentioned in section 3.2. For instance, from age 2;6 onwards (simultaneously with the emergence of the functional category INFL, see Stenzel 1994), most of her mixes concern single nouns inserted at the switch point Det/N. This observation is well in accordance with Poplack's (1980) observation that this switch point accounts for a large percentage of adults' switches, and it is also in accordance with DiSciullo, Muysken and Singh's (1986) government constraint.

6 Conclusion

We believe we have shown that changes in the formal properties of the mixed speech of bilingual children are closely related to grammatical development. Specifically, the appearance of the functional category INFL seems to account for major qualitative changes like the transition from mixing of 'function words' to mixing of lexical categories (especially nouns). It also appears to be a prerequisite for the ability to respect grammatical constraints on intra-sentential code-switching.

Table 13.1   *Mixing – Ivar*

	Utterances – German			Utterances – French			Single words – mixed German & French	
Age	Total	Tot. mix	% mix	Total	Tot. mix	% mix	% function	% lexical
1;10,12	119	25	21	134	13	9.7	59.5	40.5
1;10,30	164	45	27.4	197	28	14.2	57.7	42.3
1;11,17	159	33	20.8	93	12	12.9	69.2	37.8
2;00,02	227	34	15	92	36	39.1	57.8	42.2
2;00,29	217	32	14.8	249	61	24.5	43.1	56.9
2;02,07	200	41	20.5	207	71	34.3	53	47
2;03,05	256	23	9	287	142	49.5	60.8	39.2
2;04,09	144	46	31.9	129	44	34.1	36.1	63.8
2;05,07	282	12	4.3	191	11	5.8	26.1	73.9
2;06,06	233	10	4.3	224	9	4	36.8	63.2
2;07,17	—			—				
2;08,15	—			205	1	0.5	100	0
2;09,18	270	1	0.4	205	7	3.4	42.9	57.1
2;10,24	—			—			—	—
2,11;21	170			255	5	2	20	80
3,01,03	185	4	2.2	312	4	1.3	37.5	62.5
3;02,14	358	5	1.4	325	10	3.1	6.7	93.3
3,03;12	—			—				
3.04;23	—			—				
3;05,28	—			376	3	0.8	0	100
3;07,09	—			—			—	—
3;08,01	—			344	6	1.7	0	100
3;08,29	346	1	0.3	261	4	1.5	0	100
3;10,11	—			454	2	0.4	0	100
3;11,08	—			242	1	0.4	0	100
4;00,04	—			326	2	0.6	0	100
4;00,18	—			242	1	0.4	0	100
4;01,14	—			326	2	0.6	0	100
4;02,04	—			326	5	1.5	0	100
4;03,16	—			—				
4;04,14	—			—				

Table 13.1 *Mixing – Ivar (contd.)*

Age	Utterances – German			Utterances – French			Single words – mixed German & French	
	Total	Tot. mix	% mix	Total	Tot. mix	% mix	% function	% lexical
4;05,00	—			331	1	0.3	0	100
4;05,28	—			—				
4;06,20	—			261	1	0.4	100	0
4;07,24	—			—			—	—
4;08,17	196	1	0.5	—			0	100
4;09,05	—			248	2	0.8	0	100
4;10,15	261	1	0.4	303	3		0	100
4;11,14	—			211	3	1.4	33.3	66.7
5;00,25	—			309	1	0.3	0	100
5;01,22	—			—			—	—

(— = recording without mixes)

Table 13.2 *Mixing – Annika*

Age	Utterances – German			Utterances – French			Single words – mixed German & French	
	Total	Tot. mix	% mix	Total	Tot. mix	% mix	% function	% lexical
1;05,09	19	3	15.8	34	6	17.7	66.7	33.3
1;06,06	54	1	1.9	36	13	36.1	85.7	14.3
1;07,02	25	2	8	14	5	35.7	100	0
1;07,26	26	7	26.9	36	9	25	100	0
1;08,09	34	1	2.9	32	6	18.8	85.7	14.3
1;08,23	57	1	1.8	40	9	22.5	100	0
1;09,07	130	2	1.5	55	20	36.4	90.9	9.1
1;09,21	24	2	8.3	66	11	16.7	69.2	30.8
1;10,03	57	3	5.3	34	8	23.5	36.4	63.6
1;10,18	—			77	16	20.8	87.5	12.5

Table 13.2 *Mixing – Annika (contd.)*

	Utterances – German			Utterances – French			Single words – mixed German & French	
Age	Total	Tot. mix	% mix	Total	Tot. mix	% mix	% function	% lexical
2;00,10	114	2	1.8	74	9	12.2	90.9	9.1
2;00,17	177	2	1.1	289	4	1.4	50	50
2;00,27	240	1	0.4	—			0	100
2;01,10	—			171	1	0.6	100	0
2;02,22	—			—				
2;03,16	228	1	0.4	147	3	2	25	75
2;04,18	—			—				
2;05,18	230	4	1.7	303	1	0.3	20	80
2;06,18	—			370	2	0.5	0	100
2;07,29	—			133	2	1.5	0	100
2;08,19	246	1	0.4	229	3	1.3	75	25
2;10,00	—			—				
2;10,27	270	1	0.4	352	1	0.3	100	0
2;11,27	—			140	1	0.7	0	100
3;01,00	—			—				
3;01,26	—			274	5	1.8	0	100
3;02,24	—			154	7	4.6	14.3	85.7
3;03,21	—			—				
3;05,04	—			219	3	1.4	0	100
3;05,30	—			179	6	3.4	0	100
3;07,02	—			198	5	2.5	40	60
3;07,13	—			256	8	3.1	0	100
3;08,24	—			161	4	2.5	50	50
3;09,19	—			320	1	0.3	100	0
3;10,26	—			244	3	1.2	33.3	66.7
3;11,10	—			103	1	1	0	100
4;00,25	—			—				
4;01,25	—			155	5	3.2	0	100
4;02,26	—			135	4	3	0	100

(— = recording without mixes)

The development of pragmatic functions of code-switching, however, seems to be related to grammatical development only in a more general sense. Remember that language choice according to the interlocutor may occur at sentence boundaries and, consequently, does not need to observe grammatical constraints. Rather, pragmatic aspects of code-switching, largely influenced by external factors like language use in the family, the parents' expectations about language choice and their reactions to mixing, etc., may contribute to an early separation of languages as well as to the development of specific strategies helping to avoid mixing.

What needs to be investigated in more detail are the causes of early mixing: are there any pragmatic motivations for mixing of 'function words' (e.g. mixing of deictic elements and yes/no), or does this kind of mixing indeed indicate fusion of both language systems? In addition, we have to ask whether the correlations which we found between grammatical development and formal aspects of language mixing are indeed universal. What has to be done, in fact, is to analyse the mixed speech of more children, acquiring different languages, with respect to these questions. Finally, the role of grammatical development in the acquisition of constraints on code-switching has to be further explored. Here, it might be promising to examine more closely Bickerton's (1990) hypothesis: is early child language indeed a kind of 'protolanguage' (i.e. lacking syntactic structures) and can the 'onset of syntax' really be located chronologically and developmentally at the precise point suggested, around age 2;0? Under Bickerton's hypothesis, the classification of young bilinguals' speech as 'fusion of two systems' as well as the notion of 'system' referring to early child language, should be reconsidered.

Notes

[1] 2;0,0 = years; months, days.

[2] This is not to say, however, that every case of violation of constraints on code-switching needs to be explained as resulting from lack of grammatical or pragmatic knowledge. It has often been reported that older children and even adults mix if they do not know a word or construction in one language, and even when this expression is only momentarily not available. In our data, we find numerous examples of such mixes which typically concern the insertion of isolated lexical items into an utterance of the other language. Given that in most of the cases, the children show by self-corrections, hesitations or laughter, that they are aware of mixing, we would like to suggest that these conscious mixes should, more appropriately, be characterised as 'flagged switching' (Poplack & Sankoff 1988). With respect to the results presented in section 5, it is interesting to note that flagged switches first occur at exactly the same age when important

changes in grammatical development, as well as in mixing behaviour, could be observed.

[3] McClure (1981: 74) states that up to the age of around five years, children are not able to assess their interlocutor's (relative) linguistic competence in a second language, whereas our own research seems to indicate that such judgments may influence the children's language choice much earlier – see Köppe (1990).

[4] See Auer (this volume) for a detailed description of the mechanisms underlying such 'participant-related' switching.

[5] For a detailed discussion of Redlinger and Park's results as well as of their methodology, see Meisel (1989, 1994a) and Veh (1990).

[6] DUFDE = Deutsch und Französisch – Doppelter Erstsrpacherwerb (German and French – Simultaneous Acquisition of Two First Languages), a research project made possible by several research grants (1986–92) from the Deutsche Forschungsgemeinschaft to Jürgen Meisel. During the period when this chapter was written, the researchers in this team were Caroline Koehn, Regina Köppe, Natascha Müller and Achim Stenzel. Students collaborating as research assistants were Cornelia Hußmann and Christophe Bresoli. Suzanne Schlyter, who has been a member of the team for three years (1986–9), initiated the analysis of language-mixing and code-switching in our group; see Schlyter (1987). We want to thank all of them for their most valuable help, and we also want to thank Birgitta Veh for her comments on an earlier version of this paper.

[7] The abbreviations F, G and M refer to the French and the German interviewer and to the (French) mother. Switches are given in italics.

[8] As most sentential subjects consist of pronouns rather than Det + N sequences, such switches rarely concern the subject NP.

[9] An explanation for these differences is offered by Köppe (1990) who states that in Annika's family, a very rigid language separation is observed, i.e. the parents do not accept being spoken to in the respective other language. This may partially account for early metalinguistic awareness as well as for Annika's linguistic behaviour, as described above. Köppe concludes that the child uses strategies like simplification, avoidance of (switching) errors, etc., in order to maintain communication in French in spite of increasing problems of expression in this language.

Bibliography

Arnberg, L. (1987) *Raising children bilingually: the preschool years*. Clevedon, Avon: Multilingual Matters.

Bergman, C. R. (1976) Interference vs independent development in infant bilingualism. In G. D. Keller, R. V. Teschner, S. Viera eds., *Bilingualism in the bicentennial and beyond*. New York: The Bilingual Review/La Revista Bilingüe Press, 86–96.

Bickerton, D. (1990) Syntactic development: the brain just does it. Unpublished ms., University of Hawaii at Manoa.

Blom, J.-P. and Gumperz, J. J. (1972) Social meaning in linguistic structures: code-switching in Norway. In J. J. Gumperz, D. Hymes eds., *Directions in sociolinguistics. The ethnography of communication.* New York: Holt, Rinehart & Winston, 407–34.

Clyne, M. G. (1987a) Constraints on code-switching: how universal are they? *Linguistics*, 25: 739–64.

(1987b) Don't you get bored speaking only English? – Expressions of metalinguistic awareness in a bilingual child. Ms.

DiSciullo, A. M., Muysken, P. and Singh, R. (1986) Government and code-mixing. *Journal of Linguistics*, 22: 1–24.

Durán, R. P. (1981) ed. *Latino language and communicative behavior.* Norwood, N.J.: Ablex.

Fantini, A. E. (1985) *Language acquisition of a bilingual child: a sociolinguistic perspective.* Clevedon, Avon: Multilingual Matters.

Gardner-Chloros, P. (1987) Code-switching in relation to language contact and convergence. In G. Lüdi ed., *Devenir bilingue – parler bilingue. Actes du 2ᵉ colloque sur le bilinguisme, Université de Neuchâtel, 20–22 Sept. 1984.* Tübingen: Max Niemeyer Verlag, 99–111.

Givón, T. (1979) *On understanding grammar.* New York: Academic Press.

Grosjean, F. (1982) *Life with two languages. An introduction to bilingualism.* Cambridge, Mass.: Harvard University Press.

Gumperz, J. J. (1976) The sociolinguistic significance of conversational code-switching. *Papers on Language and Context (Working Paper 46).* Berkeley: University of California, Language Behavior Research Laboratory, 1–46.

Gumperz, J. J. and Hernández-Chávez, E. (1975) Cognitive aspects of bilingual communcation. In E. Hernández-Chávez, A. Cohen, A. Beltramo eds., *El lenguaje de los chicanos.* Arlington, Va.: Center for Applied Linguistics, 154–63.

Joshi, A. K. (1985) Processing of sentences with intrasentential code-switching. In D. R. Dowty, L. Karttunen, A. M. Zwicky eds., *Natural language parsing.* Cambridge University Press, 190–205.

Kielhöfer, B. (1987) Le 'bon' changement de langue et le 'mauvais' mélange de langues. In G. Lüdi ed., *Devenir bilingue – parler bilingue. Actes du 2ᵉ colloque sur le bilinguisme, Université de Neuchâtel, 20.–22.9.1984.* Tübingen: Max Niemeyer Verlag, 135–55.

Kielhöfer, B. and Jonekeit, S. (1983) *Zweisprachige Kindererziehung.* Tübingen: Stauffenberg Verlag.

Klavans, J. L. (1983) The syntax of code-switching: Spanish and English. In L. D. King, C. A. Matey eds., *Selected papers from the 13th Linguistic Symposium on Romance Languages.* Chapel Hill, N.C.: 213–31.

Köppe, R. (1990) *Code-switching: Strategien und Funktionen der Sprachwahl bei bilingualen Kindern (Französisch-Deutsch) im Vorschulalter.* Master's thesis, University of Hamburg.

(1994) The DUFDE Project. In Meisel (1994b), 15–27.

Lindholm, K. J. and Padilla, A. M. (1978) Language mixing in bilingual children. *Journal of Child Language*, 5: 327–35.

McClure, E. (1981) Formal and functional aspects of the code-switched discourse of bilingual children. In Durán (1981), 69–94.

McClure, E. and Wentz, J. (1975) Functions of code switching among Mexican-American children. In R. Grossman, L. San, T. Vance eds., *Functionalism*. University of Chicago, Department of Linguistics, 421–33.

McLaughlin, B. (1984) *Second-language acquisition in childhood*. I. *Preschool children* (2nd edn). Hillsdale, N.J.: Lawrence Erlbaum.

Meisel, J. M. (1989) Early differentiation of languages in bilingual children. In K. Hyltenstam, L. Obler eds., *Bilingualism across the lifespan. Aspects of acquisition, maturity, and loss*. Cambridge University Press, 13–40.

(1990) INFL-ection: subjects and subject–verb agreement. In J. M. Meisel ed., *Two first languages. Early grammatical development in bilingual children*. Dordrecht: Foris, 237–98.

(1994a) Code-switching in young bilingual children: the acquisition of grammatical constraints. *Studies in Second Language Acquisition*, 16: 413–39.

(1994b) ed. *Bilingual first language acquisition: French and German grammatical development*. Amsterdam: John Benjamins.

Oksaar, E. (1976) Code switching as an interactional strategy for developing bilingual competence. *Child Language* (= *Word 27*), 377–85.

(1978) Preschool trilingualism: a case study. In F. C. C. Peng, W. V. Raffler-Engel eds., *Language acquisition and developmental kinesics*. Hiroshima, 129–37.

Pfaff, C. W. (1979) Constraints on language mixing: intrasentential code-switching and borrowing in Spanish/English. *Language*, 55: 291–318.

Poplack, S. (1980) Sometimes I'll start a sentence in Spanish Y TERMINO EN ESPAÑOL: toward a typology of code-switching. *Linguistics*, 18: 581–618. Also in J. Amastae, L. Elías-Olivares (1982) eds. *Spanish in the United States. Sociolinguistic aspects*. Cambridge University Press, 230–63.

(1981) Syntactic structure and social function of code-switching. In Durán (1981), 169–84.

Poplack, S. and Sankoff, D. (1988) Code-switching. In U. Ammon, N. Dittmar, K. J. Mattheier eds., *Sociolinguistics II*. Berlin: Mouton de Gruyter, 1174–80.

Radford, A. (1990) *Syntactic theory and the acquisition of English syntax*. Oxford: Basil Blackwell.

Redlinger, W. E. and Park. T.-Z. (1980) Language mixing in young bilinguals. *Journal of Child Language*, 7: 337–52.

Romaine, S. (1989) *Bilingualism*, Language in Society 13. Oxford: Basil Blackwell.

Ronjat, J. (1913) *Le développement du langage observé chez un enfant bilingue*. Paris: Champion.

Sankoff, D. and Poplack, S. (1981) A formal grammar for code-switching. *Papers in Linguistics: International Journal of Human Communication*, 14 (1): 3–46.

Saunders, G. (1988) *Bilingual children: from birth to teens*. 2nd edn. Clevedon, Avon: Multilingual Matters.

Schlyter, S. (1987) Language mixing and linguistic level in three bilingual children. *Scandinavian Working Papers on Bilingualism*, 7: 29–48.

(1990) Introducing the DUFDE project. In J. M. Meisel ed., *Two first languages. Early grammatical development in bilingual children*. Dordrecht: Foris.

Stenzel, A. (1994) Case assignment and functional categories in bilingual children: routes of development and implications for linguistic theory. In Meisel (1994b), 161–208.

Taeschner, T. (1983) *The sun is feminine. A study on language acquisition in bilingual children*. Berlin: Springer.

Timm, L. A. (1975) Spanish–English code-switching: *el porqué y how-not-to*. *Romance Philology*, 28: 473–82.

Veh, B. (1990) *Syntaktische Aspekte des Code-Switching bei bilingualen Kindern (Französisch–Deutsch) im Vorschulalter*. Master's thesis, University of Hamburg.

Vihman, M. M. (1984) A developmental perspective on code-switching: conversations between a pair of bilingual siblings. MS.7, Stanford University.

(1985) Language differentiation by the bilingual child. *Journal of Child Language*, 12: 297–324.

Volterra, V. and Taeschner, T. (1978) The acquisition and development of language by bilingual children. *Journal of Child Language*, 5: 311–26.

Woolford, E. (1982) Bilingual code-switching and syntactic theory. *Linguistic Inquiry*, 14 (3): 520–36.

14 THE CODE-SWITCHING BEHAVIOUR OF ADULTS WITH LANGUAGE DISORDERS - WITH SPECIAL REFERENCE TO APHASIA AND DEMENTIA

Kenneth Hyltenstam

1 Introduction

1.1 The problem

In some of the reported cases of bilinguals suffering from brain diseases, speakers have been observed to switch between their two languages in interaction with monolingual interlocutors. There are also cases where patients try to communicate entirely in a language that is not at all understood by their interlocutor. Although language mixing and language choice are salient phenomena in the study of language disorders in bilinguals, it is, however, not the case that these linguistic characteristics always accompany neurological diseases in bilinguals. For bilingual aphasics, literature reviews seem rather to support the opposite, i.e. that language mixing occurs in a minority of the reported cases (Paradis 1977; Albert and Obler 1978; Paradis 1989). From what we know about demented bilingual speakers at this point, language mixing and problems with language choice may well be more prevalent in this group.

The main question that will be focussed upon in this chapter is whether the code-switching behaviour observed in aphasic and demented subjects is structured linguistically in the same way as that of healthy bilingual speakers. In the case of aphasic speakers, this question will be discussed on the basis of a review of cases reported in the literature and the examples of code-switching given there. For demented speakers, the discussion will be based both on a review of published results and on empirical data from an ongoing investigation into the language of demented bilingual speakers, presently being carried out at Stockholm University.

As pragmatically appropriate code-switching presupposes that a specific language choice has been made by the bilingual speaker, the question of language choice and its relation to code-switching in the actual group of speakers will also be briefly dealt with.

1.2 A brief characterisation of aphasic and demented speakers

Studies of acquired language disorders in bilingual adults have traditionally been concerned with aphasic patients, i.e. subjects exhibiting linguistic or communicative problems as a result of brain damage. These insults to the brain may affect language only, or language in combination with other cognitive or motor–perceptual functions depending on the localisation and extent of the damage. Space does not allow for a treatment of the linguistic characteristics of the various types of aphasia here (for overviews and typologies, see Caplan 1987 and Kertesz 1979). Suffice it to say that the type of language that is produced by aphasic subjects (for example, language that contains abundant verbal paraphasias and neologisms) can make the analysis of code-switching and other contact phenomena in this type of data extremely difficult.

Recently, a different bilingual population exhibiting language disorders has been addressed in research, namely subjects suffering from dementia of the Alzheimer type (DAT).[1] Alzheimer's dementia, as do other types of dementia, involves a 'chronic progressive deterioration in intellect, personality, and communicative functioning' (Bayles and Kaszniak 1987: 1). Rather than the focal brain injuries that cause aphasia, the neurological deterioration that takes place in this disease is global in nature, involving changes in the structure of the brain tissue and in the balance of chemical substances upon which the interaction between neurons is dependent. Again, due to lack of space, we will not be able to look into the characteristics of language produced by subjects suffering from Alzheimer's dementia at this point (see Obler and Albert 1984; Emery 1988; and below).

Although the term 'aphasia' is often used to cover the language disorders of both groups, in this chapter it is restricted in usage to the effects of focal brain damage. In the case of demented speakers, the term 'dementia-related language disorders' is used.

1.3 Limitations inherent in the study of acquired language pathologies

One of the main problems in addressing questions of language mixing in a person with a language pathology is to determine whether individual instances of mixing are an effect of the disease or not. A bilingual person who is suffering from a brain disease that affects language may very well, for example, premorbidly, have had the habit of extensive code-switching in his/her normal interaction with other bilingual speakers. Furthermore, the language choice in a particular situation may be more reasonable than it seems, in particular when a bilingual speaker realises that the interlocutor understands both languages, although only one of them is used in that particular conversation (see Grosjean 1989: 10). As Scotton (1988) observes, in any bilingual exchange type it is possible for a speaker to make an unexpected or explorative choice of language. In reviewing the literature on these questions, which will be done below, it is often not possible to know what the premorbid behaviour of a particular subject was, although most published case studies explicitly mention comments by family members about changes in the patient's linguistic behaviour.

Another problem in the interpretation of published data on the bilingual behaviour of patients is the lack of given detail of linguistic patterning. There are a number of reasons for this state of affairs. One reason is that much of the literature on case studies of bilingual aphasia was published in the first half of the twentieth century or in the last few decades of the nineteenth century, i.e. at a time when the lack of recording facilities made detailed documentation impossible. What we have in the best cases are fairly detailed protocols of the patient's interaction (e.g. Pick 1909: 218–34, 470–83; Stengel and Zelmanowicz 1933/1983: 359ff.), but, in most cases, examples consist of single utterances. Another reason is that these cases are generally described by neurologists rather than by linguists and therefore, in most cases, are not presented in linguistic analytical terms. At best, we can study single examples of switching that have been presented in the literature, keeping in mind that there may be problems with the accuracy of the reporting of these examples and that there are severe limitations generally in what single written examples can tell us about the more general patterning of code-switching. All this means that we are not in a position to compare aphasia data to healthy data at a qualified level. Still, it does seem worthwhile to examine the little data there is as a basis for hypotheses.

Finally, there is the problem that the literature on language disorders of bilingual or multilingual speakers[2] shares with the literature on bilingualism generally, namely that of lack of terminological clarity. What we today consider to be different phenomena are often lumped together without further specification under one label. The most common label seems to be 'language mixing', but sometimes the term 'interference' is used generically. What is meant in each case has to be determined from examples or from the description of a specific behaviour.

2 Code-switching – theoretical framework and terminology

Code-switching can obviously occur with high frequency when speakers who are bilingual in the same languages communicate with one another. Comparing the functions of, and linguistic constraints on, code-switching in different communities has been the focus of recent theoretical interest with the long-term goal of characterising code-switching universals. Thus, the most influential research of the 1980s, in this area, has revealed several of the sociolinguistic/pragmatic and linguistic/structural norms followed by healthy and competent bilingual speakers. In this context switching is considered to be intentional and purposeful, even though, as a rule, the specific intentions and purposes – just as in the case of other pragmatic and linguistic regularities – are not accessible to the speakers' conscious reflection (Paradis 1989: 132; Myers-Scotton 1990: 60).

The social significance of code-switching is generally assumed to be determined by norms developed within the cultural framework of specific communities (Gumperz 1982; Poplack 1985; Scotton 1988; Stroud 1992). When code-switching is produced by bilingual speakers out of the appropriate context, as it is by many speakers afflicted with aphasia and dementia, or, for that matter, by healthy speakers under conditions of fatigue, stress, emotion or momentary lack of attention, it is possible to describe the behaviour as devoid of its conventional social significance. This follows from the assumption that the on-line interpretation of the social meaning of code-switching is based on shared norms in a speech community, whatever the size of that community may be. If the interlocutor lacks this norm, or if the speaker him-/herself has never internalised such a norm, the social or pragmatic meaning of switches or of the mode of code-switching can certainly not be transferred. Hasselmo (1961) uses the term 'derailment' to distinguish this type of unintentional switching from 'functional switching', which is the speaker's intentional use of two languages within the same discourse. With Clyne (1987: 740) one might characterise this type of inattentional switching as psycholinguistically conditioned in contrast to normal sociolinguistically conditioned switching.

A number of structural constraints on code-switching have been suggested. These constraints are reviewed and discussed in other parts of this volume (see the chapters by Myers-Scotton, Poplack and Meechan, and Muysken). For the purpose of this chapter, which is to compare code-switching patterns in healthy and pathological data, it is important to use a framework that is sufficiently general to be applied to any language pair and at the same time sufficiently detailed and formalised for there to be no doubts about how the framework applies to the data. In my view, these requirements are fulfilled by the framework suggested by Poplack (1980) and developed by her and David Sankoff in various writings over the last decade. From Poplack's work I refer to the Equivalence Constraint, which restricts switching to syntactic boundaries around which the two languages involved have the same order of elements, and the Free Morpheme Constraint, which rules out switching between a bound and a free morpheme. The distinction between switching and borrowing is essential within this framework; the two are seen as totally different phenomena. In addition to the traditional category of borrowings, i.e. elements that are recurrent and widespread in a speech community (Poplack and Sankoff 1984; Grosjean 1989: 9), borrowing also includes what has been called 'speech borrowing' or 'nonce borrowing' (Weinreich 1953: 11; Poplack and Sankoff 1984). Code-switching and nonce borrowing are related in that elements from more than one language are drawn upon in on-line speech production.

It is important to keep in mind that the wider framework for Poplack's model is variation theory. This means that empirical evidence of switching patterns comes from frequencies of different kinds of switches observed in linguistic corpora. The constraints capture the probabilities of occurrence of a specific switch type and can therefore not be falsified by single counterexamples, only by corpora in which the tendencies or probabilities on which the constraints were formulated do not hold (see e.g. Poplack 1991). This restriction is important to keep in mind below when analysing and evaluating the single code-switching examples which we find in the literature.

Another model that will also be briefly referred to is the Matrix Language Frame (MLF) model by Myers-Scotton (1991 and this volume; for a comprehensive description, see 1993). In this model, the distinction between matrix (or base) language and embedded language is important. One 'principle' of this model that will be referred to below, the Morpheme Order Principle, states that the 'surface morpheme order' in constituents containing elements from both languages is that of the matrix language. In this model there is no distinction between nonce borrowings and switched elements based on structural criteria such as degree of morphological and phonological adaptation of the incorporated elements. Borrowing refers only to those elements that are recurrent in a specific corpus of data and to notions that are 'new' to the speech community (1991: 218). Other elements are switches.

The following terminology is adopted for the present discussion of language mixing in aphasic and demented speakers. 'Language mixing' is used as a general term for different types of interaction between two (or more) languages. 'Code switching' is 'the alternate use of two languages within the same discourse' (Poplack 1980). 'Borrowing' is a speaker's use of a lexical element from language A which has been morphologically and syntactically, but not necessarily phonologically, integrated into language B, when a speaker is using language B, or vice versa. This definition of borrowing covers both 'language borrowing', referring to recurrence and wide recognition of the borrowed item in a speech community, and nonce borrowing.[3] 'Language choice' refers to a bilingual speaker's choice of one of his/her languages, with or without in-mixing of the other, for a specific discourse (see Grosjean 1982). The 'matrix language' of a switched utterance is the language that has the most morphemes within that utterance, or, if this criterion fails to point out one language as the matrix language, the language from which most closed-class morphemes are drawn. Although I am not using the same criteria as they do, I follow Joshi (1985) and Nishimura (1986) in defining the matrix language for each utterance rather than basing the analysis on larger discourse samples as advocated by Myers-Scotton (1993: 66). The reason for this is that the subjects we will be briefly discussing make obvious and frequent changes of matrix language within one and the same interaction, which seem to be dependent on their lack of attention and assessment of the speech situation.

3 Code-switching in aphasic speakers

The literature on case studies of bilingual aphasia covers more than a hundred years of research. The main focus of the long-standing interest in language use in bilingual aphasics has not, however, been on issues of language mixing or language choice, but rather on two other related questions: (i) the differential degree to which each of a bilingual speaker's two languages has been affected by the brain damage; and, especially (ii) the predictability of the differential recovery patterns that have been observed for each language in a variety of cases.

Continuous surveys have been made of this literature, often with the particular aim of finding evidence for one or another of the hypotheses on language recovery regularities. Early studies of differential recovery suggested that it would be the language acquired earlier that would be first recovered (Ribot 1882), or, alternatively, the language used most extensively in the period immediately prior to insult (Pitres 1895). These patterns have been called 'Ribot's rule' and 'Pitres's rule', respectively. In particular Minkowski (1928, and in several later studies), discussing exceptions to Pitres's rule, has insisted on the role of affective factors in explaining differential recovery patterns.[4] Paradis (1977) identifies five basic patterns of recovery, the discussion of which is the main focus of his comprehensive review of published cases of bilingual aphasia: (i) *synergistic*, 'when progress in one language is accompanied by progress in another' (p. 65), either in a parallel mode 'when the languages are similarly impaired and restored at the same rate' (ibid.) or in a differential mode 'when impairment is of a different degree in each language and restitution occurs at the same or at a different rate' (ibid.); (ii) *antagonistic*, 'when one language regresses as the other progresses' (p. 67); (iii) *successive* 'when one language does not begin to reappear until another has been restored' (p. 74); (iv) *selective*, 'when the patient does not regain one or more of his languages' (p. 76); and (v) *mixed*, when 'the bilingual's two languages are inter-mingled' (p. 76).[5] Paradis (1989: 117) defines three additional patterns of recovery, namely *alternate antagonism*, in which 'for alternating periods of time, patients have access to only one of their languages', *differential aphasia* with 'different symptoms in each of the patient's languages', and *selective aphasia* with 'obvious impairments in one language without any measurable deficit in the other(s)'. On the issue of predictability of recovery patterns, the conclusion reached by Paradis (1977: 112) is still valid: '[T]here seems to be no rule with predictive value as to how bilinguals recover their languages. At best, post hoc explanations can be given by what factor seems to have played a preponderant role in a particular case.' For our present purposes, the surveys on bilingual aphasia are useful methodologi-cally in that they allow us to find the cases which have involved code-switching. It must be assumed that the cases surveyed by Paradis (1977), the largely overlap-ping cases that were summarised by Albert and Obler (1978), and the additional cases reviewed by Paradis (1989), comprising the studies that were added between 1976 and 1989, in fact include all published case studies of aphasia in bilinguals up to 1989.[6] In spite of the fact that precise statements as to the total number of published case studies are given in Paradis (1977) (138 cases) and Paradis (1989) (27 cases), it turns out that their exact number does not amount to a simple sum of these two figures. A cross-checking and recalculation of all individual cases men-tioned in the Paradis reviews and in the Albert and Obler (1978) survey indicate that the total number of published cases was 188 by 1989 (see appendix on p. 335 for an explication of how this recalculation was carried out).

The cases coded as 'mixed' in Paradis's classification (1977, 1989) are of parti-cular interest here. This category, though, is a broad one covering various lan-guage contact phenomena 'at the levels of syntax, morphology, and phonology and [occurs] in various ways in writing and reading' (p. 77).

Albert and Obler (1978) use a coding system in their presentation of case studies where the code '+mixing' is defined as 'patient mixed elements of two languages' and '−switch' as 'patient spoke a certain language inappropriately'

(p. 111). Cases coded with these two symbols should therefore be of particular interest for our purposes and contain possible descriptions of code-switching and language choice phenomena respectively. It is made clear that the cases coded for +mixing refer to 'people who had not mixed . . . premorbidly' (p. 110).

It is more difficult to identify cases where language choice is a particular problem in Paradis's review. It is obvious, though, that many patients exhibiting non-synergistic patterns of recovery may, at least for certain periods, produce another language than that of the interlocutor (or, more generally, than the language expected in the speech situation). Among all the cases treated in Paradis (1977), 6 were found to have an antagonistic pattern of recovery, 8 a successive pattern of recovery, and 37 a selective pattern of recovery. This constitutes a little less than 40% of the total number of cases. The probability of synergistic patterns among the majority of non-reported cases suggests that the incidence of not being able to use a specific language that was available premorbidly might be considerably lower than 40%.

Table 14.1 comprises a summary of those case studies reviewed by Paradis (1977, 1989) and Albert and Obler (1978) where we have some kind of indication of language mixing. Since the different characterisations of the same cases are less than unanimous (see again appendix), a renewed assessment as to the mixing character of the studies is also presented in this table. Furthermore, a judgment as to whether a particular study represents a clear code-switching case is carried out and marked in the CS column in the table. The criteria for seeing a case as a code-switching case are either that obvious examples of code-switching are given in the text or that it is made totally clear from the wordings that code-switching is involved, as, for example, in Schulze: 'In Russian, it was noticed that the patient frequently inserted Bulgarian words and endings and occasionally switched into Bulgarian without noticing it.' (1968/1983: 756). This criterion has, however, been used somewhat conservatively, so that, for example, even though comments such as '[d]uring attempts to talk Bulgarian he replaced forgotten words with Czech expressions' (Ledinský and Mraček 1958/1983: 576) would indicate code-switching, the study has not been marked in the CS column, since we know nothing about how this replacement takes place syntactically and prosodically.

In fact, three cases appearing in the reviews by Albert and Obler (1978) and Paradis (1989) turn out to be mixing and code-switching cases although they are not so coded in the reviews. These three are given as the last three entries of Table 14.1.

As shown in Table 14.1, according to the present assessment, a total of 31 cases exhibit language mixing. Among these, 15 cases have been identified as exhibiting

Table 14.1 *Cases of language mixing in bilingual aphasics identified in the literature and present assessment*

Case	Paradis (1977) 2.1	2.2	text	Paradis (1989)	Albert & Obler (1978)	Present assessment + mix	n a	CS
Bastian (1875)					x		x	
Dedić (1926)			x			x		
Florenskaya (1940)		x	x		x	x		
Gloning & Gloning (1965), case 2	x	x	x		x	x		x
Gloning & Gloning (1965), case 3	x	x	x		x	x		x
Gloning & Gloning (1965), case 4			x		x	x		x
Halpern (1941)	x		x					
Herschmann & Pötzl (1920)	x	x			x	x		
Kauders (1929)	x	x	x		x	x		x
Krapf (1955), case 1		x						
Krapf (1957), case 1		x						
Lambert & Fillenbaum (1959), case 3	x	x				x		
Lambert & Fillenbaum (1959), case 4	x	x				x		
Lambert & Fillenbaum (1959), case 14		x				x		
Ledinský & Mraček (1958)	x	x				x		
Leischner (1943)	x	x	x			x		
l'Hermitte et al. (1966), case 4	x	x	x			x		x
l'Hermitte et al. (1966), case 8			x					

Table 14.1 *Cases of language mixing in bilingual aphasics identified in the literature and present assessment (contd.)*

Case	Paradis (1977) 2.1	Paradis (1977) 2.2	Paradis (1977) text	Paradis (1989)	Albert & Obler (1978)	Present assessment + mix	Present assessment CS
Minkowski (1927), case 1			x			x	x
Minkowski (1964)		x				x	
Obler & Albert (1978)					x	x	
Ovcharova et al. (1968), case 3			x			x	
Perecman (1984)				x		x	x
Pick (1909), case 2					x	x	
Pick (1913)					x	x	
Pötzl (1925)	x	x	x		x	x	x
Schulze (1968)			x			x	x
Stengel & Zelmanowicz (1933)	x	x	x		x	x	x
Voinescu et al. (1977)				x		x	x
Wald (1961), case 4	x					x	x
Weisenburg & McBride (1935), case 4	x	x	x			x	
Winslow (1868)	x					n a	
Winterstein & Meier (1939)		x				x	
Mössner & Pilch (1971)						x	x
Nilipour & Ashayeri (1989)						x	x
Pick (1909), case 1						x	x

n a = not available to the present author

code-switching. The 31 mixing cases make up a proportion of 16% of the identified 188 published cases of bilingual aphasia. It was concluded by Paradis (1977)
that the number of cases where the patients mix languages inappropriately are in
the minority and not commonplace as might have been expected. Based on the
Paradis 1977 quantification, a figure of 7% has appeared in the literature (first, I
believe, in Albert and Obler 1978: 105; see also Perecman 1984: 44, 1989: 241),
although this proportion is definitely too low.[7] Our proportion of 16% makes the
condition of language mixing as a result of brain damage less rare than previous
comments would indicate, and it gives a definite reason, as others have done
before (e.g. Albert and Obler 1978: 105), to oppose the position taken by
Whitaker (1978: 28), that '[i]n view of the rarity of report of mixing or interference
in this body of literature, little would be gained by speculating on its significance'.

Table 14.2 specifies the number and type of switching examples appearing in
the descriptions of the fifteen code-switching cases identified in Table 14.1,
together with an indication of what languages were spoken by the patients.
Before commenting on the content of Table 14.2, it should be pointed out that
the analysis of code-switching examples presented there is of necessity tentative.
First of all, in many cases it is impossible to know what syntactic relationships
hold within an utterance from the written account, i.e. without having access to
the prosodic features of that utterance. Even the interpretation of utterance
boundaries is sometimes difficult. In several cases, markings of pauses and inter-
ruptions have been helpful in the interpretations. In addition, as mentioned
above, the patients' other aphasic features such as paraphasias, use of telegraphic
speech, logorrhea, etc., have made the interpretation of some examples impossible. Caution has led me, therefore, to comment on the structural features of code-
switching examples only where the words on each side of the switch were clearly
existing words in the actual languages.

The total number of examples of mixed utterances was 81. Several utterances
contained switches that were either translations or switches between asyntactically
conjoined phrases in agrammatic speech. These could not be assessed in terms of
current code-switching contraints. A total of 54 switches that were in agreement
with the Equivalence Constraint and 3 borrowings, i.e. integrated lexical items,
were identified. In addition to these, the following 6 potentially problematic
examples from Mössner and Pilch (1971) (examples (1)–(3)) and Nilipour and
Ashayeri (1989) (examples (4)–(6)) were found:

(1)   Das neue Haus ist nur März *finish*. (German–English)

        [The new house is only March *finish*.]

Table 14.2 *Examples of borrowing and code-switching in the literature (Cont.)*

Case	languages spoken	mixed utter.	borrowings	intra-sent.	comment
Perecman (1984)	M: German C: French A: English	10		7	Most typical characteristics: abundant spontaneous translation of entire phrases. Switch sites: +COMP (German–English) V+NP (English–German) Cop+Pred (English–German) V+Pred (English–German) Det+N (1 French–German) (1 English–German) Prep+ NP (English–German)
Pick (1909), case 1	M: German ?: Czech	35		12	Mostly inter-sentential switches. Switch sites: +COMP+ (5) Advl+ (2) NP+VP (2) Attr+N (2) V+NP
Pötzl (1925)	M: German A: Czech	1		1	Switch site: Det+N
Schulze (1968)	M: Bulgarian ?: German, Russian, English, French S: Latin				No examples
Stengel & Zelmanowicz (1933)	M: Czech A: German				No examples of code-switching in spite of detailed 'protocols' with many examples in monolingual German; 'spoke . . . in a mixed German–Czech gibberish' (Stengel & Zelmanowicz 1933/1983: 357); 'switched easily from one language to the other' (p. 369).
Voinescu et al. (1977)	M: Greek C: Romanian, Russian, German	2	1	1	Borrowing: Romanian vb+German infl. Switch site: NP+VP (German–Roman.)
Wald (1961), case 4	M: Russian ?: German, French				No examples.

Table 14.2 *Examples of borrowing and code-switching in the literature*

Case	languages spoken	mixed utter.	borrowings	intra-sent.	comment
Gloning & Gloning (1965), case 2	M: Italian C: German, Serbo-Croatian	3			The patient speaks in telegraphic style. Produces mostly asyntactic phrases mixed in all three languages.
Gloning & Gloning (1965), case 3	M: Bulgarian A: German	1	1	1	Due to paraphasias the examples are difficult to interpret. Borrowing: derivative N Switch site: NP (object) + Adv-V
Gloning & Gloning (1965), case 4	M: Hungarian C: German	Only single words	1		Patient partly logorrheic. Borrowing: compound (*heftag* Hungarian *heftö*, German *Montag*) Also examples of phonol. blends.
Kauders (1929)	M: German S: English, French	3		3	The patient speaks in telegraphic style, probably with pauses between phrases. If possible to see these as intra-sentential CS: Switch sites: NP+VP (Germ.–French) Det+N (German–French) Adj+N (French–English: *un petit* boy)
l'Hermitte *et al.* (1966), case 4	M: English S: French A: German	2 (written sent.)		2	Only written examples. Many English incorporations and massive paraphasias in a letter written in French; no French incorporations in a letter written in English, but a few in a writing test in English. Switch sites: V^{mod}+VP Adv+NP (*peut-et* two months)
Minkowski (1927), case 1	M: Swiss Germ. A: Stand. Germ., some French, some Italian				No examples: '[trying to speak Swiss German], he often did not succeed in finding the desired word, and replaced it with a word from the standard language … he had a tendency to switch back to Standard German' (Minkowski 1927/1983: 215f.)

Table 14.2 *Examples of borrowing and code-switching in the literature (Cont.)*

Case	languages spoken	mixed utter.	borrowings	intra-sent.	comment
Mössner & Pilch (1971)	M: German ?: English	9		9	Switch sites: V-NEG+V Cop+Pred NP (Obj)+Pred Prep+NP Adv+Adj Num+PP (*zwanzig of September*) Attr+N (3) + 3 potential violations of constraints (see text)
Nilipour & Ashayeri (1989)	M: Farsi S: English A: German	15		18	Switch sites: NP+VP (1 English–German) (2 German–English) V-Neg+NP (German–Farsi) V+NP (German–Farsi) Cop+Pred (German–Farsi) COMP+ (1 German–English) (1 English–German) +COMP (English–German) Wh+ (2 Farsi–German) Attr+N (1 German–English) (1 English–German) V+V (1 German–English) (1 English–German) V+Neg (English–German) +Co-ord+ (German–English–German) + 3 potential violations of constraints (see text)

M = mother tongue, C = language acquired from childhood, A = language acquired during adulthood, S = language acquired (primarily) at school, ? = acquisition conditions unknown

Here, the sentence is constructed according to German word-order rules with the non-finite verb form at the end. This word order is of course impossible in English and the example is thus a violation of the Equivalence Constraint. On the assumptions of the MLF model, however, the switch would be seen as grammatical under the Morpheme Order Principle, since German would be taken to be the matrix language and would thus determine the word order of the switched utterance.[8]

Under the Free Morpheme Constraint there should be no switches within fixed phrases as in (2) and (3).

(2)   Krieg und *peace*
        [War and *peace*]

(3)   Ach du *heaven*
        [Oh you *heaven*]

A similar example comes from the Nilipour and Ashayeri patient:

(4)   Again *mal*
        [Again *time* (= *once*)]

Example (4) can either be seen as a violation of the Free Morpheme Constraint, i.e. if we consider this to be a switch within a lexical phrase (*once again* and *nochmal*) or as a violation to the Equivalence Constraint, as the order between the two elements in the English and German corresponding phrases is conflicting.

The same meaning as that of example (4) is also expressed once in all the three languages (English–German–Farsi) of this patient as in (5).

(5)   One *mal* <u>dige</u>
        [One *time* <u>more</u>]

This same patient also produces (6), which would violate the Equivalence Constraint but, as with example (1) above, would be normal in the MLF model under the Morpheme Order Principle, given that German is the matrix language.

(6)   Ich habe *for her* <u>faqat âmrikâ</u> nicht gesacht (= gesagt).
        [I have *for her* <u>only English</u> not said.]

In conclusion, in spite of these examples of questionable code-switching grammaticality, I think it is reasonable to believe that the code-switching of aphasic speakers is structured according to the same constraints as code-switching in healthy speakers. The examples that were identified in the literature overwhelmingly support this hypothesis. Two of the potential violations to the Equivalence

Constraint, as we have seen, would be grammatical switches in the MLF model. The examples where we have a switch within lexical phrases do seem odd, but their low frequency in the data would indicate that they are not necessarily characteristic of aphasic speakers.

4 Code-switching in demented speakers

The literature on bilingual dementia is quite recent, if we disregard a number of informal observations of possible dementia cases made in medical accounts. Goldstein and Katz (1937) described a demented[9] 56-year-old Swedish woman who had emigrated to the United States at the age of 32 and who had become a fluent speaker of English. At the beginning of the observation period, the patient answered in English, the language in which she was addressed, and spoke only occasionally in Swedish. Later she often answered in Swedish and mixed the two languages. Finally, 'some weeks later' she spoke only in Swedish, and '[i]t did not help to tell her that [the observers did] not understand Swedish' (p. 485).

As a matter of curiosity, in an early essay on the diseases of the mind, Rush (1812)[10] comments on old Swedish immigrants to the USA in the following way:

> It is from the motion excited in the brain, by means of a fever, that persons in that disease, often recollect events and speak languages, which appeared to have perished in their memories. The late Mr Frederic A. Muhlenberg informed me that his father, who was for many years minister of the Lutheran church in Philadelphia, in visiting the old Swedes who inhabited the Southern district of the city upon their death beds, was much struck by hearing some of them pray in the Swedish language, who he was sure had not spoken it for 50 or 60 years before, and who had probably entirely forgotten it.
>
> (Chapter 10: 'Of demence, or dissociation', p. 284)

As mentioned above, linguistic studies of demented speakers have concentrated on patients suffering from Alzheimer's dementia. Compared to other dementia types – and also compared to most aphasias[11] – the relatively slow and successive nature of the deterioration in this disease makes possible longitudinal studies of the breakdown, or studies that relate a specific bilingual behaviour to a specifiable phase of the deterioration.

The questions that have been addressed in studies of bilingual dementia are very close to the ones we are specifically concerned with in the present chapter. Firstly, as language choice problems and inappropriate code-switching are frequently observed among bilingual demented subjects, one question has been whether these phenomena *always* accompany bilingual dementia. From the studies that have been conducted so far, it is clear that there are several bilingual speakers with a diagnosis of Alzheimer's dementia who exhibit only one or neither of these problems. Among four Yiddish–English subjects studied by de Santi *et al.* (1990), one, patient B, had no code-switching problems in either language and language choice problems only when interacting in Yiddish with a bilingual Yiddish–English speaker. Another patient, patient D, had no language choice problems in either language, but code-switching problems when interacting in Yiddish with the bilingual interlocutor. It is, however, questionable whether these cases should be seen as reflections of inappropriate language choice and code-switching, since, as pointed out by the authors, the interlocutor was bilingual in both cases.

One of the two subjects studied by Hyltenstam and Stroud (1989), KL, a Swedish–Finnish bilingual, produced only one code-switched utterance in a Finnish interaction with a bilingual Finnish–Swedish interlocutor and none in a Swedish interaction with a monolingual Swedish interlocutor. We concluded that she had no code-switching problems. On the other hand, this patient had clear language choice problems with 'fixation' (see Pick 1909) in one language for periods of time, irrespective of the language of the interlocutor. The other subject, GM, a German–Swedish bilingual, in an interaction with a Swedish-speaking interlocutor who had some receptive knowledge of German, produced only 5 utterances completely in Swedish, but 16 mixed Swedish–German utterances and 56 utterances that were completely in German. On the other hand, in an interaction with a German–speaking interlocutor, who was a balanced German–Swedish bilingual, this patient produced 76 utterances completely in German and no Swedish elements at all. GM had started to acquire Swedish at the age of 45 years, yet he had reached a high level of proficiency in both oral and written Swedish.

Among the six Finnish–Swedish patients studied by Hyltenstam and Stroud (1993), two subjects, MA and RA, showed only marginal code-switching problems in interactions with a monolingual Swedish speaker (2% of MA's 401 and 1% of RA's 277 utterances contained code-switches). MA showed only very marginal language choice problems; RA did not have any problems of this kind at all.

In conclusion, it is probably safe to say that neither code-switching problems nor language choice problems are necessary consequences of all stages of deterioration in dementia for bilingual speakers. Judging from the results of the two Hyltenstam and Stroud studies, it seems as if a second language acquired during adulthood is more affected by the limited processing capacity which is a typical effect of dementia, so that the patients would generally – partly or totally – revert to their first language when interacting with speakers of their second language, but not the other way around.

The correlation between severity of dementia and language choice or code-switching problems is another question that has been treated in the literature. A clear, and suggestive, correlation of this kind is actually found by de Santi *et al.* (1990) among their four subjects. On the other hand, two patients in severe stages of dementia, subject KL, studied by Hyltenstam and Stroud (1989), and subject RA, studied by Hyltenstam and Stroud (1993), produced extremely few inappropriate code-switches. However, a longitudinal follow-up on RA did show that the frequency of inappropriate code-switching increased as her dementia became more severe. Our interpretation of these results was that the degree of code-switching and language choice problems actually do correlate with the severity of dementia. The severity of dementia is, however, not the only factor that is involved. RA, although she had acquired Swedish at an adult age, had reached a near-native proficiency in her second language, and KL was bilingual from early childhood. Thus, one might be led to conjecture that a high level of premorbid proficiency in a language postpones the inappropriate language mixing behaviour possibly until several years beyond the onset of dementia (see a more extended discussion of this issue in Hyltenstam and Stroud 1993).

A third related question is whether code-switching and language choice problems are related phenomena and therefore always go together. It is clear from some of the results reviewed above that this need not be the case.

A fourth and final question discussed in relation to bilingual dementia is the one that is particularly focussed upon in this chapter, i.e. whether code-switches produced inappropriately by demented speakers are structured grammatically in the same way as those produced 'intentionally' by healthy bilingual speakers in bilingual interactions. Both de Santi *et al.* (1990) and Hyltenstam and Stroud (1989) hypothesise that demented speakers follow the same constraints that are valid for healthy speakers, but this is the question we will investigate in more detail below.

5 Present study of code-switching in dementia

5.1 Design and basic linguistic characteristics of the patients

The study I will draw on in this chapter is described in detail in Hyltenstam and Stroud (1993). The study is based on six subjects, all women in the age range from seventy-three to ninety-four years of age. They all had Finnish as their first language and had acquired Swedish as a second language in adult life. They had used Swedish on a regular basis prior to the onset of dementia symptoms. They were all diagnosed as suffering from dementia of the Alzheimer type (DAT) (see Ekman *et al.* in press).

Parallel data were collected in each language. The language data consisted of spontaneous conversational data on a number of predetermined topics regarding aspects of day-to-day life and on topics initiated by the patients. In addition, formally elicited data, comprising object and action naming, repetition, production of automatic sequences (numbers, days of the week, months of the year), translation and metalinguistic judgment, were collected. For the present analysis of code-switching behaviour conversational data and data from the naming tasks have been used. In addition, spontaneously occurring conversations during the collection of the formal data types have been analysed here.

Data on the patients' linguistic backgrounds were gathered from close relatives and comprised, among other things, information on the role of each language over the lifespan and an estimate of maximal premorbid oral and written proficiency in the second language. Also investigated was whether the patients had premorbidly engaged in a habit of mixing languages to any extent.

The Swedish data were collected by a monolingual speaker of Swedish, the Finnish data by a bilingual Finnish–Swedish speaker. The main portion of the data in each language was collected on separate days, but what we called 'bilingual' interactions, in which both interlocutors participated, were also organised in order to see whether the patients' bilingual behaviour would differ under the 'monolingual' and 'bilingual' conditions. (This aspect will not, however, be treated in the present chapter.) The collection of data was spread over a number of sessions, as the patients' condition did not allow extended periods of concentration. All the data were tape-recorded.

The framework for the assessment of the patients' degree of linguistic regression was the model developed by Obler and Albert (1984) on the basis of monolingual Alzheimer patients, specifying six phases of deterioration. These phases were summarised as early (phases I–II), middle (phases III–IV), and late (phases V–VI). Our assessment was based on a 300-word sample from each patient's conversational data which was quantified for (i) the proportion of content words, (ii) the number of deictic expressions without clear reference and other indefinite terms, and (iii) aberrant use of conjunctions. In addition, a qualitative judgment was made of the pragmatic interaction with the interlocutor, i.e. whether the patient typically made digressions and gave inappropriate answers to questions. In the naming task, the number of correct noun identifications was calculated, and the occurrence of perseverative speech, paraphasias and neologisms was noted. All these aspects are definitional points in Obler and Albert's model. The assessment of the patients' lingustic behaviour resulted in a ranking of them along a scale of regression according to the following chart. (The quantifications are presented in Hyltenstam and Stroud 1993: 230.)

Early phases:	MA
	JE
Early middle phases:	VH
	AKJ
Late middle phases:	RA
	KJ

The analysis in Hyltenstam and Stroud (1993) focussed on language choice and code separation issues, in particular the extent to which the patients' contributions in their interaction with the monolingual Swedish interlocutor were produced in each language. Table 14.3 presents the figures for utterances completely in Swedish, mixed in Swedish and Finnish, and completely in Finnish, for each subject. The table shows a large variation between the subjects in how prone they are to choose, and stay within, Swedish. JE, VH, and KJ use predominantly Finnish, while MA and RA use Swedish appropriately in almost all their utterances. AKJ has a slight preference for Swedish, but almost half of her utterances are either completely in Finnish or contain Finnish elements. Receptively, all the patients appeared to process Swedish as proficiently as Finnish, although in the

Table 14.3 *Proportion and number (in parentheses) of utterances in interaction with the Swedish interlocutor*

Subject	S		M		F		Total	
MA	96%	(386)	2%	(7)	2%	(9)	100%	(401)
JE	14%	(38)	18%	(49)	69%	(192)	100%	(279)
VH	8%	(52)	11%	(75)	82%	(561)	100%	(688)
AKJ	56%	(271)	7%	(35)	37%	(178)	100%	(484)
RA	99%	(275)	1%	(2)	0%	(1)	100%	(277)
KJ	15%	(86)	13%	(74)	73%	(429)	100%	(589)

S = produced completely in Swedish, M = mixed in Swedish and Finnish,
F = completely in Finnish
Source: Hyltenstam & Stroud 1993: 232

more severe cases it is sometimes difficult to judge the coherence of a contribution and therefore whether the subject has understood or not. Most of the time, the patients clearly exhibited unawareness of the fact that they did not use the same language as the interlocutor.

The majority of utterances not in Swedish were actually entirely in Finnish. For the three patients who spoke mainly in Finnish (JE, VH and KJ) the proportions of utterances containing material from both languages, i.e. utterances with code-switches, were 18%, 11% and 13% respectively. The proportion of such utterances in the data from AKJ, whose contributions were more or less evenly distributed between Swedish and Finnish, was 7%.

The language choice and code-switching behaviour of the six patients in their Finnish interactions has been treated briefly in Hyltenstam, Kuyumcu and Stroud (1990). Three of the subjects – JE, VH and AKJ – do not incorporate any Swedish elements into their Finnish at all, two of them – RA and KJ – have single incorporated elements, and MA, finally, has several incorporated Swedish elements in her Finnish. Obviously, the general pattern is that it is when these patients speak their second language, Swedish, that they have problems in filtering out their first language. MA is a speaker who has a near-native proficiency in Swedish. She had had only a a few contacts with Finnish speakers for a long period of time prior to the onset of dementia.

5.2 Code-switching between Finnish and Swedish

The Equivalence Constraint makes predictions for the language pair Finnish and Swedish that are similar to those formulated for Finnish and English (Poplack, Wheeler and Westwood 1987/1989). In particular, prepositions in English and Swedish correspond to postpositions and case inflections in Finnish, which excludes switching after a Swedish preposition or preceding a Finnish postposition or case-marker. The structure of the NP in the two languages differs in much the same way as between Finnish and English, although the determiner system in Swedish is formally different from the English one with the definite article being suffixed (or, under certain conditions, both pre- and postponed). In the data analysed by Poplack *et al.* involving nominals, the Equivalence Constraint predictions were not borne out in specific structures: English nouns with Finnish case markers (corresponding to either a preposition or a determiner) and isolated English nouns (where both preposition/determiner and case-markers were omitted) were 'massively' represented in the data. Based on a distributional quantitative analysis, these exceptions were regarded as nonce borrowings, or, in the case of the 'caseless nouns', 'as flagged, non-smooth single-word switches' (1987/ 1989: 150). In the present analysis, single lexical units that are morphologically and syntactically, but not necessarily phonologically, integrated are regarded as borrowings, while single lexical units that are not integrated are seen as switches.

Andersson (1992), although her data do not support a clear distinction between code-switching and borrowing but rather a view where these categories are endpoints on a continuum from zero to total integration, also presents examples of this kind from the language pair Finnish and Swedish.

5.3 Code-switching and borrowing in the patients' productions

The patients' inability to keep their languages separate in production results in a large number of mixed productions. This mixing comprises, among other things, code-switches and borrowings. One analytical difficulty with the present data, implied in the results presented in Table 14.3, is that one cannot assume that the patients have selected the interlocutor's language, Swedish, as their matrix language and, therefore, that the incorporations would be made in the direction of Finnish to Swedish. This means that the results are not immediately comparable in this respect with those of Andersson (1992) or Poplack et al. (1987/1989), as Finnish is clearly the matrix language in both these studies.

The first point in the current analysis was to determine for each utterance containing elements from both languages which language could be considered to be the matrix and which the embedded language. The results of this analysis are presented in Table 14.4. (For some of the utterances, the matrix language could not be identified with the criteria employed. These utterances are indicated in the table with a question mark.) What we can see from Table 14.4 is that the three subjects who mainly produce Finnish in their interaction with a monolin-

Table 14.4 *Identification of matrix language (ML) for utterances containing material from both languages (in per cent)*

	MA N=7	JE N=49	VH N=75	AKJ N=35	RA* N=17	KJ N=74
ML: Sw	100	12	9	67	54	31
ML: Fi	–	85	85	14	8	50
ML: ?	–	2	7	19	39	19

* For RA, additional data have been included here as compared with Table 14.3; see Hyltenstam & Stroud (1993: 236).

gual Swedish speaker – JE, VH and KJ – do indeed use Finnish as their matrix language in the majority of cases and incorporate Swedish material into these utterances. KJ differs from the other two in an interesting way though. Although her proportion of Swedish and Finnish is almost the same as those for JE (see Table 14.3), she uses Swedish as the matrix language in her mixed utterances to a much higher degree. From the transcripts, it is obvious that her ability to choose Swedish occurs in periodical sequences. In one of the recording sessions (April 1988), the thirty-two mixed utterances that occurred in that interaction were sequenced as follows with respect to their matrix language:

2 Sw - 1? - 5 Sw - 1? - 1 Fi - 2 Sw - 9 Fi - 2? - 9 Fi

It may well be significant that there is more Finnish material towards the end of this conversation, when the patient was noticeably less alert.

Those subjects who mainly produce Swedish in the interaction, MA and RA, typically use Swedish as the matrix language in their (few) mixed utterances. Also AKJ, who has a great proportion of Finnish material in her 'Swedish' interaction, uses Swedish in most cases as the matrix language.

In summary, the proportion of Finnish that is produced with the Swedish interlocutor is, to a large degree, reflected in the choice of matrix language for mixed utterances. This is clearly the case for the most characteristic speakers of each type, on the one hand MA and RA, with a largely appropriate language choice, and on the other JE and VH, who are definitely in a Finnish set even when they communicate with a Swedish-speaking person. The data of AKJ and KJ are less predictable. One might have expected AKJ to use Finnish and Swedish as matrix languages equally often, since her proportions of Swedish and Finnish utterances are more or less balanced, but despite this, she does have a definite preference for Swedish. Also, KJ has a much larger proportion of mixed utterances with Swedish as the matrix language than one would have expected from the general dominance of Finnish in her interactions.

The next point in the analysis concerns the types of elements that were incorporated into the matrix language. In this analysis, no distinction is made between code-switches and borrowings. Rather, all elements on a continuum from zero to full morphological integration have been considered. This has the advantage of allowing a comparison with Andersson (1992), even though, as mentioned above, the comparison is not very straightforward as the incorporations considered in the present analysis are taken from both directions between the languages. The results of this analysis are presented in Table 14.5. If we first look at how the results of the whole group compare to those of Andersson (1992), we can see that the most

Table 14.5 Incorporations (percentages) by word class, phrase type and word sequences that go beyond syntactic phrases in comparison with results in Andersson (1992)

	MA N = 9	JE N = 43	VH N = 72	AKJ N = 23	RA N = 12	KJ N = 54	Tot N = 214	Andersson (1992) N = 614
single noun	33	60	57	43	8	31	46	64·7
single verb		12	17	4	8	2	9	15·0
single adjective		2	6		8	4	4	8·0
interjection		2	1				1	4·7
noun phrase		5	3	4			2	3·1
adverb	11	2	1	9	17	13	7	1·8
verb phrase	22						1	1·0
conjunction	11	2	6	4	8	28	11	0·7
adverbial phrase	11	5	4	13		2	5	0·5*
adjective phrase		2					0	0·3
pronoun			1	13		2	2	0·2
numeral		5					1	
compound element	11	2				5	2	
multiword sequence			4	9	50	15	9	

*Here Andersson's PPs have been compared to my adverbial phrases, which in most cases were PPs frequent category for incorporation is that of single nouns. This is a recurrent result in studies using such frequency counts, but the proportion of single nouns is often larger than the 46% we find here: for example, 64.7% in Andersson's study of Swedish incorporations into Finnish (1992: 255), 68.2% in Poplack *et al.*'s study of English incorporations into Finnish (1987/1989: 139), 86% in Boyd's study of Swedish incorporations into English (1993: 400). This lower proportion of nouns might be interpreted as dependent on the dementia, as the patients' typical retrieval problems for content words, particularly nouns, makes the proportion of nouns generally lower (Obler and Albert 1984). The relatively high proportion of conjunctions, second in rank, may have a similar explanation (see especially KJ's 28%). A definite difference between the results of Andersson (1992) and the present results is that the proportion of 'phrases' as compared to single lexical units is very small in her study, only 4.9%, while the proportion in the present investigation is 17%. Here we have included multiword sequences that go beyond immediate syntactic phrase categories; these do not seem to occur in the Andersson study. Interestingly enough, such sequences are more frequent among the speakers who are at a more severe stage of dementia, as seen, for example, in RA's 50%, but also KJ's 15%. This means that it is a fairly prevalent feature of these speakers to switch to the other language in the middle of an utterance and continue in that language to the end of the utterance.

The most striking aspect of the results in Table 14.5, however, is the individual variation that can be observed. It is interesting to note that the proportion of incorporations produced by JE and VH, who operate mainly in Finnish, and whose matrix language in the mixed utterances is generally Finnish, shows great similarity to what has been observed in healthy Finnish–Swedish code-switching with Finnish as the matrix language (Andersson 1992). A closer look at KJ gives a very interesting picture. As we noted above, the matrix language of her mixed utterances changes periodically during the interaction. Her two most frequent categories of incorporation are nouns and conjunctions, but these have an almost complementary distribution in relation to the choice of matrix language as shown in Table 14.6. Thus, all nouns are incorporated from Swedish into Finnish, and the majority of conjunctions from Finnish into Swedish. The typical pattern is shown in examples (7) and (8):

(7)   *Ja kun niin se pannaan* knapp*illa.*
        And then   it gets-put button-*ADDESSIVE.*
        [*And then it gets fixed with a* button.]

Table 14.6 *Distribution of noun and conjunction incorporations in utterances with Finnish and Swedish respectively as matrix languages in the speech of KJ*

	noun	conjunction
ML: Fi	17	3
ML: Sw	0	12

(8)   Skalat eh *mutta* inte kokat.
        [Peeled eh *but* not cooked.]

Yet she has also a few conjunctions incorporated in the other direction as in (9):

(9)   Men *tämä on tuo*.
        [But *this is there*.]

Relevant to the interpretation of these patterns is the fact that most of the noun incorporations are taken from a section in the interaction where a naming task is carried out. The subject's task is to retrieve the right noun, but she also often gives further comments in relation to specific pictures as illustrated in example (7). A typical pattern for this subject, when she is confronted with a task that she experiences as demanding, is to think aloud, and she always does this in Finnish, even though she seems to be aware that she is to retrieve a Swedish word. The interaction in (10) illustrates this – the elements glossed 'neol.' (neologism) are newly formed words.

(10)   I: Vad är det här för nånting? (Shows a picture of a book.)
             [What is this?]
        KJ: *No en mie tiedä m- /mikä se nyt on. Kyllä sie tiedät nyt vain itse mutta*
             kun mie en muista. Näe niin mutta meillä on paljon mulla on noita eh
             'karte-' 'k-kraaka' garderobia (laughter) 'eli' niin.
             [*Well I don't known w- what this might be. You certainly know only*
             yourself but I just don't remember. Well but we have a lot I have those
             'neol.' 'neol.' wardrobes (laughter) or? so.]

The third task in the analysis was to categorise the intra-sentential switch sites and quantify these and the borrowings observed in the data. Table 14.7 presents the results of this analysis. In Table 14.7, we have first made a distinction between switches and borrowings. Borrowings, i.e. morphologically integrated single lexical units, are relatively few. The first thing one should notice is that the borrow-

Table 14.7 *Number of borrowings and switches of various types produced in interaction with a Swedish-speaking interlocutor*

	MA	JE	VH	AKJ	RA	KJ	Tot
Borrowings	1	8	13			16	38
N	1	6	6			15	28
V		2	7				9
A						1	1
Switches	10	44	69	26	15	41	203
Translations	1	11	9	3	3		27
SW → Fi		6	1	2	1		10
Fi → Sw	1	5	8	1	2		17
Intras. switches	9	33	60	23	12	41	176
+COMP+	2	7	11	1	5	23	47
NP+VP		1	1	5	1	1	9
V+NP	1	1	1	2	3	3	11
COP+Pred	2	14	20	3	1	1	41
+Advl+	2	5	12	5		9	35
Attribute+N	1	4	13	6		3	27
V+V	1			1		1	3
Lex. phrase		1	2				3

ings occur predominantly among those subjects who mainly use Finnish as the matrix language in their mixed utterances (see Table 14.4). This means that the majority of the integrated incorporations are Swedish lexical items with Finnish morphology. All of JE's 8 borrowings, all but 4 out of VH's 13, and all but 1 out of KJ's 16 borrowings are of this kind. KJ's one exception is a compound. '*kahvikau*-affären', ['*coffee-sho*- shop-the', i.e. the coffee-shop], pronounced under one single prosodic contour, with an interruption in the middle of the second element and starting anew with this in Swedish. (Compounds have been classified as Finnish or Swedish depending on the language of their heads.) The 4 exceptions in VH's data are actually instances of the same Finnish noun with a Swedish plural marker (*tipp*ar [*drops*]). VH has a very different distribution amoung nouns and verbs compared to the other subjects and to how these categories are distributed in most data. A total of 7 of her borrowings are verbs, 1 is a noun derived from a verb (box*aaminen* [box*ing*]), and 2 are nouns. Example (11) is typical of her borrowing of verbs.

(11)   *Juu ja sitä ei saisi koskaan* gråtata.
        Yes and that not would-be-allowed never cry-*INF*.
        [Yes and one should never be allowed to cry.]

It is obvious that lexical items may be more or less integrated by one and the same person, for example, integrated nouns being produced in some utterances and bare nouns in others. One particular item may even be treated differently in one and the same utterance as in (12) from KJ.

(12)   *Ja* kaffekopp*ia ja heikko (laughs) kah-* kaffekopperna *kansalla*.
        And coffee-cup*s and weak (laughs) coff-* coffee-cups-the *people*-ADESSIVE.
        [*And* coffee-cups *and weak (laughs) coff-* the coffee-cups *of people*.]

Two subjects in particular, JE and VH, but also AKH and RA to some extent, produce spontaneous translations such as (13).

(13)   *Se on talvi*, vinter.
        [*It is winter*, winter.]

VH generally translates words that have first been produced in Finnish into Swedish. They may thus be intended for the benefit of the Swedish interlocutor. For the others, the translations are as often in one direction as in the other. With such a pattern, one cannot be conclusive about any communicative function for these translations.

As for the intra-sentential code-switches, their distribution according to switch site is somewhat different from what has been seen in the Poplack *et al.* (1987/ 1989: 140) Finnish–English data as displayed in Table 14.8.[12] The two sets of data differ mainly in two respects. Firstly, the dominating switch point after *että* [that], in Poplack *et al.*'s data is not very salient here. It is actually a preferred switch point for only one of the subjects, KJ. Secondly, two frequent categories in the present data, i.e. those of switching between a copula and its nominal or adjectival predicate and after a sentence-initial, or before a sentence-final, adverbial, do not occur at all in the Poplack *et al.* data. The high proportion of the former of these categories is because of the fact that this is a preferred switch point for two subjects, JE and VH; almost half and a third of their switches, respectively, are of this kind. For the remaining four subjects, this is not a common category. The switch point in the vicinity of an adverbial is a frequent one in several studies, which means that the present data seem to be more in line with the general patterns than the Poplack *et al.* data. One obvious reason for some of the differences between the two sets of data is that in the Poplack *et al.* data the matrix

Table 14.8 *Distribution of switch sites in the present data compared to those of Poplack* et al. *(1989)*

	Poplack *et al.* (1989)		Present data	
	N	%	N	%
Comp+S	95	62	47	28
V+(Object) NP	25	16	11	6
(Subject) NP+VP	10	6	9	5
Dem+N	9	6	27	15
Adj/adv+N	11	7		
V+Infinitive	4	3	3	2
COP+Pred			41	23
+Advl+			35	20
Lex. phrase			3	2
Totals	154	100	176	100

language is clearly Finnish, while the present data consists of a composite set of material in which Finnish and Swedish function interchangeably as the matrix language.

This implies that there is also considerable individual variation among the present six subjects with regard to preferences of switch points. This may have some relationship to what the matrix language in the mixed utterances is. The two subjects who speak predominantly in Finnish and also use Finnish as the matrix language, JE and VH, typically produce syntactic frames in Finnish and insert Swedish elements in these frames, similarly to what we saw in the case of borrowings above. Subject KJ who also speaks predominantly in Finnish, but who uses Swedish as the matrix language in portions of her mixed utterances, has a more or less even distribution between Swedish and Finnish syntactic frames for her code-switches. AKJ, who overall produces equal portions of Swedish and Finnish in the interactions, actually has a definite tendency towards Swedish frames for her code-switches. MA and RA, who speak Swedish most of the time, have Swedish frames for their code-switching.

In conclusion, even though there are frequency differences in the distribution of switch sites between this study and various other studies, it would be premature to see these differences as resulting from the dementia *per se*. These differences in frequency are certainly related to, or perhaps even an automatic consequence of, the deviant relative proportions of open-class and closed-class lexical items that are found in demented speakers, but this is a more general characteristic of demented speech and not linked directly either to bilingualism or to code-switching. There may also be additional reasons for these differences such as, for example, differences in data types and the nature of the tasks of the subjects, differences in the direction of incorporations, and the effect of individual preferences in such a small sample of speakers as the one presented here. In the studies of healthy speakers that have been used for comparison, no details of individual patterns are presented.

Now, how do the switches produced by these demented bilinguals relate to the Equivalence Constraint proposed by Poplack (1980)? First, in the majority of cases when a single noun is involved in the switch, it is produced in its bare form as in (14).[13]

(14)   *Onks se* sten *vai mikä se on?*
        Is-Q it stone *or what it is?*
        [*Is it a* stone *or what is it?*]

These examples involve, in fact, violations of the original formulation of the Equivalence Constraint. In Swedish, as in English, the noun ought to be preceded by an indefinite article, and in Finnish a case-suffix is needed; the morphological marking of the noun is omitted from both languages. This kind of structure does, however, as mentioned above, occur frequently in the healthy Finnish–English speaking subjects in Poplack *et al.* (1987/1989), and can therefore not be considered to be a peculiarity of demented speakers. Other than this type there are actually only 3 switches that would potentially violate the Equivalence Constraint ((15–(17)):

(15)   *Kyllä mä* trött *olen.*
        Certainly I tired *am.*
        [*Certainly I am* tired.]

(16)   *Ja/kyll* stolen *on Lennarti tehnyt.*
        And/certainly chair-the *has Lennart made.*
        [*And/*the chair *Lennart has certainly made.*]

(17)   *En minä* mycke *ole mutta vähänhän olen.*
        not-1sg I much *have but   a-little have-1sg.*
        [*I have not [worked]* much *but I have [worked]* a little.]

Example (15) has an order between the copula and the predicative adjective that is impossible in Swedish but normal in Finnish, which should prohibit a switch between these two elements. It is possible that the Equivalence Constraint is too strong in excluding examples of this type. They would be seen as totally normal in the MFL model, where the matrix language, Finnish in this case, would determine the word order of the whole utterance. I have not seen published examples of this kind, but to my mind it is improbable that they would be restricted to the speech of demented speakers. Examples (16) and (17) may be given an identical interpretation. In (16) there are two elements, '*kyll*' and 'stolen', in the pre-finite-verb position, which is impossible in Swedish, since this language is a verb-second language. In (17) the order of 'mycke' and '*ole*' is impossible in Swedish, so a switch between these two words would not be allowed according to the Equivalence Constraint. As Finnish is clearly the matrix language in these two latter cases, they would be acceptable in the MLF model under the Morpheme Order Principle.

Even if we did consider these three examples as violations to universal constraints on code-switching, they are extremely few considering the fact that the remaining 173 switches are grammatical. The frequency is low compared to what has been found in several other investigations (cf. Clyne 1987). It is reasonable to conclude that the pragmatically inappropriate code-switching that occurs in demented speakers is structurally equivalent to the purposeful code-switching of healthy bilingual speakers.

6 Conclusion

6.1 Aphasia

We have seen that one effect of brain diseases among bilinguals is a failure, total or partial, to speak the language that is expected in a particular speech situation. The literature on bilingual aphasia shows that a considerable proportion of the cases reported – up to 40% – have difficulty in making a correct language choice. The most common interpretation of this fact in neurological terms is that 'the temporarily or permanently inaccessible language is not destroyed, but inhibited' (Paradis 1989: 134). The picture of language choice problems among aphasics is truly complex. The fact that the localisation or extension of the damage do not automatically predict which one of a bilingual's languages will be most affected, or the extent to which a particular language is affected, has made it difficult to propose a general theory for language choice in bilingual aphasia. Adding to the difficulty is the fact that some of the aphasic patients seemed to be unaware of speaking a language that was not appropriate in the speech situation, while others were definitely aware of this problem. One interpretation of this difference is that, for some of the patients, their problem is one of limited attention, while for others, it might be the case that they can very well assess the language choice requirements of the situation, but are not able to access the right language for purely physiological reasons. This possibility is probably valid for the majority of patients, since lack of attention is not a general problem in this group.

In the area of language mixing, the present reassessment of the cases where this phenomenon occurs suggests that the incidence of 7% that has generally been reported earlier is a considerable underestimate. The proportion of 16% arrived at here makes mixing a less uncommon condition than was formerly believed. This review did not look closely into the various ways in which mixing manifests itself in the different cases; the analysis was restricted to investigating the examples of code-switching presented in the reports. Suffice it to say that the reports contain examples of every conceivable type of interaction between language systems. Even in this respect, the picture is extremely complicated. Again, it is not possible to propose a general theory for language mixing in bilingual aphasia.

As regards code-switching, the result of our examination of examples of code-switched utterances presented in the literature gave the result that the vast majority of such examples were structured grammatically in accordance with constraints or principles suggested for code-switching among healthy speakers. Out of sixty switches, only four were identified as clear violations of these constraints. Because of the existence of a wide range of linguistic structural deviances characteristic of the various types of aphasia, these results are, however, somewhat weakened: it was impossible to interpret the exact nature of some utterances possibly containing switches, especially for those patients with telegraphic or agrammatic style (see Menn and Obler 1990). Since these examples had to be excluded from the analysis, we may have missed a small number of violations, although certainly not more than three or four. If, however, the breakdown affects grammatical systems as it does in these cases, code-switching by implication also ought to be affected. However, as this would result from a general difficulty with grammar, it cannot be interpreted as a specific difficulty with code-switching. I believe that we can tentatively say that aphasia does not affect the ability to code-switch according to existing constraints.

6.2 Dementia

In the case of dementia-related language disorders, the picture seems clearer. Generally, the background for language choice problems in this group is a problem of attention, which in itself would be a result of the limited general cognitive processing capacity known to exist in demented patients. Such an explanation is not sufficient, however, since it would predict the same kind of difficulties in interactions in each language. This is not what we have seen, but rather a pattern that is more systematic than haphazard. Those demented speakers who have acquired their second language in adulthood have a tendency to choose their first language or switch into their first language when they are assumed to be speaking their second language, but the opposite is not true. This pattern is especially salient, it seems, in those cases where the second language has not been acquired to a high level of proficiency. We have also seen that the patients can handle the second language more appropriately in comprehension than in production and that they are generally unaware of speaking an inappropriate language. (For a comprehensive discussion of this issue and an interpretation within an information-processing model of linguistic functioning, see Hyltenstam and Stroud 1993.)

In the same way as for aphasic speakers, code-switching among demented speakers was found to generally obey structural constraints and principles that have been formulated for healthy speakers. The differences in relative frequencies of incorporated elements that we have seen in the data presented here compared to studies of healthy speakers have a tentative explanation in the fact that it is a characteristic feature of demented speakers to have a lower proportion of content words, especially nouns, in their speech than healthy speakers. The differences in relative frequencies among the demented speakers are thus implied by these general effects of the disease, which means that they are not peculiar to code-switched utterances.

6.3 The universality of structure in code-switching

The fact that code-switching seems to be structured in the same way in data from aphasic and demented speakers as in data from healthy subjects supports the view that a specific code-switching grammar does not need to be postulated as one of the grammatical systems of bilingual speakers (see Pfaff 1979; Lederberg and Morales 1985). Rather, the way in which code-switching is carried out grammatically is an automatic consequence of knowledge of the grammars of each of the languages that interact with each other. In particular, as several of the cases that have been reported in the aphasia literature, and also the majority of our own subjects, are claimed not to have been members of code-switching speech communities, then this, if true, means that they cannot have acquired the grammar for code-switching between their two languages (see Hyltenstam and Stroud 1989: 224). The simultaneous activation of their two languages, although non-intentional, results in the processing of both language systems and keeping track of possible switch-points in the same way as the intentional use of both languages in bilingual conversations among healthy speakers.

Acknowledgments

This research was supported by grants no. F 635/87, F 502/88 and F 541/89 from the Swedish Council for Research in the Humanities and Social Sciences (HSFR). I would like to thank Christopher Stroud for continual fruitful discussions of the issues treated in this chapter and Eija Kuyumcu for co-operation in the project. Eija Kuyumcu also helped with translation and interpretation of examples as did Riikka Alanen, Birgitta Englund Dimitrova and Leyla Naseh. I also wish to thank Don Kulick for comments on an earlier draft of the chapter and Sarah Williams for helpful revision of my English.

APPENDIX

On the identification of bilingual aphasia cases exhibiting language mixing

The total number of published cases of bilingual aphasia

Both Paradis (1977) and Albert and Obler (1978) present the cases they have reviewed in tabular form; Paradis, actually, does this twice. In one table (his Table 2.1), he correlates patterns of recovery with characteristics of the language recovered (whether or not it is the patient's mother tongue, his/her most fluent language and what the language of the surroundings is). In another table (his Table 2.2) the context of acquisition and use of particular languages is correlated to pattern of recovery and type of aphasia. A quick count shows that Paradis's first table (Table 2.1, pp. 68ff.) enumerates 122 cases, 14 of which are mentioned only in this table. His second table (Table, 2.2, pp. 102ff.) comprises 121 cases, 13 of which are mentioned only here. This means that the total number of cases he presents are 135 (the 108 cases mentioned in both tables + the 27 cases mentioned in only one of the tables) rather than 138, as is stated in Paradis's text (p. 67). This difference in number is not particularly important for Paradis's argument, and it is certainly not my intention here to be a fault-finder. This point is valid also for what is said below. However, if this chapter can save others from the trouble I have had in the different treatments of the same cases in previous reviews, it should be of some value.

Albert and Obler (1978), who do not claim to have carried out a complete survey, present 108 cases of bilingual aphasia, 26 of which are not mentioned in the Paradis review. Among the 135 cases reviewed by Paradis, 53 are not mentioned by Albert and Obler. This means that the number of cases reviewed by either Paradis or Albert and Obler – or by both reviews – amounts to 161 (the 135 cases in Paradis + the 26 cases mentioned only in Albert and Obler; alternatively, the 108 cases in Albert and Obler + the 53 cases mentioned only in Paradis). To arrive at the total number of cases published up to the present time one should add the 27 recent cases reviewed by Paradis (1989), thus reaching the figure of 188.

The total number of cases exhibiting mixing

There is a problem in deciding how many cases of mixed recovery Paradis (1977) in fact presents. Although he gives specific numbers for all the other types of recovery patterns, he does not give a figure for the mixed cases in his text. The problem arises from the fact that Paradis does not present all cases in both his tables and that some cases that appear in both tables are classified as mixed in only one of them (13 cases are classified as mixed in both tables, 4 cases that appear in both tables are classifed as mixed in only one of them and 4 cases appearing in only one table are coded as mixed). Adding to the confusion is that fact that only 10 of the cases coded as mixed in the tables are commented upon in the text, whereas 6 other cases, *not* coded as mixed in the tables, are given as examples of language mixing in the text (Dedić 1926; Gloning and Gloning 1965, case 4; l'Hermitte *et al.* 1966, case 8; Minkowski 1927 (case 1 or 2?); Ovcharova *et al.* 1968, case 3; Schulze 1968). In his two tables we find altogether 21 cases that have been coded for mixed recovery. This would give 16% (21 out of 135). Adding the 6 cases commented upon in the text, but not coded as mixed in the tables, we reach the considerable proportion of 20%. If we use the +mixing cases in the sample reviewed by Albert and Ober (1978), which amount to 12, we would arrive at a proportion of 11% (12 out of 108). This low number of mixing cases seems to depend on an under-identification though, since 5 additional cases, identified as mixed by Paradis and in the present assessment (see my Table 14.1), are in fact included in Albert and Obler's sample without being coded as mixed. In the more recent sample of 27 cases reviewed by Paradis (1989), only 1 is claimed to have mixed recovery in the text (p. 119), although in Table 1 (p. 118) two cases carry the symbol M for mixed recovery. Altogether, 36 cases were identified in the 3 reviews. 2 cases (from 1868 and 1875) were not available in the present assessment, and 3 were not judged as mixing cases, thus giving 31 cases. The 31 cases identified make up 16% of the total number of 188.

Notes

1. Dementia of the Alzheimer type is the most prevalent category among the dementias. The other most common type is what is referred to as multiinfarct dementia (MID) the causes of which are repeated minor cerebrovascular accidents. The reason why patients suffering from Alzheimer's dementia have been the focus of linguistic studies is that the linguistic deterioration in these cases is assumed to be more uniform, since the development of Alzheimer's disease is relatively gradual compared to the more abrupt changes that can take place in MID. A less prevalent type is Pick's disease.

   A distinction is often made between Alzheimer's disease (AD) and senile dementia of the Alzheimer type (SDAT) according to age of onset – before or after age 65 respectively. However, the terms 'Alzheimer's dementia' or 'dementia of the Alzheimer type' (DAT) are used to cover all age ranges by some authors, while in other cases the term AD is used as the generic term (e.g. in Bayles and Kaszniak 1987).

2. In much of the neurological and psychological literature that will be referred to in this chapter the term 'polygot' is used instead of 'bilingual' or 'multilingual'. I will use only the term 'bilingual'. This refers both to speakers of two, and to speakers of several, languages. The rationale for this is that most of the speakers who will be discussed here are indeed bilingual and not multilingual, and that the neuro- and psycholinguistic aspects of processing two or more languages must be assumed to be the same. Also, when I use wordings such as 'one language and the other', 'the other' is meant to cover also 'the others'.

3. The adoption of the terminological distinction between code-switching and borrowing does not imply a theoretical stance on the psycholinguistic difference between the two. This discussion is beyond the scope of the present chapter. The categories are used rather for instrumental purposes.

4. Minkowski is interesting from a sociology of science point of view in that for forty years he repeatedly published on cases where he considered the affective factor to have explanatory power. The following example illustrates how loosely this causal relationship is sometimes argued for. In Minkowski (1964/1983: 676) we encounter a case where an L1 speaker of German, after having functioned in his L2 Spanish for twenty-three years, recovered German but not Spanish, thus being an exception to Pitres's rule. The affective basis for this is explained in the following way: 'Through my previous experience with the importance of intimate, affective factors in the particular determination of aphasia in polyglots . . . , I asked the patient if he had ever fallen in love with a German-speaking woman in his youth. He shivered, covered his face with his hands, and began to cry. For obvious reasons, I did not pursue the matter.'

5. It is interesting to note that writers have found it troublesome to decide how many patterns of recovery are indeed suggested by Paradis. Paradis himself (1977: 65) says that '*at least* five basic patterns are encountered' (my emphasis). Whitaker (1978: 25) says that 'Paradis identified four such modes or patterns of recovery' and mentions *synergistic* (with its subcategories *parallel* and *differential*), *antagonistic*, *successive* and *selective*. Albert and Obler (1978: 104) mention the five basic pattern as suggested by Paradis, but Paradis (1989: 117)

says that the review in Paradis (1977) 'revealed six basic patterns of recovery: parallel, differential, successive, antagonistic, selective, and mixed'. One reason for this little problem seems to lie in the fact that Paradis suggested one category, *synergistic*, comprising two subcategories, *parallel* and *differential*. However, it is my view, and the reason for my mentioning this point, that the issue can also be seen as related to the logical–definitional problem inherent in Paradis's categories, some of which exclude each other, while others can be combined in a single case. For example, the category of *mixed* involves a totally different dimension (interrelationship between language systems) as compared to the others (degree and time sequencing). In addition, some categories, especially the additional ones presented in Paradis (1989), are defined more on the basis of type and degree of impairment than on pattern of recovery. It is, however, beyond the scope of this article to discuss these issues at any length.

[6] A bibliographical search, carried out by the present author in October 1992, for both journal articles and books published from 1990 onwards on all combinations of the cue words 'aphasia' and 'dementia' on the one hand, and 'code-switching', 'language/code mixing', 'language choice', 'bilingualism', and 'second language acquisition/learning' on the other, gave no results. Some study of bilingual aphasia or dementia may have slipped through this net, but it is reasonable to believe that no significant study of *code-switching* in bilingual aphasics or demented speakers has been published during this period.

Another important research tool for the present chapter is the 800-page volume comprising a collection of 94 of the most important articles on bilingual aphasia (some of which appear in summary form), published betwen 1843 and 1974 (Paradis 1983). All articles in this book that were not originally published in English appear in their English translation. As useful as this volume is, for the purposes of this chapter it is unfortunate that in some of the articles originally published in German (e.g. Gloning and Gloning 1965), not only the text, but also the examples produced by patients partly or totally in German, have been translated into English. This makes it impossible to study their original linguistic form, which means that one still has to consult the original German version of the texts for this information.

[7] It is difficult to know how the figure of 7% for inappropriate language mixing has been arrived at. As Albert and Obler refer to Whitaker's (1978) discussion of the Paradis data on the same page as they present the proportion of 7%, a reasonable guess would be that the figure is based on Whitaker's (erroneous) claim that 'Paradis notes that only 10 of the 138 cases in the literature discuss [mixing or interference between languages]' (p. 28). 10 constitutes exactly 7% of 138.

[8] This example also contains an instance of interference. The word *nur* [only], in *nur März* would come from 'only' in English; in German it would be *erst* [first], as in *erst im März*.

[9] The patient was diagnosed as suffering from Pick's disease, but the symptoms described could as well be typical – or more typical – of Alzheimer's disease (observation made by L. K. Obler, personal communication).

[10] I am grateful to Loraine K. Obler for showing me this chapter.

[11] Developing aphasia resulting from the growth of a brain tumour is an exception.

[12] The categories in Poplack *et al.* (1987/1989) and in the present analysis are compatible although they are expressed slightly differently. Comp+S corresponds to +COMP+; in the present data, switches are made both before and after a complementiser. Dem+N and Adj/adv+N correspond to one category in my analysis, Attribute+N. The other differences should be self-explanatory.

[13] In some cases it has its morphology from the embedded language.

Bibliography

Albert, M. and Obler, L. K. (1978) *The bilingual brain. Neuropsychological and neurolinguistic aspects of bilingualism.* New York: Academic Press.

Andersson, P. (1992) Finns and Americans in Sweden: patterns of linguistic incorporation from Swedish. In G. Extra, L. Verhoeven eds., *Immigrant languages in Europe.* Clevedon, Avon: Multilingual Matters, 249–69.

Bastian, C. (1875) *On paralysis from brain disease in its common forms.* New York: Appleton.

Bayles, K. A. and Kaszniak, A. W. (with the assistance of Tomoeda, C. K.) (1987) *Communication and cognition in normal aging and dementia.* Boston: College-Hill Press.

Boyd, S. (1993) Attrition or expansion? Changes in the lexicon of Finnish and American adult bilinguals in Sweden. In Hyltenstam & Viberg (1993), 386–411.

Caplan, D. (1987) *Neurolinguistics and linguistic aphasiology. An introduction.* Cambridge University Press.

Clyne, M. G. (1987) Constraints on code-switching: how universal are they? *Linguistics*, 25: 739–64.

Dedić, S. (1926/1983) Zur Aphasiefragen. *Zeitschrift für die gesamte Neurologie und Psychiatrie*, 106: 208–13. English translation: Questions in aphasia. In Paradis (1983), 199–204.

de Santi, S., Obler, L. K., Sabo-Abramson, H. and Goldberger, J. (1990) Discourse abilities and deficits in multilingual dementia. In Y. Joanette, H. Brownell eds., *Discourse abilities and brain damage: theoretical and empirical perspectives.* New York: Springer Verlag.

Ekman, S.-L., Robins Wahlin, T.-B., Viitanen, M., Norberg, A. and Winblad, B. (in press) Preconditions for communication in the care of bilingual demented persons. *International Psychogeriatrics.*

Emery, O. B. (1988) Language and memory processing in senile dementia Alzheimer's type. In L. L. Light, D. M. Burke eds., *Language, memory, and aging.* Cambridge University Press, 221–43.

Florenskaya, I. A. (1940/1983) Sluchai rasstroistva rechi pri organicheskom zabolevanii s korsakovskim sindromom. *Trudy Tsentral'nogo Instituta Psikhologii*, 1: 333–46. English summary: A case of speech disorder during the course of an organic disease, in the presence of a Korsakoff syndrome. In Paradis (1983), 396–8.

Gloning, I. and Gloning, K. (1965/1983) Aphasie bei Polyglotten. Beitrag zur Dynamik des Sprachabbaus sowie zur Lokalisationsfrage dieser Störungen.

Zeitschrift für Nervenheilkunde und deren Grenzgebiete, 22: 362–97. English translation: Aphasias in polyglots. Contribution to the dynamics of language disintegration as well as to the question of the localization of these impairments. In Paradis (1983), 681–716.

Goldstein, K. and Katz, S. E. (1937) The psychopathology of Pick's disease. *Archives of Neurology and Psychiatry*, 38: 473–90.

Grosjean, F. (1982) *Life with two languages. An introduction to bilingualism.* Cambridge, Mass.: Harvard University Press.

(1989) Neurolinguists, beware! The bilingual is not two monolinguals in one person. *Brain and Language*, 36: 3–15.

Gumperz, J. (1982) *Discourse strategies.* Cambridge University Press.

Halpern, L. (1941/1983) Beitrag zur Restitution der Aphasie bei Polyglotten im Hinblick auf das Hebräische. *Schweizer Archiv für Neurologie und Psychiatrie*, 47: 150–4. English translation: Restitution in polyglot aphasia with regard to Hebrew. In Paradis (1983), 418–22.

Hasselmo, N. (1961) *American Swedish.* Unpublished Ph.D. thesis. Harvard University.

Herschmann, H. and Pötzl, O. (1983) Bemerkungen über die Aphasie der Polyglotten. *Neurologisches Zentralblatt*, 39 (1920): 114–20. English translation: Observations on aphasia in polyglots. In Paradis (1983), 148–54.

Hyltenstam, K., Kuyumcu, E. and Stroud, C. (1990) Svenska som andraspråk hos äldre dementa. In G. Tingbjörn ed., *Andra symposiet om svenska som andraspråk i Göteborg 1989.* Stockholm: Scriptor, 275–87.

Hyltenstam, K. and Obler, L. K. (1989) eds. *Bilingualism across the lifespan. Aspects of acquisition, maturity and loss.* Cambridge University Press.

Hyltenstam, K. and Stroud, C. (1989) Bilingualism in Alzheimer's dementia: two case studies. In Hyltenstam and Obler (1989), 202–26.

(1993) Second language regression in Alzheimer's dementia. In Hyltenstam & Viberg (1993), 222–42.

Hyltenstam, K. and Viberg, Å. (1993) eds. *Progression and regression in language. Sociocultural, neuropsychological and linguistic perspectives.* Cambridge University Press.

Joshi, A. K. (1985) Processing of sentences with intrasentential code-switching. In D. R. Dowty, L. Karttunen, A. M. Zwicky eds., *Natural language parsing.* Cambridge University Press, 190–205.

Kauders, O. (1929/1983), Über polyglotte Reaktionen bei einer sensorischen Aphasie. *Zeitschrift für die gesamte Neurologie und Psychiatrie*, 122: 651–66. English translation: On polyglot responses in a sensory aphasia. In Paradis (1983), 286–300.

Kertesz, A. (1979) *Aphasia and associated disorders: taxonomy, localization, and recovery.* New York: Grune and Stratton.

Krapf, E. E. (1955/1983) Über das Sprachverhalten hirngeschädigter Polyglotten. *Wiener Zeitschrift für Nervenheilkunde*, 12: 121–33. English translation: On the linguistic behaviour of brain damaged polyglot patients. In Paradis (1983), 552–62.

Lambert, W. and Fillenbaum, S. (1959/1983) A pilot study of aphasia among bilinguals. *Canadian Journal of Psychology*, 13: 28–34. Summary in Paradis (1983), 626–35.

Lederberg, A. R. and Morales, C. (1985) Code switching by bilinguals: evidence against a third grammar. *Journal of Psycholinguistic Research*, 14: 113–36.

Ledinský, Q. and Mraček, Z. (1958/1983). Vliv poranení temporálního laloku dominantní hemisféry na recové funkce u polyglota. *Ceskoslovenská Neurologie*, 21: 207–10. English translation: The effect of damage to the temporal lobe in the dominant hemisphere on the function of speech in a polyglot. In Paradis (1983), 574–8.

Leischner, A. (1943/1983) Die Aphasie der Taubstummen. Beitrag zur Lehre von der Asymbolie. *Archiv für Psychiatrie*, 115: 469–548. English translation of excerpt: Aphasia of deaf-mutes. In Paradis (1983), 423–45.

l'Hermitte, R., Hécaen, H., Dubois, J., Culioli, A. and Tabouret-Keller, A. (1966/1983) Le problème de l'aphasie des polyglottes: remarques sur quelques observations. *Neuropsychologia*, 4: 315–29. English translation: The problem of polyglot aphasia: comments on a few observations. In Paradis (1983), 727–43.

Menn, L. and Obler, L. K. (1990) Theoretical motivations for the cross-language study of agrammatism. In L. Menn and L. K. Obler eds., *Agrammatic aphasia. A cross-language narrative sourcebook*. Amsterdam: Benjamins, 3–36.

Minkowski, M. (1927/1983) Klinischer Beitrag zur Aphasie bei Polyglotten, speziell im Hinblick aufs Schweizerdeutsche. *Schweizer Archiv für Neurologie und Psychiatrie*, 21: 43–72. English translation: A clinical contribution to the study of polyglot aphasia especially with respect to Swiss-German. In Paradis (1983), 205–32.

(1928/1983) Sur un cas d'aphasie chez un polyglotte. *Revue Neurologique*, 49: 361–6. English translation: On a case of aphasia in a polyglot. In Paradis (1983), 274–9.

(1964/1983) Sur un nouveau cas d'aphasie avec des réactions polyglottes particulières. *Comptes rendus du Congrès de psychiatre et de neurologie de langue française*. Marseille, Paris: Masson. English translation: On a new case of aphasia with particular polyglot reactions. In Paradis (1983), 673–80.

Mössner, A. and Pilch, H. (1971/1983) Phonematisch-syntaktische Aphasie. Ein Sonderfall motorischer Aphasie bei einer zweisprachigen Patientin. *Folia Linguistica*, 5: 394–409. English translation: Phonological–syntactic aphasia. A rare case of motor aphasia in a bilingual patient. In Paradis (1983), 767–82.

Myers-Scotton, C. (1990a) Intersections between social motivations and structural processing in code-switching. In *Papers for the workshop on constraints, conditions and models*. (Held in London 27–29 September 1990.) Strasbourg: European Science Foundation, 57–82.

(1991) Whither code-switching? Prospects for cross-field collaboration: production-based models of code-switching. In *Papers for the Symposium on Code-switching in Bilingual Studies: theory, significance and perspectives I*. (Held in Barcelona, 21–23 March 1991.) Strasbourg: European Science Foundation, 207–31.

(1993) *Duelling languages: grammatical structure in code-switching*. Oxford: Clarendon Press.

Nilipour, R. and Ashayeri, H. (1989) Alternating antagonism between two languages with successive recovery of a third in a trilingual aphasic patient. *Brain and Language*, 36: 23–48.

Nishimura, M. (1986) Intrasentential code-switching: the case of language assignment. In J. Vaid ed., *Language processing in bilinguals: psycholinguistic and neuropsychological perspectives*. Hillsdale, N.J.: Lawrence Erlbaum, 123–43.

Obler, L. K. and Albert, M. (1978) [Case study presentation]. In Albert and Obler (1978), 131.

(1984) Language in aging. In M. Albert ed., *Clinical neurology of aging*. New York: Oxford University Press.

Ovcharova, P., Raichev, R. and Geleva, T. (1968/1983) Afaziia u Poligloti. *Nevrologiia. Psikhiatriia i Nevrokhirurgiia*, 7: 183–90. English translation: Aphasia in polyglots. In Paradis (1983), 744–52.

Paradis, M. (1977) Bilingualism in aphasia. In H. Whitaker, H. Whitaker, eds., *Studies in neurolinguistics* III. New York: Academic Press, 65–121.

(1983) ed. *Readings on aphasia in bilinguals and polyglots*. Quebec: Didier.

(1989) Bilingual and polyglot aphasia. In F. Boller, J. Grafman eds., *Handbook of neuropsychology* II. Amsterdam: Elsevier Science Publishers, 117–40.

Perecman, E. (1984) Spontaneous translation and language mixing in a polyglot aphasic. *Brain and Language*, 23: 43–63.

(1989) Language processing in the bilingual: evidence from language mixing. In Hyltenstam and Obler (1989), 227–44.

Pfaff, C. W. (1979) Constraints on language mixing: intrasentential code-switching and borrowing in Spanish/English. *Language*, 55: 291–318.

Pick, A. (1909) Fortgesetzte Beiträge zur Pathologie der sensorischen Aphasie. *Archiv für Psychiatrie und Nervenkrankheiten*, 37: 216–41, 468–87.

(1913/1983) Geheilte tuberkulöse Meningitis: zugleich ein Beitrag zur Aphasie bei Polyglotten. *Prager Medizinische Wochenschrift*, 38: 635–6. English translation: Cured tuberculous meningitis: at the same time a contribution to the study of aphasia in polyglots. In Paradis (1983), 102–7.

Pitres, A. (1895/1983) Études sur l'aphasie chez les polyglottes. *Revue de Médecine*, 15: 873–99. English translation: Aphasia in polyglots. In Paradis (1983), 26–49.

Poplack, S. (1980) Sometimes I'll start a sentence in Spanish Y TERMINO EN ESPAÑOL: toward a typology of code-switching. *Linguistics*, 18: 581–618. Also in J. Amastae, L. Elías-Olivares (1982) eds. *Spanish in the United States. Sociolinguistic aspects*. Cambridge University Press, 230–63.

(1985) Contrasting patterns of code-switching in two communities. In H. J. Warkentyne ed., *Methods V: Papers from the Vth International Conference on Methods in Dialectology*. University of Victoria Press, 363–86.

(1991) Discussion of paper of Stig Eliasson. In *Papers for the workshop on constraints, conditions and models*. (Held in London, 27–29 September 1990). Strasbourg: European Science Foundation, 51–5.

Poplack, S. and Sankoff, D. (1984) Borrowing: the synchrony of integration. *Linguistics*, 22: 99–135.

Poplack, S., Wheeler, S. and Westwood, A. (1987/1989) Distinguishing language contact phenomena: evidence from Finnish–English bilingualism. In P.

Lilius, M. Saari (1987) eds., *The Nordic languages and modern linguistics*, 6. University Press, 33–56. Also in Hyltenstam and Obler (1989), 132–54.

Pötzl, O. (1925/1983) Über die parietal bedingte Aphasie und ihren Einfluß auf das Sprechen mehrerer Sprachen. *Zentralblatt für Nervenheilkunde und Psychiatrie*, 96: 100–24. English translation: On aphasia of parietal origin and its influence on the speaking of several languages. In Paradis (1983), 176–98.

Ribot, T. (1882) *Diseases of memory: an essay in the positive psychology*. London: Paul.

Rush, B. (1812) *Medical inquiries and observations upon the diseases of the mind*. Philadelphia: Kimber & Richardson.

Sankoff, D., Poplack, S. and Vanniarajan, S. (1990) The case of the nonce loan in Tamil. *Language Variation and Change*, 2: 71–101.

Schulze, H. A. (1968/1983) Unterschiedliche Rückbildung einer sensorischer und einer ideokinetischen motorischen Aphasie bei einem Polyglotten. *Psychiatrie, Neurologie und medizinische Psychologie*, 30: 441–5. English translation: Varied restitution of both a sensory and an ideokinetic motor aphasia in a polyglot. In Paradis (1983), 753–60.

Scotton, C. Myers (1988) code-switching as indexical of social negotiations. In M. Heller ed., *Codeswitching: anthropological and sociolinguistic perspectives*. Berlin: Mouton de Gruyter, 151–86.

Stengel, E. and Zelmanowicz (1933/1983) Über polyglotte motorische Aphasie. *Zeitschrift für die gesamte Neurologie und Psychiatrie*, 149: 292–311. English translation: On polyglot motor aphasia. In Paradis (1983), 356–75.

Stroud, C. (1992) The problem of intention and meaning in code-switching. *Text*, 12: 127–55.

Voinescu, I., Vish, E., Sirian, S. and Maretsis, M. (1977) Aphasia in a polyglot. *Brain and Language*, 4: 165–76.

Wald, I. (1961/1983) Problema afazii poliglotow. *Voprosy Kliniki i Patofiziologii Afazii*. Moscow, 140–76. English translation: The problem of aphasia in polyglots. In Paradis (1983), 645–69.

Weinreich, U. (1953) *Languages in contact*. The Hague: Mouton.

Weisenburg, T. H. and McBride, K. E. (1935/1983) *Aphasia: a clinical and psychological study*. New York: Hofner. Summary of pp. 160–82 in Paradis (1983), 376.

Whitaker, H. A. (1978) Bilingualism: a neurolinguistic perspective. In W. C. Ritchie ed., *Second language acquisition research. Issues and implications*. New York: Academic Press, 21–32.

Winslow (1868/1983) *On obscure diseases of the brain and disorders of the mind* (4th edn). London: Churchill. Excerpt in Paradis (1983), 7.

Winterstein, O. and Meier, E. J. (1939/1983) Schädeltrauma und Aphasie des Mehrsprachigen. *Der Chirurg*, 11: 229–32. English translation: Skull fracture and aphasia of a polyglot. In Paradis (1983).

15 CONCLUSION: CODE-SWITCHING RESEARCH AS A THEORETICAL CHALLENGE

Andrée Tabouret-Keller

1 Introduction

This concluding chapter is designed to suggest how the reader might move towards a synthesis of the wide range of material presented in earlier chapters, to consider some interrelationships and to raise some broader issues. We can begin by assessing the value of the opportunity provided by the European Science Foundation, over a period of three years, of convening three international workshops, a large international colloquium and a school where young researchers could work out their ideas with established scholars, in order to allow researchers in this field to focus intensively on key issues in code-switching research. Chapter 1 comments in a general way on the value of this ESF initiative, but we can now go a little further in view of the results of the work of the ESF Research Network as they appear in this volume. However, it is worth emphasising before we proceed further that these pages are not the only product of several intensive research meetings; scholars from different countries and a range of different research traditions learnt to appreciate approaches other than their own, and established lasting networks of friendship and scholarly collaboration. This is an important achievement in a contemporary world fraught with divisions and conflicts, not all of them academic.

As we saw in chapter 1, the study of bilingualism has historically been associated with practical issues such as educational policies, the development of writing systems and, more generally, with the numerous political and policy issues raised by the existence of bilingual populations. While these practical and applied issues are still central concerns of many scholars, the European Science Foundation Research Network on Code-Switching and Language Contact has, as this book shows, developed a more detached perspective on bilingualism than that of the earlier studies described in chapter 1. The starting point of the Network's discussions was the simple fact that bilingual individuals normally mix languages in their everyday speech. They alternate from one language to a different one in different situations, they code-switch within the same conversation, they communicate by mixing languages even when they are fluent in both and seem equally able to use them separately. Furthermore, when conversationalists have no common language they build up an original mix, an instant pidgin. It is not sufficient to say that such behaviour needs to be described; it also needs to be explained not only in terms of social and behavioural variables but also in terms of theoretical linguistic models and possibly also with reference to biological or neuro-psychological models.

The aim of this concluding chapter is to set out and explore, making use of some tentative diagrammatic representations, the theoretical questions raised by the wide range of research reported in this book. The results of this research are, we must remember, deduced from data which are themselves derived from procedures bound either to discipline-specific methods, or to interdisciplinary methods. They are also set within the frameworks provided by a wide range of models which, in turn, affect the interpretation of specific aspects of the very heterogeneous material which researchers all describe as 'data'. At a time when the physical sciences (physics, in particular) are seeking a unified theory, the behavioural and social sciences are far from realising such an ambition. However, this does not mean that no attempt should be made to explore at least some of the most obvious difficulties in formulating a unified theory – in this case, of code-switching.

2 Variable and complex constraints

Our network meetings have gone a long way towards specifying clearly the constraints on code-switching. The composition of the chapters of this book involved a good deal of co-operation with other authors and with the editors, and each author re-evaluated his or her own contribution in light of the comments of others. Although some chapters are more practical in their orientation and others more theoretical, the book as a whole presents a comprehensive account of the state of the art in each discipline and field of enquiry represented by the section and chapter headings.

Whatever the orientation of the research – broadly social/historical, linguistic/systemic, psycholinguistic/neurological/biological – the issues faced can be summed up as follows: the code-switching process involves constraints, both variable and complex, which are in each case described according to a disciplinary point of view involving choices with respect to both methodology and concepts within a theoretical framework. We are therefore not dealing with empirical objects but with constructs. Our task is to provide an account of a variety of constraints, inferred from data which themselves are constructs rather than empirical objects insofar as they are set forth within specific theoretical frameworks. This general postulate is valid for both 'applied' and 'theoretical' approaches. The first approach gives rise to questions concerned with (for example) avoiding, controlling or supporting these constraints in pursuit of specific goals like a language policy, or an educational policy or a general communication and information policy. The second suggests the need for a general model which would show the *interrelationship* between constraints along with an account of their respective weight in any given situation. We can therefore start with the following tentative generalisations:

(i)   the three sets of constraints which we have defined (social, linguistic and biological) are of necessity interrelated;
(ii) the strength of the constraint varies in different cases of language contact.

When we read the chapters of this book it is clear that each type of constraint is itself complex with respect to both its internal constituents and specific external determining factors. For example, Heller in her account of language practices in Quebec, shows how these practices are bound up in relations of authority and power (language-use legislation) which are themselves embedded in more abstract ideologies. In the Quebec context, Heller shows what might be described as an 'intra-social' interrelationship between constraints – between power and solidarity, between individual and collective. While she deals with a range of different processes, nevertheless they are all clearly of a social type. Auer, who deals with bilingualism from a conversation analytical perspective, shows that the sequential embeddedness of code-alternation in conversation can be characterised as a relatively independent and autonomous phenomenon. For him, the basic principles by which codes are alternated in conversation can be stated independently of both the grammars of the two languages and the macro-social context of code-alternation. In such a case we are concerned not with specifying the relationship between our three basic types of constraint but with the complexities within one of them. In contrast, the Matrix Language Frame model, developed by Myers-Scotton, is an attempt to integrate both psycho- and sociolinguistic processes with structural principles of well-formedness which in turn depend on the highly abstract hypothesis of a control centre in language production. Heller and Auer thus deal with the social type of constraints, while Myers-Scotton deals with a complex construct which involves both linguistic and cognitive types of constraints by means of a model designed to accommodate cross-linguistic data. Here we are looking on the one hand at (external) interrelationships between our three basic types of constraint but also at internal relationships within at least two of them: linguistic constraints which attempt to account for a large variety of restrictions on intra-sentential code-switching data, and social constraints which attempt to account for particular instances of code-switching. We now turn from these initial observations to examine the manner in which models of code-switching might be represented. We then turn to the question of developing a more general theory of code-switching and language contact.

3 The representation of models

While certain theories lay claim to universality, they nevertheless emerge at a historically definable point in time at a geographically definable point in space. I would argue that the influence of this historical and spatial context means that theories which claim universality are in fact *local*. These contexts also provide criteria for situating each local theory within a more general theoretical framework. The term 'local' is thus understood to refer metaphorically to both time and place.

Concerning local theories, the first observation we shall make derives from 'socio-linguistics' (written with a hyphen) originally conceived as an interdisciplinary field, interfacing with both sociology and linguistics. However this original conceptualisation of sociolinguistics has changed (it has in fact progressively been elaborated by some practitioners as a unified discipline) and whatever the practical and theoretical issues involved, the two poles 'language' vs 'society' nevertheless remain in the background. Sometimes indeed they provide the starting point for an immense field of on-going research, of which this book gives evidence.

A first glance at many of the chapters of this book clearly reveals a 'language–society' bipolarity of the kind illustrated by Figure 15.1. Such a bipolar representation suggests that particular pieces of research may be located at different points between these two extremes; one where the process of contact between different languages is conceptualised as stemming from the formal properties of the languages themselves, the other where it is considered to stem from situational contexts. We can take as an example of the systemic or language pole Muysken's account of code-switching and grammatical theory. Muysken deals with intra-sentential switching in order to give an account of grammatical notions relevant to code-switching, holding firmly to the Saussurian principle, according

language   society

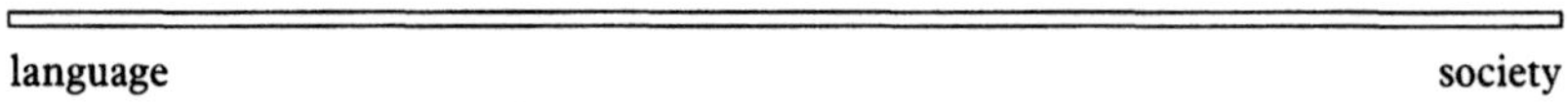

Figure 15.1 The language/society axis: a bipolarisation

to which a language event is described in terms of the language to which it belongs. The sharply opposing social pole is exemplified by Martin-Jones's paper on code-switching in classrooms as analysed over the last twenty years; she deals with the need to integrate such different dimensions as the social conditions operating in different types of classroom, and the manifestations in bilingual discourse practices of the different views about the value and purpose of bilingual education. The term 'local' consequently acquires a third sense additional to those specified at the beginning of this section: it refers to theories made specific insofar as they are dealing primarily with systemic (linguistic), or with social, constraints. Like all good metaphors, the signifier 'local' thus condenses several paradigms.

The disadvantage of the graphic presentation set out in Figure 15.1 is that it places local theories on a line that it is all too tempting to interpret as a continuum. Such an interpretation is not defensible for at least three reasons. First, it cannot be claimed *a priori* that it *should* be possible to locate all theories about language contact between the two poles. Second, certain theories refer to both poles but give priority to a third – for example, some work is based on the notion of fundamental cognitive processes of analysis which are associated with linguistic and language-processing universals. Third, with respect to each piece of research which we attempt to locate on a language–society continuum, the concepts and the system employed constitute a discrete set, the heuristic value of each concept, however, depending on the limits imposed on its use. For example, as noted in Chapter 1, although various scholars employ the same terms, they are often used with different meanings: the term *code-switching* itself is a good illustration of this point. Furthermore, we also find that the same concepts are used by different authors, linked however to one or more different concepts. In such cases, one can postulate discrete sets even if they partially overlap. However, the main point which we need to make is that, despite its attractive simplicity, it is difficult to exploit a two-pole model because it represents an idealisation focussed on specific disciplines, a narrow classification of 'research objects' rather than an instrument for conceptual analysis.

Although it would not be difficult to list the theoretical options represented in this book (which imply also methodological ones) it is more difficult to put them into some kind of order, because such an ordering involves choices. Since there is no real reason to discard the 'language–society' bipolarity, I have maintained it,

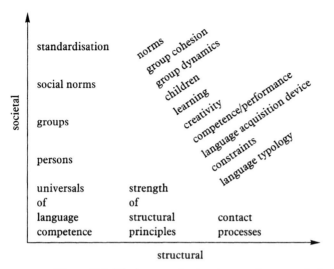

Figure 15.2 The language/society intersection: an orderly dispersion

though deliberately avoiding any interpretation in terms of a *continuum* which, as I have shown, creates certain problems. Instead of two poles, we can think of the language/society area as a flat space where various topics in the field which fall between the two extreme points are dispersed in an orderly way (Figure 15.2). Such a representation makes no theoretical claims, but serves to identify empirical local complexities and to show at least some of the issues which each of them raises. Suppose 'children' is chosen as the starting point for a piece of research on code-switching; this choice raise the issues of 'creativity', 'learning' and, via the competence/performance model, the hypothesis of an innate language acquisition device.

It is immediately clear that a surface ordering of the heterogeneous range of topics in the field, such as that attempted in Figure 15.2, conceals more problems than it solves. First the numerous points at which the two axes can be shown to intersect suggest a range of correlations which, given the current state of our knowledge, we cannot at present handle: this problem reflects the difficulty which bedevilled all our various attempts, at the three ESF workshops, to set out a hierarchy of constraints. We discussed such issues as the following: are neuro-psychological constraints universal and therefore the primary constraining factor? Are structural constraints universal or not? Are social constraints always relevant, or can certain types of data be explained without them? The answers to such questions tended to vary in accordance with the theoretical perspective adopted.

A second problem with Figure 15.2 springs from the need to represent on each of the axes complex issues like the question of social norms or the strength of structural principles. However, each of these in turn opens up a further range of problems, such as that of underlying dynamics, of relative laxity or cohesion – in the case of social norms – or issues relating to language typology when the strength of structural principles is considered. If one allows that the social dimension can be organised in terms of variables like laxity (or strength) of norms, group cohesion, group dynamics, then the social axis will be the locus of a certain number of empirical realities. However, these are interpreted differently by different authors – as being either inevitable constraints or, more simply, variables which must be accounted for.

Another difficulty springs from the need to locate the assumption of innateness, in whatever form it is expressed. As a first step I have placed this universalistic assumption at the intersection of the two main axes, societal and structural, because some social (including ethnomethodological) approaches assume universals of communication, while general linguistics assumes structural universals; an example of such an intersection is provided by Poplack and Meechan's chapter, which makes use of a clearly sociolinguistic variationist methodology but employs the structural notion of 'equivalence site' which assumes variable, but nevertheless universal, constraints on switching.

Some constraints however can be adequately located neither on the societal nor on the structural axis. For example, an assumption of neuro-psychological constraints underlies Grosjean's chapter. Here he uses experimental procedures to explore the psycholinguistics of language processing in bilinguals, with partciular attention to lexical access of code-switched and borrowed items. Hyltenstam's psycholinguistic study compares the code-switching behaviour of demented subjects with that of healthy bilingual speakers. He concludes that a specific code-switching grammar does not need to be postulated as one of the grammatical systems of bilingual speakers; rather, the way in which code-switching is carried out (grammatically speaking) is a consequence of the extent of the speaker's spared knowledge of the grammar of each of the languages involved.

One could of course multiply the number of axes and work with a multi-dimensional space; however this does not help with the task of working out relationships and correlations relevant to specific hypotheses. In practice, the representation set out in Figure 15.2 opens up possibilities of uncertain relationships and thus fails to address the question of a hierarchy of the constraints which restrict patterns of language contact – a question central to code-switching research. That alone is sufficient reason to discard Figure 15.2 and we must conclude that, though this representation has the advantage of integrating large quantities of information and of allowing the identification of various problems, it has few positive heuristic qualities. We must therefore look for another way to schematise constraints on code-switching.

We noted earlier that three sets of constraints are needed to represent the totality of our theoretical and methodological options: structural, social and neuro-psychological constraints. The advantage of a representation in terms of set theory, associated with Venn–Euler diagrams, is that they can be expressed formally as well as graphically. When the three sets are expressed graphically, they can be shown individually or joined (in twos or altogether), either with or without an overlap. Individual representations of sets correspond to a monodisciplinary approach; overlapping sets to a multidisciplinary approach; sets which are joined with no overlap to an interdisciplinary ideal. These various representations make it possible, it seems to me, to accommodate all the approaches discussed earlier in this chapter. Of course, since language is the focus of our concern, they all, by necessity, deal with language data; therefore the linguistic set is in a sense redundant since a focus on language and code-switched data is already assumed. As this argument might be equally valid for the necessarily social characteristics of languages as such, and indeed for its neuro-psychological foundations, it should be stressed that our goal is to develop procedures for explicitly accounting for systemic, social or biological *constraints*.

Four examples will illustrate these points in the case of primarily social approaches. Milroy and Li's study attempts, in terms of the concept of 'social networks' to develop a coherent account of the relationship between code-switching and language choice in individual speakers, and of the relation of both to the broader social, economic and political context. Giacalone Ramat's study explores situations where the languages in contact are the *standard language* and a genetically related *dialect* where the author tries to relate various code-switching patterns to the very general issue of language shift and/or language maintenance. The chapter by Dabène and Moore, which focusses on the language behaviour of *migrant groups*, concentrates on the issue of bilingual behaviour in the specific context of labour migration in Europe. Gardner-Chloros discusses the status of the concept of code-switching itself (which refers implicitly to finite systems) arguing however that discreteness of linguistic systems and of their components should be recognised as a myth. We are certainly dealing in these four chapters with research which falls within sociolinguistics – in other words, within the intersection where the 'language' and the 'social' sets overlap.

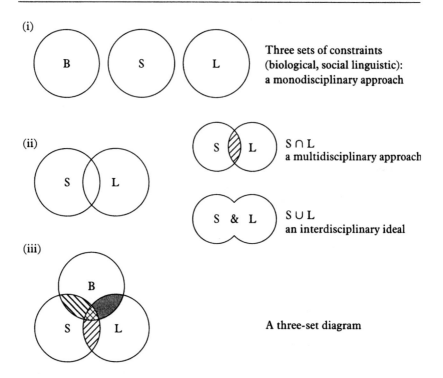

(i)

B   S   L

Three sets of constraints
(biological, social linguistic):
a monodisciplinary approach

(ii)

S   L

S   L   S ∩ L
a multidisciplinary approach

S & L   S ∪ L
an interdisciplinary ideal

(iii)

B

S   L   A three-set diagram

Figure 15.3 Types of constraints: an application of Venn-Euler diagrams

A chapter like Muysken's offers a sharp contrast in that it focusses firmly on the set of linguistic constraints: a strong system-oriented perspective is adopted according to which code-switching is viewed as impossible in principle; however, a range of procedures for resolving the system conflict are discussed. In contrast, the chapter by Köppe and Meisel would fit into the overlapping intersections of our three sets, since its orientation is biological, social and linguistic. Thus, the advantage of a Venn-Euler diagram is not that it represents a theoretical model in itself, but that it reveals the assumptions underlying the models employed by researchers in the field of three broad categories of constraints: the linguistic, the social and neuro-psychological. If one accepts that all the frameworks used in code-switching research can be subsumed under these three categories, we surely have the foundations of a general model.

4 Towards a general theory of code-switching and language contact

In Lüdi's (1990) review of the work presented at the third workshop (held in Brussels) on the relevance and the interdisciplinary impact of research on code-switching (1990: 1–3), he points out that the participants in all three workshops felt the need for a general model that would allow integration of the following constraints: the linguistic (formal properties of linguistic systems), psycholinguistic (the properties of the human mind) and socio-pragmatic (the social and interactive properties of social systems in general, and/or specific social systems). This seems to challenge us to develop a very general and robust theory of code-switching which can be applied in a full range of contexts.

The three types of constraints specified by Lüdi can of course be represented by sets, in isolation or intersecting (see particularly Figure 15.3(iii)) as discussed in the previous section. However, with respect to research on code-switching and language contact, the problem is to go beyond the discrete character of the three types of constraints, not by bracketing them out but by integrating them into an

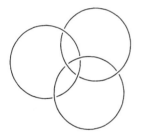

(i) The Borromean knot

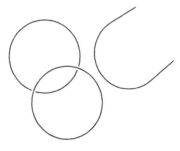

(ii) The untied knot

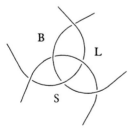

(iii) The necessary knotting of
the three fields of constraint:
biological (B), social (S), linguistic (L)

Figure 15.4 Code-switching: an application of the Borromean knot

appropriate model. One can thus move beyond the model suggested by Venn–Euler diagrams suggested in our earlier discussion, to a somewhat more complex topological model represented by the so-called Borromean knot, as illustrated in Figure 15.4(i) (Soury 1986–8). The chief characteristic of this knot is that, while each of the three loops can slide on top of the two others, when any one of the strands is cut the other two are released and become independent of each other (Figure 15.4(ii)). The three types of constraints can here be seen as fields whose topological properties can be defined. According to the first property of the knot, the areas of intersection of the three fields may vary considerably. In the case of scholars who stipulate that syntactic constraints are nothing more than neuro-psychological constraints, the two fields (the linguistic and the neuro-psychological) would largely overlap. A further advantage suggested by the Borromean knot is that one does not need to specify whether the three fields have finite or non-finite properties. For example, we do not need to specify in advance whether a language is a finite object rather than one with fuzzy edges (or perhaps no edges at all; see for example Gardner-Chloros's discussion of this issue). This example illustrates an important property of a model such as that presented in Figure 15.4: although we do not need to specify in advance certain properties of the constraints, doing so can help us to define and explicate our assumptions.

A representation like Figure 15.4 is furthermore capable of showing each of the three sets of constraints as distinctive while insisting that all be tied. Untying one of them entails the loosening of the other two (Figure 15.4(iii)). On rereading the chapters of this book, it seemed to me that this provides a good representation of one of the tasks we must tackle if we want to make any kind of headway. The implication is that, whatever one's viewpoint, the idea (at least in the form of a hypothesis or of a question) of some type of interrelationship, subsequently to be defined in association with the other categories of constraints, has been accepted.

5 Conclusions: the issue of assumptions

We asked a question at the outset about how representations of broad theoretical frameworks might be linked to representations of constraints on patterns of code-switching. This question seems to make sense only in terms of a further question about assumptions underlying our discourse. One such assumption is that of a distinction between theoretical and empirical objects. In raising this issue, I am taking sides in a debate which was sometimes explicit but more often implicit in our research meetings. However, whatever side we take in that debate, it is surely true that our knowledge of language contact phenomena depends on an accumulation of descriptive studies and on our ability to handle this accumulation. A systematic broadening of the data base is a necessary step in developing a sound theory; we do not yet possess sufficiently diversified data, although large amounts of relatively homogeneous data are available. Although these data are indispensable, they are nevertheless biased in the direction of certain types of contact situations and certain types of language. It is for this reason that the idea of developing a data-bank was proposed at the ESF network meetings, and indeed this idea should be further explored.

We can conclude by citing three examples, one for each of the fields of constraints defined, to illustrate the importance of unstated assumptions in code-switching research. In the field of neuro-psychological constraints, the weightiest assumption seems to me to be that of the innateness of certain basic elements of linguistic competence; in the field of structural constraints, the discreteness of linguistic systems can be mentioned. I call these postulates 'weighty', because as soon as they are specified they give rise to a second assumption; namely that such constraints are universal. For it is also clear that the idea of the internal coherence of grammars is itself seen as an intrinsic property of language, and thus as a fundamental constraint. Finally, in the field of societal constraints, there is an assumption that language behaviour is (relatively) independent of linguistic and neuro-psychological constraints. While the influence of such constraints is not entirely denied, they are seen as subordinate to the needs of communication.

The research represented in this book is thus truly avant-garde in the sense that it leads us to take stock of two general questions which are currently highly revelant – is the distinction between natural science and a science of human culture a pertinent one, and further, where is linguistics located with respect to this distinction?

Bibliography

Lüdi, G. (1990) Synthesis. In *Code-switching and language contact: impact and consequences: broader considerations*. Strasbourg: European Science Foundation, 22–4.

Soury, P. (1986–8) *Chaînes et noeuds* I–III. Paris: Michel Thomé and Christian Leger.

INDEX

Printed in the United Kingdom
by Lightning Source UK Ltd.
134848UK00002B/74/A